T0146998

HITLER

HITLER

COULD IT HAPPEN AGAIN?

PAUL LEFORT, MD

HITLER
COULD IT HAPPEN AGAIN?

iUniverse books may be ordered through booksellers or by contacting:

iUniverse
1663 Liberty Drive
Bloomington, IN 47403
www.iuniverse.com
1-800-Authors (1-800-288-4677)

Because of the dynamic nature of the Internet, any web addresses or links contained in this book may have changed since publication and may no longer be valid. The views expressed in this work are solely those of the author and do not necessarily reflect the views of the publisher, and the publisher hereby disclaims any responsibility for them.

Any people depicted in stock imagery provided by Getty Images are models, and such images are being used for illustrative purposes only. Certain stock imagery © Getty Images.

ISBN: 978-1-5320-5906-3 (sc)
ISBN: 978-1-5320-5907-0 (e)

Print information available on the last page.

iUniverse rev. date: 10/27/2018

Contents

*To all the democracies in the world, which,
however imperfect they may be,
form a bulwark against barbarism and
remain the guardians of civilization.*

Introduction

The Nazi dream of a millennial *Reich* came to a brutal end on April 30, 1945, at 3:15 pm, in the underground sitting room of the *Reich* Chancellery. After twelve years as its reigning leader—through six years of peace and six years of war—Adolf Hitler had just shot himself, leaving behind him the destruction of Germany, the collapse of the Nazi empire, and millions of deaths. While his suicide would allow him to escape the court of law, he would eventually come to be judged in the pages of history.

* * *

On April 29, 1945, shortly after midnight, the wheel-grinding squeal of Russian tanks could be heard in the streets of Berlin. In the underground bunker of the Reich Chancellery, the fifty-six-year-old dictator who terrorized Europe was now a pale shadow of himself. Prematurely aged and a bit unsteady on his feet, he signed the marriage certificate with a trembling hand. Eva Braun, his faithful and discreet companion of the past few years, was now his wife. After a brief celebration, punctuated by the rumbling sound of Soviet gunfire circling the city, Adolf Hitler retired to his apartment and wrote his political testament in the presence of Martin Bormann, his private secretary, Paul Joseph Goebbels, minister of Propaganda, and his secretary, Frau Traudl Junge. He reiterated his faithfulness and love for the German nation, blaming the war on Jewish political interests.

In the afternoon, he ordered his secretaries to burn confidential documents. In the evening, he walked silently amongst the officers and staff and went to his apartment while those closest to him kept watch until the morning. The next day, around noon, he met one last time with his military staff before retiring to his apartment. The Soviet troops were practically at the gates of the Chancellery. Shortly after, a gunshot shook the stuffy atmosphere in the bunker. Shocked by the horrible fate of Mussolini, who was exposed to an angry crowd and hanged by the feet, Hitler has shot himself in the head at 3:15 pm while his new bride Eva Braun swallowed a cyanide pill. Alerted by the detonation, Heinz Linge, Hitler's valet and Martin Bormann found the two dead spouses side by side on a sofa. As per the last wishes of the Führer, the two bodies were soaked in gasoline and burned in the garden of the Chancellery. The Reich of a thousand years, which was Hitler's dream, barely lasted more than ten years.

Adolf Hitler was able, and we still wonder how, to mobilize hundreds of thousands of honest citizens and convince them that they could build a new civilization over the bodies of children, women and men whose only fault was to live in Europe. The grandiose dream of this megalomaniac dictator died when Germany was destroyed by the Allies' massive bombing, but also in the ashes of twelve million people whose bodies were cremated. In World War II, the number of deaths was five times that of World War I, the highest toll humanity ever had to pay for a natural or human hand disaster. We will never know the extent of the pain in the body and soul of the survivors who returned to their homes. Hitler left behind an indelible mark in the collective human conscience.

For the descendants of the conflict's victims, Jews and Poles in particular, the wound remained open and will, for many of them, stigmatize future generations as well.

For all those who experienced nothing of this conflict, World War II is summed up in a sequence in war movies, a few pages in a history book or a few testimonials half-listened to. Yet, all these people live in a world transformed in the wake of Hitler. Without him, Israel would not exist. Without him, there would have been no division between East and West Germany. He brought the hegemony of two superpowers and sped up independence movements in the European colonies. He destroyed Germany and part of Europe. He moved a population of over thirty million people. He made several generations of Germans feel guilty and reinforced Jewish solidarity. In occupied countries, he created dissents and hatreds between collaborators and resistance. He also changed something in each of us: he sowed in the collective consciousness an agonizing doubt about our ability to contain the perversity and the destructive fury of the human soul, aggravated by the hatred of our fellows.

Was it an inadvertent error of human nature?

The explosion of barbarism in Germany cannot be considered a momentary collective deviation or an inadvertent discrepancy in the history of humankind, given the premeditated perversion of codes of social behavior via a wild theory of the laws of nature, the tacit acceptance of or submission to that theory by tens of millions of people, the research protocols leading to outrageous medical experiments on human beings by Nazi doctors with the blessing of the government, the development of industrial methods of mass killing made profitable by the recovery of useful human remains, and the contribution of major German industries to the Nazi extermination project.

These findings always bring back the same haunting questions. Why and how did it happen? Had we lived in Germany at that time, would we have been sadistic executioners, complacent witnesses, blind citizens or brave opponents?

It is tempting to trace the problem to a racial or German cultural characteristic. Unfortunately, Japanese and Russians were also guilty of unspeakable cruelties and mass extermination that compare with German standards at the time. On the other hand, several occupied European countries collaborated with alacrity to the Jews extermination and even mobilized forces to increase the number of men in the SS troops in 1944. Among the thirty-eight Waffen-SS divisions, nineteen were made up mostly of foreigners from almost all countries of Europe. Finally, several Jews assuming the role of guard in the extermination camps reassured their people with deceptive words to calm their fears as they walked to the gas chambers.

To make sense of the events, we need to consider the ability of the human soul to react in a morally acceptable way in a context of social and economic deprivation, of continuous misinformation and indoctrination, intimidation and terrorism, when individuals and families are left to the discretionary power of an institutionalized mafia, without any legal recourse.

Eyewitness accounts of the collective angst caused by the Nazi horrors, as recorded in hundreds of thousands of written documents, have not yet exhausted the subject and even nowadays, articles, analyses, and books are published at a pace that does not slow down. Often a source of great controversy strongly flavored with resentment or guilt, they inevitably bring back the same questions about a civilization backslide never equaled in the history of humanity, that has perplexed many historians. In the preface to the autobiography of Rudolf Höss, who was commander of the Auschwitz concentration camp, Geneviève Decrop wrote the following: How is it possible that a man with no political or military training, who had been a bohemian artist and an underachiever in school, came to exercise such a grip on the German people? Why did Hitler, an Austrian by birth, feel a pressing need to adopt the Aryan cause and call upon the German people to dominate the world? How could a very ordinary man exert such dominion over his colleagues who, with few exceptions, refused to blame him and expressed their loyalty by making the Hitler salute before dying on the scaffold?

In 1944, before the fall of the Nazi regime, Konrad Heiden questioned the nature of the people who had become ruthless criminals. In turn, Alain Desroches wondered how a civilized nation that produced Goethe, Beethoven, and Kant could have become complicit of such a hideous project.

Hitler exercised a powerful magnetism on his men. Hermann Göring, second strongest man of the Nazi regime, was relieved of his duties by Hitler shortly before the suicide of the latter, but remained an unconditional advocate of the Führer and his policies during the Nuremberg trials. Also surprising is the fact that none of the Nazi leaders brought to justice felt the need to shift the responsibility on Hitler for the events leading to criminal charges. On the contrary, before being hanged, some of them renewed their inalienable fidelity to the Führer and Germany, convinced that history would eventually prove them right.

By extension, we can also question the role of the Nuremberg trials. Was it a form of collective exculpation? What was the social impact? Why is it that, individually or collectively, few Nazis admitted their guilt for the atrocities of World War II? At the Nuremberg trials, where Nazi leaders were accused of war crimes and crimes against humanity, it was stunning to listen to the testimony of the defendants—most of them were disconcerted by the accusations, and to discover the horrors of the concentration camps from those who denied having participated in the Jewish genocide and killed people who were enemies of the state. In the final pages of his autobiography, Rudolf Höss defends his actions in having approved the extermination, having abused or killed inmates and having tolerated the abusive conduct of his subordinates.

Why another book on Hitler?

As a medical doctor, I have developed an expertise in psychiatry and an inexhaustible interest in research on human behavior. The Nazi adventure is filled with behaviors defying comprehension. Human beings display their true character in the face of tragedy. And no episode in the history of humanity was more tragic than World War II. The executioners, victims, actors, witnesses, those who committed the acts of cruelty and those who ignored their barbarism, those who cooperated passively and those who had the courage to stand up, each of them revealed the many faces of who we are. The discovery of those faces and the resonance they can find within each of us are mirrors of the soul, and may help us know better who we are.

The internal logic of human behaviors

To understand human behaviors, one needs an essential tool called empathy, which is the ability to see the problem with another person's eyes while remaining in one's own shoes to keep in touch with a certain objective reality. Grasping this reality with the eyes of the patient requires a leap of imagination. In the absence of comparison to apply to our reality, it is difficult to imagine the consequences of extreme situations. Therefore, if I tell you that in 1922 inflation reached unprecedented levels, you will have an intellectual perception of this fact, but it is very likely that the color of this reality will quickly fade out after having read a few pages. If I create an image reflecting your reality and explain that the rate of inflation was such that a house sold for $100,000 in 1922 saw its value drop to a few dollars two years later, you can easily imagine the impact of this economic situation if it applied to you.

Grasping the reality experienced by others is not enough. We still need to identify the internal logic of behaviors. No one takes the most insignificant or commonplace step without real benefits. Who is really aware that the instinctive muscular stretching in the morning aims to eliminate muscle edema due to immobility during the sleep and regain flexibility? Due to behavioral automatism, these benefits are almost always unconscious and defy the sagacity of the observer. We should now apply what psychological therapy calls the patient agenda, such as benefits that justify what looks like an abnormal, unacceptable, inadequate or counterproductive behavior. We must be suspicious of *post hoc* justifications that we invent to prove our good intentions.

Human behaviors are often automatic responses based on unconscious beliefs influencing our perception of reality. They provide the structure of an analysis grid that could be compared with corrective lenses through which we grasp our inner reality. The grid, based on educational and cultural elements as well as life experiences that are unique to each individual, determines beliefs that can be true or false. In turn, those beliefs generate emotions that lead to appropriate or inappropriate behaviors. Those beliefs determine the internal logic of the individual. Distortions in the vision of reality typically induce maladaptive behaviors that cannot be modified unless perception errors are corrected. Therefore, a bank teller affected by post-traumatic stress following an armed robbery may imagine in the next few months that every customer is a potential criminal. Innocuous situations such as a customer keeping his hands in his pockets will create anxiety for the bank teller who has suspicious and defensive behaviors.

In the observer's reality, some of our acts or attitudes may look wrong. But, in the subjective reality, we are always right. And the reality remains our subjective reality when compared to someone else's. Maturana and Varela have shown that the reality is not transmitted, but transformed by our perception. The uniqueness of our perceptions is shaped by their structure rather than the nature of the information. According to other authors, this structure is linked to elements such as the personality, the temperament and the educational and experiential contexts, which make the belief system act as a prism and distort the perception of reality for each individual. Basically, the knowledge of these real or false beliefs helps us understand, at least partially, the cause of behaviors and attitudes otherwise unexplainable. Therefore, since the reality is never transmitted as it is and becomes the perception of the observer, we can say that there is simply no objective reality.

The result of this observation is crucial to understand human beings: living systems do only what their structure allows them to do and they are always justified to do what they do as long as we accept that the reality in which they live may be different from ours.

If this approach aims to identify the perspective of another individual and the underlying objectives of the maladaptive behaviors, it does not imply that we share his vision of reality or believe that the behaviors are justified. Sympathy has an emotional connotation while empathy has a cognitive connotation. However, since empathy does not convey a value judgment, it may falsely suggest a subscription to the values or options of the other individual. And it is the danger of this book, especially when it becomes necessary to find culprits to blame to ensure that we are cleared of any wrongdoing.

It is difficult to apply this approach to one person only. When a group is involved, it is even a more complex task due to the infinite number of driving forces between individuals and groups that are likely to influence individual behaviors and mass movements. Nevertheless, we can reasonably believe that the information obtained through historical research will allow everyone to develop areas for future research and more nuanced opinions on a topic very likely to create controversy.

What will you find in this book?

This book draws on the incredible volume of documents published on the subject, the relevant parts of a historical case, enabling us to understand the personality of Hitler and the global context in which the nazi adventure took place. Without contextual repositioning, it is illusory to imagine finding a meaning to those disturbing events and we must rely on reductive simplification to satisfy our desire to understand.

This book is divided into three parts. The first three chapters describe in chronological order the life of Hitler before his entry into politics, the birth of the National Socialist Party, and the accession to power until the outbreak of World War II. The election of Adolf Hitler to the head of Germany within a certain constitutional legality is a symptom of social dysfunction that cannot be understood without a deep awareness of the social, economic and political context, as well as the sequence of events that led to his election. In fact, nazism seeped slyly into German democracy, exactly like cancerous cells that silently invade vital organs, use body energy to their benefit, in order to sow anarchy and sabotage the normal functions of healthy cells. As a result, after Adolf Hitler's rise to power, the army was forced to swear an oath of allegiance—not to the German nation as it should have been, but to the Führer himself. The first three chapters help understand how Hitler was able to recover the German social institutions and make them subservient to nazi goals.

The seven following chapters describe the progression of the nazi cancer to the death of Germany. They scrutinize several important historical aspects of the nazi regime: the outbreak of the war, the military operations until the final defeat, the policing organization, the nazi terrorism, the persecution and the concentration camps, the resistance and, finally, the Nuremberg trials. They review the human aspects of the tragedy—the actors, the perpetrators, the victims, the collaborators and the witnesses, and the extremely complex organizational aspects that helped write the most sinister pages of human history. The takeover of most of the mechanisms correcting the excesses and dangers of people in power is also discussed in a few chapters: the propaganda, the educational ideology imposed early on to the German nation, the monitoring of communications, the political police crackdowns and the principle of absolute authority for the leader. The Holocaust is treated in a central chapter. We will see how the link between the different events gradually brought ordinary people to become instrumental in a large-scale crime and the German people to blindly follow the most abject directives of their Führer.

Finally, the last two chapters are devoted to examining Hitler's personality and the German nation in order to identify ways of understanding why and how was created between the man and the nation the strange link that led to their destruction. Information on the results of psychological and psychiatric research provides great insight into the mechanisms underlying deviant behaviors. Adolf Hitler was able to use his personality strengths, and above all to take advantage of his extraordinary organizational skills, to build a political structure granting, in an apparent legitimacy, the unlimited power that he used to take Europe to the abyss. However, if Germany had not reached out and given him a dictatorial power in exchange for a promise to save the nation, he would have been reduced to total powerlessness.

For that reason, the story is centered on the political events in Europe, rather than those in Africa or Asia. The military facts are basic. The character of Hitler and the contents of his book *Mein Kampf* have received a great deal of attention due to the spotlight they shed on Hitlerian opportunism. Strangely, the reading of *Mein Kampf* could have predicted the future. However, few people at the time believed that this redundant, crazy and poorly written drivel would become a crystal ball that revealed the painful story of Germany in the next twenty years.

Although rewriting the patient's history is often a long and painful therapeutic process, it is also the first step toward healing. As the pieces of the puzzle fall into place, an image takes form, blurred at first, then clearer for the therapist and the patient. The latter relives simultaneously past experiences that can be extremely painful, but the reactivation of his buried emotions influences their integration into cognitive experiences in a new way and with a new look that may be compatible with the current experience. The healing process begins with the clearing of prior trauma history. The cognitive integration of highly emotional experiences has a curative effect.

Historical facts must be engraved in our memories and we must take stock of the events in order for us to recover from this tragedy.

To develop a draft response to those questions, we must break from our life and cultural environment, jump back in time more than one hundred years ago, and relive with our heart and reason the main moments of the drama, with the actors who wrote it.

What are your own biases about Nazism?

No page in history has stigmatized mankind as deeply as that of Nazism. When the last victim of the concentration camps will be dead, millions of men and women who are the descendants of the persecutors and persecuted will carry deep inside the fate of their parents. And beside them, a large part of humanity will seek to understand the why and the how of this slippage.

The Germans did not hold a monopoly on barbarism in the twentieth century. It is shocking that Emperor Hirohito was not tried for war crimes and continued to govern after 1945, given the cruelty of the Japanese army during the war. They had nothing to learn from the SS: mass executions with a bayonet, dismembering of victims, and vivisection and inoculation of deadly poisons were part of the treatment of the prisoners of war. It is also shocking to see that the Soviet Union sat as a judge at the Nuremberg tribunal, given that twenty million Russians were killed by Stalin before the war. And there were countless cases of horrible racial wars in the past ten years.

If Nazism embodies a typical case in history, it is because no other similar tragedy is as rich in publicly accessible documents. Furthermore, a wide range of the actors concerned have published their memoirs, allowing for an analysis of the problem from various angles.

Public discussions of Hitler and Nazism keep triggering controversy about the interpretations given to the facts or the perspective from which the problem is analyzed. This is why some people fear that an empathetic look at Hitler could exonerate him from any blame. Those who try to collect objective data are said to be detached and they are criticized for not reflecting the reality. Those contentions are mostly explained by different perspectives that can be put together in groups associated with the four phases of grief.

1. Individuals simply deny the reality or minimize the seriousness or significance of the events and claim, for example, that the Nazi persecution has been greatly exaggerated. We often hear that the figure of six million victims comes from the Jews themselves and does not reflect the objective reality.

2. It can be compared to a roller coaster of emotions. When expressing their opinions, individuals often show anger, irritation or intolerance. The victims of the Nazi persecution or their relatives are often found in this group.
3. Individuals streamline and intellectualize in order to conceptualize the sequence of events and manage its integration into daily life in an acceptable manner.
4. Individuals have developed a perspective of Nazism that provides satisfactory answers and allows everyone to integrate this tragedy into a global vision of humanity.

Trying to explain the atrocities of World War II can give the reader the impression that it is providing him with a rationale. Since the executioners had their own reasons to do what they did, their actions were justified as if the moral aspect of the act was based on the reason for doing it rather than on the act itself. It is tantamount to saying that the end justifies the means, which was exactly the moral code of Hitler. However, Nazism has tarnished our collective consciousness and touches deeply many of us to varying degrees, depending on our closeness in the face of this tragedy.

Stages of grief	Denial	Ventilation	Understanding	Integration
Mechanism	Denial of the loss	Release of emotions	Intellectual analysis	Acceptance of the loss
Purpose	Avoid unbearable suffering	Transfer the evil to the guilty	Find an explanation	Integrate loss into one's reality
Example of thought	The events have been greatly exaggerated	Hitler was crazy, a psychopath, the incarnated evil	Hitler and the German nation were targeting different goals	We have closed one of the darkest chapters in history

Table 1 – The clearing process of a loss

An intellectual approach strips nazism of its emotional content and will seem outrageous to many readers who are filled with horror and repulsion by the narrative of the events. They will feel that such a vision squeezes out the responsibility of those who have committed the criminal acts. However, this book does not intend to determine the guilt or the innocence of the Germans: it seeks to understand the stated or hidden, normal or pathological motives, explaining those horrendous crimes as if they were trivial behaviors or daily routine.

When we speak of nazi barbarism, it immediately evokes the Jewish persecution and the Holocaust. We should recall that the Jews were not the only victims of the Nazism. A large number of Poles, Russians, Communists, Gypsies and political opponents, many of whom were Germans, died at the hands of the SS. Here, the Jewish genocide remains a point of reference because of its historical importance. Approximately six million Jews were exterminated in the concentration camps and some claim that this figure is exaggerated. The exact figure has no importance whatsoever. The fundamental question is: How could a small group of fanatics led by a sick mind manage to lead Germany, impose its law almost all over Europe and pervert the moral sense of a culturally and industrially developed nation?

This book uses World War II to explore human nature and try and make sense of events that we cannot explain. It does not look for the demons behind the actors in this drama. It seeks to lift the veil hiding the most formidable, monstrous or repugnant urges in human beings, specifically, this aspect of ourselves that we would like to ignore. Some readers will probably be frustrated to find no condemnation of the perpetrators of objectionable or contemptible acts. This approach is not a moral judgment or condemnation, but an exploration of the elements that allowed the events to happen.

Respectable Germans

Several actors in this drama belonged to respectable walks of society. It is in the most traditional occupations that the Nazi Party recruited the highest percentage of members: 45 percent of the German doctors belonged to the Nazi Party and 22 percent were members of the SS. In

1938, 18.7 percent of the SS generals were aristocrats. Most of them made an opportunistic choice. The Nazis subverted the law and then observed the letter of the law, as respectable citizens, turning a blind eye to morally unacceptable situations from which they draw obvious advantages. Which ones? Why? How?

This debate will remain open for a long time. I hope that this book will allow many readers to become aware of the dangers of power and the fragility of the human soul where the best and the worst interact each day. At the end of the road, we may very well discover our own intolerance, aggressiveness, thirst for power, passivity in the face of injustice and ease to absolve our own faults.

Chapter 1

Adolf Hitler's youth: The birth of a doctrine

Adolf Hitler's family

Adolf Hitler was born on April 20, 1889, in the small town of Braunau am Inn in Austria, near the German border. The future dictator of Germany kept a slight accent, a reminder of his Austrian origin.

His father, Alois Heidler, was an Austria customs officer and probably the natural son of a travelling miller, Johann Georg Hiedler, and a peasant, Maria Anna Schicklgrüber. During the Nuremberg trials, the Nazi Governor of Poland, Hans Frank, claimed that Alois' father was Jewish. The validity of this statement was challenged for two reasons: Hans Frank's testimony was unreliable, due to his mental health problems, and several of his statements proved to be inaccurate. On the other hand, the German newspaper *Der Spiegel* checked the records of the city of Graz and noted that there were no Jewish residents at the time. However, Johann Georg married Anna Maria five years later. Alois was ten years old when his mother passed away. Shortly after, his father disappeared for approximately thirty years.

Young Alois went to Spital to live with his father's brother, Johann von Nepomuk Hiedler, where he learned the shoemaker trade. Alois bore his mother's name, Schicklgrüber, up to the age of thirty-nine, when his father, who was eighty-four years old, reappeared and claimed paternity. Alois changed his name to Hiedler. But due to a transcription error, the name registered was Hitler.

From a modest background and despite a very rudimentary education,

Alois owed his respectable social position to his hard work and a few weddings to women who brought a large dowry. At the age of eighteen, he worked as a shoemaker in Vienna and decided to enlist as a customs officer in Salzburg.

Alois was thirty-six years old when, for better or for worse, he married Anna Glassl, who was fifty-one and financially secure. The household settled in a hostel and the worst was to come. Soon after the wedding, Anna became ill and Alois brought his niece, Klara Pölzl, to be a housekeeper. Despite her blood relationship to him, she soon became his mistress. However, Alois was keeping his eyes open and was also attracted to a servant of the hostel, Franziska Matzelberger, with whom he had an intimate relationship at the same time. Anna tolerated the situation for a few years before asking for a divorce. After the separation, the relationship between Alois and Franziska continued and, in 1882, she gave him a son, Alois Jr. The couple was married the following year. Franziska became pregnant again after the wedding and gave birth to a daughter, Angela. Shortly after, she developed a lung disease and, once again, Alois brought his niece Klara as a governess. When Franziska died at the age of twenty, Klara was already pregnant and Alois offered to marry her.

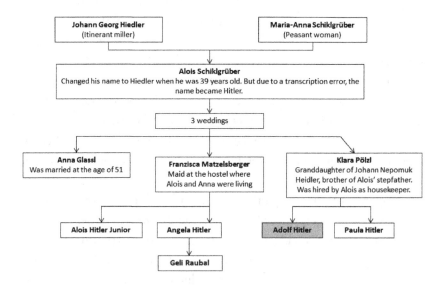

Table 1 – Adolf Hitler's family tree

Klara was also from the small village of Spital where Alois lived after his mother's death. She was the granddaughter of Alois father's brother, Johann von Nepomuk Hiedler. This close kinship required an Episcopal dispensation for a religious marriage. The couple had five children, but three of them died at an early age. Adolf, the third child, and his youngest sister Paula were the only ones who lived.

Adolf Hitler also had a half-brother, Alois Jr., and a half-sister Angela. Later, Angela married a civil servant named Raubal and gave birth to Geli Raubal, a blonde and elegant young woman who probably was the only person that Hitler loved deeply.

The German domination in Austria and the birth of a German imperialist current at the end of the nineteenth century

For centuries, Eastern Europe had been troubled by ethnic tensions. Inhabited by peoples of various nationalities, who spoke different languages and had different beliefs, those countries saw their geographic boundaries change to the rhythm of the conflicts that arose due to ethnic claims. Hitler, who was an Austrian citizen, later gained German citizenship. At the time he was born, there were a dozen nationalities in Austria. Yet, the German-Austrian minority, accounting for approximately one third of the population, emerged by imposing its language and culture to the rest of the Austrian empire. This is when Hitler became aware of the German race supremacy that was to be the foundation of his political action. He was convinced of the superiority of the Germanic race, because of the influence of that minority on the life and culture of fifty-two million Austrians. He even said that Austria could have been mistaken for a German state.

After 1850, the German domination started to weaken and other Austrian ethnic groups felt a sense of nationalism that created a growing need for autonomy. At the same time, the working class got organized and demanded democratic rights. Hitler perceived those changes with bitterness, convinced that Austria was wrong in letting the inferior races influence the state decisions. According to him, the best avenue remained the one determined by the absolute authority of the German race. This German nationalism, expressed very early in Hitler's life, increased in an uncontrolled way and became a fanatical belief, totally destroying the main values that are the basis of human relationships, such as honesty, sincerity and tolerance.

The German bourgeoisie of the ninetieth century was responding to the antihumanist school of thought inspired by the literature published between 1850 and 1900. Charles Darwin, an English biologist, had developed a theory on the origin of species based on the natural selection of the fittest. Published in 1859, his book *On the origins of species by means of natural selection* won a strong scientific interest and the opposition of theologians. Deducting simplistically that the strongest are necessarily the best, Hitler raised this principle to a moral level: The strongest were to guide the nation according to the objectives that they considered appropriate.

Count Joseph Arthur de Gobineau, a French writer and diplomat, went further than Darwin and proposed a classification and prioritization of human races. Around 1855, he published an essay on the inequality of human races that summarized the racist thinking at the time. Houston Stewart Chamberlain, an English-born German music critic and Wagner's son-in-law, published in 1899 *The Foundations of the Nineteenth Century*, a best-seller that restated the same arguments attributing racial superiority to the Germanic blood.

On the other hand, Friedrich Nietzsche, a German philosopher who died in 1900, questioned the humanistic values, treating them as a reaction of the weakest dominated by the most powerful. He opposed to those values the life affirming position through the superiority of a strong human being. With his superman doctrine dividing humanity into a race of lords and a race of slaves, he certainly supported German imperialism, although he never emphasized the superiority of the Aryan race.

Adolf Hitler's youth

Young Adolf entered primary school at the age of six. He ranked above average despite frequent changes of school due to the different assignments of his father who was a customs officer.

If the temperament is inborn to a certain degree, the personality develops during the teenage. For Hitler, it was very revealing. In 1900, Alois decided to send his eleven-year-old son to high school and enrolled him in Linz College. Driven by legitimate pride due to his social rise and wanting nothing less for his son, Alois was already planning for him a career in the Austrian civil service. Alois was authoritarian, probably like many men at that time, a trait that was accentuated by his professional experience. His son Alois Jr. had left home at the age of fourteen due to his difficult relationship with his father. Historians describe a stormy relationship between Adolf and his father, but Hitler's statements suggest that the situation was not as difficult as they say. In his book *Mein Kampf*, Adolf Hitler speaks of his father with respect and admiration, highlighting the courage of the dear old man who left the family home at the age of thirteen and managed to step up the social ladder. Adolf certainly inherited his father's egocentric, authoritarian and domineering temperament, but was far from sharing his views. In fact, his father was an Austrian nationalist showing contempt for the Prussians while Adolf admired the German nation. Alois believed that success is the result of a constant effort while Adolf showed an aversion to anything that was of no interest to him.

Adolf did not have the temperament, the taste or the interest to follow in his father's footsteps and he stubbornly resisted any attempt to do so. In order to sabotage his father's plans, he neglected his studies and failed his examinations. In fact, he continued to get good grades in subjects such as geography, history and especially drawing. But he did not do so well in subjects that were of no interest to him or that he deemed unimportant. Brilliant when he was in primary school, he failed to get his high school diploma. One day, exasperated by this oppositional behavior, Alois Hitler asked his son what he wanted to be. The young Adolf answered with determination "an artist"! Taken aback by this answer, Alois insisted, but Adolf resisted with all the stubbornness that would remain his dominant personality trait.

In 1903, Adolf was thirteen years old when his father died from a stroke. Despite being relieved of his father's pressure that pushed him to get educated and to whom he attributed his failures, he continued to neglect his studies. Throughout his life, he was unable to sustain an effort.

With Alois' pension and his profitable past investments, the family enjoyed a comfortable financial situation. Adolf went to school in Steyr, a nearby city, and Klara paid his room and board in a host family close to the school, hoping that her son would improve his academic performance. He led a solitary life, limiting his contacts with the family and staying mostly in his room. However, his marks did not improve.

During the summer of 1905, at the age of sixteen and on the advice of his physician, Adolf took a one-year break. The affection he suffered remains obscure. Pulmonary infections were common at the time, and it was the type of illness that killed Alois' second wife Franziska. However, historians wonder about the possibility of a psychosomatic or pure fiction health problem. Whatever it was, Adolf went to live with his mother and his sister Paula. Alois Jr. had already left the house and Angela had married Leo Raubal Sr. Free of obligations, he engaged in his favorite activities, touching up his sketches and compulsively reading Fennimore Cooper and Karl May, fascinated by their stories about the American Indian life. During all those years, he was also very interested in the military books that he discovered in his father's library.

He dreamed of being a great artist and frequented the Linz Opera House. He was particularly fascinated by the music of Richard Wagner, his favorite composer, who celebrated the glory of Germany in epic operas that Hitler kept seeing over and over as they enhanced his nationalist fervor. At that time, he started to befriend August Kubizek, who shared his dream of becoming an artist.

It was during those years that Adolf Hitler began to change. He grew a mustache, dressed smartly and often sat at the opera with the upper class of Linz. He did not seem to be comfortable with or attracted to young women his age. He merely fantasized about beautiful blond Nordic women who symbolized the greatness of the German race. He was sporting the image of a young student financially secure who could afford leading a life of luxury. In 1906, his mother offered him a one-month trip to Vienna, where he admired the architecture. He did not return to school after and lived on revenues from his mother, surviving from one day to the next and refusing to work in order to live decently.

However, in January 1907, Adolf's mother was diagnosed with breast cancer. Sensing her imminent death, she handed her son his inheritance in the fall of that year, hoping that he would begin a more productive life and enroll in the school of fine arts. With no skills and no job, he decided to move to Vienna at the age of nineteen.

His stay in Vienna (1907-1913)

Hitler rented a room in Vienna and, convinced of the importance of his natural talent, immediately applied to the Academy of Fine Arts. To his dismay, he was rejected since his drawings did not show enough talent. He then requested an interview with the director of the academy who recognized a certain talent in his sketches of buildings and structures and advised him to enroll in the school of architecture. To be eligible for the school of architecture, he was lacking a certificate of school completion that would have been easy to get. He never initiated such action, did not inform his mother of the failure of his request, and remained in Vienna, immediately falling into the life of idleness with no liability that had become his favorite lifestyle since he had interrupted his studies at the age of sixteen after a vague illness.

He was still in Vienna when his mother died in the fall. He felt a genuine sorrow for the woman who had always surrounded and protected him. He revered his father, but he loved his mother.

After the passing of his mother, he refused to seek work, claiming for the benefit of his family that he was pursuing studies in fine arts. He returned to Vienna, where his friend August Kubizek joined him and shared his apartment. Kubizek studied music and went to the academy early in the morning while Hitler slept in, a habit that he kept until the end of his life. Hitler spent his time reading, strolling in the city and sketching on paper his observations of the magnificent Viennese architecture.

In that period, Kubizek repeatedly witnessed Hitler's emotional instability. He had extreme exaltation peaks and unrealistic dreams followed by a period of deep despair during which he accused everyone of undermining their implementation.

His readings reflected his immediate interests and predicted his evolution. He read political writers, Georges Sorel, Nietzsche, Schopenhauer, historians and technical manuals. Those who knew him considered him knowledgeable in mechanics and problems pertaining to armament. For the rest, he had a superficial and varied knowledge, supported by an exceptional memory, that enabled him to take sides on all matters.

According to his own testimony, he made his political apprenticeship in Vienna. Witnessing the Austro-Hungarian monarchy being torn by nationality claims amplified his belief in the superiority of the German nation. At the time, antisemitism was more violent in Austria than in Germany. A German member of parliament in Vienna had even proposed to legalize the killing of a Jew. In 1904, an antisemitic Austrian party had emerged, the German Workers' Party. In 1918, the party changed its name to the National Socialist Austrian Party. And another antisemitic movement that brought together members of the German bourgeoisie and Czechs from Vienna, the Christian Social Party, had gained momentum under the leadership of an intellectual, Dr. Karl Lueger.

Blessed with a strong personality, he had become the powerful mayor of Vienna. Hitler admired the apparatus that surrounded his party, such as parades to the sound of music, with banners and uniforms. He admired Lueger's personality, even if the latter did not share his overflowing nationalism. His antisemitism was not as radical as Hitler's, but would have been at the origin of his racial beliefs, not only because of Lueger's opinions, which were moderately antisemitic, but mainly because his opponents belonged to the Socialist Party. In Europe, a relatively high percentage of Jews were in the top management of socialist parties. The intellectuals of the upper crust had not yet discovered the political strength of the workers, but they knew that the base of the socialist movement needed educated leaders. Most of the time, Jews were the only candidates. They often had a university degree gained in Austria, Germany or Russia and, therefore, could become judges or government agents. This situation created the impression that the socialist movement members were mainly Jews. Hitler hated the principle of justice and respect for human rights, that he called morality of mercy. He was more following Nietzsche's line of thought for whom the strongest had always been right. Throughout his life, he adhered to the principle that the end justifies the means.

Hitler was shy, withdrawn and almost asocial in his daily life. However, when discussing politics, he was exuberant, interrupted people and strongly expressed his views. He sometimes went to taverns, where he drank a beer and entertained the clients with his political beliefs.

Around July 1908, Kubizek went back to Linz after completing his studies in Vienna. Hitler remained alone and left his boarding room without providing a forwarding address. Hitler was humiliated for having been rejected a second time by the Academy of Fine Arts in Vienna, but he was also trying to escape mandatory military service in Austria, where he hated the government.

If the following years were difficult for Hitler, they probably had a decisive influence on his journey. He became withdrawn, solitary, and spent most of his time reading and drawing. He had depleted his savings and moved several times. He experienced hunger, financial insecurity, and physical and moral distress. In Vienna he lived the life of a tramp, finding casual employment as a construction craft worker, selling drawings, living in poor housing and attending soup kitchens. Those years of humiliation certainly fueled his future resentment toward the society that had rejected him. It is believed that his life in the lowest strata of society was a source of inspiration for his description of human distress in his book *Mein Kampf.*

Two years later Hitler met Reinhold Hanisch, another tramp not as shy and more extroverted, who was an artist manager. He convinced Hitler that an association with him could be beneficial and undertook to sell his partner's art work. They spent the following years in a kind of shelter for men where Hitler installed a workshop and painted Viennese scenes or buildings.

Hanisch knew how to sell and their association became financially viable. However, Hanisch, who has been in jail before, decided to increase his earnings by copying Hitler's art work. The latter took him to court and ended their partnership.

During those years, Hitler spent much of his time reading and reflecting. He further developed his nationalist convictions, devouring books with a selective perception of history, eliminating the elements that were not in accordance with his beliefs and integrating those that fed his vision of things. This inability to grasp reality with clarity became a caricature toward the end of the war, when his staff kept the bad news from him for fear of triggering the hysterical fury attacks that were shaking the generals. This period also gave him the opportunity to develop his demagogic skills. It is in Vienna that he developed his abilities as a speaker, giving booster talks to the disadvantaged people he met in the shelters or soup kitchens.

Hitler's antimarxism

When Hitler arrived in Vienna, the Germans were a minority in Austria and the Slavic peoples, especially the Czechs, were constantly eroding the German domination. In the previous fifty years, the population of Vienna had nearly tripled, causing a social crisis due to unemployment, low wages and a lack of available housing. A large number of Czech workers moved from the countryside to Vienna and, satisfied with lower wages, were competing for jobs with the better paid German workers. The social democratic party was aligned with the aspirations of a large number of those disadvantaged workers when denouncing the exploitation of the working class by the bourgeoisie and attacking the nation, the authority of laws and everything that was used to exploit the proletariat. This Marxist rhetoric shocked Hitler, who saw the different peoples work together, which, in his opinion, was in contradiction with the natural principle of inequality among individuals and races, and inexorably led to the degradation of the nation. Being an ultranationalist, Hitler was convinced that only a purified and strengthened Aryan race would improve the nation.

Discovering that he often ran out of arguments in discussions opposing him to the Marxists, he started devouring books, newspapers, pamphlets, everything concerning the social democracy that he disliked so much. This is how he learned the importance for a political party to intoxicate the crowds with a subtly maintained propaganda and the need to control them by skillfully dosing terror. He realized that the crowd will follow the stronger master and that tolerance was a weakness that undermined authority. He concluded that violence allows the firm establishment of an ideology for those who fight fire with fire, and that equal brutality can be used against the social democratic poison.

Thanks to his phenomenal memory, he was able to hide his lack of critical judgment and nuances behind the figures, quotes and historical anecdotal accounts with a self-assurance that confused his opponents. He quickly became a formidable political discussion partner. However, Hitler was not the only one in Austria to defend those positions. An anonymous party founded in Austria in 1904 and led by a similar inspiration, the

German Workers Party (GWP), was opposed to the Social Democratic Party of Austria.

Contempt for democracy

In his free time, Adolf Hitler enjoyed reading, observing and reflecting. He discovered the parliamentary system and developed a growing contempt for this democratic institution. After attending the debates of the National Assembly, he felt revulsion at the inability of the parliamentarians and the institution to make informed decisions and assume responsibilities. He soon drew the conclusion that democracy was a dead-end path.

Hitler described democracy as a step in the continuum of Marxism. He saw parliamentarism as unproductive discussions, which rarely lead to concrete and socially valuable projects. His selective vision highlighted in an apparent but biased logic the gaps and weaknesses of parliament and passed under silence the benefits of democracy. He will later use this half-truth rhetoric to rally the masses to his ideology. Moreover, at the end of his speech, Hitler never allowed for a period of questions or discussion that might have shed a different light on the topic.

In Hitler's view, the nation could not progress, unless one man, a political genius, of course—had the absolute power and did not risk being defeated by the mass of citizens.

He subsequently reached the inescapable conclusion that parliamentarism failed to straighten the society and redefine democracy as a government system allowing for the harmonious development of the nation, since democracy as perceived no longer represented a political system where people exercise sovereignty in the free choice of its laws, institutions and representatives. For Hitler, democracy consisted of exercising absolute control over the masses, in order to implement the objectives aimed at improving the physical and moral individual qualities in a nation that created the means for that achievement. In his opinion, it was the control of the masses for their greater good that characterized true democracy.

This concept was opposed to true German democracy, in which the freely chosen leader must take full responsibility for his actions. Such democracy did not admit that the different issues be settled by a majority vote. Only one person decided and took ownership of the outcomes of his decisions.

Hitler's antisemitism

The origin of Hitler's antisemitism is controversial among historians. Some argue that it could have been created by conflicts with some of his Jewish teachers, or that it would have developed following the death of his mother, who had been treated by a Jewish doctor.

In *Mein Kampf,* Hitler stated that he had not developed antisemitism before his move to Vienna. He says that the newspapers, which had the bad taste of showing their repugnant cult of France, were very critical of German affairs. He stopped reading those newspapers and started to read the *Volksblatt,* that he considered intensely antisemitic, but where the general comments were treated more appropriately.

The mayor of Vienna, Dr. Karl Lueger, seems to have played an important role in the development of Hitler's political concepts. He led the Christian Social Party, which supported the fight against capitalism, deemed to be under Jewish control, and against the Social Democratic Party, whose Marxist philosophy was inspired by the Jew Karl Marx. Originally opposed to Lueger's ideas, Hitler later endorsed them.

Hitler's antisemitism seems to have gradually developed. In 1857, there were six thousand two hundred seventeen Jews in Vienna, representing 2 percent of the population, as compared to one hundred seventy-five thousand three hundred eighteen in 1910, or 8.6 percent of the population. Despite their minority status, the Viennese Jews were noticeable in two ways. A limited number of educated Jews held a disproportionate place in professions, education, finance and the arts. On the other hand, those who were poor—many of whom had emigrated from Eastern Europe and whose appearance was strange, were concentrated in a few neighborhoods of Vienna and more visible.

Hitler began to read antisemitic books and pamphlets that did not convince him that Jews could be a social danger to the Viennese community. In the following months, his views of Vienna changed. Wherever he went, he saw Jews and learned to distinguish them from the other men, particularly Germans. From then on, his antisemitism developed very quickly. He said that he had identified the ethnic trait of Jewry, which he called the Zionism. According to him, liberal Jews stood apart from Zionism, but it did not change the solidarity that united them.

In *Mein Kampf*, the abusive and racist comments took precedence and became part of almost all of Hitler's speeches in his conquest of power.

Reviewing the areas in which there was Jewish activity—press, arts, literature, theater—he used the terms moral plague, black death and littering in the face of humanity. Searching for literary trash, he assigned nine tenths to the Jews, who accounted for less than one hundredth of the country's population. He even held them responsible for prostitution and white slavery in Vienna.

Hitler closed the loop when he found Jews in an unexpected place, in the heart of the Marxist ideology, and discovered that they were the leaders of Social Democracy. Hitler later wrote that Marxist theories can only be explained and justified by the Jewish plans to destroy the society, the nation and the humanity. That was when he really understood the problem. The scales dropped from his eyes and it was the end of a long inner struggle.

With this new reading of reality, he developed the sick antisemitism that helped him discover the evil Jewish omnipresence, which stood in the way of the German nationalism momentum. He then reviewed the social democratic press and newspapers that were not adopting the nationalist ideology and discovered that Jews were everywhere.

This is how he developed block by block a doctrine, which, when fully applied, would lead the German people to give full powers to one man and engage in a destruction never known before. In 1924, the detailed program established by Adolf Hitler was recorded in a book that was printed in millions of copies that neither the Germans nor the Europeans of other nationalities could read and understand. No doubt that this blindness can be explained in part by a denial mechanism that prevents us from seeing what no one can conceive, but also by the fact that this destruction without historical precedent could not be taken seriously on such a large scale. However, even after the invasion of Austria and Czechoslovakia by Germany, European leaders still had their eyes closed.

His stay in Munich (1913-1914)

After a six-year stay in Vienna, Adolf Hitler went to Munich on June 26, 1913, and explained to his companions that he would be studying at the Academy of Fine Arts.

Hitler moved to Munich as a painter and writer and began to sell paintings. He did not enroll at the Academy of Fine Arts, nor did he look for work. He stayed with a family and continued to paint scenes of Munich, surviving through the sale of a few paintings and leading a more solitary life than in Vienna.

His interest in politics was growing. He read a lot, got a closer look at the relations between Marxism and the Jewry and had heated political discussions in the cafes of the city. That was when the Austrian authorities were able to join him in Munich and called him up for compulsory military service.

In 1909, Hitler had failed to register for military service. He had no desire to serve in the Austrian armed forces. In January 1914, he was ordered to report to the Austrian consulate to explain his desertion. Pretending that he had never been called up, he requested to be exempted on the grounds of a lack of resources, poverty and an infectious disease. His presentation was so impressive that he was declared unfit for combat and unable to bear arms due to his physical debility.

A few months later, Archduke Franz Ferdinand was assassinated in Sarajevo and Germany entered World War I. Germany's entry into war raised an extremely powerful nationalist feeling in the population and Hitler's enthusiasm was particularly intense as he was finally seeing his nationalist dream take shape and expressed in an unprecedented patriotism. For Hitler, the outbreak of World War I was the most important event in his youth.

Hitler gave a meaning to the conflict between Austria and Serbia. It was the fight of Germany for freedom and the future of the German nation. He heard an inner voice pushing him to stop reading and win the battle, and this is precisely what he did. He asked King Ludwig III to be permitted to join a Bavarian regiment and soon wore the uniform, filled with joy and recognition. He was a brave and bold soldier who seemed to be frenetically attracted by the dangers and torments of war. For two years he remained on the front lines, volunteering for all dangerous missions and systematically refusing the leaves of absence that were offered to him.

Noted for his bravery in battle, he was promoted to the rank of corporal and awarded the Iron Cross First Class that he proudly wore throughout his reign in Germany. Tireless, ignoring danger, he impressed his comrades by his bravery, but irritated them as well since they did not necessarily share his attraction to war. His psychological instability and problems with establishing good relationships deprived him of the possibility to be promoted to a higher rank of command. From those years of war, he retained the mysticism of the heroic German soldier fighting for his homeland.

Hitler's attraction to war is a phenomenon that deserves to be highlighted. In fact, Hitler's experience was considerably different from the usual human experience, which sees war as a plague leaving a trail of death and destruction.

Hypersensitive to negative comments about everything affecting the glory of Germany, Hitler blamed the press for its lack of support to the nation and felt a great bitterness for what he perceived as a reservation with respect to the achievements of the German army at war. He blamed this attitude on the Jewish Marxist poison that the emperor failed to stop. He deeply regretted that the authority had been unable to brutally suppress this movement. He advocated for drastic intervention measures, which clearly foreshadowed the future of Germany under his leadership.

However, he stressed that a brutally repressive force and persecution may create an increasing resistance, unless an ideology justified these actions.

The end of World War I and the Treaty of Versailles

In 1917, the German army was leading on all fronts and victory seemed assured. In the summer of 1918, German forces were exhausted and a British counteroffensive launched on August 8, 1918 suggested the possibility of a defeat. The German high command made an approach to discuss the terms of peace while concealing the seriousness of the situation of the German army, which felt close to victory. In October 1918, it was no longer possible to hide the truth and the nation learned with dismay the news of the German defeat.

On November 10, 1918, with mixed feelings of shame and despair, Hitler learned that Germany had been defeated. He said that he cried for the first time since his mother died. After reflecting on the sacrifices of the Germans who had lost their most courageous sons, he decided to take up political work.

The Jews were once again identified as the source of Germany's misfortune and Hitler would in the years to come burden them relentlessly with every evil that was to affect the nation.

Meanwhile, in Europe, the German troops were defeated and the Allies claimed victory. It was the armistice. Kaiser William II abdicated the throne of Germany, but wanted to keep the Kingdom of Prussia. He was forced into exile in the Netherlands. King Ludwig III of Bavaria was forced to flee as well. Other kings and princes were driven out. The German monarchy was eradicated.

In Berlin, the birth of the Free Socialist Republic of Germany was proclaimed. The military authorities were willing to work with the new government of socialist Friedrich Ebert. At the same time, councils of workers and soldiers—called soviets, were formed to exercise the sovereignty of the nation. The Social Democratic Party of Germany joined the revolution and negotiated with the councils the establishment of a new government based on the Russian model that gave the executive and legislative powers to the Council of the People's Deputies. It was the birth of the Weimar Republic, a fragile democracy shaken by a divided left, since social democrats and communists were engaged in a trench warfare and criticized by the right, which attacked the Republic with demagogic accents, holding it responsible for the ills of war and the Treaty of Versailles.

In May 1919 in Paris, the Allies were laying out the conditions of peace to the German delegation, but the latter rejected them as being unacceptable. Faced with the threat of an immediate resumption of hostilities, the German National Assembly was forced to ratify the treaty on June 28, in the midst of political resignations and popular demonstrations through Germany. Under the terms of the treaty rejected by the United States Congress, Germany was mainly to blame for World War I and was amputated of seventy thousand square kilometers of territory, including many farmlands, and five and a half million inhabitants. The creation of the Danzig Corridor deeply humiliated the Germans. Since 1793, Prussia had been controlling that strip of land between the Baltic Sea and Poland. The Treaty of Versailles gave Poland a corridor twenty to seventy miles wide, giving access to the port of Danzig and the Baltic Sea. For the

Germans, this clause broke the country as it separated East Prussia from Germany. Furthermore, the Treaty required Germany to deliver much of its raw materials and agricultural production to the Allies. An extremely heavy fine phased over forty years was imposed. Prohibition of military service and heavy weapons, an army limited to one hundred thousand men and the extradition of war criminals were part of the German bill. Philipp Scheidemann, who was the head of the National Assembly, refused to sign the treaty and resigned. The Social Democratic Party and the Center Party formed a new government under the leadership of Gustav Bauer, who signed the Treaty.

If the Treaty of Versailles contained the seeds of World War II, the theoretically democratic Weimar Republic introduced in its constitution the key that would allow Hitler to take power in Germany. At the time, nobody suspected the scope of article 48, which gave to the president the right to legislate without the *Reichstag*.

This article provided that if a state did not comply with the tasks imposed by the constitution or legal authority, the president had the power to use the army to force the state to meet its obligations. In addition, the article authorized the president to use all necessary means, including military service, when order and security were endangered within the federation. Finally, in an emergency situation, article 48 of the Weimar Republic authorized the president to suspend the liberties of German citizens, even if their rights were guaranteed by the constitution. The article opened the door to the dictatorial powers that Hitler will exercise in 1933.

In Munich, on September 12, 1919, less than three months after the ratification of the Treaty of Versailles, Adolf Hitler, who was a complete stranger, delivered a speech at a meeting of the National Socialist German Workers' Party. The wolf was in the sheepfold.

Chapter 2

The birth of the Nazi Party (1919-1925)

1919-1925: The illegality

The end of the Second Reich and the birth of the Weimar Republic

After the Prussian victory, Austria was excluded from the Holy Roman Empire. In 1871, Germany became a federation of twenty-five relatively autonomous states under the authority of Prussia, which was exercising a discretionary power on foreign policy and the conduct of the war on behalf of the German Confederation. In fact, the King of Prussia was the Emperor of Germany. The *Bundesrat* was the Assembly consisting of representatives from the twenty-five states chaired by the Reich chancellor appointed by the Emperor of Prussia. The prime minister of Prussia and Reich chancellor were the same person, thus celebrating the Prussian hegemony.

At the end of the ninetieth century, Germany was engaged in a remarkable technological and industrial development, which, in 1914, had propelled the country to the second rank of the world's industrial power, immediately after the United States of America.

However, Germany was suffering from a major political and economic backwardness. Inside of a decidedly feudal system, the aristocrats held a disproportionate share of power while the workers expanded a collective awareness of their value that started an economic power shift in their favor, leading them to demand further political power. At the beginning of the ninetieth century, the German society was composed of three distinct groups: the aristocracy and the bourgeoisie; the middle class or lower bourgeoisie, comprising officials, merchants, and artisans; and the workers and peasants. The electoral system allowed each group to elect one third of the deputies. But obviously, aristocracy and bourgeoisie, which represented 3.5 percent of the population, held a disproportionate power over the workers, who elected the same number of deputies although they represented more than 84 percent of the population.

At the end of World War I, it became necessary to set the record straight on the industrial era, but the economic misery and unemployment resulting from the war precipitated Germany in political and social upheavals. In October 1918, communist left-wing political groups proposed to create councils (*soviets*) of workers and soldiers who were demanding improvements in their working conditions, the right to vote, the right to strike and the right to unionize following the Russian model. The revolutionary movement first involved sailors and shipyard workers who went on strike. The German Communist Party was founded in January 1919 and became the center of radical revolutionary claims. A Soviet Republic was even proclaimed in Bavaria on April 7, 1919. The movement was repressed by the Social Democrats who sent soldiers from Berlin, and by the Corps Francs delegated by the monarchy and the bourgeoisie. On May 1, 1919, hundreds of Communists were massacred.

According to Rudolf Höss, the Corps Francs were paramilitary groups consisting of soldiers unable to adapt to civilian life, adventurers, young enthusiasts and unemployed. Governments used them when police or military personnel were inadequate and could disown them once the danger had passed. Frequently, those troops took the law into their own hands and improvised courts where those who were considered traitors were condemned and executed. In fact, Höss was sentenced to ten years of forced labor in 1922 for the murder of a man suspected of being a communist spy.

The political situation turned to utter confusion when the German army high command proposed to support the socialist majority if they committed to protect order, fight against communism and support the army. At the elections to the Constituent Assembly on January 19, 1919, a coalition composed of the Social Democrats, the Catholic Centre Party and the German Democratic Party won 75 percent of the votes.

Name	Years	Period (years)	States (number)
First Reich (Holy Roman Empire of the German Nation)	962-1806	844	
German Confederation (Bundt)	1815-1866	51	
Second Reich	1871-1918	48	25
Weimar Republic	1919-1933	14	17
Third Reich	1933-1945	12	

Table 1 – The political structures of Germany

Prince Max von Baden, a cousin of the Emperor, resigned and appointed to the chancellery the leader of the Social Democratic Party, Friedrich Ebert. Protected by the army, the National Assembly undertook to draft a new constitution in the city of Weimar. On July 31, 1919, the Constitution of the Weimar Republic was adopted at the third reading and Friedrich Ebert became the first president. The new republic consisted of seventeen states called *Länder,* under a central Reich responsible for foreign policy and military affairs, previously assumed by Prussia.

For the aristocrats, there were too many changes, but for the workers, they were insufficient. Few Germans derived benefits from the new Weimar Republic and the dissensions were dramatically amplified by the post-war economic poverty.

The first act of history: Munich, Bavaria

After the revolutionary government crackdown, Bavaria became the rallying point for the German ultranationalist movement. The Thule Society was the Bavarian branch of the *Germanenorden* (Order of Teutons), where German nationalism and antisemitism were preached in a medieval esoteric atmosphere. Several future Nazis, such as Himmler, Rosenberg, Hans Frank and Rudolf Höss, were already active supporters of that ideology. The newspaper *Münchener Beobachter* became the *Völkischer Beobachter,* the official newspaper of the Nazi Party.

In fact, few people in Bavaria were really satisfied with the new republic. The military wanted the return of the monarchy. The working class continued to claim their rights. The middle class feared the proletarianization. The bourgeoisie, the monarchists and the industry, who feared for their privileges, reacted to the revolutionary movement initiated by the working class by entrusting the army officers, who were born monarchists, with the creation of troops of Corps Francs, mainly active at the borders and whose mission was to destabilize the communist revolution. Political crimes became forgiven, since their objective was to defend the homeland, foreshadowing the philosophy that Hitler would impose to the German nation. Clashes between the disinherited left and the right seeking to preserve its privileges soon became part of the daily life. The fight against communism was reviving antisemitism. The founder of communism was a Jew, Karl Marx, and many communist leaders belonged to the Jewish community.

Political regimes followed one another, punctuated by putsches and assassinations. Political parties proliferated and tried to attract demobilized soldiers who, facing poverty and unemployment, easily used brutality and violence. Parapolitical and paramilitary groups were proliferating and many of them had retained their combat weapons. The attacks were widespread. Germany was then a republic administered from Berlin. But a few provinces were trying to distance themselves from the central government. In Munich, a Bavarian city, Gustav von Kahr had seized power, supported by the army and General Ludendorff, head of the divisions stationed in Bavaria.

Having traditionally supported the monarchy, the army was not yet adapted to the new post-war Republic and had formed a political office to monitor the emergence of "dangerous" groups advocating democracy and socialism. Adolf Hitler, who was in Munich at the time of the government crackdown on communist revolutionaries, was appointed an officer-instructor by the army. He was responsible for propaganda activities and facilitated civic education sessions for the military. The army provided the propagandists with a small bookshop where Hitler certainly drew much of his convictions on bolshevism and antisemitism.

There was resentment against political authorities who, on the advice of General Ludendorff, had signed the surrender because they believed that a defeat was unavoidable and they wanted to negotiate peace on the best possible terms. Although the enemy had not yet set foot on German soil, defeat seemed inevitable and many exploited politically the demand for surrender, calling it a stab in the back. An armistice request to limit the losses in Germany could have been described as a responsible and patriotic gesture, but Hitler, who was to do exactly the opposite at the end of World War II, would not refrain from condemning such cowardice.

At that time, the army was doing politics and offering training sessions to the *Reichswehr* soldiers in order to protect them from democratic influences and to fight socialist ideas. Hitler was appointed instructor following a few interventions where he amazed his superiors with his powers of persuasion. He refined his speaker talent, promoting at the same time the ideas that he always defended.

The political assembly at the Sternecker Brewery

The military closely watched the political groups of workers to detect socialist or communist threats against the regime. On September 12, 1919, Hitler was commissioned by the army to attend a meeting of the DAP (German Workers' Party). The party was founded on January 15, 1919 by a locksmith, Anton Drexler, and a sports journalist, Karl Harrer. When Hitler arrived at the Sternecker Brewery, he found about twenty-five people gathered in the basement. The main speaker was Gottfried Feder, whom he had heard a few weeks earlier at a policy briefing for soldiers. Feder was defending economic ideas, rejecting the speculative capitalism in the hands of the Jews in favor of a productive capitalism generating goods and services. Already sharing Feder's antisemitism, Hitler said that he understood the pernicious nature of marxism when listening to his speech. During the discussion following the conference, a participant who was a professor of history challenged some points raised by Feder and proposed instead to separate Bavaria from Prussia and annex it to Austria. This proposal collided head-on with Hitler's ultra-nationalism who saw Austria annexed to Germany. Shocked by the idea of a fragmented Germany, Hitler gave an impassioned speech and made a strong impression on the six members of the party leadership. At the end of the meeting, Anton Drexler, still amazed by what he had heard, gave Hitler a brochure entitled *My political awakening*, that explained the ideology of the party.

Back home, Hitler read the document and was pleasantly surprised to find in it a political roadmap that matched his own. Apparently, he was not planning to go to other DAP meetings; however, a few weeks later, he received a membership card and an invitation to the next meeting of the party committee.

Hitler spent a few days thinking about it. He had no intention of joining an existing party. He wanted to create his own. Moreover, he was not impressed by the narrow scope of the DAP leadership members, who handwrote the invitations to political assemblies and distributed them to passersby, thus attracting a very limited audience. Hitler already had a sharp political instinct that did not fit easily into a weak organization. Nevertheless, guided by an opportunistic flair that he will have throughout his career, he decided to attend the meeting of the party local executive.

The founder of the party, Anton Drexler, was a sickly and poorly educated man who worked in the railway shops in Munich. He shared with Hitler a vigorous nationalism and an intense antimarxism, but he had no speaker talent and was unable to disseminate his beliefs. The party president, Karl Harrer, was a journalist who wrote well, but did not have the gift of speech. The two men belonged to the Thule Society, a secret racist association that supported the DAP. On the given day, Hitler went to the assembly where he was invited.

He had to go through a lounge before entering a room lighted with a half broken gas lamp where four men were sitting around a table. He was greeted as if he was a member of the party. They read the minutes of the last meeting. Then, the treasurer handed his report establishing the assets of the party to seven marks fifty pfennigs, and he was confirmed in his post. Finally, the group examined one of a few letters and concluded that this exchange with other organizations was a sign of health for the German Labor Party. Hitler was astonished by the lack of organization of the party, that he compared to a house club at its worst.

He pondered back and forth for a few days and decided to join the DAP, thus becoming the seventh member of the committee. He became responsible for recruitment and propaganda.

Hitler seizes control of the DAP

Hitler was well ahead of several members of the party executive. His arrival on the committee caused a major reorganization in the direction of the party. Hitler was often opposed to Harrer on the precise role that he should play on the political level. Moreover, Harrer left the party on January 5, 1920, less than four months after his first contact with Hitler. Subsequently, the latter had the opportunity to meet prominent figures who joined the party and shared his convictions, and without whom his incredible political ascension would have seemed impossible.

He immediately befriended Captain Ernst Röhm, who was one of the few to be on first-name terms with the Führer. A professional soldier, a rugged adventurer and openly gay, Röhm was a harsh character, stocky built, his face covered with scars. He shared the unconditional nationalism of Hitler and his resentment against the humiliating Treaty of Versailles. Röhm was also an exceptional organizer, respected by his men. Hitler will later entrust him with the leadership of the SA, also known as the Brown Shirts. Very popular with the army, Röhm contributed to the recruitment of a large number of former military personnel, who formed an important nucleus within the party. But he also had a significant political influence that generated the tolerance of both the government and the Bavarian police, when confronted with the violence that soon became the trademark of the party.

Dietrich Eckart was also part of the party's leadership committee and probably the man who exerted the strongest influence on Hitler. Bavarian and twenty-two years older than Hitler, Eckart showed a path strangely similar to Hitler's. He had failed law school because he drank too much and did not study hard enough. He was a brilliant journalist who had led an idle life in Berlin when he was in his forties. Pretending to be a poet and playwright, he lived as a tramp for a few years, blaming the failure of his life on a Jewish conspiracy. Due to his abuse of alcohol and morphine, he had to be treated in a psychiatric hospital where he staged plays for the patients. After the war, he returned to Bavaria and made political speeches focused on the German nationalism, the exclusion of the Jews from Germany and the elimination of the central government in Berlin. It was also the main thrust of the theses supported by Hitler, and Eckart sensed that he had found the man that the party needed to grow. He took Hitler under his protective wing. He recommended appropriate readings to him, helped him improve his German language and introduced him to the Munich society, which, besides financially supporting the party, also arranged for him to meet several future key men such as Rudolf Höss and Alfred Rosenberg. Moreover, it was through his contacts that the party was able to buy a newspaper that became its instrument of propaganda. General Franz von Epp, of whom Röhm was the right-hand, raised funds that enabled Eckart, in February 1923, to buy a newspaper, the *Völkischer Beobachter,* to be managed by Hermann Esser, another DAP leader. The newspaper became a powerful propaganda tool and the official organ of the Nazi Party until the fall of the regime. Hitler's speeches were regularly printed in the newspaper.

Finally, Gottfried Feder, an engineer and self-taught economist, impressed Hitler with his theory that speculative capitalism was responsible for the problems afflicting Germany. True to his habit of drawing here and there evidence validating his own convictions, Hitler saw in Feder's language a thought likely to become the core ideology of the party and to generate the slogans that were essential to an effective propaganda.

After several attempts to increase the participation in political assemblies, Hitler took over their organization. He replaced the handwritten invitations with printed ones, increased the number of invitations and published advertisements in the newspapers. He innovated by collecting an entrance fee from those who showed up. The assemblies began to attract more and more curious onlookers. One evening, one hundred eleven people were in a room that could contain one hundred thirty, and Hitler took the floor as second speaker. At the end of his thirty-minute speech, people were so impressed that their donations amounted to three hundred marks.

Political assemblies followed at a fast pace, attracting more and more participants whose entrance fee ended up in the party's coffers. The party became more structured and, in April 1920, Hitler changed the name of the German Workers Party (DAP) to German Workers' National Socialist Party (NSDAP for *National-Sozialistische Deutsche Arbeiter Partei*).

The NSDAP dictatorship

Hitler refined his speaking style. He oversimplified the complicated issues, refuted the expected objections, used a popular language often rude and marked with jokes in bad taste, and aligned gestures with pitch modulations to magnetize the crowds. However, several members of the leadership committee were irritated by his style a bit too popular, his frequent mood swings and his arrogant attitude. In the summer of 1921, there was a dissension on how to increase the strength of the party. Hitler favored a more aggressive propaganda and Drexler a merger with other parties pursuing similar objectives. Drexler's option gained ground despite Hitler's arguments, as he feared that it would dilute the control over the party. In a work session, an irritated Hitler offered his resignation and slammed the door. Fearing that he would create a new party or take with him a significant number of members, the leadership surrendered to Hitler, who was now requiring dictatorial powers. The committee wanted to avoid taking the feud before the general assembly of the members, but, on July 29, 1921, Hitler summoned an extraordinary meeting and won his point. This is when Hitler was called Führer or leader for the first time. His magnetism and speaker talent soon attracted around him many of the future nazi leaders: Alfred Rosenberg, a Moscow architect, Rudolf Höss, who had a degree in political science, Hermann Göring, Julius Streicher, and many others.

This victory consecrated the supreme authority of Hitler on the leadership of the party and helped make him the depositary of absolute truth.

To create an element of gathering and unity within the party, Hitler endowed the organization with a red flag with a black *swastika* in the center of a white circle. An armband with the swastika was also adopted and worn with pride by all members of the party. Banners modelled after those of imperial Rome lined the walls of the rooms hosting the political assemblies or were held by a large number of party members during parades. They contributed to give a solemn atmosphere to the NSDAP and sent to the German nation the message that a new order had just arrived. There is no doubt today that such a grandiose staging strongly impressed the German people at a time when they were desperately looking for a lifeline, and it became an instrument of propaganda that no other political party had the ability to use. Albert Speer, Hitler's personal architect, was to amplify the dimension of that staging.

Hitler's messages

Like Röhm, Hitler felt painfully humiliated by the Treaty of Versailles and he attributed to the Berlin regime the responsibility for the defeat in the war. He believed in the rebirth of a strong Germany reunified by an authoritarian political party supported by the crowds. Today, historians agree that the Treaty of Versailles, signed on June 28, 1919, was the first step toward World War II. Germany was not alone in considering the imposition of the treaty as a senseless decision and an unacceptable outrage. In disagreement with the terms of the treaty, the United States had withdrawn from the table prior to the signing of the document. Besides amputating Germany of its colonies, having the army occupying the Rhineland—a strip of territory between Germany and France, limiting the forces of the German army to one hundred thousand men, and prohibiting any form of heavy armament, the Allies imposed a huge debt that was to be phased over the next forty-two years. Even the British Ambassador to Germany, Sir Nevile Henderson, denounced in 1938 the destabilizing effect of the Treaty of Versailles on the political scene in Europe.

Although several German political groups had raised protests against this Treaty, Hitler emerged with his strong conviction and his magnetism on his audiences with his ability to express his ideas in simple words that crowds could understand. In his first speeches as head of the Nazi Party, Hitler claimed with force that the protests against the Treaty of Versailles would be short-lived unless Germany regained its former power. Hitler made this issue his number one priority and, during the Nuremberg trials, Joachim von Ribbentrop, foreign minister of nazi Germany, and Hermann Göring, second most powerful man in the regime, justified their membership in the Nazi Party by the belief conveyed by Hitler that the treaty needed to be revised. Hitler was the only one who proposed a vision of Germany that matched their own. Julius Streicher was a teacher who joined the party in 1921, after hearing Hitler speak for three hours and energizing the audience. He explained that an inner voice suggested that he had to talk to that man and offer his services. He became general of the SA, *Gauleiter* of Franconia and editor of a newspaper, *Der Stürmer,* supporting antisemitic propaganda. Schirach, head of the Hitler Youth movement, joined the Nazi Party in 1925, after hearing a speech in which Hitler promised work, wealth and happiness for Germany. He confessed that he saw him as the man who could release Germany from the Treaty of Versailles and, at the Nuremberg trials, he said that he believed that Hitler owed his meteoric rise to the treaty.

As for the racist theories of the NSDAP, they were explicit from the outset of the party program. Only a member of the race could be a citizen, and a member of the race could only be one who was of German blood. Consequently, the reunification of all Germans, in particular those who lived in the territories bordering Germany, in neighboring countries, as well as the expanded territory, was to allow the Aryan race to develop. Therefore, the party propagandized the master race, but, at the Nuremberg trials, Hjalmar Schacht noted that the concept was ridiculed by the German public opinion. In fact, the emaciated Hitler, the short Goebbels born with a club foot, and the obese and whimsical Göring who was also a drug addict, did not reflect the master race that they were advocating.

This racist theory led to a large number of consequences whose future implications might not have been obvious at the beginning. In the midst of the claims about the Treaty of Versailles supported by the German citizens, this racist theory created some confusion. The German nation was to develop enough power to abolish the unacceptable principles of the Treaty of Versailles. However, once the power was restored, the regime had a tool that could be used for many other purposes. This is how Adolf Hitler prepared the ingredients for his expansionist project, the *lebensraum,* the annexation of the territories of neighboring countries largely inhabited by Germans, but also other territories to the East, at the expense of Russia, a huge country. A reunified and purified Germany would then be able to develop its vital space. To support his project, he needed a committed Germany and to cunningly acquire portions of adjacent territories. He mobilized the German citizens in a reconstruction project by no means lacking in attractions, in view of the unemployment, social violence and rampant inflation that Germany was experiencing. For the sake of a regained pride, the project developed, supported by a propaganda monitoring unrelentingly everything that was published, and social organizations that were repeating the same message to all age groups. All that mattered was the greatness of Germany, where the individual was only a tool. The catastrophic effects of this principle on the population were not correctly evaluated. The result was total conformity of individuals, fanaticism, militarism and exaltation of the masses. Territorial aggression policies became a natural consequence of this social project.

For Hitler, it was clear that those goals could not be achieved without a bloodshed. Hitler added explicitly in his book *Mein Kampf* that it may be necessary to eradicate France to allow the German nation to expand in another direction. Those statements did not create waves at the time, in Germany or in the rest of Europe. It is quite difficult to imagine that a politician at the head of a civilized country could willfully break all the rules governing its relationships with other countries and indulge cynically in an international banditry. European leaders for their part completely ignored the warnings. The most striking example is Neville Chamberlain, who went back to Great Britain with a peace letter signed by Hitler, that the latter subsequently ignored. Shortly after having reassured the international opinion by presenting to the Assembly of the United Nations with consumed cynicism a list of countries that he was not planning to invade, Hitler admitted to those close to him that a treaty was something to be torn up.

Those objectives could not have been achieved without an aggressive and ruthless organization of political institutions. For Hitler, the two principles of management (*Führerprinzip*) were authority and totalitarism. The leader concentrates all power in his own hands, which leads to the principle of infallibility of the Führer (the party's manual stated that the Führer was always right) whose power has no political or legal limit. The authority can be delegated and must be accompanied by an absolute and unconditional loyalty to the immediate superior. At the time, the culture was conducive to such an attitude. Most Germans had been taught to respect authority in all its forms, and Hitler's message seemed as incongruous as it could have been in America at the time and even more nowadays. At the very edge of the abyss, short of money, employment and bread, unsecured by governments that barely lasted a few months, shocked by the multiple political groups that cultivated physical violence, Germany discovered a leader who promised greatness, power, and economic and social stability for the nation. With great art, Hitler was whipping up the patriotic sentiment among the Germans. Opponents who criticized the means to achieve those objectives were considered to be enemies since real Germans could not reasonably oppose them. In any case, the German citizens never questioned where the objectives would lead them. They wanted to know if there would be bread on the table the next morning and if they would find a job the next week. It looks like Hitler was the only one who knew the path on which he was leading the German nation and he had clearly explained it in the party program.

Due to some of his political ideas, Hitler soon clashed with the president of the party, Karl Harrer, who was opposed to Hitler's violent antisemitism for fear of alienating the support of the working classes. He argued that Hitler did not express himself correctly in front of a crowd. When Hitler decided to organize an important political assembly to present the party program, Harrer resigned in protest and was replaced by Drexler. Now, nothing prevented Hitler from taking over the party's leadership.

The NSDAP creates a 25-point program

Hitler quickly realized that if the party wanted to play an important role on the political stage, it needed a specific program. With Feder and Drexler, he wrote a program containing the essence of their political philosophy.

On February 24, 1920, a large assembly attracted two thousand participants at the Munich Hofbrahaus. After several interruptions quickly mastered by the service responsible for maintaining order, Hitler listed twenty-five proposals that he asked the crowd to repeat after him. They were all accepted unanimously with enthusiasm. The Nazi Party had just achieved its first huge success.

Although Hitler captured many of those points in his *Mein Kampf* manifesto, they can be summarized under five main themes.

1. Racism. German citizenship applies exclusively to individuals of German blood. Jews will be subject to the laws on foreigners and forbidden to hold any position in the public service or to own land.

2. Foreign policy. All Germans must, under the right of the people to self-determination, be brought together in a greater Germany. Therefore, all the Germanic strains must be regrouped within the same borders: ethnic minorities of Denmark (Schleswig), Poland (Posnania, Upper Silesia), Czechoslovakia (Sudetenland), Italy (South Tyrol), and France (Alsace-Lorraine). This reunification must take place without violence (in a plebiscite) and Germany bears the responsibility for ensuring that these German minorities are not oppressed in their host home country.

   Without offering specific ways to achieve this, the program denounced the loss of their colonial empire with the Treaty of Versailles and proposed the concept of living space (lebensraum) that will give the German nation the territorial space conducive to its prosperity. This vital space needed to develop in Europe.

3. Economic and social policy. Work is a duty imposed on every citizen and any idea of profitability has to give way to the goal of meeting the needs of the country. As a result, a proto-socialist policy should restrict private interests' powers, so that the state alone may decide to work ineffectually in certain sectors that seem to be important.

   However, there was some confusion with those principles, since private property was still recognized and Germans could freely use the product of their labor.

4. Reform of the law, education, etc. The program forbids Jews to collaborate with German newspapers. The Roman Law (the Napoleonic Code) must give way to the German law, less focused on materialism.

   Education must give significant importance to physical development, provide adequate civic education, and teaching must become practical. For example, stop teaching languages that will never be used by the vast majority of students.

The program gives freedom of religion insofar as it does not go against the plans of the state.

5. The form of the state. The program allows for a central parliament, but proposes to waive the parliamentary party system. Parliament is an advisory body only and at all levels, responsibility is assumed by one man, and the state is based on a strict hierarchy. It is the Führerprinzip.

The creation of the SA division

The political assemblies continued to attract more and more curious onlookers. Fought by other competing political groups, the party attracted opponents who loudly disrupted the political assemblies. With the exception of Röhm, no member of the Leadership Committee of the party had military experience. Therefore, Hitler recruited demobilized soldiers, tough ones who joined the party and silenced the opponents, and put them at the entrance door when needed. Violence became a routine during the party's assemblies and, at the beginning of the meetings before calm was restored, the usual show was repeated. Hitler was peacefully standing on stage and the women seated at tables covered their heads with their arms while mugs of beer were flying in the air. After a while, the thugs of the party restored calm and Hitler began to speak, literally hypnotizing the participants with his extraordinary talent.

The security forces quickly became an instrument of violence when Hitler decided, in turn, to use them to disrupt the political assemblies of the other parties. In Vienna, he had become convinced that brutality was an irreplaceable propaganda tool. He led his troops to sabotage the assemblies of other political parties and, in 1921, he was sentenced to three months in jail for having assaulted a speaker. He was in jail one month only. At the time, each political party had a security team, but in Hitler's mind, the SA division was to become a private army that could be used in a coup d'état. The uniform was intended to give a formal look to impress enemies as well as supporters.

But the SA troops were also a propaganda tool. When they paraded in the streets of Munich and sang *When Jewish blood flows from our knives, things will go much better*, they had an irresistible impact on the population. Five hundred SA who walked in a row projected more power and authority than ten police officers on horseback.

Hitler's driver, Emil Maurice, was the first commander of the shock troops, who looked more like a sports organization to counter the police efforts and avoid attracting the attention of the Berlin government. On October 5, 1921, they were officially named *Sturmabteilung*, or Storm Sections (SA). The members of the troops wore brown shirts and terrorized Germany for a decade.

July 29, 1921: Hitler's appointment as NSDAP president

Hitler took on an increasingly important role and began to create a powerful political party from a small racist club. He gathered around him men who were to become famous: Röhm, Höss, Rosenberg, Göring, Streicher, Goebbels, and Himmler.

Even in 1921, the movement was primarily a Bavarian phenomenon, spreading little further than Munich. Then, the party began to establish contacts with other nationalist parties, but Hitler opposed that those parties be combined with his. With an amazing audacity, he demanded that people resign from their party prior to enlisting in the NSDAP. Hitler's opponents in the party saw an opportunity to confront him, but that is precisely what he expected. He threatened to resign and agreed to reconsider his decision if he was granted dictatorial powers. At a meeting on July 29, the party gave in once again.

A disastrous economic crisis

In the early 1920s, Germany was starting to show social stability and, if that trend had been maintained, the NSDAP would have become a short-run phenomenon. However, in 1921, the Great Depression began to sweep away everything. Unemployment increased significantly, the German mark fell dramatically, and the bourgeoisie lost their life savings. Observers noted that the German government was taking advantage of the inflation and repaying war damage liabilities with devalued currency.

In 1922, Germany requested a moratorium on the reparation payments to the Allies. In Berlin, the Reich chancellor Joseph Wirth said "First bread, then reparations." Reparation payments, threats from the Allies in the event of non-payment and the inflationary policy of the *Reichsbank* created a disastrous fall of the mark on the international equity markets. In July 1914, the dollar was worth 4.2 marks. In January 1922, it was worth 191.8 marks and in November 1923, 4,200 billion marks. Stamps were no longer printed since their price changed on an hourly basis. As a result, postal workers had to handwrite them. On November 1, 1923, one loaf of bread cost 260 billion marks.

Date	U.S. Dollar	German mark devaluation	Devaluation of a $100,000 house	Impact of inflation on a $10,000,000 war debt
1922 (January)	$1.00	191.80	$100,000	$10,000,000
1923 (July)	$1.00	353,412	$54.27	$5,427.09
1923 (August)	$1.00	4,620,455	$4.15	$415,11
1923 (October)	$1.00	25,000,000	$0.76	$76.02
1923 (November)	$1.00	4,000,000,000	$0.004	$0.48

Table 2 – German mark devaluation and its impact on the assets of German citizens and the war debt

The economic crisis affecting Europe was unimaginable. Life savings became worthless. One who believed that he was worth a small fortune could have received a letter advising him that the bank was unable to manage his deposit of 68,000 marks because the administrative costs were disproportionate compared with the amount deposited. As a result, the bank was forced to return the capital to the client. And due to the lack of low-denomination banknotes, the bank had to round up the amount to 1,000,000 marks. The cost of the postage stamp on the envelope was 5,000,000 marks.

The inflation growth was senseless. At the grocery store, the waiting time for the clients in the line could double the price of their purchases. In the restaurants, the price of the meal could have doubled between the time you ordered and the time you paid for it. A house worth $100,000 in January 1922 was worth less than a dollar two years later.

Within a few years, the Germans had lost their Kaiser, and part of their territories and colonies. They had also lost their political and economic stability. They were now faced with unemployment, poverty and social misery. The properties were losing most of their value and even those who had money could not buy anything. The mark had become a ridiculous and unnecessary currency. In the worst moments of German history, money had always been a way to survive. In the Great Depression, money could not buy anything. Men were used to assess their value in terms of money. According to their financial value, they could go up or down the social ladder. Before, money had permanence and reference value. All that no longer existed. The changes were weakening the minds, making them vulnerable to anyone who could stir up their emotions and express their anger. And, basically, Hitler who believed that misery and chaos were necessities of fate rejoiced in their misfortune. He knew how to steer a revolt, but also how to obtain obedience. He added that the liberation of Germany was based on anything else than economic policies. To be free, it took pride, commitment, challenges, and hatred—especially hatred.

The RUHR occupation stirs hatred in Germany

In December 1922, the Reparation Commission noted that Germany intentionally failed its deliveries of coal and telegraph poles to France. On January 11, 1923, despite numerous warnings, French-Belgian troops occupied the Ruhr area covering two thousand and one hundred square kilometers, with three million inhabitants. Germany vigorously protested against the military occupation, stopped all deliveries to France and Holland, and ordered passive resistance in the occupied territories. Tension rose by several notches when France adopted retaliatory measures such as the occupation of industrial installations, the confiscation of wages, taxes, customs revenues, and the establishment of police roadblocks. Mass demonstrations multiplied. German protesters and French soldiers were killed and the occupying forces soon organized the deportation of one hundred fifty thousand Germans from the occupied territories. Others were sentenced to ten or twenty years in jail. Those who remembered that period said that it was worse than the Russian occupation at the end of World War I.

The atmosphere was explosive when the NSDAP held its first official congress in Munich at the end of January 1923. Hitler cleverly used the accumulated frustrations of the nation to stir up agitation in Germany and demand outright repudiation of the Treaty of Versailles. In an atmosphere of national suffering, he promised to tear up the Treaty of Versailles and his words provided hope. The party membership increased rapidly. Hitler began to see himself as the leader of the nation, and not of a political party only. As a result of the agitation raised by the NSDAP, several cities decreed the dissolution of the party that had become a threat to homeland security.

In June 1923, the Reichsbank has no more control over the German currency and a few months later, the government used the Emergency Powers Act to put into circulation a currency guaranteed by land holdings, commerce and industry as well as banks. Those measures put an end to inflation, but overthrew the Gustav Stresemann's government following a non-confidence vote by the Social Democratic Party.

The failed Beer Hall Putsch in Munich (*Hitlerputsch*)

When Mussolini marched on Rome and took power on October 29, 1922, the Bavarian Germans saw that as a great example of seizure of power of a central state by a regional political force. Hitler felt helpless and frustrated by the success of Mussolini's seizure of power while his own party was being attacked by the Bavarian government, which had banned the NSDAP meetings and made impossible the raising of troops. Therefore, he tried to bring together the nationalist parties in Bavaria and promoted the idea of a march on Berlin.

One of his contacts was General Otto von Lossow, commander of the Seventh Reichswehr (Army) Division stationed in Bavaria. He told him that a coup d'état was being prepared and asked for weapons to fight it, which the general refused, explaining that his troops were able to suppress a coup. Nonetheless, Hitler had built a secret arms cache, but the coup failed during the protest because Röhm did not arrive in time. Retaliation was prevented by the inability of the government to react.

In September 1923, faced with the deterioration of the political and social climate, the government repealed its directive of passive resistance given to the Germans in the Ruhr area occupied by France and Hitler took the opportunity to accuse the government of cowardice. The Bavarian authorities being in disagreement with the central government, the latter revoked the Bavarian government and appointed Gustav von Kahr to the position of state commissioner-general. He, in turn, entered in conflict with Berlin, but made two important allies, General von Lossow and the head of the State Police, Hans von Seisser. The situation came to the brink of civil war since von Kahr wanted the separation from Germany and the return of the monarchy in Bavaria. His plans were in direct conflict with those of Hitler, who advocated a strong central power in Berlin, gathering under his wing the German provinces. He feared above all to be outpaced by von Kahr and find himself in an independent Bavaria.

Therefore, he began to prepare and used his troops, having in mind to present the Kahr-Lossow-Seisser trio with a fait accompli. It was to take place on November 10, 1923, but the date was moved up two days when Hitler learned that the trio would be at a membership meeting of von Kahr's party. Hitler was aware that the army allegiance was to the Bavarian government rather than the central government in Berlin. And he feared the announcement of measures leading to the independence of Bavaria. His political philosophy was at the extreme opposite. Far from fostering a dismemberment of Germany into more or less autonomous states, he dreamed of a strong Germany, capable of asserting its hegemony over Europe. Above all, he feared a secession project initiated by the military that would jeopardize the work done by the party in the past two years.

On November 8, 1923, he went to the meeting, walked through the crowded auditorium and forced the trio into an adjoining room at gunpoint where he tried unsuccessfully to convince them of his coup d'état. The arrival of General Erich Ludendorff, who supported the idea, and the enthusiasm in the hall staggered the resolution of the three prisoners, who agreed to shake hands with Hitler in front of a cheering assembly. After leaving the brewery, Kahr, Lossow and Seisser changed their mind and, the following day, von Kahr disavowed the forced statements of the previous night.

The next day, Hitler and Ludendorff organized a march through Munich, but the police who had been alerted had set up roadblocks.

Shots were fired, sixteen people were killed, and Göring who walked next to Hitler was wounded in the abdomen.

Hitler's project was abruptly put on hold. Between 1923 and 1929, Germany was relatively quiet and the National Socialist Party was barely visible.

His time in the Landsberg jail was as good as a stay at the hotel

Hitler was arrested two days after the march. The trial began on February 26, 1924 and lasted nearly six weeks. With a certain complacency of the Court of Justice, Hitler used the Court as a political forum to attack his opponents, develop his political ideas and pose as the defender of the German nation. The trial roused public opinion and granted Hitler an unexpected visibly, as he was on the front page of almost every German newspaper for the duration of the trial.

On March 29, 1924, he was found guilty and sentenced to five years' imprisonment in the fortress of Landsberg, a small village located approximately fifty miles west of Munich. The NSDAP was also to be dissolved. The newspapers criticized the Court for the lightness of the sentence imposed, and the Times claimed that a breach of the Constitution was not considered a serious crime in Germany.

The conditions of detention imposed on Hitler were more in line with a holiday in a luxury hotel. He had a spacious and sunny cell, spent a lot of time outdoors in the gardens, received all the visitors that he wanted, and all the newspapers and books that he asked for. Among the other prisoners, many belonged to the NSDAP and Hitler exerted a certain ascendant over them. He always had the best place in the dining room of the prison where the food was tasteful, and detainees stood at attention until he sat in his chair.

During his stay in prison, he used his extraordinary power of persuasion to convert the staff to the principles of national-socialism. From the cleaners to the governor of the prison and his wife, all were blown away by his magnetism. Raf Leybold, governor of the prison, enrolled later in the National Socialist Party with his wife and children. When Hitler came to power, he rewarded him by appointing him director of all German prisons.

Mein Kampf

Hitler took advantage of his stay in prison to write his political autobiography, initially helped by Emil Maurice. The latter, who liked street battles, had joined the Nazi Party in 1919. He was Hitler's driver and bodyguard and, after his release from prison, he remained his driver. Maurice soon left his position as secretary to Rudolf Höss, a German born in Alexandria, Egypt, who had been sent to Germany by his father to pursue his university education. Höss was fanatically devoted to his chief. Hitler, who had not completed high school, took advantage of Höss' suggestions and knowledge to put in writing the story of his life and his political thoughts. The result was a rather disorganized and narcissistic book, full of monotonous repetitions, half-truths and oversimplifications. The topics, such as his youth, the superiority of the Aryan race and the associated threats, the political education and the means to be used to develop the spiritual strength of the nation, spread over a few pages and do not interact very well with each other. The style is more spoken than written language.

The first part of the nazi bible, *Mein Kampf*, My Struggle, was published on July 18, 1925. The second part was dictated in 1928, but not published immediately, possibly so as not to interfere with the sale of the first volume. The manuscript of the second volume was found in 1958 and published in 1961. For the first volume, Hitler had originally proposed the title *Four and a Half Years of Struggle Against Lies, Stupidity and Cowardice*. The editor, Max Amann, reduced the title to two words. Amann was the director of the *Völkischer Beobachter*. He managed the financial problems of the party and wanted a provocative best-seller. But Hitler had no narrative talent and, for political reasons, did not wish to cause a stir in the Bavarian and Berlin governments. The book was not well received by the public. In 1925, he sold only nine thousand four hundred copies, but after the accession of the ruling party, not having a copy at home was considered a shame. In 1933, he had sold a million copies and the profits generated were his main source of income.

Hitler was released on December 20, 1924, after only nine months in prison. Meanwhile, the political and social situation in Germany had improved. The mark was stable at the end of 1923. The parliamentary system functioned reasonably well, supported by the majority of the Center Party. On August 16, 1924, the Dawes plan, named after Charles Dawes, an American banker tasked with suggesting solutions to the combined problem of Germany's payment of war reparation and the resulting inflation, was approved by the London Conference. The main aspects of the plan were the evacuation of the Ruhr, a reduction of Germany's payments for war reparation and a loan to Germany to spur an economic recovery.

When Hitler was released from prison, the party was disorganized and only a handful of supporters were present. Some Nazis were still in prison, others had resigned and several members blamed Hitler for the failed putsch. He was accused of lacking political instinct and being responsible for the fall of a party that seemed promising. Since the NSDAP was banned under the new Bavarian government, Hitler did not give a speech. A fresh start was necessary. However, he had learned one very important lesson and he now knew that brute force only did not lead to power—bullying, lies, and deceit worked better. He was going to prove in the years to come that he was mastering those tools.

After the Munich putsch, the decline of the other far right parties enabled the NSDAP to quickly regain its popularity. In February 1925, the official newspaper, the *Völkischer Beobachter* reappeared with an editorial signed by Hitler in which he stated that he had given up power plays and would follow the path of democracy. The wolf was now dressed like a law-abiding citizen respectful of society and his party will again be allowed in early 1925.

In the presidential election of April 26, 1925, the seventy-seven-year-old Field Marshal Paul von Hindenburg was brought to power as a result of a coalition with the Bavarian People's Party, the German National Party, the German People's Party, and the Bavarian Peasants' League. He was President of the Republic until 1933, when Adolf Hitler succeeded him.

Chapter 3

The seizure of power and the establishment of dictatorship (1925-1939)

1925-1933: The legality

On February 25, 1925, the party newspaper was published again and announced a Party rally. At the meeting, Hitler explained that he will become the undisputed leader of the party or stand back and see it disappear. At the end of the speech, an enthusiastic crowd jumped on the tables. After the meeting, letters of support came from all over Germany. Thereafter, Hitler showed signs of a sincere conversion to democratic legality, offering to participate in the functioning of the German Republic.

The creation of SS groups

Meanwhile, Hitler was preoccupied by the troops led by Ernst Röhm, who was unconditionally loyal to the army rather than Hitler. He knew that if there was a crisis, the SA would join the army. Feeling the need for personal protection against his opponents at political meetings, he mandated his driver, Julius Schreck, to put together a troop of SS (*Shultz Staffel* or protection squadron) that was to give their allegiance to him only. The group was to be composed of steadfast men likely to fight against their own brothers. Very restrictive selection criteria led the SS to see themselves as an elite corps of whom the SA were jealous. They were street fighters that the German citizens feared and Hitler realized that they had a negative impact on his image. Much to the displeasure of the party leaders and the SA, Hitler established from the outset the independence of the SS from the Nazi Party.

On January 6, 1929, when Heinrich Himmler, the chicken breeder who looked like a schoolmaster, became head of the SS, the party leaders showed great satisfaction, thinking that they would easily dominate the timid and frail man. That was a big mistake. Himmler was about to transform the troop into an almost monastic order and become the most feared leader of the Third Reich. Under his command, the SS became elite troops. Despite being outnumbered by the SA, they saw themselves as a superior race with their black uniforms. Through an extensive screening process over a period of two years, Himmler had sixty thousand men expelled, mainly alcoholics or homosexuals. With approximately two hundred men at the beginning, the SS units had grown to fifty thousand men when Hitler became chancellor of Germany in 1933.

Leibstandarte-SS Adolf Hitler

Hitler was constantly afraid of being assassinated. Himmler fueled this fear by foiling plot after plot. If some of them were real, the others were most likely part of Himmler's strategy to consolidate his position with Hitler. He ordered Himmler to create an elite guard consisting of one hundred twenty handpicked SS to form three human ramparts around the Reich Chancellery. Hitler's level of satisfaction with this elite corps was such that, during a rally in Nuremberg in September 1933, he named the troop Leibstandarte-SS Adolf Hitler, allowing it to carry his own flag, and appointed a brutal man, Josef Sepp Dietrich, at the head of this elite corps. Himmler now had a small military unit that would grow to compete with the German army in the following years. It is the unit that was used on June 30, 1934 to decapitate the SA leadership in the Night of the Long Knives.

The end of democracy in the NSDAP

From the beginning, Munich was the birthplace of the NSDAP. But when it became a national movement, a dispute arose within the other cells of the party, mainly because of the influence of some deputies of Hitler at the party headquarters. In Thuringia especially, there was a rebellion against the Munich hegemony and the meaning of the directives from headquarters. The leader of the Thuringia party was Gregor Strasser, assisted by his brother Otto, and Paul Joseph Goebbels, holder of a doctorate in literature. Gregor Strasser was an idealistic intellectual, whose enthusiasm for the NSDAP had led him to sell his pharmacy in 1924, in order to devote himself to the affairs of the party. This man who had been a deputy in the Reichstag was a happy-go-lucky person who felt right at home in politics. Goebbels who worked as editor for a weekly national socialist newspaper had been trying his hand at writing during a few years, after lengthy studies in literature and philosophy at six universities. Strasser's and Goebbels' political objectives were different from those of Hitler. Goebbels even wrote a letter seeking a rapprochement with the communists, that Hitler saw as a sacrilege. Hitler promised to maintain private property while Strasser proposed to end free economy. At a meeting organized by Strasser in Hanover on November 22, 1925, the Gauleiters (party leaders of regional branches of the NSDAP) of northern Germany, many of whom had been appointed by Strasser, were invited to discuss the program they proposed. One of the participants yelled that they should not have to take orders from the pope of Munich, and Goebbels asked that the idiot Gottfried Feder, who was sent by Hitler as an observer, be expelled from the meeting.

Hitler used the same technique. He invited the Gauleiters of southern Germany in Bamberg on February 14, 1926, but most of them had not been appointed by Strasser. The Strasser brothers and Goebbels attended the meeting, which was a political point-scoring between Hitler and Gregor Strasser on topics such as workers, socialism, economy, possible alliances with Russia, and the concept of revolution. At the end of the discussion, Goebbels stood up and publicly announced that he was supporting Hitler, admitting with emotion that he had been heading in the wrong direction with Strasser. The latter had just lost the game.

Goebbels soon became one of the most ardent admirers of Hitler, skillfully flattering his narcissism. He shared with Hitler the amorality that allowed them to use lies, misrepresentation, cheating, deceit and violence, when those means helped achieving their goals. He made the SA wear a red head bandage to let people think that the party counted several heroes who did not hesitate to shed their blood for the cause. Using a pen name, he wrote in the *Völkischer Beobachter* about his own heroic adventures. Once, he reported that feeling unsafe on a trip, he stopped the vehicle and discovered that one of the wheels was attached to the hub by a single nut, another Jewish conspiracy.

On November 1, 1926, to test his new lieutenant, Hitler appointed him head of the Berlin cell, where a mutiny had broken out. An aggressive and radical Goebbels used ruthless methods to control the rebellion led by Kurt Daluege, a leader of the SA troops in Berlin. He gained the favor of Hitler, who appointed him minister of Propaganda in 1928, a position he held with an undisputed success. Hitler was very close to Goebbels' family, who perfectly complemented his chief by materializing projects that otherwise could have remained at the planning stage.

In May 1926, Hitler invited the Munich party members to a meeting where it was decided that the Munich cell would be the official voice of the NSDAP, and its leader automatically became the head of the NSDAP at the national level. The president had the authority to appoint or dismiss the Gauleiters across the country. This is when the Führerprinzip (Führer principle) was established. Authority was delegated by the immediate superior, who derived his authority from his own immediate superior. At the top of the pyramid was the chief vested with unlimited power and authority, the elected head of the NSDAP. Hitler's party was no longer a democratic party.

On his way to power

The Nazi Party had managed to undermine the regime from the inside, eroding the loyalty of the public servants, many of whom were spies paid by the party. Those spies gathered secret information from the government and forwarded it to a central office of the party led by Rudolf Höss, Hitler's right arm. One day, the minister of the Interior wrote a confidential decree ordering the secret police to monitor the meetings of the National Socialist Party. The party leaders were informed of the decree before the secret police was aware of it.

The introduction of the Hitler salute at the first congress of the NSDAP

On July 4, 1926, the NSDAP held its first congress since its reconstitution in Weimar, Thuringia, one of the few regions in Germany where Hitler still had the right to speak in public. He greeted the crowd with an outstretched arm. Later, a group of five thousand men in uniform greeted him with this salute. At that time, the party had twenty-seven thousand members and the growth of the party was phenomenal. In November, the party had forty-nine thousand members. This is when a youth division of the SA was created, the Hitler Youth.

Year	Number
1925	700
1926	49,000
1927	70,000
1928	100,000
1932	850,000
1933	8,000,000

Table 1 – Number of members of the Nazi Party from 1925 until the takeover

The ban on public speaking in Bavaria was lifted on March 10, 1927, and in Prussia on September 28, 1928.

In the following years, Hitler had plenty to do, as he was struggling to navigate between the intense scrutiny of the judiciary and the Party members, on which he exercised a very relative control. The SA troops openly defied his authority, spontaneously murdering whoever they wanted, and sometimes looked like a hotbed of homosexuals. Aware that he must depend on the SA, he tolerated and excused unacceptable behaviors. Sometimes he was filled with fear and trepidation due to the risk of deportation associated with some enthusiastic leaders of the SA, who dreamed of fomenting a rebellion in the army and taking it over. Violent discussions often opposed him to recalcitrant SA leaders. As for the Gauleiters, a few of them used their power to divert the funds of the party and several were projecting a questionable morality.

1925	Publication of the first part of *Mein Kampf*.
	The party newspaper is published again.
1926	First congress of the NSDAP in Weimar. Adoption of the Hitler salute.
1927	First congress of the NSDAP in Nuremberg. 30,000 men are in uniform.
	Party members: 70,000
1928	The NSDAP wins 12 seats in the Reichstag.
	The organization is divided into 34 Gaue (administrative regions).
	Party members: 100,000
	The second part of *Mein Kampf* is still an unpublished manuscript.
1929	Election of 107 deputies in the Reichstag.
	The SA has 100,000 members, more than the regular army.
1932	The SA has 400,000 members.
1933	Hitler is elected chancellor of Germany.
1934	The SA reaches 500,000 members.

Table 2 – Milestones on Hitler's path to power

And then, Hermann Göring, who was in contact with Italian princes and would become the link between Hitler and Mussolini, returned from exile. Moreover, Göring, a distinguished aviator, was also in contact with Erhard Milch, technical director of Lufthansa, who played an important role in the rearmament of Germany.

In those years, public interest in the party declined. The departure of the occupying troops in Rhineland on June 30, 1930, five years before the scheduled date, decreased the tension in Germany. In the 1928 election, the party obtained only 2.6 percent of the vote, but Goebbels and Göring were elected deputies and the party was setting foot in the German parliament.

This is when the party took advantage once again of a state of crisis that would bring many benefits. The Dawes plan, that was merely spreading the World War I reparation payments of Germany, was replaced by the Young plan, proposed by the American banker Owen T. Young and adopted in August 1929. The new plan reduced further annual payments and spread them over the next sixty years, placing on the unborn German grandchildren the burden of a debt they had not incurred. Hitler used this crisis as a springboard and made an alliance with some industrialists of the German right-wing who openly criticized the acceptance of the plan. His contacts with respectable and influential people allowed Hitler to bail out the party, whose emblems began to proliferate in Germany. Goebbels was appointed minister of Propaganda and, under his leadership, Hitler's party was to take precedence over the others. After getting off the ground at the national level, his party flush with money, Hitler ended his relationship with the industrialists he had been courting since 1928. The party could finally embark on a national campaign on a scale never envisaged before.

On October 24, 1929, the Wall Street Crash and the Great Depression completely destroyed the Germans' confidence in parliamentary democracy and made them receptive to Hitler's speech promising work and bread. As a result of the economic slowdown caused by the recovery of Europe helped by the United States and the prohibitive prices impacting personal consumption, thirteen million shares lost 30 percent of their value and thousands of investors were wiped out entirely. Spectacular suicides were reported and that day went down in history as the Black Thursday. The economic recovery in Germany was too fragile to avoid a backlash and unemployment rose at a frightening speed. In September 1930, there were three million unemployed in Germany, and that number doubled over the next two years. Again, Hitler took full advantage of the situation. Knowing how to increase the nervousness and anxiety of various segments of the German population, he gathered huge masses under the banner of his party. The Nazis organized their own groups in offices and factories. Agitators were in the streets to talk to the unemployed. The party had really taken off. The communist elements consisting of the workers and disadvantaged of other parties warned the population against the words and actions of Hitler and Göring, who returned the attacks against their opponents. They found a sympathetic ear in the bourgeoisie frightened by the prospect of a workers' revolution. Germany was cleaved between the nazi far right and the communist far left.

The party attracted young people, especially in the academic world, who enlisted in large numbers and sometimes threatened the lives of their peers and teachers who did not participate in this mobilization, or denounced their Jewish colleagues. For the campaign in the parliamentary elections of September 14, 1930, an important organization joined the entire population, even in the hamlets, and used visual techniques, including gatherings at night under spotlights, and parades in the light of torches. The ballot exceeded all expectations. With one hundred seven seats, Hitler's party won the second place in parliament, behind the Social Democrats, who had one hundred forty-three seats, and far ahead of the Communists, who had seventy-seven seats only. However, Hitler had not been elected, as he was ineligible due to his Austrian citizenship. But the NSDAP became an important stakeholder on the political scene and was able to form a coalition with the moderate block. In fact, a coalition between the NSDAP, the National Socialist Party and the main right-wing parties expressed its intention to overthrow the democratic regime of the country. The successive votes of non-confidence in the government of Chancellor Heinrich Brüning created an instability that worked to the advantage of Hitler. The chancellors and their government began a stunning game of musical chairs while President Hindenburg was forced to rule by decree, as allowed by article 48 of the Constitution.

However, the social democratic Chancellor Brüning was in a hopeless situation. He did not have an absolute majority and could not count on a coalition due to the distribution of seats. The solution he adopted provided Hitler with an important precedent. As German chancellor, he took the position of government advisor to the president of the Republic, and Field Marshal Hindenburg ruled through presidential decrees, applying austerity measures that met opposition in Germany.

President Hindenburg was an eighty-two-year-old war hero, whose popularity came from his success as commander of the German army in 1916. He felt a strong antipathy for Hitler. In 1932, he was up for reelection. Since Chancellor Brüning did not want a new campaign, he attempted to amend the Constitution in order to extend the mandate of the president for two years. However, since he needed the consent of the National Socialist Party members, the chancellor was forced to meet with Hitler. Hitler was facing a dilemma. If he accepted, he lost the chance to become president of the republic with absolute powers; if he refused, he would be insulting a respected man on the German political scene. After long days of hesitation, he refused both alternatives and managed to expose Brüning's dealings in an attempt to cling to power. Presidential elections had to be called and Adolf Hitler decided to seek the presidency.

The election campaign was one that the country had never seen. Nazi banners were present everywhere and Hitler smartly planned to travel by air, impressing the population across the country. He promised to rid Germany of the thirty parties that had created a political chaos. The newspapers were full of articles and photographs, and the theaters showed ten-minute advertising spots before the movie. The nazi electoral successes caused an upsurge in violence in the streets and bloody confrontations made many victims. The government was forced to introduce emergency measures and the SA and SS groups were dissolved on April 13, 1932. Hitler ordered his SA and SS troops to join the party. In the second round of voting, Hindenburg was reelected with 53 percent of the vote while Hitler had only 36.8 percent.

1933-1939: The seizure of power

The presidential election was a bitter disappointment for the Nazis. Having gained enough confidence to take measures against the Nazis, Chancellor Brüning ordered the disbandment of the SA and SS under a decree that prohibited uniformed political organizations. Many nationalist groups had their own uniform and the decree was not exclusively intended for the Nazis. Consequently, the chancellor was the subject of campaigns using offensive language throughout Germany. The relationship between the chancellor and Hindenburg got so bad that the latter dismissed the chancellor on May 30, 1932, on the charge of having Bolsheviks in his cabinet, and replaced him with Franz von Papen, whose cabinet included a high proportion of large landowners such as Hindenburg himself. Under the new chancellor, the uniform ban was repealed on June 16, 1933. The enthusiastic Nazis worked to aggravate the disorders that prevented the government from taking action. The country was on the verge of a civil war while the Communists and the Nazis frequently clashed.

At the legislative elections of July 31, 1932, the German nation showed its determination to put an end to a long series of governments unable to manage the republic. The Nazi Party won two hundred thirty seats in parliament and no majority could be guaranteed without their collaboration. Chancellor von Papen declared in an interview that the time had come for the National Socialist Party to closely engage in the reconstruction of Germany. Since the NSDAP had no absolute majority, the other political parties believed that Hitler would have no choice but to compromise.

Political parties	May 1924	Dec 1924	May 1928	Sept 1930	July 1932	Nov 1932	March 1933
NSDAP	32 6.5%	14 3.0%	12 2.6%	107 18.3%	230 37.4%	196 33.1%	288 43.9%
Social Democrat	100 20.5%	131 26.0%	153 29.8%	143 24.5%	133 21.6%	121 20.4%	120 18.3%
Communist	62 12.6%	45 9.0%	54 10.6%	77 13.1%	89 14.6%	100 16.9%	81 12.3%
Catholic Center	81 13.4%	88 13.6%	78 12.1%	87 11.8%	97 12.5%	70 11.9%	93 11.7%
National Far Right	95 19.5%	103 20.5%	73 14.2%	41 7.0%	37 5.9%	52 8.8%	52 8.0%
Others	102 27.5%	112 27.9%	121 33.0%	122 25.3%	22 8.0%	35 8.9%	23 5.8%

Table 3 – Distribution of the seats and percentages of the vote in the general elections of Germany between 1924 and 1933

Against all odds, Hitler asked von Papen to abdicate in his favor, so that he could be appointed chancellor by President Hindenburg. Franz von Papen answered that the president did not know him well enough and offered Hitler the position of vice-chancellor, with the promise to grant him the chancellery when he becomes known. Hitler declined von Papen's offer, bluntly replying that he had no intention of playing a background role, given the importance of his party's representation in parliament. Since Hitler was inflexible, von Papen proposed to defer the question to the president.

On August 13, Hitler met with Hindenburg, who appealed in vain to his sense of patriotism. Hindenburg remained firm and refused to give him the position of chancellor, unless his party could form a coalition that would give him a majority of seats. Hitler slammed the door, saying that his party would support the government insofar as the policies implemented were consistent with the program of the National Socialist Party.

The Reichstag was convened on August 30 and, on that day, Göring was elected president of the chamber, since he was the representative of the party having the largest number of elected deputies. On September 12, at the first parliament meeting, von Papen presented an economic recovery plan, but before the end of his presentation, a Social Democrat, Communist and National Socialist coalition led by Göring adopted a motion of non-confidence in the government. A general pandemonium followed and von Papen laid on Göring's table a decree ordering a new dissolution of parliament. He immediately left the assembly while Göring, deliberately ignoring the decree, was collecting the deputies' votes. The government was defeated by four hundred twelve votes against forty-two. It was only after the vote that he read the Decree of dissolution of the Parliament chamber and invalidated it since the government had just been defeated. He tried to cancel the decree without success.

After the fall of von Papen, a new election on November 6, 1932 granted one hundred ninety-six seats out of five hundred ninety-four to the National Socialist Party. Hitler's party had lost two million votes to the other parties. Once again, the government was unable to achieve a majority without the support of Hitler. Discussions with other political parties failed. Obviously, the National Socialist Party was the only one that could put in power a majority government, if it was supported by the Centre Party, which had 70 seats. Having exhausted all his resources, Hindenburg offered the chancellery to Hitler, but the latter declined, demanding a presidential cabinet. Hindenburg was in a hopeless situation.

Hindenburg appointed the scheming General Kurt von Schleicher to the position of Reich chancellor. The Socialist Party's financial resources were being drained by its election efforts and all support was crumbling. Hitler was challenged even within the party, and the members began to say that he was losing opportunities to seize power. Schleicher made an attempt to reconcile the National Socialists by contacting Gregor Strasser instead of Hitler. Out of loyalty, Strasser refused, but Hitler had him executed in 1934. That was when Hitler was put in contact with a Cologne banker, Baron Kurt von Schroder, who promised to support the party. Schleicher was upset and managed to alienate Hindenburg, who had appointed him chancellor. A by-election in Lippe confirmed the popularity of the Socialists and Chancellor von Schleicher realized that his days were numbered.

Meetings and discussions followed, recalling backstairs influence. Otto Maissner, secretary of state for the presidency, participated in the discussions and convinced Hindenburg that his rights as president of the republic and head of the army would be respected by the Nazis. For his part, von Papen reassured Hindenburg, believing that the Nazis would be defeated as the result of the mobilization of the christian and conservative forces. Furthermore, Hitler's party required two Nazis only in key positions: Wilhelm Frick at the ministry of the Interior for the Reich, and Hermann Göring, commissioner of the Interior for Prussia. Hitler alleged that changes in the Prussian police had become necessary, due to the communist threat. Franz von Papen reassured the president, arguing that two Nazis only in the cabinet could not have a significant degree of control compared with the eight other ministers who were more conservative. That was a huge mistake. He believed that the political institutions were strong and stable enough to allow genuine democracy. He wrote in his memoirs that, at the first cabinet meeting, Hitler was angry and protested against the manifestations of antisemitism in his party, promising to rein in his unruly troops. The sincerity that he showed did not augur that the party leader, who advocated discipline among its members, was the one who, in his quest for absolute power, would eliminate political parties and social institutions.

On January 22, 1933, Hitler met with Franz von Papen and Oskar von Hindenburg, the son of the president. That meeting sealed the fate of Germany. After granting tax-exempt land to the Hindenburg family and the vice-chancellorship to von Papen, Hitler became chancellor of Germany on January 30, 1933. The political class was reassured by the fact that the cabinet was made up of five conservative members, who should be able to effectively control the three nazi members who complemented the government. However, among those three Nazis, Göring was head of the police services and Hitler was chancellor. It was clearly written in the Constitution that the chancellor could use exceptional powers if the state security was threatened. It was a door that Hitler was able to open. In Berlin that night, hundreds of thousands of Nazis participated in an imposing torchlight march that lit the streets from the Brandenburg Gate to the chancellery. However, the flame of democracy would soon be blown out.

We now leave the German history to enter the history of the world.

The establishment of the dictatorship

When Hitler was appointed chancellor in 1933, Germany was going through a deep crisis of confidence in its political institutions. The population believed less and less in the democracy of the Weimar Republic. For more than a decade, governments had succeeded one another at a fast pace, none of them being able to solve the economic and social issues. But, due to the power of conviction of its leader and the importance given to the magnificent public manifestations meant to hit popular opinion, the NSDAP was standing out from the other parties. Hitler had succeeded in giving the Germans hope for a political revival. And the army, despite its oath of loyalty to the new republic, remained an imperial army, watching with great reserve the governments in power. The NSDAP exerted a strong appeal on the army and some officers even felt that the SA troops could play the role of a parallel army, for example, in monitoring the border. Enjoying with his usual opportunism the political uncertainty experienced by the population and the army, Hitler ran a series of projects characterized by short but massive and unexpected interventions that prefigured the *blitzkriegs*, the sudden and overwhelming military attacks that will enable him to invade Austria, Czechoslovakia and Poland without any resistance.

February 27, 1933: The Reichstag fire

Twenty-eight days exactly after his appointment as chancellor, an unexpected event put the key to power in Hitler's hands. On the evening of February 27, 1933, Berliners who lived close to the Reichstag saw a yellow and glossy reflection in their windows. The Reichstag was ablaze. Nazi leaders rushed to the scene. Göring, sweating and puffing and beside himself with excitement, was already there declaiming to heaven, as von Papen later recalled, that it was a communist crime against the new government. Göring blamed the communist revolution and stated that the government would be merciless in repressing the political chaos.

Several troubling circumstances suggested that the fire was ignited by the Nazis themselves. At the Nuremberg Tribunal, Göring was asked how he could, one hour after the fire, issue a statement attributing to the communists the responsibility for the fire. Göring said that he had no recollection of that statement and suggested that the idea came from Hitler. However, he was forced to admit that Hitler could not have had valid evidence in such a short period of time and that a list of five thousand communists had already been prepared and was ready to use the day after the fire. During the trial, General Franz Halder also testified having heard Göring boasting at a luncheon in 1942 that he had set the parliament on fire. In fact, a mentally retarded pyromaniac of communist allegiance, Marinus van der Lubbe, was found at the crime scene and sentenced to death in December 1933. Experts argued that Lubbe was unable to set a fire of that magnitude, considering that the flames were raging in the large central hall, two and a half minutes after the start of the fire. If the project was the work of the communists, it is unlikely that they would have entrusted the task to a half-wit such as Lubbe. Underground tunnels connected the parliament with the palace of the President of the Reichstag Hermann Göring. The most probable assumption is that SA members used the tunnels to spread gasoline in the parliament and paid Lubbe to be on the scene at the appropriate time.

Unlike the communists who had no acceptable justification for carrying out that project, Hitler was clearly prepared to take advantage of the fire. In one of his interviews on August 21, 1942, Hitler said that he went to the *Völkischer Beobachter* office that night to immediately use the Reichstag fire for his own purposes.

The next day, Hitler met with President Hindenburg and persuaded him to sign a decree abolishing civil and individual liberties of citizens, for the protection of the German people and the German state. The freedom of speech, the freedom of the press, the freedom to organize and assemble, and the right to secrecy of communications were abolished. The state was also attributed the right to search and detain suspects. The day after the fire, political authorities claimed that a thorough investigation incriminated the communists. Four thousand Communists were arrested and incarcerated. A large number of communist deputies were incarcerated despite their parliamentary immunity. Supported by the authority of Göring, minister of the Interior of Prussia, which represented two-thirds of the German territory and traditionally gave the tone to Germany, the SA troops replaced the police forces. They entered homes, made arrests and used torture under the stunned eyes of a population still under the shock of the events. The prisons being crowded, Heinrich Himmler, the nazi commissioner of the Munich Police, created the first concentration camp in Dachau on March 20, 1933. In a fast, brutal and efficient way that would remain his trademark, Hitler had just eliminated the communist opposition a few days before the election scheduled on March 5, a week later. This dramatic purge was also meant to make the electorate aware of the alleged danger of a communist revolution and rally votes for the Nazi Party. Göring blamed the communist revolution and stated that the government would be merciless in repressing the political chaos.

The Reichstag fire was the first demonstration of the effectiveness of an unexpected intervention that would allow Hitler to use an element of surprise to eliminate all resistance to his projects. This is how he easily obtained emergency powers enabling him to eliminate trade unions, political parties, and invade Austria, Czechoslovakia and Poland. It was also the first demonstration of a large-scale deceit, which has always been part of his repertoire of political tactics. In 1939, he will use a similar sham in the false flag attack on a German radio station close to the Poland border to justify the invasion of the neighboring country. No one can say that Hitler was covering his tracks. As early as 1926, he wrote in *Mein Kampf* that the big lies are more credible than the small lies.

The last democratic elections in Germany

The last democratic elections were held in Germany on March 5, 1933. The vote was secret, but the ballots were marked to identify those who voted against Hitler's party. A minority of Germans (17,269,629 people) voted for the National Socialist Party (43.9 percent of the votes) and 22,054,834 votes went to the fourteen other parties. This significant increase, when compared to the twelve million votes four months earlier, suggests that many Germans surrendered their freedom to win security six days after the Reichstag fire. But the party still did not have a majority. The fifty-two nationalist seats added to the two hundred eighty-eight nazi seats gave the government a majority of sixteen votes only in the Reichstag.

In any case, Hitler did not intend to govern with the support of the Reichstag. Ten years earlier, he had written in *Mein Kampf* that the power should remain in the hands of one man directly responsible for his decisions, and not with a handful of irresponsible people who were no longer accountable at the end of their mandate. The last election had given him an apparent legitimacy and he was about to impose a totalitarian regime to the German nation.

Hitler (national socialist)	Chancellor
Von Papen (center)	Vice-chancellor
Von Neurath (no party affiliation)	Foreign minister
Frick (national socialist)	Minister of the Interior
Von Krosigk (no party affiliation)	Minister of Finance
Von Blomberg (no party affiliation)	Minister of Defense
Hugenberg (dnvp)	Minister of Economics
Göring (national socialist)	Minister without portfolio
Rust (national socialist)	Minister of Education
Seldte (steel helmets)	Minister of Labor
Von Eltz-Ruhenach (no party affiliation)	Minister of Communication
Gürtner (dnvp)	Minister of Justice

Table 4 – Hitler's cabinet in January 1933

March 23, 1933: The Enabling Act and the end of democracy

In order to establish the legality of his dictatorship, Hitler needed a parliamentary vote that gave him legislative authority for a period of four years, in order to put an end to the misery of the people and of the Reich. Taking advantage of the confusion created in Germany by the Reichstag fire and using his power of persuasion, he told the members of parliament what they wanted to hear. He talked about morality, peace, and economic independence of Germany and managed not to arouse the vigilance of the members of parliament. He had them ratify the Enabling Act, granting the chancellor the power to enact laws without the involvement of the Reichstag, which was to be informed of governmental measures.

The Communist Party being forbidden in parliament, the Social Democratic Party was the only one to rise against this law that virtually put an end to what remained of democracy in Germany.

The Catholic and Democratic Centre Party having received from Hitler the written promise—never held, that he would abide by the veto of the president, voted for the Bill. It was March 23, 1933, and democracy was legally dead.

In the following days, Hitler banned all the political parties in Germany and, on July 24, the NSDAP became the only authorized political party, the other parties had been dissolved voluntarily. Now Hitler was free to disregard the constitutional guarantees and had just achieved the incredible feat of legally establishing his dictatorship in Germany.

The nazification of Germany: From the Länder to the Gaue

When Hitler came to power in 1933, Germany was a federation of fifteen provinces, basically equal, but largely dominated by Prussia, which occupied a territory four times larger and had a population five times greater than Bavaria, its nearest competitor. In the thirteen other provinces, each had less than 5 percent of the geographical area of Germany and, apart from Saxony, less than 5 percent of its population. Three independent cities completed the German territory.

For administrative purposes, the Nazi Party had divided the German territory into districts called Gaue.

In April 1933, Hitler began to choose governors, called Gauleiters, to head the districts. Those officials, from the Nazi Party and loyal to Hitler, were appointed by the old President Hindenburg, who saw the power slip slowly through his fingers. The Gauleiters enjoyed an almost absolute power, often more important than that of several cabinet ministers. In 1938, there were thirty-two Gaue in Germany and forty in 1942, due to the annexation of Austria, and the Czechoslovakian and Polish territories that became part of Germany. The occupied territories will be administered by a Reich commissioner or a governor.

Date	Law decree	Objective
February 28, 1933	Presidential decree for the protection of the German people and German state	Abolition of civil and individual liberties
March 23, 1933	Enabling Act	Gives the chancellor the power to enact laws without the involvement of the Reichstag and abolishes the parliament
April 7, 1933	Law for the Restoration of the Professional Civil Service – authorizing the appointment of *Gauleiters* for each district	Hitler abolishes the local governments and appoints nazi governors with the sanction of President Hindenburg
January 30, 1934	Law for the Reconstruction of the Reich - which transferred the states' powers to the Reich	Traditionally autonomous provinces now answer to the minister of the Interior
August 1, 1934	Law giving presidential power to the chancellor	Gives the chancellor presidential powers until the next election
August 3, 1934	Law combining the office of Reich President with that of Reich Chancellor	Gives the chancellor presidential powers as long as necessary
August 20, 1934	Law making mandatory for the army to swear an oath of allegiance to Hitler	Each soldier must swear an oath of allegiance not to the constitution or the president, but to Hitler

Table 5 – Hitler's accession to dictatorship: The legal steps

A new law proclaimed on April 7 assigned to each state of the German republic a member of the Nazi Party as Reich governor, who deposed local governments, dismissed judges and officials, and whose mission was to follow the policies dictated by the chancellor. Hitler was putting an end to the traditional autonomy of the German provinces and creating One People, One Nation, One Leader. On January 30, 1934, a law officially recognized the transfer of sovereign powers to the states under the authority of the Reich, and the appointed governors reported to the minister of the Interior.

One by one, the German institutions were crushed by the nazi steamroller.

On May 1, 1933, Hitler proclaimed Labor Day as a paid national holiday, and the party organized reassuring mass rallies where it was said that the revolution was not against German workers, but for them. He launched with enthusiasm a slogan emphasizing the respect due to the workers. No later than the next morning, Hitler promulgated the dissolution of all trade unions in Germany and the seizure of their assets and properties to be transferred to one single union, the German Labor Front, headed by Dr. Robert Ley, leader of the Nazi Party in Cologne, that all German workers were required to join. The GLF abolished collective bargaining, prohibited strikes and regulated working conditions.

Political instability had apparently come to an end in Germany, but it was replaced by a social instability encouraged by a political mafia. Social and political stability are essential to the successful conduct of business. However, during that time, the SA were calling the shots, arresting and beating up citizens while the police chose not to intervene. Even the judges were intimidated when they had to render a verdict of guilt against the SA in obvious situations such as cold-blooded murder.

In his memoirs, Vice-Chancellor Franz von Papen explained that his office became somehow the complaints department of the Reich, due to the growing number of protests in the population about the excesses of the Nazi Party. He added that the freedom of press limitations imposed earlier by the nazi regime prevented the mobilization of the public opinion against the government.

The swastika becomes the emblem of nazi Germany

Hitler attached paramount importance to external events likely to strike the imagination, such as uniforms, flags, emblems, rallies and parades. The most representative and ubiquitous symbol of the nazi power remains the gammadion cross or swastika, that we still see nowadays when neo-nazi movements arise. The name swastika was loaned from the Sanskrit terms *su,* meaning well, and *asti,* meaning is. It was originally a Hindu symbol of India, reminding of a rising sun, standing on one branch, its points directed to the left. The swastika has been part of many cultures over the centuries. It was recovered and adapted as their emblem in the early twenties by an antisemitic nationalist group best known as the Thule Society, founded in 1919 in Munich. Several future Nazis such as Max Amann, Anton Drexler, Dietrich Eckart, Hans Frank, Rudolf Höss, Alfred Rosenberg, and Gottfried Feder were members of the Thule Society. Hitler used the swastika as an Aryan symbol of the purity of the Nordic blood. It was incorporated in the German flag in September 1935, after turning the points to the right and rotating the emblem to give an impression of movement.

The swastika became the symbol of conformity to the nazi orthodoxy and unity. Distributed as a red armband with the swastika inside a white circle, it was worn on the left arm over the sleeve of civilian clothes, or police or military uniforms. The army vehicles, airplanes, official cars and military decorations displayed the swastika. The ubiquitous emblem was even found in consumer products such as bottles of wine and neckties. At political rallies, thousands of flags fluttering in the wind gave the impression of a red sea with shades of white and black.

As Führer and Chancellor of Germany, Hitler used the swastika standing on one branch without the rotation applied to the national emblem, to give an impression of stability. At official ceremonies, this version of the swastika was often topped by a huge eagle with outstretched wings.

There were many variations on the same theme. For example, Hitler Youths wore a red armband with a white stripe through the center and a white patch with a black swastika stitched in the middle of the armband. The SS wore the standard armband bordered in a black rayon tape at the top and bottom edges.

Different versions of the swastika with curved branches inspired other symbols such as the SS letters representing two parallel lightning bolts meant to inspire terror under the nazi rule.

1933-1935: The beginning of the Jewish persecution and the Nuremberg Laws

The end of March 1933 saw the beginning of the persecutions against Jews, whom the Nazis equated with the Communist Party and described as opponents of National Socialism. In Europe and America, protests arose in Jewish communities, calling for a boycott of German products. In retaliation, the German government called for a boycott of stores owned by Jews, as well as Jewish professionals, such as lawyers and doctors. In Prussia, under the authority of the Minister of the Interior Göring, several measures were first implemented to oust Jews holding positions of responsibility in the public service as well as in academic and cultural spheres, where it was recommended that they spontaneously resign. In all major German cities, in an extensive process of intellectual uniformity, a cultural cleansing led to the burning of all non-German books.

Between the seizure of power in 1933 and the promulgation of the Nuremberg Laws in 1935, the path of antisemitism illustrates in abundance the chaotic aspect of the leadership established by Hitler. Sometimes he used his authority as leader of the Nazi Party, other times his authority as head of the government to issue guidelines addressed to the party members or government circles. Several governmental directives were piggybacking on spontaneous initiatives of the party and were nothing more than a political sanction against the behavior of the most radical nazi elements.

Antisemitism, which became more and more evident starting in 1933, suited many people for different reasons. The Jewish omnipresence in several key positions in Germany was an annoying obstacle for Hitler, whose objective was to develop a pure Aryan race. After the murder of Ernst Röhm, he brutally removed the obstacles preventing him from achieving his purposes. Here again, intentionalists and structuralists will find considerable matters of debate to defend a logical path without deviations or a circumstantial and organizational improvisation, to explain the relationship between Hitler's intentions and their materialization. Hitler wanted to eliminate the Jews in Europe. His intentions resulted in the extermination of the European Jews. The big question is to what extent can we attribute to Hitler, intentionalist hypothesis, or other nazi leaders, structuralist hypothesis, the final form of achievement of this objective?

The Führer would certainly not have shied away from this initiative, regardless of where it came from. His visceral and even pathological hatred of the Jews, which was a considerable part of his rhetoric since 1919, somehow forced him to be coherent and support the party's initiatives in line with the racial discrimination path he had traced. However, he never showed a marked propensity for details, always preferring to give general instructions verbally, leaving to his subordinates the task to put in writing what they had understood. This disregard for details gave those who were implementing his directives unhoped-for room in their personal initiatives largely linked to their powers. Thus a large number of nazi initiatives can be considered as spur of the moment decisions likely to be institutionalized when they brought the expected results.

For the radical Nazis, antisemitism was a way to boost the nationalist fervor of the working class as it designated a culprit for society's problems. In the euphoria of the taking of power, the party's radical elements took the initiative to trigger a wave of anti-Jewish violence without a formal directive from the government or the party. On April 1, 1933, Hitler was forced to proclaim an official boycott of Jewish professionals' shops and offices to support the antisemitic movement, but especially to give the impression that he was leading the wave. Criticized outside the country, denounced by German conservative elements and not supported by President Hindenburg, the Jewish boycott was a fiasco and the antisemitic movement began experiencing a lull in the summer of 1933, although the violence against Jews by the SA and extremist elements of the party never ceased.

It must be said that for some sectors of the German population, the Jewish elimination offered major economic benefits. It removed an unwelcome competition for many non-Jewish businesses, and even gave to several Germans the opportunity to buy successful businesses at a ridiculous price. Some people were pleased with this redistribution of wealth, since they were jealous of the excellent economic positioning of several members of the Jewish community.

On September 15, 1935, at the seventh national congress of the NSDAP, Hitler proclaimed the Nuremberg Laws. As was his custom, Hitler was at the last minute. The content of the laws was improvised in one hour the evening before their promulgation. They recognized German citizenship to citizens of German blood and excluded the Jews from the right to vote and occupy a position in the public service. Moreover, any union, extramarital relation or marriage abroad between a German and a Jew was invalid in Germany. Jews were not allowed to employ in their households females of German or related blood who were under forty-five years of age, and were forbidden to fly the Reich flag. In late December, Jewish physicians working in public hospitals were forced to resign. Jews were no longer German citizens, but pariahs living in Germany.

The laws raised the indignation of part of the population and officially marked the beginning of the persecution that escalated and ended with the Holocaust.

When Germany celebrated Christmas in 1933, the country was almost completely nazi. Under the responsibility of the SA, concentration camps were full of political prisoners. The Reichstag had become a democratic decoration, political parties and trade unions had been dissolved, the administration of the nation rested with members of the Nazi Party, the freedom of the press had been silenced and the individual freedom suppressed.

May 17, 1933: Hitler reassures the world

On May 17, 1933, Hitler gave a speech, a masterpiece of deceptive propaganda meant to reassure the German people and the outside world about his peaceful intentions. He was responding to President Roosevelt, who had sent a plea for disarmament to the chiefs of state of forty-four nations. With unparalleled cynicism, he congratulated Roosevelt for his peace proposals and asserted that Germany stood behind the United States for this project, if the neighboring countries were doing the same thing. And he was ready to sign a solemn pact of non-aggression to prove his sincerity.

In October 1933, his power consolidated but embarrassed by the constraints exercised on his foreign policy, Hitler withdrew Germany from the League of Nations on the grounds that it did not have the same rights as the other nations. In order to ratify his leadership, he called an election in November 1933 and asked the citizens to answer yes or no to a question about the government disarmament policy. The Nazis won 92.1 percent of the votes.

September 4, 1933: The Nazi Party Congress in Nuremberg

The Congress of the National Socialist Party, which took place in Nuremberg on September 4, 1934, gave Hitler the opportunity to capture the popular imagination more than ever. It was an unexpected opportunity to increase his prestige outside Germany. He took advantage of the countless delegations and foreign visitors to project an image of power and he was highly successful. Even nowadays, the photographs, showing hundreds of thousands of Germans standing in impeccable rows before a huge stage decorated with a monumental eagle head framed with swastika banners, are spectacular.

Hitler owed to his architect, Albert Speer, the realization of the stage work. For the night events, Speer had asked Göring to provide more than half the strategic reserves of powerful spotlights that the army kept in case of an air raid. Göring was reluctant, but Hitler liked the idea, especially since this exhibition would give other countries the impression that Germany had a large number of those projectors. In his memoirs, Albert Speer admitted that one hundred thirty sharply defined beams, placed all around at intervals of forty feet and projecting columns of light at more than twenty thousand feet in the sky, gave a surreal impression that surpassed what he had imagined. It was like a huge Gothic cathedral supported by one hundred thirty pillars, rising into the sky. Speer believed that this stage work was his most memorable architectural creation and Sir Nevile Henderson, the British ambassador to Germany, mentioned in his writings the solemn and grandiose scene that gave the impression of being at the center of an ice palace.

The streets of Nuremberg were decorated with an orgy of swastika flags and banners were suspended from one house to the other, creating the illusion of a veiled sky. By projecting the image of a powerful and prosperous nation, Hitler echoed the deepest desires of the Germans. In one of his fiery speeches, he hammered the same themes and the crowd sang songs celebrating the glory of Hitler, the memory of the nazi martyrs and the greatness of Germany.

The elimination of the right and left wings of politics

One year after Hitler's rise to power, the disenchantment was total. Hitler had been unable to satisfy anyone and he was trapped between the right-wing conservatives, who were hoping for a return of the monarchy, and the left-wing revolutionaries, who kept repeating the same thing despite the National Socialist Party's rise to power.

The German right-wing was recruiting the former regime's bourgeoisie and aristocracy, where von Papen came from, and complaining to the vice-chancellor, who shared many of the concerns brought to him, but had very limited authority within the cabinet. Unsatisfied citizens openly criticized the abuse of the National Socialist Party and dreamed of the return of the monarchy in Germany.

On June 17, 1934, in a speech delivered at the Marburg University, von Papen criticized the enslavement of the press by the ministry of Propaganda headed by Goebbels and the antidemocratic policies put forward by the leaders of the National Socialist Party. It was to be the last manifestation of freedom of expression in Germany until the end of the war. On that same evening, Goebbels prohibited that von Papen speech be broadcasted on the radio. Outraged, the vice-chancellor went to Hitler to complain about the gesture of a minister who, theoretically, had less power than him, and offered to submit a letter of resignation to President Hindenburg. Conciliatory, Hitler shared the indignation of his vice-chancellor, convinced him that the incident was an isolated act, and proposed a three-party meeting with the president. He promised to lift Goebbels' ban and asked von Papen to postpone his resignation until the meeting with the president, which never took place. Franz von Papen said that he learned at the Nuremberg trials that Hitler had met with President Hindenburg to complain about his inability to govern with a vice-chancellor whose political thinking had a significant deviation.

In the days that followed, Edgar Jung, a Munich lawyer at the center of a conservative group resisting the national socialism and a close collaborator of von Papen—he had written the speech delivered by the vice-chancellor at the University of Marburg, was arrested by the Gestapo and executed. It was the first step in the elimination of the right-wing. Hitler took advantage of the Night of the Long Knives to order the Gestapo to invest the vice-chancellor' offices, and arrest and execute without warning several officials of von Papen as well as influential members of the conservative right-wing. Franz von Papen was not arrested. However, put under house arrest, he was unable to communicate with President Hindenburg.

Using the crisis situation to their advantage, Göring and Himmler pretended that there was a national conspiracy against the government. On June 25, Werner von Fritsch, the commander in chief of the army, put the army on high alert, cancelling all leaves and asking his troops to stand ready to intervene.

The German population criticized the regime for not fulfilling its promises. Six months after the rise to power of the nazi regime, despite a 33 percent reduction of the unemployment, life in Germany was not easy. Wages determined by the state had significantly decreased and the German worker had become an industrial serf linked to his employer, in the same way peasants were the property of the lord of the manor in the feudal system. Consumer prices were higher and significant or abusive constraints were attached to the social protection policies. The government had set up a product marketing system that satisfied neither the consumers nor the peasants, since its application was not entirely successful. Perishable products were rotting in trucks sitting idle pending bureaucrats' clearance to make deliveries.

The bureaucracy had become problematic. Several positions were occupied by members of the SA troops. In many cases, they did not have the expertise required, and the positions they held were a way for the socialist party to reward them for their participation in the takeover. However, it is precisely this seizure of power that helped widen the gap between Hitler's interests and those of the SA.

The SA troops consisted mainly of Germans of humble social status who wished to derive some benefit from their participation in the meteoric rise of the Nazi Party. After 1933, the Brown Shirts continued to promote revolutionary goals, but for Hitler, the national socialist revolution had ended. The SA troops had played an undeniable role in the seizure of power with the terror that they instilled in the population and remained useful during the first months of the regime by supporting the bringing to heel of Germany by the National Socialist Party. However, once the political parties were dissolved, the trade unions eliminated and the associations silenced, the SA troops became annoying in many ways for a government that wanted to look democratic. The excessive violence of the SA members, who never shied away from senseless murder or their extremist and revolutionary ideals, so useful before the rise to power, was no longer serving the interests of the Party. After the elimination of the sources of political opposition in Germany, Hitler was facing another opposition within the Party. The ill-disciplined SA troops recognized Röhm's authority over that of Hitler. Unfortunately, Röhm did not know how to navigate in politics. Being arrogant, he had a special way of provoking the hostility of several powerful leaders of the National Socialist Party. He drew a fierce opposition from most of the army officers who refused to accept the inclusion of the SA in the army. He also irritated Hitler, whose ideas on the role of the SA were in conflict with those of Röhm, who insisted that they be used in the German rearmament projects.

Hitler had not forgotten that shortly before the Reichstag election of September 1930, the SA troops under Walther Stennes, commander of the SA in East Germany, had presented him with an ultimatum demanding permission for the SA leaders to enter the Reichstag, a decrease in authority for the Gauleiters, and a compensation for the SA who maintained order in political rallies. Hitler had ignored their demands and the SA had withdrawn from a political assembly during an election campaign at the Berlin Sports Palace in protest. Goebbels and the nazi supporters, outnumbered by the opponents, were in a bad position. The assembly was saved by Himmler, who called his SS to the rescue. Later, Stennes reconciled with Hitler, but the message had been fully understood: Hitler could rely on the unwavering loyalty of the SS, but not of the SA. Even the arrival of his old friend Röhm at the head of the SA shortly after did not improve the situation.

Röhm had a very real power that overshadowed Göring, the first leader of the SA. In the spring of 1934, the SA were a force of over three million men and an indisputable threat to the army, thirty times smaller. At the beginning of 1934, frequent physical incidents involved members of the SA and soldiers of the army. Röhm despised the army and had come into conflict with Baron von Fritsch, chief of staff of the army. Hitler had been embarrassed when Fritsch had asked him to decide once and for all in favor of the army. Hitler, who was indebted toward Röhm for his political rise, did not want to offend him, but he needed the support of the army to carry out his plans. As usual, he avoided to take a stand in the debate. However, taking advantage of the concerns of the chief of staff, he promised to increase the size of the army and reduce that of the SA, in exchange for his military support, should he decide to be the successor to President Hindenburg. And, to appease the SA, he published in the Party newspaper a letter stating that he recognized the essential role played by the SA during the revolution, and he appointed Röhm cabinet member on December 1, 1933. However, the problem was still there and it became quickly obvious that Hitler's interests were more in line with those of the army. The head of the Gestapo, Heinrich Himmler, was about to help correct the situation.

For Himmler, the SA troops cast a shadow on his own troops. When he learned about the plots involving Ernst Röhm, Gregor Strasser and General von Schleicher, he did not hesitate to amplify the seriousness of the events. He told Hitler that a coup was underway and it was imperative to act quickly. Hitler took a few days to think it over and, since he was naturally suspicious, he agreed with Himmler. On the eve of the Night of the Long Knives, the Reichswehr Minister von Blomberg had publicly linked the fate of the army to the state by announcing in the Party's newspaper, the *Völkischer Beobachter,* that the *Wehrmacht* and the state were only one. The Chief of Staff von Blomberg, General von Reichenau and the Chief of the Military High Command, General von Fritsch, were aware of the operation Night of the Long Knives and put army equipment at the disposal of the SS.

On June 30, 1934, hundreds of leaders of the SA troops throughout Germany were awakened by the SS led by Josef Sepp Dietrich and killed without any form of trial. Hitler dithered for two days before approving the execution of Röhm, who refused to commit suicide and was shot point blank. Göring and Himmler took advantage of the situation to settle old scores by adding to the list of suspects other troublesome opponents. Many SA were killed for having opposed Hitler in the past and others were murdered because they knew too much.

This brutal repression has gone down in history under the name of the Night of the Long Knives, because the SA carried a knife in their belt. In the following days, the cabinet declared that the purge was necessary for the protection of the state. This episode marked the beginning of assassination as an instrument of political management for the nazi regime. Marshal von Blomberg, commander in chief of the Reichswehr, compromised the German army by congratulating Hitler on that sinister political massacre, which was only a prelude to the bloodshed that will stain the military uniform. He informed his officers and troops of the tragic events of June 30, and acknowledged the loyalty and courage of the soldiers who had ended the activities of many traitors and killers.

Through its dealings with Hitler and the tacit approval of the executions that followed, the great and proud German army had compromised its integrity and sold its soul to the devil. Having largely benefited from that operation, the army could no longer disassociate itself from the most barbarous nazi policies to keep their hands clean. On August 2, the army formalized its Nazi Party membership by swearing an oath of allegiance to Hitler.

On July 3, von Papen, who was still under house arrest at Göring's order, received a phone call from him. Göring pretended to be surprised that the vice-chancellor was not at the last meeting of the cabinet to provide an update on the events of recent days. Angry, von Papen met with Hitler, only to be told that more serious events needed his attention at the moment. He subsequently learned that hundreds of victims, including two army generals, had been brutally murdered for reasons unrelated to the putsch staged by the SA. However, von Papen was unable to meet with President Hindenburg, who was sick and died a month later, on August 2, 1934. Hindenburg's death removed the last obstacle to the absolute control of Hitler in Germany.

To apply a semblance of democracy, in the days that followed, Hitler conducted a large-scale propaganda campaign to direct popular opinion toward feelings of gratitude and admiration for the Führer, who had been able to quickly control elements that could have seriously endangered the stability of the state. Little aware of the details, the Germans did not disapprove his actions.

Even if the army largely benefited from the operation, the SS troops also established themselves by clearly demonstrating their ability to execute diligently and efficiently the most sordid tasks required by the regime in power. They also took advantage of the vacant space left by the disappearance of the SA to dramatically increase their power in order to compete with the army.

The taking of absolute power

Several members of the Reichstag had underestimated Hitler, convinced that President Hindenburg, who despised the little corporal, would control him. When Hitler came to power, the old president was tired and sick. Therefore, he was never able to impose his authority over Hitler.

In his memoirs, von Papen recounted the events surrounding the death of President Paul von Hindenburg on August 2, 1934. The day before, the cabinet had voted a law merging the positions of Chancellor and President of the Republic, to come into force on the day of the death of the President. The law was partially in accordance with article 51 of the Weimar Constitution, which gave the chancellor presidential responsibilities until the holding of an election. However, an amendment to the Constitution Act pertaining to full powers, voted by parliament on March 24, 1933, allowed the Chancellor to enact laws without the involvement of parliament, but not to abolish the position of President of the Republic. Article 2 stated that the national laws enacted by the Reich Cabinet may deviate from the Constitution as long as they did not affect the position of the Reichstag and the Reichsrat. The powers of the President remained undisturbed.

A second law voted the day after the death of Hindenburg proclaimed that Hitler had the rights and powers of the President. Franz von Papen, questioned at the Nuremberg trials on the fact that the two documents carried his signature, denied having signed such documents.

Shortly after, Hitler usurped the loyalty of the army. General von Blomberg, minister of the Reichswehr, agreed to request the army to swear allegiance not to the Constitution or to the President of the Republic, as was the tradition, but to Hitler personally. On August 20, 1934, another law gave legal weight to the oath of allegiance of the army.

In August 1934, the generals who could have overthrown Hitler rallied behind him and took an oath of obedience, thus confirming his supreme legal authority. Their loyalty to the Führer, assured by their sense of honor, prevented them to engage in risky military activities. But at the same time, the oath offered several officers the possibility to transfer on Hitler the responsibility for their war crimes.

Hitler had become Führer, in other words, the guide and chancellor of the Reich. He had managed to combine the positions of head of state and supreme commander of the armed forces. According to von Papen, only those who had been educated in the Prussian tradition of loyalty and obedience could foresee the disastrous effects to come. Any general who wished to distance himself from the power was faced with a breach of what he considered all his life as an absolute—loyalty to his oath.

In order to give a democratic flavor to his illegal takeover of power, Hitler plebiscited the population two weeks later and 90 percent of the voters approved his decisions. Adolf Hitler had absolute power in Germany. The parliament remained a democratic front. The cabinet meetings became less frequent and stopped from 1938 onward. His dream of a Thousand-Year Reich of blond, blue-eyed master race was now in sight. Hitler had just opened the last door to absolute power. He could now focus on his expansionist plans.

The economic miracle

During his first years in power, Hitler was able to help bring about impressive changes in Germany because of his unlimited power over the economy. The dumbfounded European countries observed the reconstruction of Germany, where Hitler almost looked like a magician.

When Hitler became chancellor of the Reich in 1933, he inherited a disastrous economic situation with a record number of six million unemployed and a country afflicted by violence, misery and hunger. With no economic knowledge, but innate political instincts, he appointed Hjalmar Schacht director of the Central Bank and, subsequently, minister of Economics. Three years later, unemployment in Germany was practically history and the country seemed to be a wellness oasis in the European continent devastated by the economic depression, watching with envy and disbelief the improvement of living standards of the Germans. In Germany, the misery and hunger had given way to a modest but quiet prosperity.

However, the improvement of the German economy came at a price.

The financing of the economic recovery was coupled with an inflationary trend that had to be overcome by a rigid control of salaries and consumer prices. It was also necessary to limit all external trade. Hitler had the power to exercise all those controls, thanks, among other things, to the dissolution of trade unions. From then on, individual freedom had to be sacrificed for the greater good of the nation. The state would take care of that. Any trade with the outside world without permission, any increase in consumer prices, any request for a salary increase or any strike could lead to a rehabilitation stay in a concentration camp.

This is how Germany adopted a project to improve infrastructures such as roads, diversified its production of consumer goods and, above all, devoted huge sums of money to finance the military industry.

The military miracle

In 1933, Germany had an army of one hundred thousand men and rudimentary equipment. Five years later, the army had become one of the most powerful in Europe. On March 14, 1935, Hitler proclaimed the reinstatement of compulsory military service in Germany, in violation of the Treaty of Versailles. The former Reichswehr of the monarchy became the Wehrmacht, comprising ground, naval and air forces.

If Schacht played a critical role in the economic miracle, Hitler himself gave the impetus that led to the restoration of the German military force. It was Hitler who introduced the concept of the independent tank squadrons that revolutionized the military strategy. This new weapon will take by surprise the French military, who strongly believed that the Maginot line could not be crossed, as it was a line of concrete fortification that spread along the German border almost to the sea. The German tanks crossed the line quite easily. General Heinz Guderian and a few other generals introduced this type of artillery. European countries followed suit shortly afterward.

The economic and military miracle made a profound impression on the German people who saw their Führer as a Providence-sent Messiah. If the National Socialist Party was never very popular, the Führer was, which led to say that the Germans were more Hitlerian than socialist. Those who criticized the Führer were rebuffed by their fellow citizens. Finally, national pride was reborn after two decades of humiliation and the hope to avenge the Treaty of Versailles became an achievable dream. Hitler was freeing Germany of the chains imposed by the Allies at the end of World War I.

Hitler was at the peak of his popularity in 1939 and 1940 when, against all expectations and ignoring the warnings of his generals, he successfully invaded Austria, Czechoslovakia, Poland, the Netherlands, Denmark, Norway and France, without significant military loss. Whether they were civilians or military, all those who had criticized the Führer were silenced. The Germans did not clearly realize that those victories occurred when Germany was not at war and the infallibility of the Führer myth began to spread. In fact, the invincible military leader had never won a war against an opponent with a power comparable to that of Germany. His victories were against weakened opponents or those who were unable to put up a significant resistance. In terms of foreign policy, he gave the image of an extremely capable strategist. People came from London, Paris, Prague, Rome and Moscow to negotiate and seek compromise. Hitler took advantage of the good faith, gullibility and weakness of his opponents. He kept flouting international negotiating rules based on sincerity and respect of the obligations attached to the signature of an agreement. A large number of his diplomatic victories were due to his routine use of outright lies, dramatic settings, misleading impulses of sincerity, perfidious tricks and backroom dealings that were his negotiation tools in terms of foreign policy. His diplomatic victories were not the result of his ability to create stable alliances or to negotiate advantageous terms for Germany, but rather his use of deceit and bogus peace treaties that he tore up as soon as they became cumbersome.

Instead of declaring war on Poland, he created a scenario to make it look like the aggression was imperative to protect Germany. SS members disguised as Polish soldiers attacked a German radio station near the Polish border. The German nation went to war without understanding and enthusiasm, but carrying a new pride and convinced that the Führer was acting for the greater good of Germany and the German people. They saw the restoration of the pre-1914 borders of Germany. However, what was the end for the German people was only the beginning for Hitler. Endowed with full powers, having wiped out the state institutions, eliminated all opposition, able to block all resistance with the help of the SS police, Hitler had a powerful and well-oiled machine to achieve his personal goals. It was the first move toward war.

Chapter 4

The instruments of nazi power

When negotiating with the nazi government, the representatives of the European nations were unaware that they were dealing with a real mafia that had usurped the German constitutional powers to divert to its benefit the interests of the citizens. They were also unaware that Hitler was several steps ahead as he had knowingly decided to boycott the rules of foreign policy and that his signature on a treaty was meaningless. No one wins against a cheater. This is what Chamberlain learned when he returned triumphantly to Great Britain, waving like a flag a letter signed by the Führer ensuring the British government of his peaceful intentions, a few weeks before the invasion of Poland that triggered World War II.

During his time in government, the National Socialist Party broke the record of the worst crimes committed by any international mafia. Stealing: Göring assembled the biggest art collection of Europe, stealing or buying at a ridiculous price masterpieces that his SS were seeking out across the continent. Fraud: After the Night of Broken Glass, the Nazis decided that the compensation the Jews were entitled to for the destruction of their property belonged to the state. Kidnapping: After having held the wealthy Vienna banker Baron Ferdinand de Rothschild in the Mauthausen concentration camp, the Nazis tried to obtain a significant ransom from the English branch of the family. Protection racket: In April 1940, despite a non-aggression pact signed a year earlier with Denmark, Germany invaded Denmark and Norway under the pretext of protecting those countries. In fact, Germany needed the Norwegian iron and feared an alliance between Norway and Great Britain. Counterfeit money: The technical division of the Security Service of the Reichsführer-SS or SD printed and uttered large quantities of pounds sterling in order to destabilize the British currency. Lie: When there was none, Himmler created a homosexual story to eliminate Baron Werner von Fritsch, commander in chief of the Wehrmacht and potential successor to the minister of the Armed Forces. A parallel investigation conducted by the army clearly showed that the principal witness worked for the SS, but Fritsch was nonetheless eliminated. Arson: In order to accuse and imprison a large number of communists, Göring ordered the burning of the Reichstag a few days before an election. Perfidy: It is the simulated attack on a German radio station by SS members disguised as Polish soldiers that allowed Hitler to invade Poland. Murder: The nazi regime alone eliminated more opponents than all the gangsters of the planet over hundreds of years. Unlike mafia, service records and friendship meant nothing in terms of security: Despite his long friendship with Hitler and his invaluable contribution to the political success of the Führer, Röhm was ruthlessly killed like a thug.

The new order imposed to Germany by the National Socialist Party was essentially based on a balance of power between the party and the government, then between the government and the German citizens, and finally between the nazi leaders. The autonomous, political, administrative or governmental organizations defined their field of competence from their struggles, the most powerful trying to expand its influence. Their cooperation, information sharing and contribution to a joint task became situations likely to transfer power to the opponent and weaken one's own structure. As a result, the conflict zones multiplied and the completion of a task became problematic. If in a democratic state the first objective of the Charter of Human Rights, often translated by specific laws in each country, is to protect citizens against the arbitrary use of power by the state, in nazi Germany, it protected the state against citizens and democracy.

The totalitarian power of the nazi government was the result of an operation carried out in several stages described by Göring at the Nuremberg trials.

Steps	Objectives
1	The Führerprinzip: Total and blind allegiance to the leader
2	Discrediting of the regime in power
3	After taking over the administrative apparatus, development of a political structure where the party is synonym of state
4	Systematic elimination of organized opposition
5	Elimination of political parties to take control of the legislative power
6	Control of the dissidents in the population
7	Creation of a secret police force and special prisons

Table 1 – Steps toward the establishment of the nazi government

The Führerprinzip

The nazi power was structured like a pyramid. At the top of the hierarchy, Hitler had absolute power. He dominated seventeen *Reichsleiters* or ministers, who reported directly to the Führer. The party was divided into regions (*Gaue*), districts (*Kreise*), groups (*Ortsgrupen*), cells (*Zellen*) and blocks (*Blocke*). There were thirty-two regions in Germany and ten in the occupied territories.

The leadership of the Reich was carried out by the Reichsleiters or ministers who were responsible for departments such as justice, finance, armaments, propaganda, external affairs, etc. The *Landesinspekteures* were under the authority of the Reichsleiters and responsible for four regions or Gaue. Decisions were taken at the highest level and communicated to the base. Conversely, a *Blockleiter* was responsible for approximately forty to sixty people he knew well and he was required to report to his superior any behavior or comment that deviated from the nazi orthodoxy.

Adolf Hitler wanted absolute power. The Führerprinzip represented for him the indispensable instrument to remove the obstacles and help the Germans walk toward their glorious destiny. It is the principle of the absolute leader, whose decisions go beyond the popular opinion, and legal and judicial instances. Without such an instrument, no success was possible.

After the merger of the positions of chancellor and president, Hitler became the most powerful political leader of Germany. When the Enabling Act was voted, he was no longer accountable to the Reichstag, which he never consulted subsequently.

The chancellor of Germany: Adolf Hitler
⇧
The cabinet ministers:
Reichsleiters (17)
⇧
The party inspectors:
Landesinspekteures
⇧
The regional leaders:
Gauleiters
⇧
The district leaders:
Kresleiters
⇧
The local chapter leaders:
Ortsgruppenleiters
⇧
The cell leaders:
Zellenleiters
⇧
The block leaders:
Blockleiters
⇧
Population units:
40 to 60 people

Table 2 – Pyramidal structure of the nazi power

The Gaue and the Gauleiters

There are few examples in history of a dictatorship so concerned about establishing its power on constitutional foundations. Seeking a democratic alibi, Hitler decided to retain the existing governmental structures and top them with a parallel system stemming from the party and having the real power. In doing so, he created quite an administrative disaster in the workings of the state.

The National Socialist Party had divided Germany into administrative regions called Gaue. The number of regions varied slightly during the twelve years of the nazi regime, and, toward the end of the war, there were more than forty regions. Major cities could be an autonomous Gau within a larger Gau. The territories annexed to Germany were also divided into Gaue. Austria, for example, had seven Gaue and, in Czechoslovakia, the Sudetenland became a Gau. Occupied territories did not have that structure, but were incorporated into the adjacent Gau, as for the protectorates of Bohemia and Moravia.

Each region was governed by a Gauleiter from the party. His power came directly from Hitler to whom he was answerable without an intermediate. The Gauleiters were intensely loyal and trustworthy to their leader who was trying to limit their power without upsetting them. Inside their administrative territory, they were masters after God, namely Hitler. Their power was neither supported by state bureaucrats nor limited by the central leadership of the party, or even submitted to the cabinet ministers.

On October 6, 1943, Albert Speer, minister of Armaments, asked the Gauleiters to stop blocking the repeated requests to transfer a number of German workers to the production of armaments. Explaining the critical military situation created by the insufficient production of weapons, Speer threatened to impose, with the agreement of Himmler, the closure of consumer goods industries in the next two weeks if the Gauleiters did not collaborate. Infuriated that Speer could impose his decision with authority, they noisily expressed their disagreement. Informed of the controversy and without providing a reason, Hitler told Speer that the Gauleiters were angry, but refrained from taking sides. Faced with the need to increase the war effort, and despite the importance that he gave to the German military power, Hitler preferred to spare his political support and to divide and rule.

On March 12, 1945, Cavalry Captain Gerhardt Boldt attended a meeting at the Reich Chancellery, where the *Panzer* General Dietrich von Saucken was invited by Hitler to discuss new military strategies. General Guderian presented his report on the military forces in Eastern Prussia and the Danzig region, and Hitler gave Saucken instructions pertaining to the combat operations for his divisions. After a short pause, he added that in the regions where he was to fight, the general's responsibilities were limited to military action. For anything else, he would be under the authority of Gauleiter Albert Foster. He concluded that the final responsibility and ultimate authority remained in the hands of Foster. There was a silence, and to the amazement of all, Saucken replied calmly that he had no intention of taking orders from a Gauleiter. For a few moments, Boldt said that they could have heard a pin drop. For the first time, a German general was challenging a Führer's order. General Guderian and Hitler's personal secretary tried in vain to reason with the general. Finally, Hitler gave up and agreed that he assumed command. When Saucken left the meeting, Hitler did not shake his hand. Hitler's power was beginning to crumble.

With unlimited power, the Gauleiters could easily block the state apparatus. Each Gauleiter had his own interpretation of Hitler's instructions and applied them with more or less significant distortions. Even for the leaders of the Reich, it was difficult to have a comprehensive plan uniformly applied throughout Germany.

Several Gauleiters abused their power and some of them built a political empire. But it was not an occupation without risk. Fifty-six percent of the fifty-two Gauleiters died prematurely. Thirteen of them committed suicide in 1945, eight were executed as war criminals, and eight others were killed by the Gestapo, by resistance activists or during Allied attacks.

The men in power

In Hitler's circle, the most stable people were those who said what the Führer wanted to hear.

Wilhelm Keitel was one of them and toward the end of the regime, most generals of the German general staff had given up on providing objective information. They fed Hitler the good news only.

Next to this line of authority were the ministries whose organization enabled them to apply the decrees and regulations issued by the government. This second army of performers was joined by the ad hoc organizations that Hitler created when an important project needed to be carried out. Those were usually headed by power-hungry leaders skilled in backroom games, who in turn tried to develop their organization to gain more control.

Almost always, the ad hoc organizations, government institutions and Gauleiters competed in the areas of power. Hitler, who wanted to preserve his personal image and was not interested in addressing their disputes, was unable to make a decision and let the events fix the problems for him.

Without the help of the dominant elite in the Nazi Party, it seems unlikely that Hitler would have been able to take over and stay in power until 1945. With the exception of the generals who were killed in the defeats or eliminated, according to the Führer's mood, two dozen names pop up all the time, each occupying a zone of variable influence depending on the intrigues and their proximity to Hitler. The latter had developed a flair for taking advantage of rivalries between various factions struggling to get special favors and he was almost using that as a political management tool. His choices seem to have been closely linked to the control he could exert on these men. The only nazi leader that Hitler really feared was Himmler. Goebbels and Göring were strong personalities who showed a fanatical dedication to the Führer, whose ideology they totally embraced. Moreover, Goebbels committed suicide with his family at the same time as his leader and Göring was the most ardent defender of the nazi regime at the Nuremberg trials.

Name	Position
Bormann, Martin	Hitler's private secretary; successor to Rudolf Höss
Dönitz, Karl	Grand Admiral, Commander in chief of the Submarine Force, Commander in chief of the Navy; successor to Raider in 1943; successor to Hitler on May 1st, 1945
Frank, Hans	Governor of Poland
Frick, Wilhelm	Governor of the Protectorate of Bohemia and Moravia
Fritzsche, Hans	Director of Propaganda (radio)
Funk, Walter	President of the Reichsbank
Goebbels, Paul Joseph	Minister of Propaganda
Göring, Hermann	Reich-Marshal, Commander in chief of the Luftwaffe
Höss, Rudolf	Hitler's private secretary until 1941
Himmler, Heinrich	Reichsführer-SS
Heydrich, Reinhard	Director of the Gestapo
Jodl, Alfred	Chief of the Operations Staff of the Armed Forces High Command
Keitel, Wilhelm	General, Head of the Supreme Command of the Armed Forces
Ley, Robert	Minister of Labor
Raeder, Erich	Grand Admiral, Commander in chief of the Navy
Rosenberg, Alfred	Minister for the Occupied Eastern Territories and party ideologue
Sauckel, Fritz	General Plenipotentiary for Labor Deployment
Schacht, Hjalmar	Former Minister of Economics, President of the Reichsbank before Funk
Seyss-Inquart, Arthur	Austrian Minister of the Interior
Speer, Albert	Hitler's architect; Minister of Armaments and War Production
Streicher, Julius	Editor of the newspaper *Der Stürmer*; Gauleiter of Franconia
Von Neurath, Konstantin	Protector of Bohemia and Moravia; former Minister of Foreign Affairs
Von Papen, Franz	Vice-Chancellor of Germany
Von Ribbentrop, Joachim	Minister of Foreign Affairs
Von Schirach, Baldur	Head of the Nazi Youth; Gauleiter of Vienna

Table 3 – The men in power

The cultural control

Totalitarian regimes often fall into cultural monotony. Along with terror, propaganda is their basic ingredient. The communication media become the means to convey political messages and stifle openness to different cultural styles. Goebbels used an iron fist to impose a nazi favored cultural orthodoxy and his ministry of Propaganda became the watchdog of the politically correct.

From the beginning of his political thinking in Vienna, Hitler saw the need for an orchestrated and pervasive propaganda to promote an ideology. He resumed in *Mein Kampf* the key features of an effective propaganda that delivers simple messages and touches the emotions. Hitler's speeches were not meant to provide information on the policies that he wanted to implement. His goal was to provoke an emotional response to his expressions of outrage that sparked enthusiasm.

Soon after the seizure of power, Paul Joseph Goebbels was appointed minister of Public Enlightenment and Propaganda. He mobilized the radio, the press and the cinema in order to flood the nation with the German ideology. Documentaries promoting the nazi regime were mandatory in all movie theaters. Goebbels was well aware that the image is more powerful than the spoken or written word.

Simultaneously, a cleansing of libraries eliminated subversive literature. Even if it was impossible to prevent radio waves from crossing the border, many messages left thinly veiled threats hang over the offenders. A movie theater advertisement showed a German listening to foreign broadcasts. He was rebuked by another actor who suggested that the German worked against Germany. "But no one sees me!" said the first actor. "Everything comes out in the end!" replied the second actor in a forceful language.

Goebbels proved to be very inventive when he took control of the culture. On September 22, 1933, shortly after the creation of the ministry of Propaganda, Goebbels established a Reich Culture Chamber for each instrument of culture, such as radio, cinema, theater and newspapers. No one could perform in public without being registered in the corresponding chamber, entitled to exclude any activity that did not comply with the nazi ideology. Open dissent meant a one-way train ticket to a concentration camp specialized in rehabilitation.

The proximity of the Führer ensured an almost unlimited power, but the differences in thinking patterns were not tolerated. In June 1942, the Governor of Poland, lawyer Hans Frank, delivered a speech before the Academy for German Law, where he advocated the return to obedience to the laws. He claimed that no civilized nation could allow arbitrary arrests and imprisonment without a trial as did the SS and the Gestapo. When he repeated his speech at the Munich University, where he had graduated, the law students stood up to applaud him with enthusiasm. He was immediately reprimanded by Hitler, who, because of his service to the party, minimized his ideological deviations as transient errors in judgment and served him a severe warning engaging him to follow the party lines. Frank went immediately back into the ranks.

The creation of the SA

When Hitler joined the DAP in 1919, he soon befriended Ernst Röhm who, like him, felt humiliated by the Treaty of Versailles and attributed to the Berlin regime the responsibility for the defeat. Like Hitler, he believed in the rebirth of a strong Germany, reunified by an authoritarian political party relying on the support of the people.

The SA was created in 1920. At the beginning, it consisted of little organized and unruly groups established by Hitler and used as a police service at the meetings of the party. At the time, several political groups were confronting one another and physical violence was the rule rather than the exception. The SA, or Assault Detachment, was aimed at maintaining order. In a context of violence, the SA squads were quickly used to terrorize the other political groups and impress citizens with their mandatory brown shirt and mass parades punctuated by war songs. The groups were often equipped with weapons retained after World War I and fatalities were not uncommon during the clashes. The SA members came from the working class and were recruited among the idealistic youths of the party.

Unlike the SS members who were selected, the SA joined together on a voluntary basis. The gigantic organization consisted of a series of grouped units whose base was the SA squad. A squad consisted of four to twelve men who shared convictions or camaraderie. Their leader gave his name to the squad and was required to report to his immediate superior. The latter confirmed the addition of a new group of SA. Three to six squads formed a troop, and two to three troops an assault section. The sections had between seventy and one hundred twenty men and were active cells of the Brown Shirts. The National Socialist Party was telling them that victory belonged to those who knew how to face death and kill, fight the enemy without mercy, and inspire terror in the adversary. The SA men, most of whom did not believe in God or human rights, became in the hands of Hitler the perfect tool to gain power.

The SA were paramilitary groups that terrorized the population. Fights, intimidation, abductions and confiscation of material goods accounted for activities that were seldom blocked by the police. Therefore, the citizens felt unprotected. The SA had to improvise holding centers for their prisoners and, one day, the SA chieftain of Dresden decided to put up a barbed-wire stockade to prevent escapes. The ancestor of the concentration camps had just been created.

With the accession to power of the Nazi Party, the size of the SA increased from three hundred thousand to three million members between January and December 1933. The SA were to take an extreme-left political tangent, with an anticapitalist economic conviction opposed to that of Hitler, courting the industry with the ambition to replace the Reichswher with a party army embracing the national socialist goals. There is no doubt that in the Night of the Long Knives, the passive collaboration of the army reflected the satisfaction to see the elimination of a power that had become annoying due to the high number of SA members.

In 1934, Göring increased the number of police officers by incorporating the SA and SS troop members who were all wearing a single white stripe on the arm. In March 1933, he made no mystery of the expanded powers conferred upon the public order policing. Göring gave clear guidelines to the police claiming that they would be supported by the SA. If one of them killed someone, they would not be held responsible, since he would fully endorse the responsibility as if he had fired the shot himself.

Except for health reasons, no one could get out of the SA, at the risk of being perceived as a state enemy. From then on, quitters were ostracized and it was impossible for them to find a job. Their livelihoods such as work and pension were compromised. They were putting at risk the existence of their family.

After the purge of June 1934, the SA organization lost its main leaders. It is estimated that the number of victims was between four hundred and four thousand. Furthermore, the seizure by the SS of one hundred seventy-seven thousand weapons made the organization toothless and harmless.

Less than a month later, on July 26, Hitler rose the SS organization to the rank of an independent organization of the National Socialist Party, in recognition of the services rendered.

The power and the domestic policy

Being head of state did not alter the personality of Adolf Hitler. Naturally messy when he was a student, he hated writing and he mostly gave verbal instructions to his subordinates.

His lack of interest left plenty of room for power struggles, each subordinate interpreting the instructions in his best interest. All means were good to eliminate an opponent and the proximity of Hitler made the envy of the top nazi officials who could take advantage of the vulnerability of a competitor. Hence, Albert Speer, who had gained a great deal of power when he became minister of Armaments, had the misfortune of being hospitalized in January 1944 for a pain in his knee. He was under the care of Dr. Gebhardt, president of the German Red Cross. Dr. Gebhardt was a SS and an intimate friend of the Reichsführer Heinrich Himmler. Without creating direct opposition, Himmler was offended by the favorable position of Speer with the Führer. Speer had no confidence in the SS. While his hospitalization extended inexplicably, Saukel, minister of Labor, Göring, minister of Aviation, and Saur, whose star was rising, tried to erode some of Speer's power. Dr. Gebhardt justified the length of the hospitalization by the severity of Speer's illness He said that his patient was spitting blood without providing more details and spread in the close circle of the Führer the rumor that Speer had a potentially fatal condition. Speer insisted on being transferred, but Dr. Gebhardt used his medical authority to keep him, claiming that a transfer would be disastrous for his condition. Deeply worried, Speer's wife made representations to the highest authorities of the regime to get her husband out of the impasse. She contacted Dr. Brandt, Hitler's personal physician, who ordered Dr. Gebhardt to transfer the patient to Dr. Friedrich Koch, an internist in Berlin. Dr. Koch suspected pulmonary embolism and maneuvered to help Speer leave the hospital where he was practically a prisoner.

Even if the interior political management was chaotic and ineffective, the power concentration allowed Germany to rebuild at a remarkable pace.

The dictatorship crushed any form of opposition that could have slowed down the speed of change. The Germans believed that they had found the master builder for the reconstruction of Germany. But at the end of the war, before the Nuremberg tribunal, Grand Admiral Karl Dönitz recognized that it was a mistake with far-reaching consequences. He pointed out that the leadership principle had been a well-proven military approach worldwide. But, in the final analysis, if this principle has generated nothing else but the misfortune of the German people, it must be false. It meant that human nature was unable to use power in an acceptable manner.

The events surrounding the Crystal Night are a good example of the anarchy that resulted from the fragmentation of power with respect to domestic policy. On the evening of November 9, 1938, after the assassination of the secretary of the German embassy in Paris by a young Jew, Goebbels, minister of Propaganda, took upon himself to organize anti-Jewish riots everywhere across the country and, under his initiative, an indescribable violence spread like wildfire. This decision, which had unfortunate consequences for Germany, does not appear to have been orchestrated by the party.

Walter Funk, minister of Economics, accused Goebbels of tarnishing the German prestige abroad while Göring spoke of an irresponsible conduct that would harm the economy. The two leaders were right. The world press unanimously denounced those acts of violence and the boycott of German products considerably intensified thereafter. As for Hitler, he avoided to take a clear position, an ambivalence that was to become his trademark. He excused Goebbels, but added that such a thing should not happen again.

The following example shows the improvisation that characterized the policies of the Führer. The Nuremberg Law for the Protection of Blood and German Honor represented an extremely important step in the anti-Jewish escalation leading to their extermination. The laws were introduced at a special meeting convened at the annual Nuremberg rally of the Nazi Party in 1935. Had this decree been long-prepared after careful consideration? No. On September 13, on the eve of the congress, Hitler ordered that a decree be written in two days and Frick, minister of the Interior, was forced to summon from his ministry two experts who started to work as soon as they landed.

After their arrival on the evening of September 14, the two exhausted experts immediately began to work and completed the drafting of the Citizenship Act at 2:30 am. Running out of paper, they wrote the document on old menus.

Despite Hitler's power, many political decisions appeared to escape his control, especially those in the hands of the main nazi leaders such as Göring, Goebbels and Himmler, who had carte blanche to do whatever they wanted. But even when Hitler issued clear guidelines, the fragmentation of the interlinked centers of power and the cumbersome administrative procedure often made the guidelines unnecessary, due to the delays in their application or the fact that their transformation rendered them inoperative.

The lack of a centralized administration resulted in the fragmentation of the operations. The competition for control between rival factions entailed an important waste of energy and a remarkable disorganization in the management of Germany.

This distribution of power that Hitler fully used as a political management approach significantly impaired the implementation of the decisions by extremely slowing down the state machine and limiting the smooth application of overall policies. The more rational decisions could be changed fundamentally when applying them since everyone submitted objections that had to be taken into account.

The chaotic nature of the Third Reich government was reflective of its leader who showed little availability to receive his ministers, was often away resting at his country home and liked to stay up late and sleep in. During the Normandy landings on June 6, 1944, a detachment of the *Leibstandarte Adolf Hitler SS* was immobilized for hours because nobody dared wake Hitler, the only one who could have given the order to join the divisions in trouble.

Adolf Hitler certainly had a great deal of power, but his power was unable to effectively deploy due to structural flaws, especially in the state management.

On the whole, Hitler showed a remarkable consistency in one area, his ideology. From Vienna, where he had developed his theories, to the Landsberg prison, where he wrote *Mein Kampf,* and to the Reich Chancellery, where he delivered his political testament before dying, he endlessly repeated the same themes, which were the superiority of the Aryan race, the dream of a millennial Reich, the inescapable need to eliminate the Jewish race poisoning Germany and the obligation to expand the German lebensraum with the conquest of foreign territories.

Notwithstanding his decisions in the military area, he frequently avoided making comments on controversial matters. The narcissistic importance that he placed on his image forced him to wait until the events followed their natural course and then he sided with whoever was in the best position.

In the last years of the regime, Hitler became increasingly isolated, leaving his omnipresent secretary Martin Bormann manage his meetings and execute his orders. In those years, Germany accumulated defeats and, fearing the hysterical reactions of the Führer, the generals, Keitel in particular, refrained from mentioning the disasters, modifying the truth to make it acceptable to their leader.

The Führerprinzip could have become a formidable instrument of power if Hitler had been able to use it in a consistent manner by creating administrative and organizational structures and granting them delineated power and responsibilities to meet state and war requirements. Instead, Hitler turned it into an instrument of personal control, arbitrarily taking the power away from those who frustrated him and transferring it to those he wanted to reward or whose loyalty he wanted to win. What could have become a well-oiled machine with perfectly adjusted gears quickly became an anarchic organization whose gearwheels jammed each other.

The power and the conduct of the war

From a military standpoint, Hitler remained true to himself. Since his childhood, he had always been almost pathologically fascinated by war. The opportunity for him to play a decisive role in the conduct of the war was completely unhoped for. He skillfully maneuvered to acquire full powers over the armed forces.

Before 1938, the supreme authority of the Wehrmacht rested in the hands of the Minister of War, Werner von Blomberg, and his Head of the Ministerial Office, Walter von Reichenau. The army, under the Commander in Chief of the Army General Werner von Fritsch and his Chief of the Army General Staff General Ludwig Beck, was the most important of the three services. There was a conflict between Blomberg and

Reichenau of the ministry of War, and Fritsch and Beck, head of the Land Forces, about the collaboration of the army with the nazi regime. Fritsch and Beck believed in the traditional values of the Prussian army and did not like the frequent political interference of the government in the army.

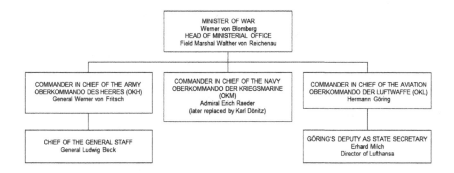

Table 4 – Organizational chart of the Wehrmacht before 1938

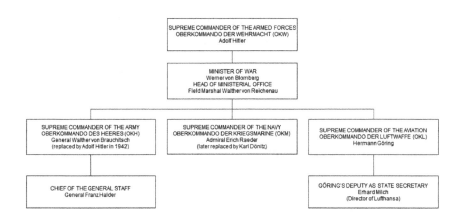

Table 5 – Organizational chart of the Wehrmacht after 1938

Hitler took advantage of the power games to establish his authority on the Wehrmacht. In 1938, the power-mad Göring managed to eliminate the minister of War Werner von Blomberg, using information provided by Blomberg's son-in-law who claimed that his step-father's new wife was a convicted prostitute. Hitler, who was reluctant to give more power to Göring took over Blomberg's former responsibilities by creating for himself the position of Supreme Commander of the Wehrmacht. In order to give the army an illusion of independence, he also created an intermediate body, namely the Department of the High Command of the Wehrmacht. It was actually a phony war ministry under the leadership of Field Marshal Wilhelm Keitel, the most servile of Hitler's collaborators, unable to come up with a different point of view. He was the laughing stock of the military and nicknamed the lackey, a pun on his name that sounded like the word lackey in German language.

At the same time, the Commander in Chief of the Army General Werner von Fritsch was falsely accused of homosexuality and a separate Wehrmacht investigation showed that it was a set-up on the part of Himmler. When he was forced to resign, his outraged Chief of the Army General Staff General Ludwig Beck tended his resignation. Several senior officers, revolted against the loss of Beck and the independence of the army from political power, took over the leadership of a resistance movement against Hitler that would lead to the failed Stauffenberg bomb plot in 1944. Hitler appointed Walter von Brauchitsch to replace Fritsch, but had to take over his position in 1942 following the German military disasters in the Russian countryside. As for Beck, he was replaced by General Franz Halder.

Wehrmacht, which means defense force, used the acronym OKW (*Oberkommando der Wehrmacht*). It was the supreme command that exerted control over the three commands:

- Ground Force High Command or OKH
  (*Oberkommando der Heeres*).
- Naval Force High Command or OKM
  (*Oberkommando der Kriegsmarine*).
- Air Force High Command or OKL
  (Oberkommando der Luftwaffe).

Table 6 – Acronyms of the German armed forces

The independence of the Wehrmacht from the political power had come to an end. This is how the interests of the National Socialist Party, the political leadership of the German Reich government, the supreme command of the Wehrmacht and the megalomaniac pretensions of a dictator ended up in the hands of one man.

Chapter 5

The SS empire: Terror in Europe

When Hitler left the Landsberg prison on December 20, 1924, he had gained a few pounds and his face looked rounder. The day he left, the director of the prison and the guards surrounded him and warmly shook his hand. The director looked more like a *maître d'* muttering with an obsequious smile: "We hope you enjoyed your stay and we look forward to welcoming you back again soon!"

Hitler had every reason to be satisfied. In nine months, he had converted to his nationalist convictions the staff of the institution, from the director to the head of maintenance. When the prison doors closed behind him, he drove in an old gray car to a place where a few supporters were waiting for him. He already knew that the task ahead would be difficult. He was no longer allowed to make speeches and the NSDAP and SA troops were banned in Prussia and Bavaria, virtually everywhere in Germany. Several members of the party had resigned, others were still in prison. The improvement of economic conditions in Germany had led to the decline of far-right parties.

However, he had a few tricks up his sleeve. His trial had ensured him an enviable reputation throughout Germany, where people saw him as an ardent patriot. He was now the main standard-bearer of German ultra-nationalism. In addition, he had learned a major political lesson. Deceit and lies were more powerful than violence or brutal force. As for morality, it established that good was anything that brought Germany closer to its destiny and whatever evil that kept it away from it. Finally, the writing of *Mein Kampf* had channeled his mental energies and deepened his belief that he was the instrument of a sacred mission in the advent of a new order built on the foundations of a regenerated civilization.

At the beginning of 1925, Hitler was keeping a low profile and was no longer a concern in the Bavarian government circles. He was again allowed to speak in public. The party had become a cluster of branches loosely attached to their headquarter in Munich. In the provinces, his leadership and political judgment were openly criticized. Dissident currents emerged, especially in Lower Bavaria, where the local Gauleiter Gregor Strasser was more popular than Hitler, who knew that the party had to become a national organization or disappear. It was time to start campaigning throughout Germany.

The first nazi SS sold classified ads

In the postwar years, violence had taken root in Germany. The assemblies of many political parties frequently attracted opponents who disrupted the meetings with their heckling. They did not hesitate to use force against militant members or speakers. Gunshots and murder of political supporters were part of the daily life.

Outside Bavaria, the allegiance of the NSDAP supporters often went to the regional leaders and Hitler did not feel safe since the SA troops were prohibited on most of the German territory, a ban that will be abolished in 1926. He often said that an idiot would be able to kill him and sabotage the grandiose project awaiting the German nation. He decided to create roaming bodyguard units who would swear allegiance to him and be responsible for his protection in stormy political assemblies.

He then entrusted to his driver, Julius Schreck, the responsibility of gathering a few men, handpicked on the basis of their stature, fitness and moral integrity, to form the Protective Echelons or *Schultzstaffel*, also called SS.

In September 1925, Schreck issued a circular letter to the regional groups of the party, instructing them to set up SS units consisting of one officer and ten men from the SA troops. They were called Groups of ten or *Zehnerstaffel*. Schreck established rigorous selection standards that he did not meet. The candidates had to be between twenty-three and thirty-five years of age, strong and healthy, lead an exemplary life, have no criminal record and provide at least two respondents. No one could become a SS just like that. Schreck dissolved a SS unit formed spontaneously in Munich with former members of the SA. He stated that the SS group was created on a solid base and could not be imitated. Their shirt, hat and black tie clearly distinguished the SS from the brown shirt SA troops.

Recruitment was to remain under the SA supervision and their number was not to exceed 10 percent of the SA strength. The beginnings of the SS units were rather humble. If their purpose was the protection of Hitler, in their free time they also had to attract advertisers for the party's newspaper, the *Völkischer Beobachter,* and recruit new members.

However, the SS leadership was unsatisfactory. Schreck showed complacency in recruiting the SS. In April 1926, he was replaced by Joseph Berchtold, a journalist and nazi businessman who preferred to be in the newsroom of the *Völkischer Beobachter* rather than in the role of a policeman. He was unable to manage the tension between the SS troops and other power groups. He resigned eleven months later and was replaced in March 1927 by Erhard Heiden, a former police informant whose reputation was less-than-spotless. The number of SS increased slowly, reaching two hundred eighty men in 1928. Less than two years later, Heiden was replaced by an enigmatic person, Heinrich Himmler.

Shy and frail as a child, Heinrich Himmler became the worst mass murderer in Europe

It is in Munich, the cradle of the NSDAP, that the future Reichsführer SS was born. On October 7, 1900, Gebhard Himmler and Anna Maria Heyder celebrated the birth of their second son, named Heinrich in honor of Prince Heinrich of Bavaria, who had agreed to be the godfather of the child. Heinrich's father was a respected catholic monarchist and the tutor of the Prince of Bavaria. A third son was born in 1905.

In his boyhood, Heinrich was puny and reserved. He received a severe education that made him develop a poor temperament, meticulousness and a remarkable thoroughness. He loved to read about the history of great civilizations. Very early, he became interested in the history of his ancestors and Germany. He liked to sit on his father's lap and listen to the story of his military exploits on the battlefields of Greece. In their house, a room had become a kind of sanctuary for books and objects that perpetuated the knowledge of the family ancestors. A graduate in philology from the University of Munich, Professor Gebhard Himmler had a passion for German history. His financial situation allowed him to engage in archaeological work, looking for objects likely to demonstrate a link between the Roman and German civilizations. When the young Heinrich entered high school, his knowledge of German history was comparable to that of his teachers.

As a teenager, Heinrich remained a loner who brought very few friends home. He was not accepted in the groups. Due to his frail stature and severe myopia, he showed no interest in sports. He attempted to learn piano without success and had language-learning difficulties. But he pretty much excelled in history.

In 1917, he joined the army, hoping to repeat the achievements of his grandfather, but the German defeat halted his plans. He left the army and enrolled in agronomy where he became interested in the development of new varieties of plant strains through interbreeding. After his graduation, he worked for a chemical fertilizer company. Around 1922, Himmler shared the post-war disillusionment of the German nation. He was drawn to extreme right-wing political movements and even joined the Corps Francs. Having heard Hitler's speeches on several occasions, he had been touched by the nationalist ardor of the Austrian.

A train called Strasser

On a morning of April 1923, Himmler went to the NSDAP office in Landshut, where his family lived, in order to register as a member of the party. The man sitting behind the desk was none other than the Gauleiter of Lower Bavaria, Gregor Strasser. As they were filling the registration form, the two men discovered some common ground. Strasser, who was a pharmacist, shared with Himmler an interest in the secrets of chemistry. A friendship developed between the two men and ten months later, in June 1924, Himmler was appointed private secretary to Strasser. The latter proved to be an effective assistant, running with thoroughness and dedication the many administrative tasks that were entrusted to him.

Himmler was a shy small man who looked like a school teacher with his round glasses, a round face sporting a narrow mustache and a small chin. He worked with the SS members who were selling ads to increase revenues for the *Völkischer Beobachter* and was sometimes assigned to assist reporters in the collect of information on the communists and socialists. He was appointed head of the tiny local SS unit.

During Hitler's imprisonment in Landsberg, Strasser came close to forming a new nationalist party from the branch of the national-socialist party he led. Hitler maneuvered skillfully and summoned a special meeting of the party during which the two men faced each other. Abandoned by Goebbels who changed sides, Strasser finally joined Hitler in February 1925. The following year, in September 1926, Strasser was appointed Reich propaganda leader and Himmler followed him to the headquarters within the select circle of nazi leaders. At the end of 1932, Strasser had a heated exchange with Hitler and tendered his resignation to the Nazi Party. Strasser was murdered in the Night of the Long Knives. Hitler was avenged.

In 1927, while on a business trip in Berlin for the Nazi Party, Himmler met Margarete Boden, a blonde nurse with blue eyes who was eight years older than him. They were married that year. Margarete had a certain wealth that allowed Himmler to buy the following year a land where he built a poultry farm. He experimented to improve the quality of the poultry and increase their productivity.

The beginning of Himmler's rise to power

Pretty much all nazi leaders had megalomaniac visions. Walther Darré, the future minister of Agriculture, and Alfred Rosenberg, the theorist of the party, shared with Himmler a deep passion for the origins of the German nation.

Rosenberg harbored a deep hatred for the subhuman Slavic race and kept telling Himmler that the development of the Nordic race's origin consisting of tall, blond individuals was lost in the mists of time, but their survival was indicative of the quality of the breed. The importance of the race and its determinants became a source of constant concern in discussions. Himmler fed his beliefs in foraging information here and there without discriminating between facts and huge assumptions that could become absolute certainties. His medieval chivalrous idealism mixed with his racial idealism, drawing in his mind an ethereal vision of the future of the German race and the role that it should play to save humanity.

Darré was an agronomist. He was writing a book on the principles of the enhancement of Nordic blood, *The Peasantry as the Life Source of the Nordic Race,* that Himmler kept on his bedside table. He believed that the Aryan superiority was genetic, and that German peasantry was the gene bank of the Nordic race, which needed to spread to dominate Europe. Darré pointed to Himmler that instead of investing in chicken breeding, he had two hundred unique German specimens in the SS troops who could represent the germs of a civilization of masters of the world.

Darré's suggestion made Himmler aware of the opportunities available to him. He decided to meet with Hitler later and offered to assume the leadership of the SS in order to use this pool of pure Nordic elements that embodied the German power symbol and could become the precursors of a pure and regenerated race. Hitler, who was busy rebuilding the Nazi Party, could not figure out who could be entrusted with the SS leadership. He jumped on the offer. Himmler's racial projects matched Hitler's racial obsessions. On January 6, 1929, he appointed Himmler head of the SS, who were about one thousand men at the time. Heinrich Himmler was to remain the undisputed SS leader until his death.

The organization of the Nazi Party approved without reservation Himmler's appointment as Reichsführer-SS. They were lulled by the ordinary looks of a man who definitely did not appear to be gifted for backroom games. It proved to be a fatal mistake. Behind his hesitancy and blandness, he hid his fanaticism and the ability to carry out the cruelest orders with an extreme coldness. While criticizing Göring's cruelty as a hunter, he ordered the execution of thousands of victims without feeling the smallest regret.

Himmler was an unfailing admirer of Hitler, who affectionately called him My faithful Heinrich. He indiscriminately endorsed the most ludicrous theories of the Führer, whose words put him in a state of quasi-mystical ecstasy. The fact that Himmler was drab and timid may have enabled him to avoid arousing a strong opposition in the political backrooms were was played the decisive card that made him one of the most feared men in Germany.

Between 1929 and 1933, Himmler increased the number of SS to approximately fifty thousand men. The SS remained citizens who worked in a trade or profession and voluntarily devoted part of their free time to train and undergo indoctrination of nazi ideology.

The German resistance to nazism

When Hitler was brought to power in January 1933, the German population was far from being nazified. Between 1933 and 1938, four hundred thirty-five thousand Germans were sentenced by the courts of the Third Reich for crimes and political offenses. About eight million citizens had voted for the Communist Party. And even in the election of March 5, 1933, the NSDAP collected only 44 percent of the votes, unable with two hundred eighty-eight seats to get a majority in the Reichstag. The Communists had 4.8 million votes, despite being accused of having set fire to the Parliament a few days earlier.

Those who refused to believe that it was the end of democracy in Germany argued with figures at hand that Hitler would be unable to impose his will with a parliamentary minority. Even in the ministerial cabinet, he had a minority with only three members out of eight belonging to the National Socialist Party.

Hitler played a game other than that of democracy. Having failed to have more members of his party elected, he came to the same result by reducing the number of opposition members. A few weeks after the elections, Hitler had approximately eighty communist deputies imprisoned in the SA camps.

A significant proportion of the population hated the SA, who imposed their laws and terrorized with impunity the major cities of Germany. Nine months prior to Adolf Hitler's rise to power, representatives of several states ruled by Prussia and Bavaria had requested from the central government the outright ban of the SA, which was promulgated by President Hindenburg on April 14, 1932. Political schemes within the army forced the government, led at the time by von Papen, to remove the ban two months later. Hitler took advantage of the visibility of the SA when his party wanted to differentiate itself before the electorate. After the seizure of power, the image of indiscipline and anarchy projected by the SA troops became counterproductive. For Hitler, the first revolution was over and it was time to foster an image of fight against the enemies of the party and the opponents of the government in power. The SS troops, better organized and more disciplined, represented a much more suitable tool to achieve those goals.

On December 19, 1945, during the SS trial at the Nuremberg international tribunal, Commander Warren F. Farr, the American prosecutor, said of them that the creation and development of such an organization were essential to the implementation of the conspirators' plans. The radical program and measures that they prepared and applied could not be fully achieved by using the government or the party mechanism. The responsibility of what was going to be done could not be openly assumed by a government agency or a political party—not even by the Nazi Party. It had to be a particular kind of body or organization, linked somehow to the government and having received its official support, enjoying an almost independent status while its actions could not be blamed on the government or the entire party. The SS played that role.

Year	Number of SS	Stages
1924		Hitler is released from prison in December and starts rebuilding the NSDAP at the national level
1925		The first SS units are created in September
1928	280	
1929	1,000	Himmler is appointed Reichsführer SS in January
1932	50,000	There are 700,000 SA
1933	100,000	The Waffen-SS doubles the number of SS
1934		The SA are eliminated in the Night of the Long Knives
1939	240,000	A little more than 10% of the SS belong to the Waffen-SS
1944	1,000,000	Of this number, 600,00 are Waffen-SS

Table 1 – Chronological order of the developmental stages of the SS troops

When the Nazi Party was elected, about fifty thousand SS were ready to fill different positions in the government services. With the complicity of Hitler, a real kidnapping of power took place, deflected into the hands of an organization that would use those levers to bring about a new order, whatever the cost.

Himmler and his obsession with the SS elitism

The SS were probably the most fascinating and sinister by-product of the Third Reich. Popular imagination still uses the term Gestapo to describe a threatening and malicious inquisitive attitude.

Between 1933 and 1939, Germany was booming. The country was rehabilitating its economy by preparing for war, and the reduction of unemployment amazed several of its European neighbors. The systematic dismantling of all democratic institutions, the nazification of social organizations and a good propaganda gave the nation the impression that an exciting social project was finally going to happen. Every German was hoping for a better world. The incredible successes of Hitler in the escalation that will lead to World War II suggested that the most fantastic projects could materialize if they were endorsed by the Führer.

Those closest to the Führer were thinking big. If Hitler was dreaming, Himmler was certainly not going to wake him up, because he was going as far as him, if no further, in his dreams of a Nordic race sanitized, regenerated, and able to impose a new world order and inaugurate a new civilization.

For Himmler, the responsibility entrusted to him by Hitler was a sacred mission. He became the custodian of the jewel of German civilization that was to dominate Europe first and then the world. In Himmler's mind, the applicants selected for the SS were to become the fathers of the new Germanic race, exempt of its contaminants and generator of the future civilization. Hitler had no doubt that in a few hundred years the entire German elite would be a product of the SS. Himmler presented himself as a gardener, aiming to purify a contaminated strain by a careful selection. He was going to carry out his task with a merciless resolution.

Upon his appointment, he undertook to increase the strength of the SS and pushed for a more rigorous selection process using racial and morphological criteria, as well as a stratification of the value of the candidates based on pseudo-scientific classifications. It was necessary to trace and exclude the subjects who displayed morphological characteristics of inferior blood, such as bulging cheekbones indicating Slavic or Mongolian origins.

He developed a pseudo-scientific structure around him, as well as a Research Institute of the Nordic race, and surrounded himself with scholars whose mandate was to investigate the characteristics thereof. He asked Professor Bruno K. Shultz to create morphological criteria in order to filter prospective SS and only admit those who, with their perfect physical condition, would create a race and a nation of lords. The candidates had to achieve a specific score before being admitted to the SS family.

The contrast is striking between the thorough elitist selection of the SS members, the undeniable quality of their organization and their cruelty and barbarism in the execution of their criminal missions. Himmler had taught them in a harsh way that human life has no value in itself. At the Nuremberg trials, Professor Gebhardt, head of the SS medical services, reported that Himmler had ordered the SS to use real bullets for their live-fire practices, which rarely ended with no loss of lives.

In his speeches to the SS troops, focused on the survival of the Aryan race in a great Germany, Himmler continuously strengthened the will to destroy the Jewish people. Addressing the SS major-generals, he recommended to maintain cordial relations with their fellow Germans and to show contempt for foreigners. And although they were not interested in those people, they should learn everything useful about slave needs, for the benefit of developing the German culture. He concluded by saying that the German nation was the only one to have positive feelings toward animals and that they should have the same attitude toward those human beasts.

The SS were convinced that they were writing a glorious page in their history, since they had a moral right and even the duty to their country to exterminate the Jewish people who wanted to destroy them. Himmler was essentially a bureaucrat, not an organizer or a schemer. He established the ideological base of the SS philosophy in 1931, and then discovered an assistant who would become the perfect complement to lead the destiny of the SS organization. With no philosophy or morality, cruel, treacherous and unforgiving, if the devil existed, his name was Reinhard Heydrich.

The devil became SS: His name was Reinhard Heydrich

Even though Himmler was the undisputed head of the SS, the quality of the organization of the SS troops should be credited in large part to one who was unquestionably the best recruit within the SS, Navy Lieutenant Reinhard Heydrich. This virtuoso came from a bourgeois family and his father was director of the Conservatory of his hometown.

An anecdote gives a remarkable description of the cynicism of the man who became a terribly ingenious and efficient right-hand man for Himmler. Heydrich was a handsome man with blond hair and a broad forehead. He was a gifted musician. He appealed to women. In 1931, he was an officer in the intelligence and telecommunication services of the Navy. He was in love with the daughter of a high-ranking engineer and they were engaged. Unfortunately, she became pregnant and the father decided that the couple should marry quickly. Heydrich refused immediately and explained to the angered father that he would never marry a woman who had sex outside of marriage, even with him, and that an officer and a gentleman should not marry such a girl. The woman's father took his case to the supreme commander of the Navy who asked Heydrich to resign to avoid the shame of being excluded from the army. The next day, Heydrich submitted his candidacy to the SS Hamburg section. Because of his military experience, he was accepted immediately.

Heydrich was extremely intelligent, quick-witted and ambitious. He was a performer capable of imagining the most Machiavellian scenarios to achieve his objectives. While Himmler was working on the morphological characteristics of his future SS, Heydrich lamented the mediocrity of the mental quality of the candidates. He suggested that Himmler open schools dedicated to intellectual training in addition to physical training. Himmler pursued Heydrich's idea and founded the so-called special *Junker Schools* or Junker-Schulen (Junker means Knights). The cadets had to get up at 6:00 am, engage in physical conditioning for one hour before breakfast, and spend the morning exercising and taking part in weapons training. Three times a week, their training involved using texts such as *The Myth of the Twentieth Century* by Alfred Rosenberg or *Blood and Soil* by Richard Darré. The afternoon was again devoted to physical training.

The SS training included knowledge of history, geography and military science, but the cadets also had to develop qualities such as leadership, self-confidence, a feeling of superiority of their race and, especially, a brutal determination excluding obsolete feelings like pity for the enemies of the Reich. At the end of their training, the SS were to have integrated the three major principles, which were human race, obedience and sacrifice.

Human race

If there is one explanation to the behavioral aberration of the SS, we must look for it in the ethnocentric and racial ideology put forward by Himmler, who never missed an opportunity to remind the SS that they were better people and better soldiers because they had a better understanding of their duties and were more intelligent than the soldiers of other nations.

To him, the struggle was engaged in the extermination of the sub-humans all over the world, who were in league against Germany, the nucleus of the Nordic race, the core of the German nation and the custodian of human culture. Therefore, the fight against this deadly danger threatening humanity was for the SS almost similar to the search for the Holy Grail, and only an organization such as the SS could and should win the fight, given their faithfulness to their purpose and their unconditional determination.

He used this noble purpose to justify the brutality of the German soldiers against the enemy. The killings would eradicate the greatest number of sub-humans and enable Germany to expand its territory.

Obedience

Befehl ist Befehl, as put it most defendants in the Nuremberg trials. An order is an order. This simple statement reflected the absolute aspect of an order for the SS. In a speech to the major-generals, Himmler demanded the unquestioned obedience of the soldiers, morning, noon and night, and the SS were to demonstrate exemplary behavior. An order could be discussed, but when confirmed by the superior officer, it was to be executed.

Sacrifice

Himmler intended to ensure the quality of the SS by imposing conditions that would eliminate all the subjects whose membership in the SS movement was related to the prestige.

He made it difficult to become a SS, because he wanted to be sure to choose highly motivated candidates. In those years, money was scarce and unemployment was high. And yet, the elected SS had to shell out their own money to buy the cap, shirt, tie, trousers and black boots. Himmler said that a candidate who was not ready to assume the cost of the uniform was poorly motivated and unreliable.

Hitler even asked his SS to sacrifice their families, if required.

The training of a SS

Anyone holding an important position in the Reich could become a SS by receiving the honorary SS rank. It explains the small obese SS who did not meet the criteria. But for the average person, becoming a SS was a privilege that came with a higher social standing.

According to the training program initially established by Himmler, becoming a SS took a lifetime. A young man applied for a position within the SS when he was eighteen. Beforehand he took an oath of loyalty to the Führer, successfully completed the examination and joined the army at the age of nineteen. After two years of military service, the SS ideology was rigorously taught. He learned about marriage laws, family legislation and organization, and the rules of honor. He was then given a dagger and had the right to defend his honor with his weapons. The SS remained active until the age of thirty-five and belonged to the reserve between the ages of thirty-five and forty-five. He had to demonstrate optimum fitness until the age of fifty.

In the early days, the SS recruited fifteen candidates per hundred applicants, after observing them for a few years in the Hitler Youth. Subsequently, the political certificates of the family, the list of ancestors since 1750, the proof of absence of hereditary diseases in the family, a medical certificate, a certificate of good conduct from the Hitler Youth and the opinion of the racial expert from the Committee of Inspection were required.

Several SS had a higher level of education and came from academic or professional circles. After the seizure of power in 1933, many aristocrats became members of the SS. Himmler regulated the SS organization with the most exemplary discipline, tougher requirements pertaining to physical appearance and a reserved stance in public. He wanted to produce a pure Aryan lineage exempt of racial contaminants and, for that reason, he could veto the prospective wife of a SS. However, after a few years, it became necessary to establish less stringent admission criteria as they were unable to recruit enough acceptable candidates. Before 1938, approximately 40 percent of the new SS had only an elementary education.

A SS proudly displayed on his belt the motto *Meine Ehre heißt Treue,* My honor is loyalty, and each of them was required to promise Hitler absolute allegiance until death.

This combination of brilliance and reserve projected an aura of mystery on the SS, increasingly envied by the SA. Although initially the number of SS was not to exceed 10 percent of the SA number, the massive recruitment of the SS unexpectedly expanded this elite group, to the delight of Hitler, who determined by decree in November 1930 the role of the SS organization as political police of the Nazi Party. Between January 1931 and January 1933, the size of the SS troops increased to fifty thousand members. However, that was not much compared to the size of the SA, which had increased from three hundred thousand to three million in the year following the takeover. However, Himmler had to weed the garden quickly and eliminate a large number of SS who were lacking the physical or social criteria, in order to meet the most stringent selection standards of the SS.

From then on, the SS organization developed ramifications in several subgroups that could address the many repressive needs of a dictatorial regime. However, this expansion was made at the expense of the initial selection criteria and, in the occupied countries, many non-Germans were incorporated into the SS organization.

Ultimately, it is their style that differentiated the SS from the other formations of the Third Reich. The SS conveyed a certain heroic realism, which was a pure contempt for one's own life and that of their opponents.

Such an attitude and a total lack of ethics created the most infamous genocide in history.

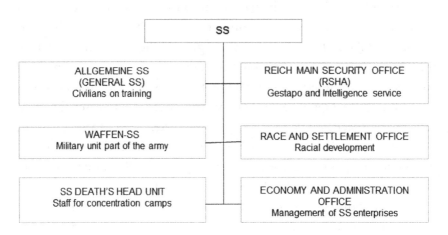

Table 2 – Administrative subdivisions of the SS

The SS troops rapidly increased in number. In the middle of 1933, the SS organization had eleven thousand members. Barely 10 percent of them were full-time members, the others being a reserve group that met twice a week, but could be used in case of emergency. On July 20, 1934, Hitler recognized by decree that the SS organization was independent of the party and removed all SS control over the SA. A masterful reorganization carried out by Heydrich led to the creation of several offices, consolidated between 1933 and 1935 by the exclusion of sixty thousand members who, due to their behavior or defects, did not meet the elitist criteria and tarnished the image of the organization.

The SS army: The Waffen-SS

When the Nazis rose to power, another troop was assigned to the national security of Germany, the *Verfügungstruppe*, which later became the Waffen-SS. It consisted of combat and reserve units. In 1942, in order to hold on to power in an extremely fragile political and military context, Hitler decided that the Waffen-SS would be the most important part of the army. At the beginning of the war, the Waffen-SS men were twenty eight thousand. At the end of the war, they were six hundred thousand and one fifth were strangers. Of its thirty-eight divisions, nineteen consisted mainly of foreigners such as Dutch, Norwegians, Danes, Finns, Swedes, Swiss, and citizens of a dozen other European countries.

The Heydrich plan: The reorganization of the SS services

During a visit to the Hamburg section, Himmler showed great interest in the qualifications of Navy Lieutenant Heydrich who had worked with the Reichswehr Intelligence. He confided to him that the SS needed to develop an effective information system to track down political enemies and put them out of action. He asked him to implement a SS security service that became the *Siecherheits Dienst* or SD. At the same time, Heydrich reorganized the responsibilities in the SS structure by creating several offices, namely personnel, administration, justice, health, social services, communications and physical training. Then he added a central office, his own security office and a racial office. Each office had many divisions and the SS organization became a multi-headed bureaucratic monster covering all aspects of life.

Allgemeine SS or General SS: The SS reservoir

During the first years, the SS men were civilian volunteers who had a job and devoted part of their time to train and learn the SS philosophy. From 1933 onward, Heydrich detached several services whose members were chosen from a common-pool resource, the Allgemeine SS or General SS troops.

The structure of the General SS was military, with divisions in sectors, sub-sectors, and also regiments, battalions, companies and sections. These SS were easy to mobilize during protests and they represented a reliable workforce that was used before the war in the antisemitic protests.

In 1937, the General SS comprised approximately one hundred eighty thousand men with a civil occupation and only 0.4 percent of unemployed.

The RSHA: The nazification of the German police

All police services, constabulary force, criminal police and political police were brought together under the supreme authority of a branch of the SS organization, the RSHA or Reich Security Main Office. Only the army, which had its own intelligence unit—the Abwehr headed by Admiral Canaris, was totally beyond the control of the SS police.

This reorganization affected the vocation of the police services and forced them to make a one hundred eighty degree turn. In all democratic countries, police services are a state institution dedicated to the protection of citizens and the national security. The takeover of the police services by the SS organization, a subsidiary of the National Socialist Party, was to provide the political party with a privileged and extremely effective repressive tool against citizens. The party's safety became the purpose of the police services and the citizens became the enemy to search and hunt down at the slightest sign of divergence with the nazi orthodoxy. The elevation of the political police, namely the Gestapo, above the judicial authority made people more fearful of the police. No German citizen felt secure on the Reich territory. The arbitrary became the rule and an unfounded suspicion or a malicious information was sufficient to make anyone eligible to an interrogation session, a torture session or a one-way ticket to a concentration camp.

Hermann Göring creates the Gestapo

In January 1933, Germany was a Federal Republic comprising fifteen states under the control of the central government in Berlin. In theory, German provinces were all equal, but in practice, thirteen of them were crowding 20 percent of the territory. Prussia and Bavaria were the two largest provinces occupying the rest of the country, but again, there was a strong inequality between them. It should be noted that Prussia had a territory four times larger and a population five times larger than its nearest competitor. Its capital, Berlin, was also the Reich. Therefore, Prussia exercised its supremacy over the neighboring states and remained the key to power. Prussian domination was part of German history. Before the Weimar Republic, the King of Prussia was considered to be the Emperor of Germany and was responsible for foreign policy and warfare.

German states	Area (sq. mi.)	Percentage of territory	Population in 1933	Percentage of population
Prussia	113,750	62.5%	38,200,000	60.96%
Bavaria	29,486	16.2%	7,400,000	11.81%
Saxony	5,856	3.2%	5,000,000	7.98%
Württemberg	7,534	4.1%	2,600,000	4.15%
Baden	5,819	3.2%	2,300,000	3.67%
Thüringen	4,541	2.5%	1,600,000	2.55%
Hösse	2,968	1.6%	1,400,000	2.23%
Mecklenburg-Schwern	5,068	2.8%	700,000	1.12%
Oldenburg	2,479	1.4%	600,000	0.96%
Brunswick	1,418	0.8%	500,000	0.80%
Anhalt	906	0.5%	400,000	0.64%
Lippe	470	0.3%	200,000	0.32%
Mecklenburg-Strelitz	1,130	0.6%	100,000	0.16%
Waldeck	438	0.2%	60,000	0.10%
Schaumburg-Lippe	130	0.1%	50,000	0.08%
City of Lubec			100,000	0.16%
City of Bremen			300,000	0.48%
City of Hamburg			1,100,000	1.76%

Table 3 – Distribution of areas and populations of the German states

Before the Nazis came to power, the organization of the police services was relatively simple. Each state had an independent police service and no German police service was subjected to the control of the central government. However, the Prussian police force exceeded in number that of all the other states combined.

Long before 1933, the power of the regular police force had weakened significantly, due to the intimidation by well-organized and aggressive paramilitary groups like the SA. Therefore, the police services had adopted a hands-off attitude on several occasions when citizens were physically attacked by the nazi troops.

When Hitler came to power, he led a minority coalition government, and the cabinet had only two Nazis in addition to himself: Wilhelm Frick, Reich minister of the Interior, and Hermann Göring, Prussian minister of the Interior. The opposition forces were nursing the illusion that the Nazis would be unable to impose their agenda on Germany. Göring was going to prove them wrong.

In each German province, the supreme authority of the police services belonged to the minister of the Interior. Frick had very little real power compared to Göring, who controlled the powerful Prussian police. Von Papen, who was vice-chancellor and opposed to Hitler, had cleverly kept the position of president of Prussia. Theoretically, Göring was his subordinate.

Prussia had a police service consisting of two sections. The police force in uniform, responsible for the enforcement of the laws, was divided into two departments: the *Schupo*, the urban constables responsible for maintaining peace, and the *Orpo*, whose services intervened when there was a strike or a riot. Another police force in plain-clothes was also divided into two departments: the *Kripo*, or the criminal police, and the *Stapo*, the political police responsible for ensuring the security of the state. Other police forces were used in more specific areas such as shipping, railways, etc. The chief of police of Prussia was coordinating this workforce and was accountable to the minister of the Interior.

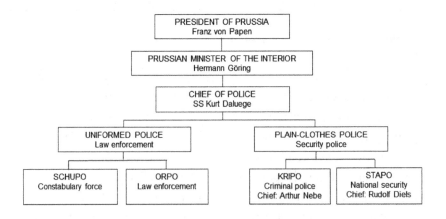

Table 4 – The police of Prussia in early 1933, after Göring's purge

Upon his appointment, Göring made very important partisan purges within the Prussian police. He dismissed twenty-two of the thirty-two police commissioners and ten thousand officials, and replaced them with members of the party. They were mostly SA, but also SS members whose loyalty to the party took precedence over their loyalty to the state.

From then on, the German police developed in an inconsistent manner and was more often involved in power struggles than emerging needs in an ordered fashion. The police network was so complex that the Germans as well as the Nuremberg tribunal lawyers found it quite confusing.

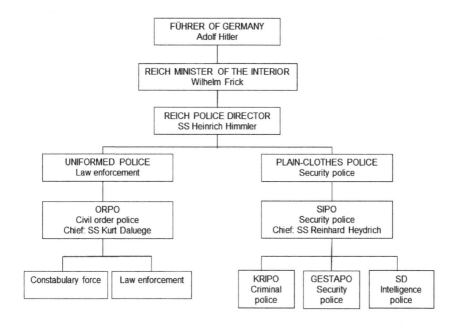

Table 5 – Structure of the German police after the centralization of the services on June 12, 1936

Upon his appointment to the ministry of the Interior of Prussia, the differences between Göring, founder of the SA, and Himmler, Reichsführer SS, started to show. Himmler and the SS will win this fierce power struggle with no holds barred.

The power struggle between Göring and Himmler

After the seizure of power in 1933, Hitler appointed Hermann Göring minister of the Interior of Prussia. Although he was technically a subordinate of Vice-Chancellor von Papen, he never reported to him. His appointment made Göring responsible for the Prussian police. He wanted to claim for himself a police force that would swear allegiance only to him and give him power by becoming a source of confidential information on political enemies and nazi leaders as well.

After severe purges to eliminate the chiefs of police who did not support the Nazis, he appointed SS General Kurt Daluege, one of Himmler's most loyal men, chief of the Prussian police services. Officially, Daluege was to assist Göring, but unofficially, he was to secure Himmler's interests and those of the SS. As chief of the Prussian police services, Daluege became technically Göring's subordinate and a subordinate of Himmler as a SS. While Göring was inviting many SA to join the Prussian police services, Daluege was doing the same thing with the SS. This is a typical example of the duplication of power that fed the image that the SS were a state within the state.

Göring hated the idea of relying on Himmler and his SS. He had detached the security police of Prussia, the *Stapo*, and obtained from Hitler, on April 26, 1933, a decree ordering the creation of the Secret State Police, the *Geheime Staattspolizei* or Gestapo, responsible for searching for political enemies and make them harmless. He quickly expanded the scope of the Prussian political police to Germany and put it under the authority of the party rather than the government. He appointed Rudolf Diels as head of the Gestapo, together with several members of the SA. Diels, the chief of police for the ministry of the Interior, was opposed to the SA and the SS. Therefore, he had his undying loyalty. Himmler did not like this appointment and, in April 1934, he managed to replace Diels with one of his most fanatical men, Reinhard Heydrich.

Himmler considered Daluege as a Berlin agent who could help him gain control of all the German police corps. The first task of Daluege was to fill the vacancies after Göring's purges. His second task was to help Himmler gain control over the Prussian police services. Daluege was able to convince Göring to appoint Heinrich Müller at the head of the Gestapo, under the authority of Rudolf Diels. Heinrich Müller was born in Munich in 1900. He dropped out of school at the age of seventeen to work as a mechanic in the aeronautic industry. He became a pilot during the war and joined the ranks of the Munich police after the war. He then specialized in the fight against socialism. He even worked against the NSDAP in its early years. With his phenomenal memory, he had the reputation of being a very effective interrogator. When the party came to power, he expected to lose his job. However, his efficient and ruthless keen sense of a bloodhound impressed Heydrich, who appointed him head of the Gestapo. At the end of the war, he disappeared in Switzerland, after emptying the coffers of the SS. Wealthy, he died in Hawaii in 1973.

Daluege also had Arthur Nebe appointed head of the Kripo, the criminal police. This is when the German police became the center of eccentric intrigues, torn by internal conflicts between the SA and the SS that reflected the friction between Göring and Himmler. As a result, Diels left his position one year later, due to the schemes of Daluege.

Members of the police services gathered in clans seeking to eliminate each other. Diels jokingly said that going in the hallway to wash their hands was a dangerous expedition that they all avoided, unless they warned a colleague of their intentions. Just like any mafia, the clans used their own services when on war with each other.

The Gestapo excelled in the discovery of conspiracies and in the fabrication of alleged conspiracies. Daluege wanted to get rid of Diels, who, according to him, was trying to undermine the influence of the SS in the organization of the police services. He commissioned SS Captain Packebush to search Diels' house in the hope of finding incriminating documents testifying of his links with the communists. Warned by his wife, Diels called on a police commander who was not afraid of Daluege. Diels went to his house with an escort of SS armed with grenades and automatic rifles. He arrested Packebush, handcuffed his men and took him to the police station where the two officers screamed at each other, Diels threatening to imprison Packebush and Packebush threatening to accuse Diels of treason.

Göring had bigger fish to fry outside police services, but for Himmler, well assisted by Daluege, it was his real spearhead and he was waiting for the right time to gain a foothold in Berlin. Made aware of the arrest of one of his SS officers, Himmler went to Berlin and protested to Göring, demanding the resignation of the chief of the Gestapo. Göring's man of trust was relieved of his duties, but was later granted an honorary position in the SS. The real winner was Himmler.

Beginning in October 1933, Hitler gave Himmler a series of appointments as chief of the police services in each of the German states and, in early 1934, Himmler was the chief of all the German police services outside Prussia, which still belonged to Göring. Ernst Röhm, head of the SA, was furious, but Hitler tried to appease him by giving him a token position of minister without portfolio. In any case, Röhm's days were numbered and the SA problem was to be definitively settled in June.

In April 1934, Himmler, who was head of the Bavarian political police, virtually took control of the Gestapo and merged with the SS. The SS being a by-product of the Nazi Party, the allegiance of the Gestapo, which was that of a government administration, became that of a political party. Also, its objectives were no longer the internal security of the state, but the security of the Nazi Party. The Gestapo was no longer accountable for its actions to the citizens, but the nazi leaders. It was no longer devoted purely to the protection of the country, but to the repression of political opponents. The Gestapo became, next to the SD, another instrument of the Nazi Party under the supervision of Reinhard Heydrich, Himmler's assistant. With extended powers, the authority of the Gestapo exceeded that of the courts and a suspect acquitted by the court could still be imprisoned by decision of the political police.

SS intrigues in the upper reaches of power

On November 5, 1937, Hitler convened the main leaders of the Wehrmacht to inform them of his military expansion project to increase the lebensraum for the German nation. In the discussion that ensued, Marshal von Blomberg and General von Fritsch raised objections on the time limits granted to the army to make it operational. Both of them insisted that they were unable to prepare the army on such a short notice for a conflict that could be global and last several years. Hitler was offended and after the meeting, he summoned Göring, Himmler and Heydrich and asked them to examine the private life of the two officers and seek, encourage or cause an accident that could lead to their dismissal.

The opportunity presented itself shortly after. In 1938, the Minister of Defense Field Marshal Werner von Blomberg had remarried with one of his secretaries, much younger than him, Fraülein Erna Gruhn. Count Wolf Heinrich Graf von Helldorf, nazi head of the Berlin police, discovered accidentally that von Blomberg's wife had a criminal record for immorality. He hid the file to Himmler and sought advice from Wilhelm Keitel, whose son Karl-Heinz was married to Dorthea von Blomberg, the daughter of Field Marshal von Blomberg, and held at the ministry of War an executive position that he owed to Blomberg. Preferring to save his position rather than Blomberg, Keitel handed the file to Göring, who informed Hitler. When Himmler took the matter in hand, Blomberg was forced to resign. Hitler took over the responsibility for the army, abolished the ministry of War and transferred it to a Joint Defense Council that included the three services of the armed forces that he headed, the OKW. Keitel became his assistant.

A petty intrigue eliminated Baron Werner von Fritsch, a former Prussian officer and austere single, who should have been the successor to Blomberg. The SS had found a member of Berlin's underworld already convicted of murder who claimed to have had a homosexual relationship with Fritsch. Profoundly offended, Fritsch asked to see Hitler, who accepted while preparing a confrontation with the accuser. Filled with shame and confusion, Fritsch was not faring well. However, the Wehrmacht, which was familiar with the methods of the Gestapo and was likely to be rocked by the scandal, undertook to conduct its own investigation, which showed that the accuser had lied and the Gestapo had taken advantage of a resemblance between the name of a genuine homosexual and that of the general of the army to falsify the police records. Fritsch was rehabilitated, but lost his position in the army and was replaced in 1938 by Walther Brauchitsch. In 1942, Hitler will grab this position and become Commander of the Armed Forces of the Reich, the OKH.

Around 1930, the SS were not yet a decisive force in Germany. They were numerically inferior to the SA, but their hierarchical structure was much more functional and the troops more disciplined than those of the SA. Heydrich knew that the SA aimed at achieving the status of parallel police or army reserve. He was also aware of the antagonism between the SA and the army, and he knew that the army was Hitler's trump card. He then urged Himmler to enlist in the SS former army officers who could make a bridge between the SS and the military.

This secret police was soon to become for the Nazi Party a tool for repression rather than a tool for ensuring the security of the state. The Gestapo owed allegiance to Göring and indirectly to Hitler, as leader of the Nazi Party. Von Papen had just been short-circuited a second time.

Meanwhile, Hitler gave to Wilhelm Frick the mandate to nazify the German government structures. In March 1933, following a putsch in Bavaria, Himmler became chief of all the Bavarian police corps, the second police force of Germany after that of Prussia. Then he appointed commissioners of police of the Reich and a *Reichstatthalter* in each German state to replace the local government, legislate in its place, and designate the official agents of the government. Himmler, who was chief of police of Munich and head of the SS troops, had a burning desire to control all the police services in Germany.

We can see two parallel structures evolve and interweave in utter confusion. The State Police Organization, with its reporting relationship, and the SS organization, with a completely different hierarchical structure. An unexpected consequence was likely to arise. Two individuals could have a similar rank in the police service, but one of them could be in a higher hierarchical position in the SS organization. Since the Nazis gave more weight to the party hierarchy than to the state, a total confusion resulted.

The political repression started with the swing into action of the Gestapo

The year of the Gestapo was 1936. In February, the Prussian government recognized the official status of the Gestapo that Göring had unconstitutionally detached from the regular police force of Prussia. A special clause raised the Gestapo above the law, since the judicial system was not entitled to review the decisions of this political police. From that point onward, any decision taken by Himmler had the force of a ministerial decree and was beyond the control of the state.

Hitler's extraconstitutional authority was now extended to the political police of the Nazi Party, against which the citizens had no legal recourse.

On June 17, 1936, Himmler was appointed chief of the German police and, on June 26, he reorganized the police service to create a law enforcement police and security service. He appointed two trusted men, Daluege and Heydrich, at the head of the two major services. On September 20, each Gauleiter and SS district was assigned a SS representative of the law enforcement police and security service. It was mandatory that the police chiefs were from the SS troops. On October 1, 1936, the Gestapo extended its authority to Germany.

The following year, Himmler managed to obtain from Hitler that the decrees issued by his office have the status of ministerial orders. He then incorporated the Gestapo into the intelligence service, the SD created by SS Walter Schellenberg. The SD was a party, not a government organization. From then on, the Gestapo belonged to the National Socialist Party and defended its interests.

The Gestapo agents, who were about forty thousand in 1944, were formed by Lieutenant General Heinrich Müller. Having closely studied the methods of the Soviet secret police, he had been impressed by the Russian government network of spies that isolated individuals by ruining their confidence in each other. He set up an extensive network of citizens with the title of honorary members of the Gestapo, who were responsible for reporting what they saw and heard. The usefulness of this system was not so much the valuable information obtained, but the fact that each German citizen became a potential target for the security police because of overheard or misinterpreted remarks.

What did a raid by the Gestapo look like?

In October 1941, the Gestapo arrested approximately fifteen thousand people per month, especially in the occupied territories. This influx of new inmates forced the nazi regime to build new concentration camps.

The *Nacht-und-Nebel-Erlass,* or the Night and Fog Decree, issued by Hitler on December 12, 1941 and signed by Marshal Keitel, shows the sinister nature of the nazi rule of terror. The decree was targeting the resistance movements in the occupied territories. In France, five thousand resistance fighters disappeared into the night and fog. Arrested by the

Gestapo without warning mostly during the night, the victims were taken to Germany, where, dead or alive, they were never heard from again.

While waiting for the bus, a Berliner complains about the work conditions since the abolition of the trade unions. A witness hears the conversation, identifies the man and warns the police services. Two days later, around 5:00 am, a big black car stops in front of the building where the complainant lives. Four men in civilian clothes disembark and three of them run upstairs. Pounding on the door, they shout: "Achtung! Gestapo! Schnell!" The family is abruptly awoken and the terrorized neighbors don't move. Someone opens the door to prevent breaking it down. Without explanation, the three men rush to the bedroom, get the victim out of bed and handcuff him. He just has time to put his slippers on. Still in his pajamas, he is taken to the car waiting for him on the street. He will never be seen again and his friends and acquaintances are terrified that their names could be mentioned in the interrogation room. It was the night and fog Gestapo. An opponent of the regime has vanished in the night.

The torture techniques used by the Gestapo had nothing to envy to the medieval ones. To the conventional slaps in the face or body punching with a whip or the butt of a weapon, they added a variety of options. They especially liked the suspension by the arms brought back that caused a painful shoulder dislocation. Nails pulled out, electric shocks to the genitals, head immersed under water, ice water baths, burns with a cigarette butt, a soldering iron or an iron, and crushing the bones of the hands and feet were the basic elements of a much larger and more sadistic repertoire of tortures.

The military were the only ones who escaped the SS in Germany. Although not allowed to arrest a military officer, the Gestapo was requested to inform the intelligence services of the army, the Abwehr, under the command of Admiral Canaris. This immunity enabled Canaris to infiltrate a group of officers opposed to Hitler, who will plan the failed assassination attempt by von Stauffenberg in 1943.

The SD: The ears of the Gestapo

In order to act, the Gestapo needed information. If the Gestapo was the punitive arm of the nazi government, the SD was its ears.

At Himmler's request, Heydrich set up in Germany an intelligence service responsible for collecting information on the enemies of the Nazi Party and for examining the party members. This information service was detached from the General SS in 1931. Initially, the SD was a structure exclusive to the SS, but Heydrich made it such a sophisticated spy organization that it became the only intelligence and counterintelligence office of the Nazi Party in 1934. In 1939, it was attached to the RSHA, the Nazi Security Office. The SD was in constant opposition with the Abwehr, Wilhelm Canaris-led army counterintelligence service, which, for reasons of military security, was beyond the control of the Nazi Party. This distrust of the SD was justified since the Abwehr became the sole institutional nucleus of resistance to nazism in Germany.

With close to four thousand members, the SD coordinated its activities with those of the Gestapo, the two organizations being complementary. The SD had set up a complex system to identify the vote on a ballot and determine who voted no and who deliberately cancelled their vote. The information was then transferred to the Gestapo to take appropriate measures.

In their weekly newspaper, the SS used blackmail and persecution against the opponents of the regime, who, because of their prestige or notoriety, could not be arrested without creating social unrest. The newspaper was drawing information from the secret files of the SD, mixing truths and lies to humiliate those people or reduce their influence.

The Gestapo: The arm of the SD

Although the Gestapo never had much more than forty thousand members, its work practices became an instrument of terror and repression across Europe. The law of January 25, 1938, promulgated by Frick, minister of the Interior and Himmler's immediate superior, gave to the Gestapo the right to take people in protective custody. Therefore, the Gestapo could arrest and detain a defendant as long as they wanted, even if he had been found guilty and had served his sentence. With this law, the accused no longer had to commit a fault. He simply had to be suspected of the intention to commit the fault. Citizens were no longer protected from the Gestapo.

Relying on voluntary action, the Gestapo had set up a network of voluntary informants among ordinary citizens, which gave the impression of a constant monitoring encouraging discretion and reducing the risk of political plots. Each group of workers had a member who represented the ears of the Gestapo. Janitors were on the lookout for suspicious words. Employees were encouraged to watch their immediate superior, and children to report their parents' or teachers' comments that could be harmful to the regime. Most of the time, the information gathered was unimportant, but a moment of inattention, words said inadvertently made the citizens vulnerable and contributed to an atmosphere of mistrust and terror in the population. It was no longer advisable to ask with insistence about a friend suddenly gone on a trip. Knowing someone arrested by the Gestapo meant being a bad German and becoming a suspect. In 1938, the denunciation had reached such a level of exaggeration that a monetary reward was offered to those who denounced a false informer.

The Death's Head formations

The first nazi concentration camp began operating in 1933. The concept was created by the SA in Breslau, near Berlin, because the prisons were full of political prisoners. The SS, subordinate to the SA in Munich, built their first concentration camp in Dachau, near Munich. After the burning of the Reichstag, many communists, opponents of the regime and common law criminals were imprisoned. Himmler believed that he would be able to prevent the growth of communist organizations in Germany, making it impossible due to a lack of members since all German suspected of communist allegiance had been imprisoned.

That year, Himmler formed special units exclusively attached to the concentration camps. They were the *Totenkopft societies* or Death's Head formations, and the only ones authorized to wear the skull-crossbones insignia on their hats. Candidates were mostly military personnel who had worked for the Wehrmacht previously. Upon completion of special training, they were to provide twelve years of service in the concentration camps. However, after 1938 and with the outbreak of the war, several men in those units were transferred to the Waffen-SS and replaced with volunteers from the General SS.

Theodor Eicke made history as the great coordinator of barbarism in the nazi camps. Eicke had a visceral hatred of Jews and Communists and a past rife with political violence. In 1920, he attempted to join the police, but was rejected due to a lack of training and his repeated implication in violent political protests. He became a member of the Nazi Party in 1928. In 1932, he was sentenced to two years in prison on charges of preparing terrorist attacks against political opponents. He escaped the verdict as a result of an intervention by the minister of Justice and went to Italy on the advice of Himmler. He returned to Germany in 1933 after the seizure of power by Hitler and joined the SS troops.

Eicke was a brutal and ruthless man who will execute Ernst Röhm in the Night of the Long Knives. On June 28, 1933, Himmler entrusted him with the command of the Dachau concentration camp. Upon his arrival, he imposed a code of discipline on the SS and demanded blind submission to his guidelines. He also put in place a regulation governing the discipline and punishment of the detainees. It specified that tolerance was a weakness and resulted in penalties for the SS who displayed humaneness. In October 1933, he presented a document that codified a list of prisoners' behaviors that called for specific punishment, but he left the SS determine the nature of the fault. This regulation was designed to break the prisoners psychologically and physically by creating an atmosphere of terror. He was targeting behaviors whose identification could be very subjective, such as making a speech, holding a provocative meeting, doing politics, gathering with others with the aim to steer revolt. Anyone breaking these rules could be immediately shot or hanged. The procedure was so effective that it was exported to other concentration camps.

On July 4, 1934, impressed by these results, Himmler appointed Eicke Concentration Camps Inspector and Commander of the SS Death's Head Units. On October 16, 1939, Hitler authorized the integration of the SS Death's Head units in the Waffen-SS and Eicke was transferred to the front, keeping the command of his SS division. Following in the steps of its commander, this SS division stood out by its brutality and fanaticism, murdering with indescribable savagery military and civilians. Eicke died on February 16, 1943, when the reconnaissance aircraft he was boarding was shot down by Soviet troops.

The SS and the mass extermination

As soon as Germany entered the war, SS extermination groups were created. The *Einsatzgruppen* or task forces were first deployed in Poland. It was difficult to entrust the army with the task of cleaning Poland of its undesirables, the military being trained to kill armed enemies, not defenseless civilians. Therefore, Hitler entrusted Himmler to form special commandos of SS capable of killing in cold blood. Those death squads were created in late spring 1941. The Einsatzgruppen personnel came mainly from Reinhard Heydrich' security police (Gestapo, Kripo and SD), with a few Waffen-SS units. Four mobile groups of SS were formed, each comprising between five hundred and one thousand men. They followed the occupying army and were charged with assassinating the Polish intelligentsia and all those who were suspected to be part of the resistance. It is estimated that the Einsatzgruppen made over one million victims.

To stimulate the enthusiasm of the SS, Himmler reminded his men the exploit of a group of Einsatzgruppen who, in the night of September 29 to 30, 1941, exterminated thirty-three thousand seven hundred seventy-one Jews in Kiev. After having asked the women, men and children to get undressed, the SS shot each of them in the back of the head. This massacre remains in history under the name of *Babi Yar*, Old Woman's Ravine. It is estimated that the Einsatzgruppen killed nearly one million civilians in the first months. It was a considerable amount of work. They needed to bring the victims together, shoot each of them in the back of the head and throw the bodies in mass graves. The SS Einsatzgruppen were unable to keep the pace after a few months in Poland. A little later, an additional workforce of approximately five hundred men, not from the SS troops, but from the Orpo law enforcement police, were added to the commandos in Russia. The meaning of the Führer's orders was that the Jews, regardless of their age or sex, were to be destroyed. The instructions given to the men allowed for the summary execution of the Jews and all those who opposed the invasion of Russia.

After attending executions where he got a splash of brains on his uniform from a victim shot in the head, Himmler had been sick. He decided that more humane measures should be proposed. Rudolf Höss was relieved when he learned that the gas chamber would be used to execute the prisoners, therefore sparing him the bloodshed.

But the use of the Einsatzgruppen showed limits in terms of efficiency, difficulty to keep the operations secret and psychological impact on the executors. It became necessary to find other solutions.

Dr. Becker, who was a SS attached to the Einsatzgruppen, suggested to use trucks crammed with the victims who were killed by carbon monoxide while the vehicle carried its human cargo to the mass grave where the bodies were disposed of. This solution appeared more effective, but included major problems that appeared shortly after. The truck drivers did not always use the appropriate procedures and the SS who unloaded the bodies often became sick, contaminated by traces of gas.

SS Christian Wirth, a former police officer, was commissioned by Himmler to find a more effective extermination method. He imagined using the shower rooms to reassure the victims and the water pipe to deliver carbon monoxide generated by vehicles outside. Those facilities were tested for the first time at the Belzec camp on March 17, 1942. The camp housed Polish Jews, who were the first victims. For the next nine months, Belzec was the main nazi extermination camp as the facilities allowed to kill up to fifteen thousand victims per day, mostly Jews. Other camps soon adopted the Belzec technology.

After the Nazis had exhausted all options to force Jewish emigration out of Europe and determined the final solution at the Wannsee conference, it was no longer thousands, but millions of Jews and Slavs who were to be exterminated. It was at Auschwitz that a subordinate of Commander Rudolf Höss developed a much more effective solution to quickly kill a large number of victims and get rid of the bodies. A German company produced the Zyklon B, a cyanide-based (prussic acid) pesticide. During an experiment, it appeared that the Zyklon B pellets released a gas that could kill a large number of victims in 10 minutes. Höss immediately ordered large quantities of Zyklon B from IG Farben, but the company opposed Höss' request to eliminate the odorous marker warning people of the presence of the gas. Apparently, this objection was not substantiated by scruples. Their patent had expired and the addition of the new molecule allowed them to apply for a new patent that competitors did not have the right to imitate. Himmler reassured the company whose dividends doubled in the following years. Moreover, the company built a rubber plant near Auschwitz, using the imprisoned Jews as cheap labor. At the Nuremberg trials, in 1948, the plant director Carl Krauch, was found guilty of slavery and mass murdering. He was sentenced to six years imprisonment.

With this technology, the gas chambers were specially designed by a German firm, German Armaments Incorporated. Special furnaces using organic fat as fuel were manufactured by another German firm, Topf and Company, in Erfurt.

The office of racial purity (RuSHA)

The mission of the office was the establishment of favorable conditions for the development of a pure Aryan race. To lead this service, Himmler selected Walther Darré who advised him to adopt policies to develop the Nordic race in Europe, using the German peasantry as a gene bank. From then on, the SS had to demonstrate a racial purity excluding Slavic or Jewish blood in their ancestry as far as 1750.

For a SS, falling in love was anything but easy. The office first ensured that the SS chose a wife who met precise criteria of racial purity. No SS could get married without the approval of Himmler. It was imperative that the bride had a file containing a medical examination report, a list of her ancestors since 1750, a medical certificate stating that her parents were in good health, an informative report from the police services, and ideological and human guarantees.

The office was responsible for the establishment of the SS, the ideological education of the family and their cultural environment.

Despite the promptings of their leader, the SS men did not fulfill the mating expectations, averaging one child per family. Himmler was convinced that his SS were manly men and that the falling birth rate was due to their wives. To compensate for their slowness in producing a master race of Aryan babies, Himmler set up the odd project of maternity homes known as *Lebensborn* or fountain of life. It is difficult to avoid comparing the reproduction of a pure German race with the poultry rearing techniques.

The breeding wards or Lebensborn

In 1936, Himmler established the Lebensborn program to promote the reproduction of pure German strains that were to give birth to the master race. There were about a dozen houses on this program in Germany where German women who met the racial requirements were encouraged to bear the children of the SS, who would become model citizens of a nation renewed and purified of its contaminants, the Jews. Those women could be the wife or the girlfriend of a SS, or a perfect stranger. In exchange, they were entitled to excellent care during their pregnancy and became eligible for financial compensation from the Reich after childbirth. The child also received the attention and financial support that he deserved as a future breeder of the master race.

On October 28, 1939, Himmler encouraged the SS to procreate out of wedlock in order to foster children with pure Aryan blood. Even teenagers were encouraged to bear a child for the Führer, if they wished. The SS were not encouraged to take advantage of the situation, but when the girls discovered their duty to the nation, the SS had to be happy to oblige. Parents who refused the involvement of their young daughter in the Lebensborn received an explanation from the SS. Parents who resisted were sent to a concentration camp. However, those programs were never popular with the SS, who much preferred their spouse to a Lebensborn stranger.

From 1975 onward, German secret documents revealed that hundreds of thousands of children in the occupied territories were stolen and brought into Germany for their favorable physical characteristics. They were adopted by German families to accelerate the creation of the superior race. And among the thousands of Polish children stolen for germanizing the Third Reich, barely 15 percent were repatriated.

The scientific research institutes to prove the value of the Aryan blood

Educated in history and archaeology by his father, Himmler set up scientific institutes to study history and engage in archaeological work to scientifically demonstrate the German presence and its development. In fact, he wanted to counter the assumption that Prussia was a Slavic land by discovering in the ground signs of the German presence centuries earlier.

With great enthusiasm, Himmler said in his Posen speech in 1943 that the German nation had a past of over a thousand years, and he wished that Germany would be more eternal than Rome, which was two thousand years old.

Chapter 6

The outbreak of World War II

World War II put an end to the poker game that had begun on March 16, 1935, and brought together two dictators and two democrats. Josef Stalin, unpredictable, calculator and paranoid, played the cynicism and trickery cards. Adolf Hitler, turbulent opportunist bereft of morality and devoid of moral conscience, played those of bluff, deceit, perfidy and falsehood. Édouard Daladier and Sir Neville Chamberlain were holding their best card, that of military power, but they chose to play naivety, good intentions, denial and pusillanimity, the weakest in the political game. At the end of the game, Russia, Germany, Great Britain and France plunged the planet into the bloodiest conflict in human history.

Four players in a triangle

World War I Allies, France and Great Britain, were recovering from their war effort and longing for peace in Europe. They were stunningly admiring the apparent economic prosperity of Germany, when that country was in fact preparing for a new war. They had a visceral fear of the new Russia, which had brutally rejected the tsars' legacy and now lived under a communist dictatorship. Marxist theories were attracting followers from the working class everywhere in Europe and threatened the stability of democracy in many countries.

Russia was a powerful country, spanning two continents and protected by the vastness of its territory that had brought down Napoleon's armies. The country had an abundance of raw materials, which meant industrial and military self-sufficiency, but had its eyes on the neighboring countries and was exploring opportunities to extend its borders. Russia had a large military force and was holding the balance of power in Europe. Any country joining forces with Russia ensured its domination on the continent.

Germany was a historically insecure country in the center of Europe, surrounded by many militarily powerful neighbors. Except for coal, it lacked sufficient raw materials to support a major war effort. The safety of Germany was based on the military caste, especially revered in Prussia. The military were the human wall that replaced the non-existent borders. The Treaty of Versailles, limiting the German army to one hundred thousand men, was crippling Germany, taking an ax to its most sacred institutions. The country, deeply humiliated by the defeat of 1918, was eagerly waiting an opportunity for revenge. Its savior, Adolf Hitler, came to power in 1933. His sharp political flair and unparalleled opportunism enabled him to become head of the party leading Germany. Convinced that a state could only be governed effectively by one man ultimately responsible for the exercise of power, Hitler was viscerally opposed to Marxism, which handed power to the working class. After 1930, the National Socialist Party seemed to be the only one capable of stopping the communist wave and brought Hitler to power. France and Great Britain, also faced with the Marxist ideology, saw nazi Germany as a shield against the communist threat.

In fact, France and Great Britain were linked by the same interests and made the same mistakes. They wanted peace at any price and feared Stalin more than Hitler. They were willing to compromise themselves in questionable diplomatic negotiations to maintain good relationships with Germany.

Stalin was aware that he was in a position of force in the triangle with Hitler and the team Daladier-Chamberlain. Courted by both sides, he was patiently waiting for the most profitable alliance. He knew that the best offers would not be presented by the democrats.

Hitler was a busy, impulsive and stubborn man. He was like those teenagers driven by wishful thinking, who believe that they are invincible and increase the risky behaviors without thinking. With no trump card in his hands, Hitler bluffed brazenly and began the betting.

Dates	Critical events
March 16, 1935	Reintroduction of compulsory military service in Germany
March 7, 1936	German troops march into the Rhineland
March 13, 1938	German troops march into Austria
March 15, 1939	German troops march into Czechoslovakia
August 23, 1939	German-Soviet Nonaggression Pact
September 1, 1939	German troops march into Poland
September 3, 1939	Outbreak of World War II

Table 1 – The escalation of World War II

The reintroduction of compulsory military service

On March 16, 1935, when Hitler got up, he had major plans for the day. He was to play his first card before the international community. He announced on the German radio that compulsory military service was reintroduced. He was telling the European countries that he did not consider being bound by the terms of the Treaty of Versailles and was making a determined step toward militarization of Germany. Deliberately violating the Treaty of Versailles, which limited the strength of the German army to one hundred thousand men, Hitler intended to create thirty-six divisions and recruit about five thousand men in each.

Despite a growing concern in Europe about the prospect of a new war, the Allies did not intervene and adopted a resigned attitude. On April 11, delegates from France, Great Britain and Italy met in Stresa, in northern Italy, but the discussions generated no concrete measures.

Upon his accession to power, Hitler had no intention to yield to the constraints of the international relations codes. He had already withdrawn Germany from the League of Nations in October 1933. The rearmament of Germany was the first step toward the realization of the lebensraum, the expansion of the German vital space. His expansionist policy had already been broadly disclosed in his book written in the Spandau prison in 1924. He had noticed an annual population growth of nine hundred thousand inhabitants that could result in a disastrous famine in the medium term.

He advocated four options: (1) artificially restrict the number of births; (2) increase the internal colonization by increasing the productivity of the soil; (3) acquire new territory; and (4) increase trade to ensure the existence of the nation through the profits generated. Obviously, the first option could not be upheld, since it would have been an obstacle to the development of the Aryan supremacy. The second option was a dead end since soil productivity would be optimal sooner or later. Hitler rejected the fourth option and explained that the third option, the acquisition of new territory to be colonized by the German surplus population, remained the only viable avenue.

The cynicism of the expansionist policy, formulated as if it was a no-brainer, came as a surprise in the traditional democratic context that prevailed in Europe and America. Hitler drew on the thoughts of Darwin and Nietzsche the natural selection arguments that explained the emergence of a species by the vigor of its survival reflex. He claimed that it was not the divine purpose that one country owned fifty times more territory than another. The territorial policy of Germany could not be exercised outside Europe. Since it was up to each individual to fight for one's existence, combat was the only way to achieve those objectives, considering an arms race.

The occupation of the Rhineland

One year later, on March 7, 1936, Hitler played his second card.

The Rhineland was a strip of German territory adjacent to the Rhine and stretching westward along the borders of France, Belgium and the Netherlands. Articles 42, 43, and 44 of the Treaty of Versailles established the Rhineland as a demilitarized zone by decreeing that no German military forces should be present on the left bank of the Rhine or within fifty kilometers of the right bank. The Treaty specified the prohibition of military maneuvers, the storage of military equipment or military fortifications in that zone. The Locarno Pact, signed in 1925 with the full consent of France and Germany, renewed the commitment of demilitarization and stipulated that a violation of those articles would constitute an act of aggression requiring immediate action. In 1930, the

French forces left the Rhineland as a gesture of goodwill, four years before the timeframe for withdrawal.

The reintroduction of compulsory military service a year earlier was not, in Hitler's mind, a simple protest against the injustice of the Treaty of Versailles. It was the first step of a well planned military aggression. In fact, in deepest secrecy, Blomberg, minister of War, had asked the three military branches to prepare a militarization plan of the Rhineland barely six weeks after the reintroduction of compulsory military service. Hitler had patiently waited for the most appropriate time to trigger the operation. On February 27, 1936, the ratification of the alliance between Russia and France finally gave Hitler the pretext he was waiting for. In the days that followed, Hitler ordered the troops to get ready to cross the Rhine, despite opposition from several of his officers who claimed that the operation was premature, since the German forces were not a guarantee of its success. Hitler laughed at their concerns and ordered to follow the plan.

When the sun rose on Berlin on Saturday, March 7, 1936, the government of the Third Reich had a busy schedule. Hitler awoke much earlier than usual to check his carefully prepared staging one last time.

At 10:00 am, Constantin von Neurath, minister for Foreign Affairs, put on his velvet glove to play the apostle of peace. He received in his office the ambassadors of France, Belgium, Great Britain, and Italy and proposed a twenty-five-year peace plan decreeing demilitarization on both sides of the Franco-German border. To ensure that France would find it inadmissible, Hitler has included a clause about the demolition of the Maginot line fortification. The peace plan also proposed pacts of non-aggression with the neighbors and the reintegration of Germany into the League of Nations. Two hours later, at noon, the ambassadors were still discussing with the German Foreign minister while Hitler was delivering a speech before the Reichstag. Now wearing the iron glove, he announced the government's intention to reoccupy the Rhineland, because of the pact of mutual assistance in the event of German aggression ratified a few days earlier between France and Russia. While the six hundred nazi deputies strongly supported the government, three battalions comprising thirty-five thousand men were goose-stepping in the demilitarized zone. Taken aback at first, the crowd became delirious. The troops had been secretly instructed to immediately retreat if the French intervened.

In Paris, there were consternation and confusion. Telephone lines between Paris and London were busy. France did not want to take military action without the support of London. For the British government, who advocated extreme pacifism, it was out of question to participate in a military operation with France, even though the Locarno Pact forced them to militarily support France in the event of an armed conflict. French general Gamelin considered that a military intervention would be risky without a general mobilization and the French government believed that a general mobilization was an inappropriate response, particularly in view of the popular resistance. The general simply aligned thirteen divisions along the German border, primarily to strengthen the Maginot Line. Paris brought the dispute before the tribunal of the League of Nations. The latter condemned Germany, but suggested that the parties find a solution to the dispute. Taking advantage of the indecision of the tribunal, Paris decided not to intervene, arguing that Germany was in fact taking back what belonged to its country. The tribunal members were less impressed than the international press by Ribbentrop's argument that the twenty-four-year peace plan presented to the neighboring countries the morning the German troops marched into the Rhineland reflected Germany's desire for peace.

This passive attitude would result in fatal consequences. For Hitler, the message was clear. If Paris did not intervene militarily, even though they were being threatened, and if Great Britain did not comply with the terms of the treaty of military assistance signed with France, there was a very high probability that the European democracies would not come to the rescue of any country in the event of a German aggression. We can blame the Germans for passively supporting Hitler, but Europe in general, and France and Great Britain, in particular, did not do any better in 1936. They found pathetic excuses to justify their passivity and encouraged Hitler to implement his expansionist projects through a skillfully dosed ratcheting. Reassuring his opponents on the nature of his intentions with all the deviousness he was capable of, he knew how to secure their acceptance to a tolerable limit. One thing leading to another, they eventually woke up faced with an unacceptable fact that they could hardly object. This technique was described as an ordinary drop of water that soon turned into a destructive torrent. Hiding behind a policy of purely defensive pacifism, Europe had given Hitler the signal to go forward.

The German general staff was opposed to the strategy of Hitler because Germany did not have enough troops when the operation was launched. When Gamelin aligned the French divisions along the German border, several officers were in a cold sweat. Blomberg, minister of War, and a large number of members of the military high command urged Hitler to bring home the divisions that were in the Rhineland. Hitler kept a cool head, even though the forty-eight hours that followed the entry of the German troops in the Rhineland were among the most trying of his career. Hitler's victory was a real rebuff for the Wehrmacht generals who were opposed to the project. A triumphant Hitler ridiculed them and mocked their cowardice. The officers, who were all driven by a strong patriotism to Germany, were deeply humiliated for having opposed a project that had given the nation a sense of pride and hope to remedy the outcry of the Treaty of Versailles. They had proven that the traditional military strategies did not carry any weight with Hitler's political instinct and that their attitude caused the German nation more harm than good. The recalcitrant fell into step, sheepish and repentant, leaving in the hands of the Führer the military authority that was theirs.

As for Hitler, this victory was the second act of a scenario that he intended to repeat, adding to his bets each time he threw the dice: the use of a brief military intervention, wrapped in his desire for peace in Europe, but full of bluff, lies and deceit. To strengthen his position, Hitler ordered the dissolution of the parliament in the following month and organized an election where voters were called to express their opinion on the nazi policy by indicating yes or no on the ballot. Hitler won a landslide victory, his policy being supported by almost 98.8 percent of the voters. The image of the Führer took divine proportions in the German population who was regaining the national pride lost eighteen years earlier. During those years, even Europe seemed to be swept away by the Hitleromania, despite evidence that the Führer was preparing for war. Several foreign visitors showed their admiration for the achievements of the NSDAP in Germany and Hitler's efforts to promote peace in Europe. The French ambassador to Germany, François-Poncet, even mentioned that Hitler generated in Europe a keen interest, along with fear and aversion, as well as curiosity and sympathy. Kings and princes wanted to meet the man who had breathed new life into Germany and who made his presence known everywhere in Europe.

During the 1936 Summer Olympics, barely a few months after the militarization of the Rhineland, Hitler won after having completely mystified the world on his real intentions. On January 30, 1937, he stated that surprises were over and that peace in Europe was now the main goal of Germany. In fact, Europe trusted Hitler and followed his path, a choice that it would deeply regret, but too late. European democracies, the German nation, the supreme command of the Wehrmacht, Adolf Hitler, and other actors were now ready to play their roles in the inevitable tragedy that was about to happen, World War II.

The annexation of Austria

In 1937, Hitler had managed not only to seduce the German population, but also the European countries that were watching with little understanding the return to prosperity of a nation where unemployment was virtually non-existent. On January 30, 1937, he proclaimed the withdrawal of Germany from the Treaty of Versailles. Then, in a bit of bluff, he occupied Rhineland. To support his policies, he found two allies: Mussolini in Italy and Franco in Spain.

1937 was the year for the consolidation of gains, and for economic and military development. Hitler deepened his ties with Mussolini, in particular, trying to get him to think that the reunification of Austria and Germany went without saying. Mussolini disapproved of any interventions in Austria. In the fall, he was invited to Germany by Hitler, whose words of praise for him would have looked suspicious if his ego had been less hungry for flattery, and if he had not been so much impressed by the ceremonies and military deployment. A few weeks later, the Duce, who in the spring had been unresponsive to the idea of annexing Austria, said that he was no longer interested in its fate.

But Hitler had an interest in Austria. Inhabited by six million five hundred thousand Germans and endowed with considerable economic resources, Austria held many attractions for Hitler, who had drawn upon military and industrial resources in order to support the war effort he was planning. In addition, the Germans living in Austria wanted to relate to Germany and were likely to be the engine that would lead many Austrians to promote this reunification, the *Anschluss*. The Nazi Party was very active. Financially supported by Germany, it multiplied the protests and acts of violence to undermine the credibility of the Austrian government. Besides, Chancellor Dollfuss had been murdered by Austrian Nazi Party members a few years earlier. Hitler was waiting for the Austrian government to decide to restore order. It would be easier than justifying a military intervention to protect the German blood.

In the fall of 1937, he communicated under top-secret cover with the key staff of the Reichswehr to inform them of the war plans and time schedule. Fearing an allied armed opposition to the invasion of Austria, Field Marshal von Blomberg, General Werner von Fritsch, commander in chief of the army, and Foreign Minister von Neurath objected an inadequate preparation to prevent Hitler from going ahead with his project. They were removed from their positions in the months that followed.

When he was vice-chancellor, Franz von Papen had tried unsuccessfully to win the Austrian Chancellor Kurt von Schuschnigg to the idea of reunificating the two neighboring countries. The political instability of Austria did not shake Schuschnigg's belief in an independent Austria. Annoyed, the Führer invited Chancellor Schuschnigg to his summer residence of Berchtesgaden on February 12, 1938. Hitler was aggressive and threatening. He ridiculed the military power of Austria compared to that of Germany. Destabilized, Chancellor Schuschnigg signed an agreement appointing the Nazis designated by Berlin to key positions in the Austrian government, including a Viennese lawyer, Arthur Seyss-Inquart, as head of the police and the army. Schuschnigg informed Hitler that he lacked the power to formally legalize such an agreement without the signature of the president, but promised to take action to convince the latter.

President Wilhelm Miklas first refused to put his signature on the German ultimatum. However, impressed by the mobilization of the German divisions at the border, he finally gave up and signed the agreement. A few days later, Hitler made a speech and demanded, in addition to other concessions, self-determination of the Germans in Austria. This time, Schuschnigg resisted stating that the independence of Austria was not negotiable. Many violent pro-nazi protests shook the country and crippled its economy due to investors and tourists cancelling their projects. In an attempt to rally part of the electorate, Schuschnigg decided to hold a plebiscite for the Austrians to vote on the independence of Austria. The vote was to be held four days later, on March 13, 1938. Caught off-guard, Hitler became angry and ordered the army to get ready to march into Austria on the eve of the vote. However, Hitler needed to protect his interests. He wrote a letter to Mussolini, justifying his intervention in Austria by the lawlessness that prevailed and the threat of invasion of Germany by an army of twenty million men gathered by Austria and Czechoslovakia in order to restore the Habsburg domination. The letter sent by Hitler was found in the archives of the Italian ministry of Foreign affairs after the war. Very mindful of the enormity of his statement, Hitler suppressed the passage when the letter was published in Germany.

On March 11, Schuschnigg cancelled the plebiscite to avoid a bloodshed. Hitler claimed that this concession was not enough and demanded the resignation of the chancellor and his replacement by Seyss-Inquart, who, as the new chancellor of Austria, was to send a telegram to Hitler to officially restore order in Austria and unofficially justify the German military intervention. Schuschnigg gave way once again, but president Miklas refused to endorse Seyss-Inquart's appointment as chancellor. Hitler had a fit of rage. In the evening, he ordered to launch the invasion and at dawn on March 12, 1938, the first German divisions marched into Austria without firing a shot. The next day, a large headline in the official newspaper of the NSDAP stated: "German Austria saved from chaos".

The first representative of the German government in Austria was the Chief of Police Heinrich Himmler, who walked in behind the occupation troops. The repression intensified everywhere in Austria and nearly seventy thousand people were arrested in Vienna. In the weeks that followed, Hitler organized his own referendum on the Anschluss. In an Austria swept by a wave of terror, the non-secret ballots, on which yes was twice the size of no, granted 99.7 percent of the votes in favor of the Anschluss. The German occupation was justified.

The European chancelleries remained silent once again. The dissenting voice of Winston Churchill rose in the House of Commons to issue a warning that was not heard.

Hitler was welcomed as a hero in Austria. In an outburst of narcissism, he proclaimed himself a messenger of God and, therefore, the instrument of the highest order. He expressed his gratitude to God who enabled him to return to his native country and ultimately brought it back into the German Reich.

The annexation of Austria had several major consequences. The image of the Führer generated adulation in a significant part of the German population, but the army staff experienced a growing resentment for being completely pushed aside. Hitler himself became dangerously convinced of his own infallibility, which encouraged him to replace a well-considered military plan with the magical thinking of a teenager convinced that hoping for something makes it happen. His predictably disastrous strategy in the Russian campaign clearly illustrates that error. Furthermore, the inertia and passivity of the European chancelleries toward his power play provided unlimited opportunities to his expansionist designs. Finally, Czechoslovakia, surrounded on three sides by the German territory, was offered to him on a silver platter.

The dismantling of Czechoslovakia

Czechoslovakia was particularly concerned about the aftermath of the occupation of Austria. Hitler was reassuring, pointing out that he intended to respect the Treaty of non-aggression.

The events that led to the invasion of Czechoslovakia deserve to be analyzed. They shed a harsh light on the sad or sordid human behavior of the actors of the dismemberment of Czechoslovakia, who posed as noble or respectable. Despite evidence of their military superiority and many messages from senior German military officers opposed to a war in Europe who were informing them of a plot to overthrow the Führer, representatives of the British and French governments demonstrated a servile abdication reminiscent of the passive collaboration of the Germans in the Jewish persecution. Keeping Czechoslovakia away from the discussions, even though they concerned the survival of the nation, the highest representatives of the British and French governments were like street peddlers, since Hitler never left Germany to buy the peace at any price, including the brutal threat of unilateral severance of a military assistance treaty with Czechoslovakia if President Beneš did not accept the agreement reached in his absence.

At the beginning of those events, Czechoslovakia was the most democratic, open to progress, enlightened and prosperous country in Central Europe.

Structured in 1918, Czechoslovakia had not solved the problem of the ethnic minorities, who were nonetheless among the best treated in Europe. Three million Germans living in the Sudetenland were looking toward Germany, one million Hungarians toward Hungary and half a million Ruthenians toward Russia. Ten million Slovaks who accounted for 25 percent of the Czech population hoped to achieve independence. In 1933, inspired by the seizure of power by Hitler in Germany, the Sudeten Germans, who accounted for 22 percent of the Czech nation, created the Sudeten German Party led by Konrad Henlein, a gym teacher. Subsidized by Berlin, Henlein met with Hitler to develop a strategy.

Hitler was always using the same tactics. First, he provoked unrest in neighboring countries, claiming to stand up for the German citizens living there. The latter organized themselves actively, anticipating their return to the homeland after the German invasion and the annexation of Czechoslovakia. A propaganda prepared by Goebbels exalted the popular resentment by showing in the cinema scenes of violence against their compatriots in foreign countries. Supporting the often inadmissible complaints of German citizens living in foreign countries, he created tensions with the neighboring governments and, to provide assistance to those citizens in distress, he self-righteously organized a rapid military intervention that met little resistance.

At the beginning of May 1938, convinced that Hitler only wanted to rescue his German compatriots of the Sudetenland, Premiers Chamberlain of Great Britain and Daladier of France began to exert pressure on President Edvard Beneš of Czechoslovakia, urging him to agree to the demands of the Sudeten Germans. At the end of May, when Czechoslovakia rejected the demands, Europe was expecting an impending war. Meanwhile, Hitler was finalizing the details of a military intervention that he intended to carry out when the situation would be to his advantage. To feed the crisis, the minister of Propaganda spread incredible stories of violence perpetrated against Germans by the Czech Republic.

President Beneš ordered the mobilization of the armed forces and the German ambassador in London was summoned to be informed of the support of Great Britain to Czechoslovakia, excluding a military intervention. On May 30, Hitler informed his staff of his irrevocable intention to invade Czechoslovakia no later than October 1. This is when several German generals realized the danger of that decision for Germany. The German military manpower being significantly lower than the French troops had virtually no chance of victory. The Chief of the Army General Staff, General Ludwig Beck, sent a memorandum to General von Brauchitsch, commander in chief of the army, to emphasize that the strategy proposed by Hitler contained serious errors and that the general staff refused to apply them. Brauchitsch kept the report to himself, not willing to upset Hitler, who firmly believed that France and Great Britain would not interfere.

Beck sent a memorandum to Hitler, asking the Führer to stop preparing for war and wait for a more favorable military situation. He considered that a military action was inappropriate, stressing that the staff officers were of the same opinion. Beck mentioned to Brautchitsch that a mass resignation of the generals would force Hitler to choose other options. He also raised the problem of obedience to the authority, which was challenged several times at the Nuremberg trials. He argued that there were limits to the duty of obedience to the authority when the consciousness, the sense of responsibility or the knowledge of some military facts are confronted with orders that appear to be dishonorable.

Beck's representations having failed miserably, he resigned as chief of the army general staff on August 18, 1938 and was replaced by General Franz Halder. Very early, Halder joined a conspiracy of generals opposed to Hitler's policies. They were planning to seize the dictator when the order to invade Czechoslovakia would be given. On September 9, Halder was summoned to the chancellery and placed in the uncomfortable position of describing the Czechoslovakia invasion plan to Hitler. He was reprimanded by Hitler, furious to have to deal with defeatist generals.

The conspirators sent an emissary to London to inform the British government that new concessions to Hitler could derail their project, but that an official warning could knock him down. British Prime Minister Chamberlain took that information with a grain of salt. Noting the lukewarm reaction of the British government, the conspirators contacted Sir Nevile Henderson, British ambassador to Germany, to inform him that a firm and immediate intervention by France and Great Britain would bring about the downfall of the nazi regime. Henderson considered the information as a mere sham. Other pressing contacts failed to shake the British non-intervention policy.

On September 15, 1938, a series of talks began between Prime Minister Chamberlain and Hitler, who aggressively demanded that all the Czech territories where more than 50 percent of the citizens had the German nationality be given back to Germany. Without consulting the Czech government, Chamberlain went back to London to negotiate with French Prime Minister Daladier an agreement pertaining to Hitler's requirements. In order to make this project more acceptable, France and Great Britain proposed to Czechoslovakia a military assistance treaty against unprovoked aggression. Chamberlain met with French Premier Daladier, who agreed that the Czechs must accept the following in order to avoid a war, even though they had not been involved in the discussions: all Sudeten territories whose populations were more than 50 percent German were to be transferred to Germany in exchange for a treaty of assistance with France and Great Britain against unprovoked aggression. The Beneš government rejected the compromise and was threatened with abandonment by France and Great Britain. Giving in to the pressure, President Beneš surrendered on September 21.

On September 22, Chamberlain met with Hitler to triumphantly inform him that all his claims were accepted. Hitler shocked him when he said that the situation had evolved and the concessions were insufficient. Hitler formulated new demands. The British cabinet refused to endorse them and France, which had signed a treaty of military assistance with Czechoslovakia, had a moral obligation to keep its word and go to war against Germany. On September 26, Chamberlain notified Hitler in writing that the British cabinet had rejected his new territorial demands. The Führer had an episode of uncontrolled anger.

True to his principle that the bigger the lie, the more credible it is, in a speech that night, Hitler described in apocalyptic terms the situation of the German minority in Czechoslovakia, quoting imaginary numbers provided by Goebbels to fuel the rage of the German population.

The parade of a German motorized division was held in the streets of Berlin the day after Hitler's speech. He expected a large and enthusiastic crowd, but Berliners sent a clear message to the Führer. The endless military parade failed to mobilize the interest of the small group who observed the deployment in total silence while the majority looked away and continued their activities. Hitler, who appeared at the window of the chancellery several times to salute the military by raising the right arm, was unpleasantly surprised by the reaction of the crowd, but did not change his plans.

The pressure continued to increase on Hitler. The same day, President Roosevelt of the United States and the King of Sweden sent to Hitler messages urging for peace and holding him responsible for the outbreak of war, if any. In the evening, he stepped back and wrote to Chamberlain that he did not wish to dismantle Czechoslovakia and was ready to give guarantees about the remainder of the Czech territory. Nevertheless, Prime Minister Chamberlain pressured President Beneš, holding him responsible for the outbreak of war in Europe if he did not surrender to Hitler. He also sent an informative message to Mussolini. This is when Sir Nevile Henderson suggested to Chamberlain the idea of a conference involving Germany, Great Britain, France and Italy. Hitler was not interested at all since an agreement could thwart his invasion plans already underway. But he did not dare contradict Mussolini who had suggested that he should participate. Hitler agreed and the pressure dropped a notch in the European chancelleries. The British House of Commons was thrilled. This Chamberlain's initiative put on hold the coup d'état planned by the German generals.

The pathway that led Germany to World War II illustrates the opportunism, cynicism and cunning that were Hitler's trump cards in his conduct of foreign policy. The European nations were deceived by a head of state who claimed to follow the ground rules of international relations, but brazenly lied to ease concerns. He put at the bottom of the treaties a signature that he had no intention of honoring, as it was for the sole purpose of manipulating to his advantage the political decisions of the European countries.

The Four Power Conference was held in Munich on September 29 and 30, 1938.

Mussolini had a long discussion with Hitler before the conference. He presented to France and Great Britain Hitler's previous requirements, in a watered-down version that Chamberlain, Henderson, and François-Poncet did not recognize. Two Czech representatives had been excluded from the conference room. An advisor to Prime Minister Chamberlain informed them of the terms of the Munich Agreement under which the German army could occupy the Sudetenland as early as October 1. Faced with their protests, a British representative threatened to let them settle their problems themselves with Germany.

As he was leaving, Chamberlain asked Hitler to sign a letter of understanding between Germany and Great Britain, stating that the two nations would not go to war against each other and would establish the mechanism for the peaceful settlement of their disputes. With a straight face, Hitler put his signature at the bottom of the letter. Euphoric, Chamberlain returned to Great Britain, wielding the agreement in front of a jubilating crowd. Except for Winston Churchill, who repudiated the agreement in the strong protests of the deputies in London, nobody had yet clearly understood that Hitler was playing a game and that his rules were different from those of his partners. On September 30, abandoned by the European nations, President Beneš surrendered and resigned a few days later. He was replaced by Emil Hachá, judge of the Supreme Court.

The consequences of the Munich Agreement were considerable. If the treaty had not been signed, Hitler would have deliberately followed his plan to attack Czechoslovakia on October 1, which would have inevitably dragged Great Britain, France and probably Russia into the conflict. During the Nuremberg trials, General Jodl admitted that with five active divisions and seven reserve divisions, it was impossible for Germany to imagine a victory against one hundred French divisions. Furthermore, the German general staff was already organized to overthrow the regime as soon as the invasion of Czechoslovakia was ordered. In fact, Hitler could have stopped there. He had obtained from the European countries the tacit acceptance of his expansionist aims and pushed the German borders beyond those that prevailed during World War I. He was at the peak of his popularity. The German nation had avenged the Treaty of Versailles, the great Germany had become a reality accepted in Europe and a new peace could have been established.

This is when he really lacked political acumen. Instead of consolidating his empire and using his power to make alliances that would strengthen his position, he made a huge mistake. He decided to further expand the living space and create alliances as unholy as the United States and Russia against Germany. What was the end of the adventure for the German nation was a beginning for Hitler. The Führer, blinded by his narcissism and megalomania, was the architect of the destruction of his own dream when Germany invaded Russia on June 22, 1941, and declared war on the United States six months later, on December 11, 1941.

But history has to follow its course. Hitler kept his objective to occupy all Czechoslovakia and submit the Czech nation to the law of the Reich. In October, Hermann Göring met with two Slovak leaders to inform them that Germany favored the independence of Slovakia, which would make the settlement of the remainder of the country easier, even with the guarantees to Czechoslovakia in the Munich Agreement. Meanwhile, in Berlin, Hitler was receiving Slovaks to whom he guaranteed the independence forthwith. On March 6, 1939, the unrest in Slovakia had reached such a pitch that President Hachá ordered the dissolution of parliament and the arrest of the Prime Minister Bishop Tiso. The transitional government then came under pressure and threat from the German government, which insisted that Slovakia proclaim its independence, although its cabinet had been hostile to a complete break with the central government. Hitler intensified the pressure and demanded that the cabinet request the protection of Germany at the time of independence. The Führer obtained what he wanted and Slovakia became independent on March 14, 1939. On March 16, it requested via telegram the protection of Germany.

The issue had come to a head. A number of Germans attempted to provoke disturbances in several Czech towns and cities and, despite the non-intervention instructions to the police, Goebbels echoed the old story in the German press about the poor Germans persecuted by the Czechs, who required an intervention to protect them. President Hachá and his Foreign minister immediately went to Berlin to discuss the political situation. They arrived in Berlin late in the evening on March 14. Hitler received them immediately, was aggressive and contemptuous toward his guests, and threatened Czechoslovakia of a bloodbath if the president did not sign the immediate capitulation. Hitler was so upset that he had to go and calm down in another room. Hermann Göring and Ribbentrop resumed the exhausting discussion with the president, threatening to send hundreds of bombers ready to take-off if the document was not signed at dawn. In the middle of the night, President Hachá lost consciousness. While Hitler's physician was administering first aid, Hitler was preparing the surrender text for Czechoslovakia. When Hachá came to, they put a telephone in the hands of the old president who contacted Prague and signed the document. On the morning of March 15, 1939, the German troops marched into Bohemia and Moravia. As for Ruthenia, Hitler had already given it to Hungary. On the day of its independence, the Hungarian army invaded the country.

During the Nuremberg trials, General Alfred Jodl admitted that if France had supported Czechoslovakia, the German invasion would have been foolish, the French and the Czechs outnumbering the Germans by more than two to one.

The invasion of Poland

In 1939, a war was threatening Europe. Separating Germany from the Russian borders, with a supply of raw material essential to Germany's entry into war, inhabited by inferior people easy to dominate, Poland represented for Hitler a key requirement for the German military power. On April 3, Hitler instructed the Wehrmacht to develop an invasion plan of this neighboring country. The first step was to ensure that Russia did not see the occupation of Poland as a threat to its territorial integrity. This precaution was all the more necessary since the invasion of Russia had been for a long time the final stage of the nazi expansionist policy.

Sent to Moscow, Ribbentrop met with Stalin and the Foreign Minister Molotov. On August 23, 1939, twenty-four hours later, a non-aggression pact was signed between Germany and Russia. Then, they secretly agreed to delimit the areas of mutual interest to be established in the event of a partition of Poland. Stalin was clearly anticipating the imminence of a German occupation of this neighboring country and intended to take advantage of the situation, convinced that the Western democracies would not dare oppose Hitler. Stalin should have read the page of *Mein Kampf* where Hitler wrote: "If new territory were to be acquired in Europe it must have been mainly at Russia's cost". [1]

When the delegation returned to Berlin, the British Foreign Minister, Sir Nevile Henderson, had already given to Hitler a letter from Prime Minister Chamberlain reminding him of Great Britain's commitment to military intervention, if the sovereignty of Poland was to be threatened. Chamberlain specified that this commitment would be supported, regardless of the nature of the agreement between Germany and Russia. He also warned Hitler that a dispute over Poland would probably not be limited, but could spread to Europe.

Deliberately ignoring that the agreement of February 1936 between France and Russia was establishing a pact of mutual assistance in the event a German aggression would be considered a threat, Hitler responded to Chamberlain that the agreement between Great Britain and Poland was to him a means to encourage Poland to keep oppressing the German minority. He denounced the regime of terror and cruelty imposed on the million and a half Germans living in Poland. He told Chamberlain that the British military operations in Poland would immediately trigger the mobilization of the Wehrmacht. Then, lying through his teeth, he also said that Russia and Germany would never go to war against each other. He offered Great Britain the German military support anywhere in the world.

An intense diplomatic activity followed at the Reich Chancellery between Hitler and the British, French, and Italian ambassadors. When the British ambassador left, Hitler sent Mussolini a missive informing him of the impending invasion of Poland and requesting that Italy support his project.

French Ambassador Coulondre, the successor of François-Poncet, met with Hitler, who reiterated his indignation at the Polish atrocities against the German minority and swore that Germany had a duty to protect the German minorities in Europe. Without losing his calm, Coulondre informed Hitler that his government was determined to strongly intervene if Poland was invaded, but also to maintain peace in Europe.

Shortly afterward, it was the turn of Attolico, ambassador of Italy, to provide Hitler with Mussolini's response. The latter said that to his great regret, Italy was not ready for war and could at the most provide support for

---

[1] Hitler, Adolf; Mein Kampf (James Murphy Translation), p. 119.

a few weeks with its current arming level. With unconcealed impatience, Hitler ordered Keitel to delay the entry of the German troops in Poland and began negotiating with his Italian partner. He asked Mussolini how Germany could help Italy to go to war. His demands were so exorbitant that Hitler was unable to comply. Exasperated, he asked Mussolini to at least pretend to prepare for war, to scare away the powers of Western Europe and keep secret the neutrality of Italy. Mussolini could hardly deny the requests.

Intensive discussions followed between Paris, London and Berlin. Daladier wrote to Hitler to reaffirm his commitments with respect to Poland. Hitler asked Daladier how he would react if Marseille was separated from France and he was denied his right to return. Shortly after, Hitler received from London a letter that Paul Schmidt translated. Chamberlain was rejecting Hitler's offers in exchange for a settlement that would be at the expense of Poland. He was suggesting direct negotiations between Germany and its neighbor to obtain guarantees for the German minority. London was ignoring, at least in formal terms, that it was the pretext Germany needed to march into Poland. Schmidt said that Hitler pretended to be interested in the British proposal. On August 28, 1939, he handed British Ambassador Sir Nevile Henderson a letter explaining the requirements of the German government. He was demanding to recover the city of Danzig and the corridor linking Poland to Danzig, as well as guarantees ensuring the safety of the German populations in Poland. To ensure that this plan would not succeed, he requested that a Polish delegate be in Berlin on August 30 to sign the relevant documents. The next day, in the face of Henderson's protest who was taking this request as an ultimatum, Hitler replied that the situation in Poland was deteriorating hourly and he could no longer wait to fulfill his obligations toward the German populations. Shortly after, the Italian ambassador returned to see Hitler and told him that Mussolini had been approached by Great Britain to act as a mediator. To cut off further discussion, Hitler replied curtly that he was already negotiating with the British government.

On August 30, shortly before the deadline expired, Henderson met with Ribbentrop and presented him with the British proposal in response to the requirements of the German government. Schmidt said that the conversation he witnessed as an interpreter was the most stormy and unusual in his twenty-three-year career. As soon as Henderson raised the problem of the lack of time to address such an important issue, Ribbentrop became furious and asked where was the Polish delegate who was to secure the Polish-German agreement. When Henderson suggested that both parties calm down, Ribbentrop blustered and stated firmly that Germany was not the aggressor. When Henderson submitted the British request for real negotiations in a more serene atmosphere, Ribbentrop crossed his arms and asked if he had anything else to say. Normally unperturbed, Henderson, crimson faced and shaking, warned Ribbentrop that London had information about Germany taking part in acts of sabotage in Poland. Ribbentrop replied that it was a damn lie.

Pointing a warning finger at Ribbentrop, Henderson said that his words were not those of a statesman. This is when Ribbentrop lost his temper and the two men came to blows. As the official interpreter, Schmidt said that he should have stood up, but not knowing what to do he remained seated and feigned to focus on his notes. Finally, the two men went back to their seats and Ribbentrop showed Hitler's proposal to the League of Nations for resolving the German-Polish dispute. Ribbentrop read the document to Henderson, who asked for a copy, but Ribbentrop refused to provide one. Believing that he had misunderstood, Henderson asked again for the document. Ribbentrop refused again and said that it was now useless since the deadline had expired and the Polish delegate never showed up. Paul Schmidt became agitated when he realized that Hitler's proposal was a mere sham and was never intended to be put into effect. It was obvious that Hitler and Ribbentrop were deliberately sabotaging a peace opportunity.

Hitler later confirmed that he needed an alibi to show the German nation that he had deployed all possible efforts to safeguard peace. He was so successful that in the aftermath of the Poland invasion people were wondering why Poland was attacking Germany. It was just another trick from Hitler. The spark that started World War II was caused by one of Hitler's frame-ups.

Operation Himmler

Gleiwitz is a small German town on the edge of the Polish border. Since August 10, SS Major Alfred Naujocks and his five men were in a hotel room on the square, eagerly awaiting Reinhard Heydrich's signal to conduct a simulated Polish attack against the local German radio station. On August 31, at 4:00 pm, Naujocks finally received a telephone call from Berlin. Heydrich said two words: "Grandmother died". Relieved, Naujocks took a deep breath. This former engineering student was an expert in the execution of such operations and the three weeks of waiting were for him infinitely more challenging than the transition to action. Before leaving, he called the head of the Gestapo, Heinrich Müller. He asked him to bring the material in a box and drop it on a road near the German station at 8:20 pm.

Hitler needed a border incident as a pretext for the invasion of Poland and gave Himmler that responsibility, which was to remain hidden even to the military authorities. When a subordinate of Heydrich asked for Polish uniforms for a covert operation conducted by the SS, Admiral Canaris, head of the German counterintelligence services, suspected that the maneuver was contrary to international laws and expressed his reluctance to Keitel. The latter replied that he could not oppose Hitler's wishes.

The operation officially bore Himmler's name, but the latter did not possess the evil intelligence and imagination of Heydrich, his right-hand man and chief of the secret police. Himmler admired Heydrich as much as he feared and hated him, knowing that his subordinate would have no qualms about taking his job. When Heydrich was assassinated by Polish resistance fighters in 1943, Himmler feigned indignation, although he felt deeply relieved.

As expected, at 7:45 am, the SS commando disguised as Polish military arrived by truck and ran into the radio station, screaming and firing shots into the ceiling. The employees did not resist. A SS who was fluent in Polish spoke on the radio for five minutes to rant and rail against Germany while his accomplices made as much noise as possible to simulate a massive attack. During that time, Müller dropped on the grounds of the radio station the bodies of prisoners of the Dachau concentration camp, dressed in Polish uniforms to confirm the thesis of a massive Polish attack.

Eighteen hours later, feigning indignation in a dramatic tone, Hitler announced to the Reichstag that, the night before, for the first time, Polish soldiers had opened fire on the German territory. Then, he ordered his troops to walk into Poland to defend Germany. The military operations began with air strikes on airports, destroying most of the Polish Air Force. The next morning, an incredulous German population questioned the rationale of the German aggression by Poland and showed reactions ranging from disapproval to going to war to a resigned apathy. One wonders how a country could go to war when its population was hostile to such an undertaking.

The outbreak of World War II

On September 3, 1939, British Ambassador Sir Nevile Henderson presented himself at the Reich Chancellery and met with Paul Schmidt, Hitler's official interpreter. He handed him the British ultimatum urging Germany to withdraw immediately from Poland and declaring war against Germany in the event of a refusal. Schmidt read the document and went immediately to the Führer's office. Hitler was discussing with Ribbentrop. Schmidt said that after hearing the translation of the document, Hitler looked stunned and remained silent for a while. The declaration of war hindered his plans since he had no intention of going to war on two fronts at the same time. He turned to Ribbentrop and said "So...?" Ribbentrop replied that a similar ultimatum was to be expected from France in the next few hours. He was not mistaken. World War II had begun.

Si vis pacem, para bellum. If you want peace, prepare for war. It is difficult to find a better example of the relevance of this adage. It is human nature to take a biased look at the reality. When analyzing a situation, we select the facts. We attach the highest importance to those likely to confirm our beliefs and we discard those that might be questioned. When Chamberlain, who was back from a meeting in Berlin, enthusiastically handed the letter acknowledging a mutual non-aggression agreement signed by Hitler and himself, he closed his eyes on the disturbing signals of an imminent catastrophe. The unilateral decision to reinstate compulsory military service and militarize the German economy, the exhortation to racial hatred in Hitler's speeches and the blitzkriegs for territorial expansion should have been seen as warning signals leading to the mobilization of the French and British military resources. Comforted by a post-war pacifist movement, they were slow to react. An early and energetic French intervention would have been a bargain price for peace. Peaceful stagnation was to raise this cost to astronomical levels.

Chapter 7

Hitler's war

In 1939, Germany, with its 70,000,000 inhabitants, was the most populous European country after Russia, whose 180,000,000 inhabitants were in an area thirty-six times the size of Germany. A bit claustrophobic, it was trapped in central Europe by nine countries sharing common borders. Its access to the sea was very limited. Except for coal, it had few raw material to fuel a war. Finally, the country was unable to develop sufficient food resources to feed the population.

Northern border	Eastern border	Southern border	Western border
Denmark	Poland	Austria	France
Baltic Sea	Czechoslovakia	Switzerland	Luxembourg
	Belgium		Holland

Table 1 – Countries surrounding Germany

The borders of Central Europe showed unparalleled mobility, following conflicts between ethnic groups with divergent interests. Several groups of different nationalities mingled and, in Czechoslovakia, the Czechs were numerically the largest ethnicity, even if barely accounting for 50 percent of the population. A large number of citizens of German nationality were dispersed in neighboring states. More than eight million Germans were excluded from the homeland. Austria hosted 2,250,000 of them and Czechoslovakia 3,250,000.

Countries	Ethnicities	Population
Yugoslavia		13,750,000
	Serbs	6,500,000
	Croats	4,000,000
	Slovenians	1,000,000
	Hungarians	550,000
	Germans	300,000
	Other (Albanians, Bulgarians, etc.)	1,400,000
Czechoslovakia		14,500,000
	Czechs	7,000,000
	Slovenians (Sudetens)	3,000,000
	Germans	3,250,000
	Hungarians	700,000
	Ruthenians or Ukrainians	550,000

Table 2 – Ethnic populations in Yugoslavia and Czechoslovakia in 1939

That context guided the steps of German expansionism that led to World War II. Initially, Hitler dreamed of a reunified Germany and rescuing the nationals who lived in the neighboring countries. The annexation of Austria and the Sudetenland was meant to repatriate them. But Hitler also felt cramped in Germany and needed space to carry out his plan. Russia with its large territory and abundant natural resources met those needs, especially since it was populated by races that he considered inferior and might serve the Aryan cause. However, Germany had no border with Russia where he could prepare an invasion. This common border was offered by Poland and, as an additional benefit, it had resources that were essential to the maintenance of a protracted war. Therefore, the entry of the German troops in Poland seemed to be a logical strategy, but it ignited a war in Europe.

Countries	German population	Total population
Germany	66,000,000	70,000,000
Czechoslovakia (Sudetenland)	3,250,000	15,000,000
Switzerland	3,000,000	6,300,000
Austria	2,250,000	6,800,000
Yugoslavia	300,000	13,900,000

Table 3 – Distribution of German populations in Europe

The German army general staff did not share Hitler's point of view. The generals concealed their contempt for the little corporal who was lecturing them. The high command favored a limited expansionism that would bring back the territories that belonged to Germany before the war, but they objected strongly to the invasion of the Soviet Union, which was for Hitler the crucial stage of the lebensraum conquest meant to establish the master race. Hitler found ridiculous the reluctance of the generals toward the Russian campaign. He rejected their warnings, seeing himself as the greatest strategist of all time, arguing that Russia was a building that would crash down when kicked in the door and that victory was a matter of eight weeks. Intoxicated by his previous successes, he did not realize that he had not been at war so far and that the initial victories without casualties were due to the wave of European pacifism rather than a military confrontation. The first real trial of strength was to be with Russia. At the end of June 1941, the Russian war established the precedence of the Nazi Party over the army command.

The period between 1939 and 1945 can be divided into three important episodes: the blitzkriegs with the rapid conquests, the Russian campaign with the defeat of the German army, and the counter-attack accompanied by the crash of Germany.

The blitzkriegs

On September 3, 1939, when Europe entered into war, the Germans were occupying Austria, Czechoslovakia and Poland. Ten days earlier, Hitler had signed with Russia a peace treaty meant to cover his backsides.

Date	Invaded countries	Result
March 13, 1938	Austria	Victory
March 15, 1939	Czechoslovakia	Victory
German-Soviet Pact, September 3, 1939		
September 1, 1939	Poland	Victory
Outbreak of war, September 3, 1939		
April 9, 1940	Denmark, Norway	Victory
May 10, 1940	Holland, Luxembourg, Belgium	Victory
May 13, 1940	France	Victory
Bombings begin in Great Britain, August 13, 1940		
April 6, 1941	Greece, Yugoslavia	Victory
June 22, 1941	Soviet Union	Defeat

Table 4 – The conquest of Europe

Hitler's blitzkrieg tactic made several European countries fall one after the other. While Russia was invading Finland that surrendered following a defense that made the Russian army look bad, Hitler decided to occupy Norway at the beginning of April 1940, despite opposition from his generals who considered the operation risky. That country was of strategic importance to Great Britain and Germany who were in need of foreign naval bases. In addition, for Hitler, Norway was the transit route of iron from Sweden. On April 3, 1940, the German Navy weighed anchor and headed for the Scandinavian countries. Despite the British aid for mining the Norwegian waters, but whose improvised land operations were a complete fiasco, thanks to the German air superiority and the complicity of Vidkun Quisling, leader of a pro-nazi political party, the army and the German police took control of the country two months later. The royal family sought refuge in Great Britain. At the same time, the German troops marched into Denmark, which offered no resistance and surrendered within a few hours.

Public opinion in Great Britain was damaged and the parliament openly criticized Prime Minister Chamberlain for his extreme pacifism. A tougher foreign policy was required. Despite his impulsive personality, the First Lord of Admiralty, Sir Winston Churchill, became Prime Minister on May 10, 1940, at the age of sixty-five. In his first speech, he said to the English nation: "I have nothing to offer but blood, toil, tears and sweat."

The German forces occupy France, Belgium, Luxembourg and the Netherlands

France was ill-prepared for World War II. The French generals limited the strategic use of tanks, finding them heavy and unwieldy in the light of the experience of World War I. They still believed in the cavalry, whereas Germany was preparing for modern war.

In the thirties, France invested a tremendous amount of money in the construction of a web of fortifications along the German border. Domes topped with guns crowned man-made hills. Those stations were linked by underground tunnels hundreds of feet deep and equipped with electric trains to move the troops consisting of five hundred thousand men. The line was named Maginot, after the French Minister of War André Maginot. The two hundred eighty miles of fortifications ended at six hundred sixty miles of the English Channel (La Manche), leaving the East flank defenseless. When King Leopold declared Belgian neutrality and closed the borders to French observers, the Maginot line was extended, but too late.

The winter of 1939-1940 was hard and demoralized the French troops. In one of the most rigorous winters in more than forty-five years, General Gamelin adopted a wait-and-see strategy, keeping his divisions at the German border rather than taking an offensive approach. A German general estimated at the time that a French offensive in the fall of 1939 could have defeated the German troops in one or two weeks due to their numerical superiority while Hitler was busy invading Poland.

On the day Churchill was elected, barely one month after the offensive in Norway, the German army aligned one hundred divisions and three thousand tanks supported by the powerful *Luftwaffe* on a very wide front facing not only France, but also Belgium, Luxembourg and Holland, countries requesting neutrality.

Concerned about the safety of France, which was the last bastion of Great Britain against Hitler, Churchill sent British divisions to prevent the entry of the German troops, especially in the zone left uncovered between the Maginot Line and the English Channel. Gamelin aligned one hundred French divisions and ten divisions of the British Expeditionary Force along the German border. Half those troops were stationed on the Maginot Line, and the other half at the Belgian border. The French general staff left a border of one hundred miles in the Ardennes almost defenseless, convinced that an attack through that route was impossible due to the thick forests and narrow roads that made it impenetrable. Only ten divisions, less trained and less equipped, ensured the security of the borders. However, the German tanks took that road.

At dawn on May 10, 1940, Hitler launched his offensive against the West and invaded Holland. After waves of bombings intended to destroy bridges, the tanks entered Luxembourg. Endless columns of vehicles and German Panzers advanced without opposition, even though they were an easy target for the French and British air forces, unfortunately busy in Belgium. After having bombed about fifty airfields, the Panzers opened up their way through the Ardennes. Three days after the beginning of the offensive, the Germans crossed the Meuse River and landed in France. On May 14, Holland surrendered and Belgium did the same on May 17. Marshal Pétain, who was eighty-four years old, was appointed prime minister and inherited a disastrous situation.

The French army was defeated and twelve million refugees were crowding the roads. On May 20, the German troops entered France and reached the English Channel. On May 28, Belgium surrendered. The British forces decided unilaterally to withdraw from Dunkirk, the only free port on the English Channel.

On June 10, the French government abandoned Paris and Pétain requested an armistice two days after the entry of the Germans in Paris.

Dunkirk: Hitler's first mistake

Within weeks, the victory was complete, the French and Belgian resistance was destroyed, and Great Britain brought its military forces home in a panic. On May 26, 1940, the French and British troops had reached Dunkirk.

The situation was catastrophic for Great Britain, which had close to four hundred thousand men in France between September 1939 and May 1940, almost all of its land forces. The war would have taken a different direction if Hitler had not ordered on the morning of May 24 to halt the progress of the armored divisions of General Guderian. They would have been able to reach Dunkirk on the evening of May 25. We are still speculating about the reasons behind this strategy. A credible assumption invoked the rapid progress of the armored divisions, leaving far behind the troops moving more slowly and at risk of ending up isolated against the enemy. Another explanation would be that Hitler believed that the Luftwaffe was capable of settling the fate of the fleeing troops and considered unnecessary the mobilization of the armed divisions.

Leaving their heavy equipment on the beaches, nearly three hundred thirty-eight thousand men were rescued in a masterful operation involving a hastily assembled fleet of over nine hundred ships. Hitler cancelled his order on May 26, but it was already too late. The operation was facilitated by the Belgian resistance, which delayed the German progress, and the Royal Air Force, that kept the enemy divisions at a distance during the seven days of the evacuation. The British Air Force was almost bled white by the loss of one hundred seventy-seven aircraft. The non-evacuated divisions surrendered on June 4, but Great Britain had saved its army. For many historians, Hitler had just lost the war.

France signs a separate armistice

On June 14, 1940, the Germans were in Paris. Two days later, a divided government under the leadership of Marshal Pétain, who settled in Vichy and worked closely with the occupants while Brigadier-General Charles de Gaulle became a leader of the Free French Forces in London, requested an armistice with Germany.

In the summer of 1940, the tramping nazi boots could be heard almost everywhere in Europe. Hitler, who had not been defeated on the continent, enjoyed unparalleled popularity in Germany, where the people could now raise their heads in pride, the humiliation of the Treaty of Versailles repaired. He also signed the surrender of France in the boxcar where the Treaty of Versailles was signed after World War I.

In Europe, only Great Britain and Russia remained outside the sphere of German influence. A determined rascal, Hitler signed a Pact of non-aggression with Russia on August 23, 1939, before the occupation of

Poland. Under the terms of the treaty, the signatories ensured a non-intervention if either party entered into war. In the summer of 1940, with complete peace of mind, he concentrated his efforts on Great Britain.

The Battle of Britain

On May 10, 1940, Winston Churchill replaced Chamberlain at the head of the British government. Great Britain was protected by its Navy and Air Forces, but the army had little trained forces and a ridiculous amount of armament compared to the modern and sophisticated equipment of Germany. The heavy artillery on the English coast did not have enough ammunition for the military exercises. The most effective protection against invading forces was the English Channel, which represented an insoluble logistical problem for the German general staff.

In July 1940, Hitler ordered to prepare the Sea Lion operation, which foresaw the invasion of Great Britain in mid-September. However, he needed to control the British airspace before landing between Brighton and Foblerstone to surround London. Germany had the appropriate military resources to invade Great Britain, but was faced with the logistical problem of deploying forces over the sea. To prevent the Germans from landing, the British had installed barbed-wire entanglements and other obstacles on the beaches. In London and major cities, one million five hundred thousand children were sent to the countryside and the British conducted a series of air raid drills.

The battle of Britain was a combat between the Royal Air Force and the Luftwaffe. German bombers began the attack on August 13, 1940, specifically targeting airports, radar stations, ports, and the aviation industry. The British airmen, who were approximately three thousand, defended their airspace with courage. They took advantage of the distance that was a problem for the Luftwaffe, whose aircraft could not exceed a twenty-minute attack without risking of running out of fuel to return to the continent. The Royal Air Force fighters returned to their base to refuel and went back to the battle. At the beginning of September, the Luftwaffe was raiding the major cities and industrial centers of Great Britain while Hitler indefinitely suspended his invasion plans.

The Luftwaffe gave little respite to the British in the two months that followed. Between September 7 and November 2, 1940, London was bombed for fifty-seven consecutive nights. Forty thousand civilian casualties, half of them in London, were attributed to the German bombings. On December 29, 1940, German bombers dropped incendiary bombs on London, igniting more than one thousand five hundred fires. They gradually self-extinguished when the city ran out of water.

Finally, the losses inflicted to the German aviation by the British pilots were such that Hitler decided to end his offensive. On May 10, 1941, Germany conducted the deadliest air raid in history, killing three thousand people. However, faced with the heavy casualties suffered by the Luftwaffe at the hands of the Royal Air Force, Hitler abandoned the idea of invading Great Britain and turned to Russia. Great Britain had survived. The victory of the Royal Air Force will make Churchill say: "Never in the field of human conflict was so much owed by so many to so few."

For several months, Great Britain stood alone against Hitler, who was controlling most of the European countries. Its survival was ensured by the American naval convoys bringing ammunition, food and raw materials. Part of the war was played in the Atlantic, where German submarines and U-boats sank a large number of ships, forcing them to move in convoys protected by destroyers.

Great Britain attempted to bomb Germany, but ill-equipped to cover huge distances, the British aviation inflicted little loss on Germany. For the British staff, the only possibility was to operate from bases in the Mediterranean, North African desert or the Balkans. For Hitler, it meant that the German army would have to fight on two fronts, Russia and the Mediterranean.

The African War

On June 10, 1940, Mussolini declared war on France and Great Britain. Already occupying Abyssinia and Libya, and carried away by his success, he now looked at Egypt, particularly interested in controlling the Suez Canal in order to cut off this route for the British. The war largely transferred to North Africa and will be known as the Desert War. In September 1940, the Italians attacked the British in Egypt from Libya. Despite their numerical superiority, the Italians were defeated by the British. Then the war transferred to the Middle East when the Germans decided to support the Iraqi revolt against the British.

In the fall of 1940, Mussolini invaded Greece, but failed to achieve a victory. He called Hitler to his rescue. The latter was compelled to intervene to prevent the British from securing a foothold in the Balkans. Mussolini moved back while the British invaded Libya, Eritrea, Somalia and Ethiopia. Compelled once again to help Mussolini in Libya, Hitler sent Rommel and *The Afrika Korps,* the Panzer divisions trained for combat in the desert. Twelve days after the landing of the troops in Tripoli, the German army drove the British back five hundred miles in Egypt and made thousands of prisoners, including British General O'Connor who had repulsed Mussolini's troops. In the summer of 1942, Rommel threatened Egypt. However, the more he advanced, the farther he was from his sources of equipment, food and fuel. In the spring of 1941, he completed the conquest of the Balkans when he occupied Yugoslavia and Greece. Crete, which was the only British Mediterranean base, fell in the spring of 1941. For the British, it was a dismal failure.

Eighteen months later, in August 1942, there was a turning point when General Bernard Montgomery took command of the British Eighth Army against the German position in Egypt. On October 23, two hundred fifty thousand men and one thousand one hundred tanks were preparing for battle at a railroad stop sixty-two miles from Alexandria, namely El Alamein. Rommel's infantry was outnumbered two to one and had two hundred tanks. Despite major losses for the British, Rommel had to retreat, even when otherwise ordered by Hitler. In ten days, the British lost thirteen thousand five hundred men and the Germans twenty-five thousand. To make matters worse for Germany, at the beginning of November, General Eisenhower entered the battle with troops landing in Morocco and Algeria. On May 12, 1943, Germans and Italians had no other choice but to surrender.

Coming from the African coast, the Anglo-American troops landed in Sicily on July 10, 1943, and were occupying the entire island one month later. Subsequently, Mussolini was disavowed. The new government signed the armistice on September 3, 1943. A little over a month later, the new Italian government declared war on Germany. Hitler sent his troops to Italy, regained control and released Mussolini. The latter led the Italian Social Republic in Northern Italy, but was murdered on April 28, 1945, a few days before the Führer's death. The Allied forces entered Rome in April 1944.

The war with Russia

Hitler had several reasons for coveting Russia. Germany had a pressing need for primary resources to support the massive war effort in Europe and Africa, and Russia had significant oil, metal and wheat reserves. But for Hitler the Russian campaign was also a holy war. Russia was the birthplace of bolshevism, the icon of evil, which had to be eradicated throughout Europe. The immensity of its territory allowed for the materialization of the lebensraum, the space required for the development of the Aryan race. In the nazi catechism, the survival of civilization was at stake. Therefore, the war with Russia had to be brutal and ruthless in order to annihilate the Russian intelligentsia and enslave its underdeveloped population. Finally, the conquest of Russia would allow Hitler to beat Napoleon on his own ground by winning where he had failed in 1812.

While Hitler was fighting in Great Britain, Stalin was invading the Baltic countries, Latvia, Lithuania and Estonia, and the Romanian border provinces. Hitler responded by building an alliance with Romania and Hungary, and signing with Italy and Japan the Tripartite Pact, also known as the Berlin Pact. Upset, Stalin sent his Foreign Minister Molotov in November 1940 to negotiate with Hitler. The meeting between those two aggressive and intransigent men turned into a disaster.

Stalin believed that he was safe from the German expansionism, especially since he had a non-aggression pact signed with Germany less than two years earlier. He attributed to the Allied propaganda the rumors of a German invasion of Russia. With his morbid distrust, he believed that Churchill's and Roosevelt's warnings were intended to mobilize Russia in order to reduce the pressure exerted by Hitler in Western Europe. He was convinced that Hitler would not dare brave the Russian harsh winter conditions and that the German army had their hands full on the Western front. The Russian army was the most powerful in the world, with more tanks and as many aircraft as the rest of the world. But it was also undergoing an intensive reorganization. Stalin's purges in the thirties had beheaded the army high command when 90 percent of the generals and 80 percent of the colonels were executed.

Meanwhile, previously impressed by the Russian army, Hitler had grown disillusioned when Stalin invaded Finland and the Russian army was held at bay by the Finnish resistance.

In the months before the German invasion of Russia, a massive media campaign code-named Operation Barbarossa attempted to convince the Germans that Europe was threatened by the Communists, the Jews and all sorts of reactionaries. The frustration of the Germans toward the Treaty of Versailles had been eased when they had recovered the lost territories and imposed their domination over Europe. They were less than enthusiastic about an expansion to the east, since the sacrifices required by an extension of hostilities were not justified by an immediate need. It was probably at that time that the relationship between Hitler and the German nation took a new turn. Unlike the German nation, Hitler was planning for a Reich that would last a thousand years. His dream led him directly to destruction since it was to be a war of extermination.

The German troops cross the Russian border

In the early morning of June 22, 1941, a few weeks after the failure of the battle of Great Britain, Hitler launched Operation Barbarossa and marched into Russia on the same day as Napoleon's armies. He aligned between the Baltic and the Black Sea the biggest military deployment in European history. Three and a half million men, three thousand tanks and four thousand aircraft were spread on three fronts, one in the north, another in the center and the last in the south. That tug of war with the Russian army was to be the biggest land battle ever known. The chief of staff was General Franz Halder. In front of them, Stalin aligned four and a half million men. The day of the German invasion, fifteen million Russians were conscripted.

Group	Military command	Objective
North (C Group)	General Von Leeb	Leningrad, Baltic Sea
Center (B Group)	General Von Bock	Smolensk, Moscow
South (A Group)	General Rundstedt	Kiev, Stalingrad, Ukraine

Table 5 – The three fronts of the German army in Russia

Obsessed with the success of his blitzkriegs, Hitler expected that the conquest of Russia would be a matter of eight weeks. When they invaded

Russia, the German divisions had a twenty-day supply and anything necessary was to be found locally. The men and the motorized vehicles were equipped to deal with a short war expected to be over before winter.

During the first weeks, the German advance was rapid and inexorable as the troops were marching sixty miles per day. A week after the launch of the military operation, they were already halfway from Moscow. The advance of the tank divisions was so fast that General Guderian, who was inspecting the front of a motor vehicle, found himself in the middle of Russian troops, so shocked and surprised that they did not even think of using their weapons. When the Germans walked into a town away from the border, Russian workers applauded them, believing they were Russian divisions.

At the beginning of the invasion, many Russians believed that the Germans were coming to deliver them from the yoke of Stalin and had sympathy for the invaders. Hitler quickly lost potential allies when, despite the opinion of the generals who wanted to support the Russian revolt against Stalin, he ordered the ruthless execution of Russian political commissioners, Jews and Slavs. The arrival of the Einsatszgruppen, the SS units responsible for ethnic cleansing, quickly made the Russians realize that they had escaped a tyrant only to fall into the hands of a worse one. The German soldiers had been prepared for atrocities by the propaganda bulletins designed by Goebbels to inform them that this war was not like any other. It was an ideological war and the issue was so vital that all the usual rules of war did not apply.

Russian losses were beyond imagination. In the first two days, the Luftwaffe destroyed two thousand aircraft, mostly on the ground. Thousands of Russian tanks burned in a black smoke in the fields. Two weeks after the invasion, the Russian losses amounted to half a million casualties and a million prisoners. At the end of September, the Soviet losses amounted to two million five hundred thousand men. Hitler, who was exulting once again, mocked the generals who had anticipated a long and costly war. But Russia did not look like the European countries. Its territory of 8,649,500 square miles seemed to be endless and its human and material resources inexhaustible.

Once the surprise effect was over, the Soviet troops conducted a costly counterattack against the German army. On August 13, which was the fifty-third day of the Russian campaign, 11 percent of the initial German army personnel or three hundred ninety thousand men were hors de combat, including one hundred thousand killed or missing. Hitler and Goebbels were forced to admit that they had underestimated the Soviet battlefield strength.

A major disagreement about the Russian campaign surfaced in July 1941 between General Halder and Hitler. The German troops were at two hundred twenty miles from the Russian capital and Halder was convinced that the fall of Moscow, which was also the most important industrial and communication center of the country, would bring Russia to a halt. For Hitler, the victory was ensured in the short term and he wanted to enter Moscow after the A and C group divisions had achieved their objectives. In the North, it was necessary to take Leningrad, the birthplace of bolshevism, and destroy in the Baltic the Russian fleet that threatened the supply of Swedish iron. In the South, he wanted to humiliate Stalin by taking Stalingrad and divert Russian oil from Ukraine in favor of the German divisions. In the center, General Bock's divisions were to maintain their defenses and support the divisions in the North and South. This is why the divisions of General Guderian were ordered to make a detour of six hundred miles to support the group in the south.

The Muscovites were enjoying an unexpected pause and questioning the reasons behind the halt of the German divisions headed for the capital. General Halder and General von Brauchitsch, supreme commander of the OKH, for whom a victory was far from certain, were desperately trying to rally a stubborn Hitler to their strategy. Finally, Halder managed to convince General Alfred Jodl, chief of the Operations Staff of the High Command of the Wehrmacht, of the need to maintain the pressure on Moscow. Based on his report, Hitler finally ordered to take Moscow before winter.

While the Soviet troops were carrying out a scorched earth policy, the German troops were engaged in a race against the clock. The planning of the Russian campaign was based on the assumption of a massive and short invasion. Hitler had rejected the demands of the high command of the army, which wanted to equip the divisions for winter. Victory had to be assured before the cold weather or the troops would experience insurmountable difficulties getting refueling, equipment and the necessary divisions on the site. The mobilization of such a massive force for a period longer than planned had a major economic impact on Germany. The soldiers in the west could not be demobilized and returned to the plants to enable them to operate. Therefore, one million and a half men had to be replaced by Russian prisoners. Göring was forced to prioritize food supply. The Russian prisoners working for the Reich were at the bottom of the list and nearly half of them were starving to death less than a year later.

The first bad news that reached Berlin concerned the errors in the assessment of the Soviet forces, which had twice as many tanks as estimated. The Russian resistance began to hold up the German troops. In September, Hitler was showing an utopic optimism about the advance of the German troops. He even anticipated that Stalin would surrender in the near future.

On October 2, a military operation launched against Moscow seemed to prove him right when seventy-three infantry divisions and seven Soviet armored divisions were put out of action. Hitler was claiming victory. Panic hit the Muscovites who organized the defense of the capital. They dug sixty-two miles of anti-tank ditches, five thousand miles of trenches, and placed one hundred seventy-seven miles of barbed wire. The first snowflakes fell on October 7. The soggy soil slowed down the vehicles that got stuck in the mud and the German divisions were moving at the most twenty miles a day. Half of the German tanks were unusable due to the fighting and soil condition. Then the cold weather came. On December 4, the temperature dropped down to minus 31°F. The roads were passable, but the motor oil froze and the engines did not start. When the engines happened to start, they let them idle, which consumed a large amount of precious fuel. Without winter clothing, the men suffered from cold and frostbite. At the end of November, the generals on the three fronts informed Berlin that they were no longer able to maintain the offensive and were forced on the defensive to secure their gains until the end of winter. On December 6, 1941, the Germans had captured 2,800,000 Russians.

However, the Soviet army was ready for the offensive with fresh, well-equipped and well-trained forces brought back from Siberia. On December 16, Hitler forbid all divisions to use a defensive withdrawal strategy and ordered that they hold their positions at any cost. Walther von Brauchitsch, who was ill, was relieved of his duties and Hitler immediately assumed the command of the land forces. A large number of generals and officers were dismissed and appointed, but it did not improve the situation.

That was when the Führer's health started to decline. His hands began trembling and his complexion turned grayish. He looked tired, listless, and his eyes were not as bright as before. When dining, he was repeating endless monologues that had a soporific effect on his audience. His temper outbursts became more frequent when he received bad news from the Russian front and nazi leaders, which led the generals to filter the information, concealing the seriousness of the situation that kept deteriorating inexorably, and feed his delusion about the inevitable German victory. Hitler always applied the same military strategy: absolute prohibition against the defensive withdrawal and retention of the positions at any price.

The winter of 1941-42 was long and cold. The German divisions were decimated as much by the cold and snow as by the Soviet bullets or artillery shells, now creating an offensive pressure on the three German fronts. The morale of the German troops was in freefall as they were discovering the endless space and an invisible enemy whose human resources seemed inexhaustible. Hitler had an urgent need for military success. In the spring, the German troops continued their advance. The good news started to arrive in the summer of 1942.

The Stalingrad defeat

In 1942, the Russian divisions organized the counteroffensive while German reinforcements were sent to the front. In the summer, an additional six hundred thousand Russians were taken prisoner on the three fronts. On July 23, Halder told Hitler that the Russians were avoiding the fight on all fronts. Hitler ridiculed his general, stating that they were simply fleeing. The same day, he issued the directive number 45, ordering a simultaneous offensive on Stalingrad to undermine the prestige of Stalin and the Grozny oil fields in the Caucasus to deprive the Russian divisions of their black gold. Despite the fierce opposition of the German high command, Hitler had weakened the position of General Paulus by sending divisions to the Caucasus. The generals explained that the forces on the ground were insufficient to support two simultaneous offensives. He accused them of cowardice.

On August 23, 1942, the Sixth Army, led by general Paulus, was finally on the Volga River, a few miles north of Stalingrad. Two days earlier, the German troops had flown the swastika on top of a peak in the Caucasus. The news had an electrifying effect on the Germans and the army. The German Reich covered Europe from the Pyrénées to the Caucasus. However, Stalin was ready for revenge.

The Germans had planned to capture Stalingrad, even with an amazing lack of information. They were unaware that this industrial center of six hundred thousand inhabitants had an unusual configuration. It stretched over nineteen miles along the right bank of the Volga River, which made the shellfire ineffective, but privileged close-combat and the use of bayonets. There was no bridge over the one mile wide river. Furthermore, they wrongly felt that it would be an easy win since the population was demoralized and already defeated. But the Russians showed great tenacity and the battle continued until the fall of 1942 without a decisive victory. The Political Commissioner of the city was Nikita Khrushchev, whose determination was as strong as his contempt for the Germans.

The intensive bombing and incessant artillery fire almost leveled the city to the ground, but Stalingrad did not surrender. Paulus' divisions engaged in street fighting until November, despite major losses, without being able to break through Russian resistance. The fighting took place in every street and every house with grenades and bayonets. The Russians were instructed to shoot at least one German soldier before dying.

And winter came. The Russians, better equipped and trained to fight in the bitter cold of winter, were preparing to counterattack and encircled the Sixth Army divisions. The offensive began on November 19 and, less than a week later, the German troops were in a desperate situation. Without winter clothing, food and drugs, men were dying of starvation and dysentery. Without oil, ammunition and reinforcement, the battle was impossible. Three hundred thousand German soldiers were trapped in Stalingrad.

Hitler promised refueling, but it could only reach the troops through the use of air means. Göring was directly instrumental in the defeat at Stalingrad. With an almost criminal recklessness, he boasted that he would be able to supply the encircled troops with his Luftwaffe, even though his officers recognized that the mission was obviously doomed to failure. Torn between the unbearable reality and his delusions, Hitler chose to believe Göring. As expected, Göring was unable to meet his commitment, due to the climatic conditions and the limited number of aircraft. General Paulus had set at five hundred and subsequently at three hundred tons per day the necessary amount of army supplies. He never received them. Although the German aircraft were one hundred twenty-five miles from Stalingrad, daily deliveries never exceeded one hundred thirty-seven tons. The Russian FLAK (anti-aircraft gun) was becoming more dangerous and the Russians mislead the German pilots by sending rockets similar to those of Paulus to guide the German aircraft to their landing fields.

On November 26, Field Marshall Erich von Manstein was recalled from Leningrad and put in charge of the new divisions intended to rescue the Paulus Sixth Army encircled in Stalingrad. In December, the German divisions led by General Hermann Hoth managed to break out of the Russian encirclement and reached Stalingrad. Unbeknownst to Hitler, Manstein asked Paulus to leave Stalingrad, but the latter did not dare defy the order of the Führer. The strength of the Prussian military tradition shows its absurdity when one realizes that the authority was never officially questioned and thousands of Germans had to choose between the needless sacrifice of their own lives and blind obedience to the orders of their superiors. Furthermore, the German soldiers who were starving and emaciated did not even have the force to retreat.

In early January, the wounded could no longer be evacuated and Paulus ordered to stop feeding them in order to maintain the strength of the fighters. The fuel for motor vehicles was now used to warm up the soldiers in the freezing cold weather. On January 8, 1943, the Russians presented an ultimatum to General Paulus, promising food, drugs, and the release of prisoners at the end of the war. Paulus begged Hitler to authorize the surrender, but the latter insisted that the German soldiers were to fight to the last drop of blood for the nation.

On January 10, the Russians began to launch bombs on the city. On January 25, Russians and Germans clashed in street fighting. On January 31, the Russians encircled Paulus' headquarters in the basement of a department store. Twenty-four generals and one hundred eighty thousand men who had survived the siege of Stalingrad surrendered. They were forced to walk to the Siberian prisons. Barely six thousand of them survived.

When Hitler learned about the loss of the Sixth Army, he flew into a rage. He accused Paulus of cowardice for having preferred surrender to suicide and even had suicidal thoughts. He acknowledged having been misinformed by Göring about the operational capabilities of the Luftwaffe, but assumed the responsibility for the defeat at Stalingrad. He proclaimed a three-day national mourning and ordered the radio stations to limit their repertoire to solemn music.

The Stalingrad defeat remains for many historians the most decisive battle of World War II. It broke the myth of German invincibility, undermined Italy's, Hungary's, and Romania's confidence in Germany, weakened Hitler's authority over the German general staff and enhanced the prestige of Stalin and the morale of his troops. It marked the beginning of the Soviet offensive, which will lead the Red Army to Hitler's bunker in Berlin two years later.

The collapse of the northern and center fronts

In July 1941, Leningrad was surrounded by German troops. A Soviet offensive set in motion in the summer created a backwash wave similar to that created by the German troops in June 1941. From the Baltic to the Black Sea, a Russian front as wide as the German front pushed the German troops back within their own borders.

Barely three weeks after the beginning of the Russian campaign, General Bock's divisions were two hundred twenty miles from Moscow. Despite opposition from his generals, Hitler diverted the Panzers to the south. In August, the Germans captured seven hundred fifty thousand Russian prisoners in Kiev, and less than 3 percent survived the German occupation.

However, the vastness of the Russian territory with its endless horizon undermined the morale of the German troops. The generals found it difficult to know which way to go and had to create landmarks. Then, Hitler ordered to take Moscow. Hundreds of thousands of Russian soldiers were taken prisoner as they approached Moscow and, in September, Russia had lost three million men over three months. In Berlin, it was estimated that the die was cast and the fall of Moscow was practically inevitable.

Two unexpected events occurred: the arrival of winter and that of General Zhukov.

On October 10, 1941, snow and freezing temperatures marked the beginning of winter. Slush turned unpaved roads into swamps where the German vehicles got bogged down. Furthermore, the soldiers were not dressed for winter, the oil in the vehicles was not designed for cold weather, and the artillery could stop working due to insufficient lubrication. Ekkehard Maurer, lieutenant of the 32nd German Infantry Division, said that the summer was beautiful. But when winter began, the soldiers were in no way prepared to complete the tasks required. He was angry because the men were not appropriately clothed for the cold weather. In early December, the temperature had dropped further and the artillery was no longer functioning properly.

The generals asked Hitler to pull back and camp for the winter, but the Führer persisted in requiring an offensive. When the ground was frozen, the German troops continued to advance and, on November 26, the first motorized units were seen thirty miles from Moscow. However, the Russian winter had arrived. Icy winds and temperatures of -40°F paralyzed men and vehicles. A commander reported that he lost two hundred of his nine hundred men due to the freezing weather.

In Moscow, General Georgy Zhukov, known as the man who never lost a battle, took charge of the defense of the city. He recalled about one hundred Siberian divisions, trained and equipped to fight in winter, stationed since June in anticipation of a Japanese attack. On December 6, Zhukov launched a counteroffensive. The German troops, some three hundred thousand men, were unable to resist the Russian soldiers who used skis and equipment well adapted to bitter cold weather. He eventually surrounded eighteen German divisions and took three hundred thousand prisoners. Two months later, decimated by the cold, the lack of food and the Russian artillery, one hundred thousand survivors surrendered. In the spring of 1944, General Zhukov crossed the Russian border and entered Poland and Romania. The demoralized German troops fell back.

The collapse of Germany

In 1943, the Americans were at war and Great Britain had recovered and rebuilt its air force while Hitler was leading the offensive against Russia in the east. The Americans and the British had a combined air force of twenty-eight thousand aircraft. Massive attacks involving up to one thousand three hundred aircraft left a trail of death and destruction in many German cities. The war industry was the first target of the bombing, but the Germans repaired the damage quickly and build underground factories. Then, German cities became the next target. On February 13, 1945, eight hundred seventy British bombers dropped explosive and incendiary bombs on Dresden, a world-class cultural center. The city turned into a huge blaze and citizens had to wet their clothes to protect themselves from a heat so intense that it burned the asphalt. There were one hundred thousand victims in Dresden and five hundred thousand through Germany.

The landing of the allied forces in Europe

The Allies could set foot in Europe from North Africa or Great Britain. Stalin had long demanded a military operation of allied forces across the English Channel. Churchill regarded the operation as risky, but managed to convince a reluctant Roosevelt of the usefulness of a limited landing test to evaluate the problems of a future larger scale invasion.

The landing at Dieppe: A military disaster

On August 19, 1942, the Allies attempted for the first time to set foot on the European continent. They wanted to test a landing of troops and motor vehicles on an eleven mile beach strip with the port of Dieppe in the center. The assault force comprising six thousand men included five thousand Canadians, one thousand British and a handful of United States Army Rangers. The troops were to remain on-site twenty-four hours, then evacuate the beach and return to Great Britain.

The beach was bristling of barbed wire and antitank devices, in addition to being protected by heavily armed German troops. To stand a chance to succeed, the troops had to operate in the dark and catch the enemy off guard. Unforeseen logistical problems turned the operation into a disaster. At 3:30 am, a fleet of two hundred thirty-seven ships and landing barges arrived undetected eight miles off the coast of Dieppe. A few minutes later, German trawlers crossed path with allied boats and raised the alarm. Less than half the boats carrying tanks managed to get close enough to the beach and offload their equipment. Worse still, the ships carrying the Canadian regiments deviated from the planned route and arrived at the designated place in daylight. The soldiers were easy targets for the German artillery and due to the number of victims, there was no time to organize an attack. More than 50 percent of the soldiers were killed or taken prisoner.

Operation Overlord: The most formidable armada ever assembled

From 1943 onward, the net was closing in on Hitler. In Russia, the German armies were routed. In the Atlantic, the German submarines that were calling the shots, sinking merchant ships and warships, were destroyed by the Allied aircraft now using radars. In May 1943, forty-seven U-Boats were sunk. In a year, two hundred thirty-seven submarines were destroyed. At the end of May, Grand Admiral Dönitz admitted having lost the Atlantic battle.

In November 1943, at the Tehran conference that brought together the heads of the Three Big Powers, Churchill proposed an Allied landing in Europe. It will be known as Operation Overlord. The landing in Normandy, in the north of France, was to be coordinated by United States General Dwight D. Eisenhower.

General von Rundstedt commanded the German divisions stationed in the west. Fifty-nine divisions comprising half a million Germans were assigned to the surveillance of what Hitler called the Atlantic wall, under the authority of General Rommel. Scattered over eight hundred miles of beach, the divisions were mostly concentrated in the Pas-de-Calais, north of Normandy, where the distance between Great Britain and France was shorter. Rundstedt believed that the Allies would be tempted by the proximity of the French coast at the Pas-de-Calais. Hitler did not agree.

He had planned the Normandy landings because of the deep-water port of Cherbourg. Bogus secret messages created by the Allied intelligence services and picked up by the Germans reinforced the belief that the landing would take place in the north of France rather than elsewhere.

At the end of 1943, General Rommel was involved in the construction of the Atlantic wall intended to defeat a possible landing of the Allies. He had planned to install on the beaches mines and obstacles ready to use, and kept in reserve five divisions able to move in less than two or three hours to threatened areas on the Atlantic coast. However, Hitler had forbidden the mobilization of those reserve divisions without his explicit order.

On June 1, 1944, after the 9:00 pm news bulletin, the BBC broadcast a personal message with a verse from Verlaine: "The long sobs of the violins of autumn... I repeat... The long sobs of the violins of autumn..." Admiral Canaris of the German intelligence service warned the high command of the Wehrmacht that this message was being sent to the French resistance to advise them of the imminence of an Allied landing. The second part of the verse from Verlaine was to be read within forty-eight hours of the landing. The Fifteenth Army was the only one put on high alert. Due to a communication problem, Rommel was not informed of the BBC message. The weather forecast being unfavorable to a landing, he decided to go back to Germany to celebrate his wife's birthday on June 6.

General Eisenhower, who was desperately hoping for favorable weather conditions, decided to trigger the military operation on June 6, despite an overcast sky. The huge naval operation would be unprecedented in human history. On June 5, at 10:15 pm, the second part of Verlaine's verse was broadcast by the BBC: "Wound my heart with a monotonous languor. I repeat... Wound my heart with a monotonous languor." The Fifteenth Army was put under maximum alert while the Allied bombers took off for Normandy and bombed in the night the German defenses on the Atlantic coast. Airborne American and British paratrooper detachments of twenty thousand men were parachuted inland shortly after midnight. Their mission was to scramble German communications, prevent the Germans from blowing bridges and create confusion to ensure the success of the landings. At dawn, the paratrooper divisions entered Sainte-Mère-Église, the first French village to be liberated.

On June 6, under the incredulous eyes of the Germans who were monitoring the coast, a fleet of approximately five thousand ships came out of the curtain of mist covering the Atlantic. It took several hours before the Germans realized that the attack was not a diversionary maneuver. The news of the allied landing reached Hitler's headquarters at about 5:00 am, but nobody dared wake the Führer who, as usual, went to bed late after taking sleeping pills. The reserve divisions could not be mobilized before Hitler's awakening, but he refused to move them, convinced that the real landing was yet to come. Those few lost hours sounded the death knell for the overstrained German army on the coast. As for Rommel, he was at his residence in Germany when he learned the news of the Allied landing around 10:15 am. It was already too late for Germany.

Despite the massive bombing of the previous night, those who came first were under intense fire. Several miles away on the French coast, the Allies—the British, the Americans and the Canadians—were unloading their heavy equipment and landing one hundred seventy-six thousand elite soldiers. It was definitely a success, but the war was not won yet.

The Germans retreat on all fronts

Two and a half months later, on August 25, 1944, the Allies entered Paris and paraded before a jubilating population. The Germans retreated, but fought desperately in the following months. Their fierce fighting enabled the Allies to liberate France and Belgium.

The next few months saw Germany caught between the Allied forces in the west and the Russian troops in the east. In December, the Germans won the last major battle in the Ardennes. Then, Germany was slowly strangled on two fronts. The Germans destroyed all the bridges over the Rhine, except for one that the Allies used.

Meanwhile, the Russians moved into Poland and discovered the horror of the concentration camps, in particular Auschwitz, where one million Jews were exterminated. When the western press agencies heard about the concentration camp horrors, they refuted the news, believing that it was Russian propaganda.

Stalin had told his soldiers: "Remember when you get into Germany, only the unborn are innocent." Russian soldiers were also told that they would not be held responsible for crimes committed in Germany. Therefore

Russian troops indulged in looting, rape and murder, creating the exodus of hundreds of thousands of Germans fleeing East Germany and Prussia to request the protection of the Americans and the British. The Russians showed no mercy for the Germans and, when they entered Berlin, German women threw the uniforms of their spouses or sons in the street, hoping that they would not be identified as soldiers. Nonetheless, the Russians deported three million five hundred thousand German prisoners. Half of them never came back.

On April 28, 1945, the Russians arrived at the gates of Berlin. Since January, the Führer had retreated in his bunker, a complex of thirty small rooms connected by narrow corridors and located sixty feet underground. He was pale, taciturn, had periods of elevated mood and obviously no longer controlled the situation. He proclaimed his faith in Germany to the very end. He ended his life on April 30, 1945.

Grand Admiral Karl Dönitz, who had been appointed by Hitler president of the Reich, signed the unconditional surrender of Germany on May 7, 1945.

The war in Asia

After World War I, an alarmingly fast-growing population created a major problem in Japan. Agriculture was unable to produce sufficient quantities of the necessary food. The influence of ultra-nationalist groups, coupled with military incidents, placed the country in the hands of the army, relegating politicians to the sidelines. Even though they had been in disgrace before, patriotic groups had managed to give the power back to the military. The army was full of extreme nationalists and the military power was similar to that of the mafia. Political leaders were assassinated by the army because of their liberal position or affinity with democracies. Emperor Hirohito, who only wanted to reign, but was influenced by the military and the government, adopted an aggressive and expansionist foreign policy on the Asian continent, which had an abundance of raw materials that Japan needed to survive. Great Britain, France and Holland had colonial possessions poorly protected in Asia. In the early 1930s, Japan had an increased control in Asia, easily occupying Manchuria without any international response other than a note from the League of Nations. Encouraged by the international passivity, Japan turned to China and invaded the country in July 1937, following a Hitler's style fake incident of alleged assault against the Japanese. From 1937 onward, there was an extremely violent war between Japan and China in the Far East. In a Chinese city, two hundred thousand civilians were killed by the Japanese military and the carnage even moved the Nazis, who proposed to act as mediators. Completely unrelated to the nazi intentions other than the creation of a Berlin-Rome-Tokyo fascist axis, Japan endorsed the imperialist intentions. The United States supported China, but did not want to intervene militarily. World War II gave Japan an unexpected opportunity to increase its influence in Asia, whereas the colonialist countries were busy defending themselves against Germany. However, Russia was opposed to this invasion and Russian and Japanese troops clashed. The Japanese suffered a major defeat and had to negotiate peace. At the same time, this situation brought them closer to Germany.

The Japanese propaganda, similar to that of the Nazis, exalted militarism and lied to the population to hide the losses that could be demoralizing. The generals were aimed at eliminating all western influence. In 1940, Japan wanted to end the war in China and admired the aggressive policies of Germany. The French occupation allowed the Japanese troops to enter French Indochina, near the Philippines, a United States' colony at the time. In 1941, the United States government retaliated by imposing a ban on iron and oil shipments to Japan. Japan had the most powerful naval force in the Pacific. Seriously lacking oil, it needed to have a free hand in the Pacific to ensure its supply.

Pearl Harbor

Aware of the United States opposition to its expansionist policies, Japan decided to remove the potential obstacle to its goals, which was the massive American presence in the Pacific in Hawaii, and made the huge mistake of bombing Pearl Harbor without warning.

On Sunday, December 7, 1941, ninety-four United States ships were berthed in the quiet waters of Pearl Harbor. Two hundred thirty miles away, thirty-one Japanese ships were silently waiting for the sun to rise. The six aircraft carriers of the Japanese fleet contained a four hundred thirty-two aircraft strike force. At 6:15 am, two hundred aircraft took off in the direction of the United States fleet without a declaration of war having reached Washington. An hour later, at Pearl Harbor, a radar officer called his immediate superior. He had just noticed on the radar screen a multitude of small dots that looked like a swarm of aircraft. The duty officer believed that it was a squadron of flying fortresses expected from California. At approximately 07:50 am, the Japanese aircraft could be seen in the sky and the American officer realized his tragic mistake. It was already too late.

Within two hours, three hundred sixty-three Japanese fighters and bombers in two consecutive waves almost completely destroyed the American fleet, with the exception of the aircraft carriers at sea. Two thousand five hundred Americans were killed and one thousand two hundred were injured, whereas the Japanese lost twenty-nine aircraft and fifty-five men.

It was a huge success, but only in appearance. Three aircraft carriers sailing off the coast escaped the attack that morning. They were precisely the ones that will avenge the insult inflicted on the Americans at the Battle of Midway. Furthermore, the Japanese decided not to launch a third attack, fearing to suffer greater losses. They did not touch the fuel tanks even though their destruction could have crippled the United States fleet for months. Most importantly, the attack was a brutal slap in the face of America, which until then was merely supporting the European War by providing material.

The United States did not want to enter into a conflict with Germany, but Hitler solved their problem. He proclaimed the state of war with the United States three days after the outbreak of hostilities with Japan. The attack on Pearl Harbor pleased one person among the Allies, Winston Churchill. America had to follow suit and he knew that Great Britain could no longer lose the war. As for the United States, the clashes would now take place in the Pacific and North Africa before setting foot on the European continent.

For a few months, Japan attempted to establish an empire in Asia, like Germany was ruling Europe. Japan extended its grip on all the islands of the Indian Ocean without encountering any real resistance. But the Japan industrial capabilities were much lower than those of the United States.

In the summer of 1942, the Americans sent an extremely powerful naval force to the Pacific. World War II would innovate once again in the art of war. The enemy battleships engaged in little fighting, leaving the battle to the carriers that sent squadrons of bombers to sink enemy ships. Tokyo was bombed by B-5 super-fortresses based on aircraft carriers. The material damage was minimal, but there was a significant psychological shock for the Japanese people to whom the leaders had promised an easy victory. The Battle of Midway was decisive, sealing the defeat of the Japanese fleet in the hands of the same carriers that had escaped the attack on Pearl Harbor. In Japan, the government concealed the defeat, misleading the population to prevent demoralization across the nation. In 1943 and 1944, the United States regained control of almost all the Pacific islands occupied by the Japanese. The combats were fierce, the Japanese fighting until annihilation. The British fought the Japanese in Malaysia, but the Allies were not faring well in the jungle. They surrendered due to a lack of men and equipment. For the Allies, Malaysia was the priority after Great Britain, the Middle East and Russia. The Japanese were close to running out of ammunition when the British surrendered. More than one hundred thirty thousand men were taken prisoner at the fall of Singapore, which was considered to be the worst disaster in British history.

The world enters the atomic age

In June 1945, Germany had surrendered and the Americans were on the doorstep of Japan. Impressed by the strength of the Japanese who frequently fought until their last drop of blood, the Americans planned to use a third invention of modern war undoubtedly more monstrous than the others, the atomic bomb. Paradoxically, this bomb was the result of a collaboration between Albert Einstein and Lise Meitner, German Jewish refugees to the United States, and Enrico Fermi, exiled by Mussolini. Harry Truman, who had been appointed President upon the death of Roosevelt a few weeks earlier, authorized the use of the atomic bomb, yielding to the advisors who believed that a United States landing in Japan would cost lives.

On August 6, 1945 at 8:15 am, a B-29 bomber dropped the first deployed atomic bomb over the city of Hiroshima, at an altitude of thirty-one thousand six hundred feet. The bomb exploded two thousand feet above the city in a blast equal to seventeen thousand tons of TNT, completely destroying 4.7 square miles around its epicenter. About one hundred forty thousand victims were counted, half of whom died instantly. Ironically, most of the industrial production centers were located on the outskirts of the city and were spared.

Three days later, a second bomb was dropped on Nagasaki at 11:01 am. The bomb was more powerful than that of Hiroshima, but claimed fewer victims due to the region's rugged relief.

At least one hundred thousand Japanese were killed instantly and probably as many died in the following months. Others died in the following weeks and months from radiation poisoning, characterized by a drop of the white blood cells and the loss of bone marrow. In the months that followed, as reported fifteen years later, abortions were over four times higher than before and there was an increasing frequency of cancer, in particular the thyroid cancer.

On August 10, 1945, Japan surrendered.

The end of the war and the end of Hitler

In the last two years of the war, Hitler no longer addressed the nation and virtually ceased to be the political mind of Germany. The country was heading for a disaster and Hitler refused to admit it. He was playing military strategist and simply applying his endless rhetoric of maintaining an offensive position and holding out to the end, even in desperate situations, even at the cost of the unnecessary loss of German lives. The army defeats were followed by the same repetitive scenario. According to Hitler, the generals had shown cowardice, spinelessness and defeatism. They were dismissed from their duties and replaced by other officers.

On August 22, 1944, after the failure of the July plot, Hitler had approximately five thousand former ministers, mayors and political officials of the Weimar Republic arrested and imprisoned to avoid a repetition of the events of September 1918 when Ludendorff had recommended that the political authorities request an armistice, the German defeat being inevitable to him.

For Hitler, the German defeat was not inevitable, it was unacceptable. Germany had to fight to the last drop of blood. Therefore, in the autumn of

1944, people's militias mobilized all the men from sixteen to sixty years of age. Propaganda supported the courage of the exhausted combatants, leading the nation to believe in the use of a secret weapon that would save Germany.

In line with his strategy of always maintaining offensive action, in spite of the fact that his generals disapproved of the abandonment of the eastern front faced with the advance of the Russian army, Hitler ordered the offensive in the Ardennes that was to be the last ditch-effort of the German army. As expected, the German army failed after a few temporary illusory victories, and the Russians quickly advanced to Berlin shattering the weak German lines. The defeat of the Ardennes in the west gave free passage to the Allies. They were about to cross the Rhine and the Russians the Oder. The fate of Germany was sealed and the stage was set for the country to be torn apart by the occupying forces from the east and west.

This is when Hitler decided to destroy Germany. On March 18, Haffner said that at the meeting of the chiefs of the general staff, Hitler ordered that the territories invaded in the west be totally evacuated by the German populations and all infrastructures destroyed, including all military transport, communication, industrial and supply facilities within the Reich territory.

When one of the generals raised the difficulty of carrying out the evacuation of the German populations because trains were no longer available, Hitler replied "Let them walk!"

In November 1941, Hitler said that if the German nation was not ready to stake its blood for its existence, then it should be wiped off the map. He shall not shed a tear.

For the first time in his life, Speer openly defied the Führer and used all the authority he had to cancel his order and protect infrastructures like bridges and energy devices against the attacks by fanatics who shared the views of the Führer. The SS were also tasked with looking for fugitives of the German army, naysayers in the population, and immediately execute those who had dropped out or were suspected of abandoning the cause of Germany. Countless Germans were then shot or hanged in the streets on Hitler's order.

No one was spared. SS Brigadier General Hermann Fegelein, Himmler's liaison officer to Hitler, had married Gretl, Eva Braun's sister, and become Hitler's brother-in-law. With Bormann and General Burgdorf, Fegelein was part of the narrow circle of Hitler's intimates in the last months of the regime.

On April 25, 1945, Fegelein exchanged his SS uniform for civilian clothes and discreetly left the bunker without warning anyone, aware of the approaching end. Two days later, Hitler noticed his absence and ordered SS Officer Högl to take a few men with him, look for Fegelein in Berlin and take him back to the chancellery. Högl went to Fegelein's home and found him lying in his bed dressed in civilian clothes. Fegelein pleaded the cause of a defeated Germany, but the SS officer refused to listen. He then called his sister-in-law, Eva Braun, and asked her to intercede on his behalf with Hitler, but she refused. Fegelein was taken back to the bunker, questioned by the SS, and Hitler ordered that he be killed by a bullet in the head the next day on a charge of treason. No one, family or friend, could escape the destiny that Hitler had forged for them.

In this atmosphere of destruction, disillusioned by the turn of events and faced with the cruel reality of what Hitler offered them, several Germans, especially in the occupied territories in the west, greeted the Allies as liberators.

In the last days of April 1945, Benito Mussolini and Clara Petacci were executed and hanged upside down, their bodies exposed to the insults of the crowd. Was Hitler aware of their execution? No one knows. But he decided to end his life to escape his destiny.

Hitler remained who he was until the very end, putting the destiny of a great Germany as an absolute value before any other humanitarian consideration. Hitler's morale was always guided by this absolute. The Jews and the Communists were to be exterminated, not because of their own nature, but because they were obstacles on the path to the Reich of the Millennium. Ironically, Germans likely to oppose this great dream were in turn eliminated. The dream was not conditional to the happiness of the German people, but found its justification and rationale in it. The broken dream was supposed to take the nation with him. Hitler intensely identified with his dream and had decided that he could not survive it. Hitler saw himself as an absolute. He transcended the law and his words were law. Amalgamated into one, the broken dream took his creator with him.

The Hitler myth

Gullibility and credulity need a minimum of evidence. Naivety fueled by propaganda does the rest. Hitler gave very little evidence that he was a military genius. Historians argue that the Allies avoided bombing the

Wehrmacht high command on Wolf' Lair to ensure that Hitler remained in charge of conducting the war. His military strategist skills were reputed to be so poor that after his premature death, his replacement by a senior soldier using wisely a powerful and sophisticated war machine could have made a huge difference in the German troops.

His initial consecutive victories made him look like a visionary leader in military strategy. In fact, those victories were the result of systematic lies and deceit. If one player respects the rules and the other breaks them, winning becomes impossible. But thanks to the blitzkrieg wins and his extensive knowledge of military weapons, he was able to impose his beliefs on the art of war to the German general staff. However, in times of armed conflict, the opponents apply the same rules. Deceit and falsehood are part of the tools of war and strategic planning becomes essential. On equal terms, Hitler played a loser's game. He paid no attention to the warnings of his generals who feared the difficulties of a Russian campaign. It was indefensible to maintain that a country as large as Russia could be conquered before winter. Busy in the Balkans, Hitler had delayed the confrontation by one month, convinced that the German troops would have sufficient time to defeat the enemy before winter. He had rejected the warnings of the general staff, concerned about sending troops into combat without appropriate equipment to cope with the Siberian cold. Therefore, the German troops engaged in the Campaign of Russia without winter clothing and equipment that would remain operational in the severe cold. It is said that the Russian winter killed more Germans than the Russian fire. And, as always, Hitler was fixated on his refusal to make a strategic retreat to save the military when the German troops were in trouble.

Beyond comprehension, while busy on two fronts and unable to go to war against the United States, he declared war on the United States in December 1941. Without a German provocation, it is unlikely that the American giant at war with Japan would have intervened directly against Germany.

Strategically, the workforce in the concentration camps could have been used since it represented a key asset and a cost-benefit solution in the war effort. The Germans were not greeted coldly when they entered Russia. The populations, mistreated by Stalin, could have been used by Hitler to overthrow the dictator. The Germans were ordered to exterminate the Russians and Hitler lost an invaluable potential alliance.

The toll of World War II

World War II was the most important large-scale undertaking of destruction, killing and cruelty in history.

Country	Population	Military deaths	Civilian deaths	Total deaths	% of population
China	480,000,000	2,500,000	7,400,000	9,900,000	2.1
USSR	180,000,000	10,000,000	10,000,000	20,000,000	11.1
USA	130,000,000	274,000	0	274,000	0.2
Japan	73,000,000	2,000,000	350,000	2,350,000	3.2
Germany	70,000,000	4,500,000	2,000,000	6,500,000	9.3
Great Britain	47,500,000	300,000	50,000	350,000	0.7
Italy	44,000,000	400,000	100,000	500,000	1.1
France	42,000,000	250,000	350,000	600,000	1.4
Poland	34,000,000	123,000	4,000,000	4,123,000	12.1
Romania	19,500,000	300,000	200,000	500,000	2.6
Turkey	16,500,000	0	0	0	0
Czechoslovakia	15,000,000	250,000	90,000	340,000	2.3
Yugoslavia	13,900,000	300,000	1,400,000	1,700,000	12.2
Canada	11,200,000	37,000	0	37,000	0.3
Hungary	10,000,000	160,000	270,000	430,000	4.3
Holland	8,700,000	6,000	204,000	210,000	2.4
Belgium	8,300,000	10,000	78,000	88,000	1.1
Austria	6,800,000	230,000	144,000	374,000	5.5
Greece	6,300,000	20,000	430,000	450,000	7.1
Switzerland	6,300,000	5,000	0	5,000	0.1
Bulgaria	6,300,000	32,000	3,000	35,000	0.6
Finland	3,800,000	84,000	16,000	100,000	2.6
Norway	3,000,000	2,000	8,000	10,000	0.3
Albania	1,000,000	28,000	2,000	30,000	3.0
Total	1,237,100,000	21,811,000	27,095,000	48,906,000	

Table 6 – Estimated military and civilian deaths in World War II, without Lithuania, Estonia, Africa and India casualties, exceed fifty-five million

The socio-political impacts of World War II were numerous. The United States and Russia fought to become the leading world power and tried to impose their respective areas of influence by dividing the Eastern and Western European countries. The reorganization of the world map in favor of the Jewish nation created the Israeli-Palestinian conflict that continues today. The technological efforts to improve the military power, such as the creation of the atomic bomb, changed the development and use of nuclear power, creating a real environmental threat. From a psychological perspective, that war left slow healing wounds and calls into question the most troubling aspects of human nature.

Chapter 8

The nazi Holocaust

It was not easy to justify the bureaucratized barbarism of the nazi regime. It became necessary to invent a holy war. Therefore, the Nazis created their golden calf, the German nation, and this god authorized a holy war to exterminate the Jews in all good conscience for the sake of ethnic cleaning: the Slavs for territorial need, which was the lebensraum, the Communists for ideological imperatives, and the chronically ill Germans for economic reasons. The number of Slav and Russian victims exceeded that of the Jews. But if we agree on a figure of six million Jewish casualties, two-thirds of the Jewish population of Europe were exterminated. In the face of a genocide, mourning the death of reality is fundamentally different for a victim, an actor or a witness.

The Jewish mourning

For the Jews, the genocide was and will remain an inconceivable and inexplicable wound that mourning will never heal completely. Elie Wiesel, who survived concentration camps, wrote that he did not understand and that the reader will not understand either and will remain on his side of the wall.

Freed from the Buchenwald concentration camp by the Allied troops on April 11, 1945, Jorge Semprún talked about the crematorium with the first soldiers he met and felt the same deadlock when he tried to communicate his experience.

Photograph 1 – Polish Jewish civilians, captured after the destruction of the Warsaw Ghetto

Photograph 2 – Close-up of truck bed piled high with the naked bodies of prisoners who died recently in the courtyard next to the incinerator plant at the Buchenwald concentration camp

In an attempt to capture the uncapturable, the reader should search for photographs of Jews at the time of their arrest or execution and take a long look at them. They are windows on history. They captured a single moment of reality that we can try to reconstruct. Examine the fearful eyes of this ten-year-old child with his cap on his head and his hands in the air, terrorized by the SS who take pleasure in pointing their machine guns at him. This picture went around the world and was used at the Nuremberg trials. The child who stands in a group of fifteen people remains a powerful silent witness denouncing the brutal and cruel racial extermination of the terrorized and helpless victims. There are several other pictures on the Web: A mother clutching her child who falls to the ground after being shot at close range by a SS standing six feet away; prisoners from concentration camps with hollowed eye sockets, an empty gaze, skeletal members, who have forgotten about life. All of them are silent witnesses of millions of unthinkable tragedies that occurred just over eighty years ago. We have to recognize that the horror of reality becomes almost impossible to recreate when we examine the images showing piles of dead bodies that trivialize death by showing it in spare parts. What is the meaning of an arm, a foot or a leg if we do not know who they belong to?

Behind the camera, an ordinary man or an ordinary woman was convinced that since the racial origin of those human beings made them dangerous vermin, it was absolutely necessary to get rid of them. And not only get rid of them, but also recycle them by retrieving all the clothes, shoes, glasses, artificial limbs, gold teeth, hair, and even fat to make soap.

Mourning requires being able to process the loss of past experiences by finding a justification that would give a meaning to the loss. But how can we explain, understand or accept that some people were subjected to such a destructive hatred simply because of their specific origin? In the natural order of things, we die from a disease, a trauma or old age. In the nazi agenda, people were dying because of their Jewish roots.

To all those who were able to find an end to their suffering, death was like a serene release. But for the survivors of the Holocaust, the murder of family members and loved ones definitely cut the roots that were vital to their own identity. Paradoxically, several Germans stressed the importance of protecting their own family against the nazi repression to justify their passive complacency toward cruelty and barbarism. And it was once again the inevitable loyalty to family roots that forced Hitler to back down for the first and only time in the history of the Third Reich: the order to exterminate the chronically ill who had become unnecessary eaters for the nazi leaders was cancelled after eighteen months, due to the popular movement of indignation it had created.

Canadian psychiatrist Dr. Robert Krell was born in 1940 to Jewish parents in Holland. He survived thanks to a family who took care of him while his parents escaped death in separating and hiding. He lost his entire family, grandparents, uncles and aunts at the same time as 85 percent of the Dutch Jewish community. Brought back with his parents in 1945, he heard from an early age horror stories defying imagination. In his childhood dreams, he was suffocating or buried or burnt alive. Krell described the Holocaust as the ultimate perversion of death to which gratuitousness removes any possibility of finding a meaning that we could ease into as an element of continuity and therefore allow to mourn the loved ones.

The German mourning

Talking about a German mourning might seem an insult to all those who suffered. But the Germans were not all Nazis, and the Nazis were not all criminals. The Germans have also lost something in the tragedy: members of their families for many, faith in the nation for several, and for others, self-respect or their own consciences.

For the actors in this drama, there is no easy exit. Among the fifty-two Gauleiters identified by Hamilton in his biographies of the personalities of the Third Reich, 25 percent committed suicide in 1945 at the end of the conflict. This figure reflects the impasse in which the leaders found themselves when they had to justify their behavior before the court for war criminals.

Most of the defendants at the Nuremberg trials pleaded ignorance of the facts, obedience to orders or no direct participation in the alleged acts. Some simply admitted their guilt. The very structure of the nazi system made cruelty easy. Those who gave the orders never killed anyone and those who carried them out were only following orders. Some had clean hands and others a clear conscience.

Sebastian Haffner was a young German trainee magistrate in Berlin.

He left Germany in 1938, disgusted by the policies of the nazi government, which left the SA spread terror without police intervention to protect citizens, and by the racist initiatives against Jews. He returned to Germany in 1954 and worked as a journalist and historian. He commented on the events before his departure by recalling that the Nazis made no secret that their goal was to eliminate the Jews everywhere in the world. For him, what was new in the natural history of mankind, was the attempt to neutralize the fundamental solidarity of animal species that allows them to survive in their struggle for existence. Once awakened, the murderous inclination of species toward their own breed is a matter of formality. The word Jew can be replaced with anything else.

The mourning of others

For non-Jews, it is not the genocide itself that raises questions. There were other genocides and there will be more. The issue is the context of the events and how they occurred.

The Jews were not exterminated because someone wanted to seize territory or even their assets. They were not exterminated following the emergence of a revolutionary group thirsty for revenge after years of injustice. Their extermination was simply part of a mature collective project and applied methodically in a modern and culturally developed society that advocated social order, physical and moral health, and love for the nation. It would have been easier to distance oneself from this drama if the German nation had advocated less traditional values.

When the extermination is the result of an explosion of violence, that people are beheaded with machetes or that murderers claim to be part of an extreme left group, it is easy to take some distance from those behaviors. For the SS who went to work in the morning, worked hard throughout the day and came out at night counting the number of murdered victims just like a factory worker would measure his productivity by the number of toasters at the end of the assembly line, it was difficult to see themselves as being fundamentally different. It is precisely this difficulty to take a distance from the executioners, to identify them as abnormal and different from us that is not reassuring. The psychiatric reports from Adolf Eichmann's trial in 1961 make one shudder at the thought that he proudly took responsibility for the assassination of five million Jews. Half a dozen experts judged him to be quite normal and even mentioned his exemplary family behavior. He did what his conscience dictated to him.

Europe's Jewish population before the war

After World War I, the Jews in Europe embodied different and sometimes opposite realities. Anne Grynberg, who wrote *Shoah: The impossible oblivion*, described the three main Jewish communities, those of Western Europe, Central Europe and Russia.

In France, Great Britain, Austria and Germany, the Jewish population comprised about one million and a half Jews who were economically and culturally integrated. Those Jews belonged to the middle class and often exercised a liberal profession, or were teachers, wealthy merchants or civil servants at all levels. They showed little signs of religious belonging and many of them no longer practiced their religion. During World War I, the German Jewish population participated with patriotism in the war effort.

Group	Origin	Number	Characteristics
Jews in Western Europe	France, Great Britain, Austria, Germany	1,500,000	Economically and culturally integrated Populations from Eastern Europe: poorly integrated
Jews in Central Europe	Poland, Romania, Hungary, Baltic republics	4,500,000	Poor, poorly integrated, traditional
Jews in Russia	Russia	3,000,000	Progressive integration into Russian society

Table 1 – Distribution of the Jewish populations of Europe

Next to the indigenous Jews were the Jewish immigrants who came from the east (Russia, Poland and Romania), lived much more modestly and gathered together in their own neighborhoods. They were committed to their religion, represented a Yiddish-speaking minority and were not well integrated socially. They were often considered as a burden by the socially integrated Jews, who feared that their congeners could stir antisemitic feelings when displaying their differences. Their poverty encouraged them to become more involved in the social struggles of the interwar period.

Poland, Romania, Hungary and the Baltic republics (Latvia, Lithuania and Estonia) had four and a half million Jews, whose national affiliation changed for many of them as the borders shifted after wars. Poland alone had three million Jews. Those populations were poorly acculturated, lived in poverty and had trade occupations such as clothing, leather and textile or were shopkeepers. Yiddish was the common language and their clothing or hairstyle made their religious traditions very obvious. Their visibility fostered outbreaks of antisemitism, especially in Poland and Romania, and violent pogroms unleashed, amplified by the opposition to bolshevism supported by the poor Jewish populations.

As for the three million Soviet Jews, their social situation improved considerably in 1917 when Lenin abolished the laws discriminating the Jews. The Jewish communities broke out and the Jews scattered over the country, but especially in Ukraine where half of them settled. The Bolshevik Revolution curbed the religious activities, but encouraged secular Jewish culture. The Jews benefited from retraining and engaged in agriculture, heavy industry, bureaucracy, education or the professions. They were gradually integrated and the youths no longer spoke Yiddish.

To sum up, the Jews of Eastern Europe, Poland, Russia and Romania retained in most cases their ethnicity, professed an orthodox religion, wore special clothing and spoke Yiddish. They were craftsmen, traders, and many were farmers or workers.

On the contrary, the Jews of Western Europe were absorbed by the populations of the countries where they lived and actively participated in the life of the nation. In fact, a large number of German Jews fought in the army during World War I. On the religious level, they were more liberal than those of Eastern Europe. Moreover, unlike the latter, they were more educated and held professional or teaching positions. Many of them occupied positions of power in the industry, finance, culture and press fields.

The antisemitism

Several societies show ethnocentric traits insofar as they consider their culture and ways of being superior to those of others. Pagans, barbarians, infidels are epithets that were used within societies at various times to discredit attitudes or behaviors different from theirs. A healthy ethnocentrism maintains stability within a group. It is referred to as patriotism or nationalism. In a society, the ethnocentrism can be overdeveloped for a variety of reasons and usually represents a defensive movement. If it becomes too evident, it can cause serious conflicts with other groups. It is then referred to as discrimination, segregation or racism from the dominant group.

Antisemitism, which is hostility against the Jews, is a multifaceted phenomenon.

The religious antisemitism

The Jews are not a race, but a religious community with a solidarity that persecution reinforced and deepened over the centuries. The State of Israel is officially multiracial. Judaism has never been a missionary religion, but has always been a competitor of Christianity.

The social antisemitism: The search for a scapegoat

There is a relentless logic to the need for a scapegoat. When things go well, it is never because of others, but because we made every effort to avoid problems. When things go wrong, it is almost always because of someone else, since no one will purposely look for complications. Our internal logic is always programmed to ensure that everything goes well. If our internal logic is based on false beliefs, we are not aware of it. Therefore, we do not feel responsible when things go wrong.

After World War I, antisemitism was not prevalent only in Europe. Despite the ideals of freedom developed in the United States, the postwar period was the scene of waves of antisemitism reflecting what was happening in Europe at the same time. American Jews were denied access to certain residential areas, hotels and restaurants. Colleges and universities used quotas to limit the number of Jews registered in their institutions.

But it was not an antisemitic extermination. People were intolerant of religious, cultural or clothing differences. They envied their business success and their traditions fostering education that gave to a significant proportion of Jews access to the professional elite. They were criticized for their solidarity. Therefore, their social situation easily became an irritant that could generate defensive ethnocentric reactions.

In Ukraine, in the first two years following World War I, more than eighty-five thousand Jews were murdered. During the same time, five hundred Jews suffered the same fate in Poland.

In France, the feudal system based on agriculture, whose ownership was mostly in the hands of the aristocratic caste, ended in 1789. The French revolution marked the beginning of Jewish emancipation and became part of the revolutionary catechism. However, during World War II, occupied France copied the German antisemitism. It sometimes reached grotesque proportions. An exhibition of drawings showing ears, eyes and noses with Jewish characteristics illustrated that it was important to differentiate from French morphological characteristics in order to detect and fight the Jews.

In Germany, the working class reacted to the Napoleonic domination, leading to the crystallization of a particularistic and exclusive national sense.

At the beginning of World War I, the Jews in Germany accounted for less than one percent of the population and two-thirds lived in Prussia. Twenty-five percent lived in Berlin and the majority of them enjoyed an enviable social status. Eighty percent belonged to the upper or middle bourgeoisie and fifty percent were professionals. Although they accounted for only five percent of the Berlin population, they paid more than a third of the income taxes. For the socially and economically disadvantaged Germans, the political repression imposed to the German Jews by the nazi regime was a fair return of fate. The leaders, including Hitler, Goebbels and Himmler, stirred up the anger of the population against the Jews. It was necessary to invent a conspiracy of the international Jewry to justify their murder.

After World War I, the Jews believed that they had proven their loyalty to Germany. More than one hundred thousand of them had fought in the Kaiser's army, most of them in combat units. But in 1922, Walter Rathenau, Foreign minister of Germany, was murdered by an antisemitic group. The antisemitism increased afterward and, at Nuremberg, over two hundred desecrations of Jewish graves were reported between 1922 and 1933.

Before World War II, the Jewish presence in the social elite and their most favored position in the professional, economic, financial and cultural circles made them powerful obstacles to the success of the Aryan dream.

In his paranoid delusions, Hitler made the fatal mistake of draining Germany of the brains that he needed greatly, if he really wanted a strong Germany. Therefore, he lost German scientists of Jewish origin, such as Einstein and Oppenheimer, who emigrated to the United States, sometimes with their students and colleagues, allowing the Americans to be the first to discover the atomic bomb. Moreover, the Jews criticized the National Socialists for ignoring the significant participation of the Jewish community in the defense of Germany during World War I.

The antisemitic current had penetrated the German society to the point that German physicians were discouraged from making a reference to Jewish physicians in their scientific papers. When necessary to refer to such work, they were required to prepare a separate reference list of Jewish sources, as if to keep the races separate and therefore protect the Aryan medicine from the Jewish taint.

The racial antisemitism

Racial antisemitism appeared in the nineteenth century in the writings advocating the supremacy of the Aryan race. The word Aryan, which means lord, originates from the Sanskrit and refers to an Indian warrior population dating back three thousand years B.C. According to a myth theory spread by German professor Friedrich Max Müller, those Indians were the pure primitive race from which the European civilizations originated. Therefore, some German nationalist elements came to imagine that those who spoke Indo-European languages descended directly from that race to which they attributed extraordinary qualities. Further research denied those beliefs that Müller himself later refuted on numerous occasions, but the myth survived nonetheless.

Subsequently, several writers helped spread the idea of the superiority of the Germanic race, heir to the Aryan supremacy. Houston Stewart Chamberlain, political writer born in Great Britain in 1855 and naturalized German in 1916, was one of the main proponents of this theory in a pseudoscientific history of civilization. According to the nazi doctrine, the German race was the purest expression of the Aryan race and had a supremacy over all the others.

When he was in Vienna, Hitler soon developed a visceral hatred for the Jews to whom he attributed all the ills of the world. To him, they were responsible for prostitution networks, architects of the white slave trade, authors of literary garbage and theatrical stupidities, promoters of lies in the written press, etc. But, as he said: "I now realized that the Jews were the leaders of Social Democracy. In the face of that revelation the scales fell from my eyes."[2]

The German antisemitism: A requirement for racial integrity

When a major problem arises, men often need a scapegoat who can take responsibility for it. Children routinely and regularly blame one or more of their comrades. In couples, spouses do the same to each other. One of the reasons for this is that we always have, individually or in a group, an internal logic that justifies our behaviors or attitudes. This internal logic is often, at least individually, based on beliefs acquired in childhood that are unconscious and never challenged, unless they become a source of repeated failures.

For the Germans, the Jews represented the source of all misfortunes. Jews occupied control positions in the financial and cultural circles almost everywhere. The reparations of the Treaty of Versailles to the Allies were routed through banks under Jewish control. According to Hitler, communication bodies such as the written press disseminated anti-German propaganda everywhere in Europe and the Jews were also there as leaders. There was an international conspiracy meant to transform the Germans into slaves and the Jews held all the strategic positions. Therefore, the salvation of Germany required the elimination of the Jews in Europe.

---

[2] Hitler, Adolf; Mein Kampf (James Murphy Translation), p. 58.

Hitler sometimes used derogatory, often vulgar or even filthy terms to describe the Jews: rogues, evil spirits leading our people astray, jelly and slime, corruptors, monsters. Later, in his speeches, he will use words such as poison to mankind, corruptors of civilization, infectious bacilli for the race, mortal threat to the Nordic race, pure evil and so forth.

According to Hitler, the Jew was first and foremost an obstacle to the realization of his dreams of a race of lords and a millennial Reich. And those dreams constituted a natural right, based on scientifically recognized racial theories. The use of force to remove the barriers was not only justifiable, it was also a national duty. It was a ruthless struggle between good and evil.

The first crackdown on Jews: Juden verboten!

The ordinance of February 28, 1933, following the Reichstag fire, was focused more on the Communists than on the Jews. It removed all fundamental freedoms in Germany, such as the freedom of expression of the press and the right to hold meetings, and paved the way for repression. The Gestapo had the right to detain anyone presumed to have committed a crime or found not guilty by the courts. Justice had been overruled by arbitrariness and everything was in place to reach the racial objectives of Hitler.

The nazi government spared no effort. Defamation was followed by Jewish discrimination. The abuses perpetrated against the Jewish community began two months after the seizure of power in January 1933. The Jewish threat was a little bit odd, considering that the Jews were barely five hundred thousand compared to eighty million Germans, or just over 0.5 percent of the total population of Germany. In the early days of the regime, the repression focused mostly on the Communists and Jews and was done by the SA.

At the seizure of power, the impunity of the SA was guaranteed by the nazi government. After 1933, their violence escalated and created a social chaos that worried Hitler, especially since he felt that he no longer had control over his troops. He was worried that he would lose the support of the German industrial and financial players of Jewish origin. However, urged by the SA, he decreed in April 1933 a boycott of all Jewish businesses in Germany. The SA monitored the shops closely, identifying the Jewish shops with the word Jew or the star of David.

The escalation of antisemitism

The first racial decree was introduced about ten weeks after Hitler came to power. On April 7, 1933, Minister Frick promulgated the Law for the Restoration of the Professional Civil Service, under which civil servants who were not of Aryan descent were forced to retire. It was just the beginning. Similar laws followed. Jews were no longer allowed to teach at a university. They were not admitted to the judiciary and not allowed to practice law or serve as physicians for insurance companies.

Later, additional special laws drove the Jews out of the cultural life, such as journalism, literature and theater. It was forbidden for them to write books or paint. The non-Jewish conductor Wilhelm Furtwängler opposed Goebbels in an open letter. Goebbels replied that art and intellect are instruments of domination.

This ideology translated into the burning on the square of a large number of books by non-Germans.

The Nuremberg laws on the Reich citizenship

On September 15, 1935, the nazi government introduced the Nuremberg laws, which related to the Reich citizenship and the protection of German blood and honor. Henceforth, the Jews were no longer German citizens and sexual relations or marriage were prohibited between Jews and Germans. But who was a Jew needed to be determined. A ministerial order dated November 14, 1935 defined the Jew as anyone with at least three Jewish grandparents or who belonged to a Jewish religious community. According to the decree, the nazi regime was to introduce an official policy on legal, political and social discrimination against the Jews.

In 1936, Germany has been elected host of the Summer Olympics and the foreign press was keeping a close watch on what was going on in Germany. Several nations were highly critical of the nazi policies and openly threatened to boycott the Olympics or to exert pressure to move them elsewhere. As a result, Hitler moderated his antisemitic politics in 1936.

After the Olympics, Jewish ostracism resumed: *Juden Verboten!* Jews were forbidden to use certain means of transport, facilities and educational services. At the entrance of cafes, cinemas, restaurants and libraries, two words were written on a sign: *Juden Verboten!* Forbidden to Jews. They were outside the social mainstream, unable to practice their profession or occupation, deprived of the rights and protection provided by the government to its citizens. Shortly after the accession of the Nazis to power, Dr. Spiegel, a Munich lawyer, had requested the assistance of the police against the terror imposed by the SA troops. Unfortunately for him, they were now an auxiliary policing service and the request of the lawyer was treated with derision. He was forced to walk around the city wearing a sign that said: "I shall never complain to the police again". The international press published a photo of the man walking in the streets under the mocking smile of passersby.

In November 1938, around one hundred fifty thousand of the half million German Jews had migrated out of Germany. Many of them did not escape the hatred and became the victims of the Nazis in occupied territories.

The aryanization of German economy

1938 was the year of the aryanization of the economy. Decrees prohibited the Jewish physicians and lawyers to deal with a non-Jewish clientele. In November 1938, all the Jewish retail shops were ordered to close before the end of the year.

However, the aryanization of the economy experienced major difficulties. It was easy to exert strong pressures on Jewish business owners who lived in Germany, but those who lived in France, in Great Britain, in the United States or elsewhere were protected by international treaties requiring fair compensation in the event of an expropriation. The nazi regime felt that any breach of a treaty obligation would result in unfortunate consequences that were to be avoided.

On the other hand, neither the party, nor the government could benefit from selling Jewish businesses at pocket-change prices to German interests. Therefore, the nazi government imposed a compensating tax to the new German owners. Due to many loopholes, it failed to bring money to the Reich.

The government wanted the Jews to emigrate, but stealing their property made the emigration impossible since the countries that accepted Jewish immigration favored those who could yield economic returns.

Dissatisfied with the number of departures, the Nazi Party decided to organize a boycott of the Jewish businesses in order to increase the pressure on emigration and exclude them from the economic life. A committee chaired by Julius Streicher was formed to organize mass rallies where the population was informed by the SA or the SS that the owner of the institution in front of which they stood was a Jew.

The boycott was subsequently extended to government administrative services. Therefore, it was forbidden to grant public contracts to Jewish businesses and the government staff was imposed the obligation to boycott the Jewish shops. The employees who consulted Jewish professionals no longer qualified for professional fee reimbursement. The compulsory boycott also applied to party members.

The Kristallnacht

On November 7, 1938, a young Jew of German origin, Herschel Grynszpan, murdered Ernst von Rath, secretary of the German embassy in Paris, to avenge the deportation of his family to a concentration camp in Eastern Europe. He also intended to raise international awareness around the plight of the Jews in Germany.

Forty-eight hours later, on the night of November 9, the most extensive antisemitic retaliatory operation that the world had ever seen was conducted in Germany. Presented as a spontaneous anger response of the German people against the Jews, the pogrom was in fact carefully orchestrated by the Gestapo under the orders of Göring and Himmler. A large number of Jewish homes, shops and synagogues were ransacked and burned. An undetermined number of Jews were beaten and murdered and the event became known as *Kristallnacht*, the Night of Broken Glass, for the shattered glass from the store windows that littered the streets. Several Jewish women were raped and the culprits were not brought to court for their crime, but for an offense under the Nuremberg laws prohibiting sexual intercourse between Germans and Jews to save the race. Those who committed murder were set free. With insulting impudence, Göring confiscated the indemnities paid to the Jews and repatriated them to the Reich to offset the damage to the German heritage. To top it all off, the Reich imposed on the German Jews a collective penalty of one billion marks. Yesterday's victims often become tomorrow's executioners. The Germans gave to the Jews part of what they had inherited after World War I.

On January 30, 1939, clouds were gathering in the sky over the German Jewish community. In a speech to the Reichstag, Adolf Hitler promised the annihilation of the Jewish race in Europe, if the international Jewish financial sector plunged the nations into a world war. The war, he was going to spark it himself.

The problem of Jewish emigration

Jewish emigration was the first solution applied to the problem of racial purity in Germany. In 1934, the nazi government asked the Jews to leave Germany. The Nuremberg laws forced many Jews to leave the country before the outbreak of war in 1939. Between 1933 and 1938, one hundred fifty thousand Jews out of five hundred thousand left Germany. But with the annexation of Austria in 1938 and Bohemia and Moravia in 1939, the Jewish population controlled by the nazi administration increased by a quarter of a million and the ethnic cleansing problem was back to square one. After the invasion of Poland in 1939, one million five hundred thousand people were added to the Jewish population.

The problem of the Jewish emigration was entrusted to a travelling salesman who joined the SS in 1932, Adolf Eichmann, born in Germany in 1906. After the death of his mother in 1910, his family moved to Linz, where Hitler had lived as a child. Lonely, shy, and not a talented student—like Hitler, he studied electricity, dropped out of school and worked as a salesman for an electrical equipment company. Then the introverted boy started to drink, drove a motorcycle and showed an outgoing personality. When he became a member of the SS in 1934, he was assigned to Reinhard Heydrich's intelligence service, where his laborious habits and effective working methods were noticed.

In the highly competitive circle of the nazi administration, he did not hesitate to exaggerate his superficial knowledge of Hebrew and Yiddish, and soon emerged as the specialist of Jewish affairs. He set up his Central Office for Jewish Emigration in Vienna, where he oversaw the departure from Austria of about one hundred thousand Jews. During the pogrom of the Kristallnacht, Heydrich gave him the responsibility of the antisemitic demonstration. Observers described the frenzied behavior of Eichmann, who ran from synagogue to synagogue, supervising their destruction.

In 1939, Hitler appointed him head of the Reich Central Office of Jewish Emigration. He quickly imagined solutions. Palestine was first considered to reinstall the German Jews, since this British colony had already been considered to create the State of Israel.

However, emigration remained limited because many Jews refused to leave Germany. On the other hand, Jewish immigration created negative reactions among Arabs and Great Britain stopped receiving Jews. Then, the island of Madagascar was proposed, but the war made the sea lanes impassable.

When the war broke out, the immigration doors closed everywhere and the nazi leaders were faced with a major problem. What could they do with the hundreds of thousands of Jews who remained to be eliminated? The invasion of Poland, where the Jewish population was about three million, created a pressing issue aggravated by the invasion of Russia.

The war began in Poland

Poland is the country that suffered the most from war, closely followed by Russia.

On September 1, 1939, at dawn, fifty-two German divisions entered Poland on three fronts. Sixteen days later, the Russian armies invaded the eastern provinces, using a pretext similar to that of Hitler. It was necessary to ensure the protection of the Ukrainian and Belorussian nationals in Poland. Caught between two giants, Warsaw capitulated on September 27. The scenario of the nazi occupation tirelessly repeated its three themes: the suspension of democracy, the exploitation of the natural resources for the benefit of the German war effort, and forced labor for the population.

The partitions of Poland began. The Baltic provinces, inhabited by one million three hundred thousand Jews and invaded by Russia, were Lithuania, Ukraine and Belarus. For its part, Germany annexed to the Reich a large area to the west of Poland inhabited by nine million people, including nearly three million Jews. The remainder of the territory in the center of Poland was now representing about 40 percent of the country's original surface area and was to become the general government under German administration. Inhabited by twelve million Poles, it will be governed by Hans Frank, a nazi lawyer who began his career by defending at no cost the SA prosecuted under the justice system. Safe from prying eyes and inhabited by a population terrorized by the persecution, the general government was to become the land of choice for the concentration camps. It will also be the provider of manpower for the Reich, with one million three hundred thousand Poles sent to forced labor in Germany.

The deportations began and focused primarily on the Jews representing 10 percent of the Polish population. In the annexed territories, the Russians deported one million and a half Poles to Siberia and Kazakhstan. The number of deported Polish Jews inflated the number of Russian Jews to about five million.

In the territories annexed by Germany, the Jews were insulted, abused and executed by the Waffen-SS. The army criticized the SS and built up a case against them. The army was not trying to protect the Jews, but to discredit the SS, who were competing with the army. The army criticism was also aimed at discrediting the amateurism of the SS, who claimed to have eliminated two million Jews with such methods while the army intended to achieve the same objective, but professionally.

Hans Frank delivered to Fritz Saukel, minister of Labor, one million three hundred thousand Poles who were sent to forced labor. He also delivered to Himmler the two million Jews who cluttered his territory. Most of them were sent to Auschwitz, where they were killed.

Himmler ordered his SS to proceed immediately with the deportation of half a million Jews among the two million who cluttered the territories under German rule, and of many Slavs who were to be immediately replaced by Germans who inhabited the most eastern territories annexed by Russia. The germanization of Poland was beginning. The names of the cities were changed and many bore a German name. The only possible destination for the Jews was the general government in the center of Poland, which no longer existed. Therefore, the Jews were crammed into freight trains and reinstalled in overcrowded and unsanitary ghettos pending a more acceptable solution. The Warsaw ghetto alone accommodated almost half a million Jews. During certain periods, sixty thousand Jews were packed in a space the size of a four hundred home neighborhood, each house inhabited by one hundred fifty people. As for the Slavs and the thirty thousand Roma (Gypsies), they were sent to concentration camps.

Hans Frank was quickly overwhelmed by the mass deportations of more than two million Jews and asked the nazi government to provide alternative solutions.

From the outset of the war, food was rationed in Germany. The ration took into account several factors such as the age of the person, a pregnancy and a job with physical work. The rations for the Jews were smaller than those for the Aryans. As the war effort intensified, the restrictions became more important and kept the Jews starving.

The Slavic genocide

For the Germans, the Slavs included several nationalities such as the Czechs, Poles, Slovenes, Croats, Slovaks, Serbs and several ethnic groups in the Soviet Union. They represented no danger to Germany, but they occupied territories that Hitler wanted to retrieve in order to expand the German borders.

Population	Number
Russians	80,000,000
Ukrainians	30,000,000
White Russians	6,000,000
Poles	7,000,000
Czechs	7,000,000
Slovaks	2,500,000
Serbian Yugoslavs	6,000,000
Croatian Yugoslavs	4,000,000
Slovenes	1,000,000
Bulgarians	4,000,000

Table 2 – Distribution of Slavs in Europe

In Poland, about 22 percent of the population was exterminated in order to make room for the Aryans. In the Soviet Union, the Slavs were deported, treated as slaves or sent to concentration camps.

The Slavs resided mainly in Eastern and Southeastern Europe. The Slavic populations spoke related languages and their birth rate was higher than that of the other European nations.

The first phase of the lebensraum began with the invasion of Poland. Hitler had made it clear that living space was needed whatever the price and he had authorized the brutal extermination of Polish men, women and children. If the Jews were somehow envied for their political and financial power, the Slavs to which the Poles belonged were downright despised by the Nazis, who considered them just above the animals, in keeping with the order of nature. They were called *untermenschen* or half men. Their fault was to live in the territories for which Germany had a pressing need and, according to the nazi ideology, the future of civilization depended on the project of an order imposed by the Aryan race. It was therefore justified, in the interest of the nations and societies, to remove any obstacles to the realization of that project.

One month after the invasion of Poland, the German army handed over the administration of the occupied territories to the SS sections. The Poles were classified according to their work, social status and attitude toward Germany. Three groups likely to oppose the nazi policies that needed to be put out of action immediately were removed from that classification: the nationalist Poles, those who belonged to the Polish intelligentsia—the professionals, teachers, clergy, and all those who had attended high school. Hitler had stated that it was necessary to prevent the Polish intelligentsia from influencing the rest of the people. He wanted cheap slaves, nothing more.

Hans Frank, governor of the occupied Poland, had confirmed that the Poles should be treated as subhumans and left to languish through an organized undernourishment and the liquidation of their elites.

In October 1939, the elimination of the Polish elites began and lasted five years, without a written order. Six million people or twenty-two of the Polish population—including three million Jews, died during the six-year war. The deculturation of a traditionally highly civilized nation was ensured. In May 1940, a memorandum from Himmler denied high school access to all non-German populations of East Germany. Obedience to the

East Germans was presented as an order from God. The application of those measures was targeting lower-class people who needed to be available to the Germans.

The task of exterminating the populations could not be entrusted to the army, since the soldiers did not have the ideological preparation required, and the SS units were better conditioned to carry out orders without discussion or even thinking. This is how the Einsatzgruppen, the killing squads, were formed. Their mission was to follow the German army and execute designated groups of victims.

Those units were created for the first time in 1938. Set up by Walter Schellenberg, one of the SD leaders, the combat troops were meant to eliminate the Czechoslovakian resistance. When used in Poland, they comprised mostly members of the Waffen-SS, but also members of the public order police, auxiliary police and state security police. At the beginning, traditional methods were used to exterminate entire populations, such as forcing them to dig their grave, then shooting a bullet in their neck. This technique was also used in Russia.

Later, the mass murder technique was improved and they used special vehicles with a hermetically sealed cabin where groups of fifteen or twenty victims were killed by inhalation of carbon monoxide on the way to their grave.

On October 9, 1939, pursuant to Hitler's directives, Himmler ordered the deportation of fifty-five thousand Jews and one million and a half Poles, to whom half a million Germans were substituted.

The Jews deported to the concentration camps found on arrival a well-run organization. Greeted by screaming SS and barking dogs, the train passengers quickly disembarked, leaving behind the bodies of those who, blessed despite their misfortune, had not survived the trip. Brutally pushed by the SS, they were immediately divided into two groups. Those who could work joined the prisoners' barracks while the elderly, disabled, women and children were exterminated.

The extermination of the sick and disabled Germans

The planned extermination did not focus exclusively on Jews, Slavs and Communists. According to Hitler, all obstacles to the Thousand-Year

Reich project had to be eliminated, even if they were Germans. His plan has been well prepared for a long time. In a decree dated September 1, 1939, two days before the declaration of war, but signed at the end of October, Hitler ordered his personal physician, Dr. Karl Brandt, to set up a humanitarian extermination program for the incurably ill Germans. In fact, the decree was aimed at the useless eaters, including the elderly. A special medical committee studied the patient files and prepared a list of those considered incurable. Between January 1940 and August 1941, seventy thousand two hundred seventy-three Germans were gazed, including three thousand children aged two to thirteen who were hearing-impaired and in public care.

The parents of the victims received a death notice that made many of them suspicious. The official document had a diagnosis of acute appendicitis, even though the child previously had an appendectomy. Or it was a heart disease in a young person with no family history. Errors in the selection of the victims attributed the death to a temporary condition, but the families received later a letter expressing the government regret over the death of their parent caused by a cancer.

On August 3, while delivering a sermon, the bishop of Munster described the practice of euthanasia put in place by the government as a pure and simple murder. Openly defying Hitler, the bishop printed and distributed thousands of copies of the text of his sermon that rallied a large number of Germans. The extermination program lasted eighteen months and was brought to an end by Hitler on August 24, 1941, as a result of the Church and German public protests. One hundred thousand sick Germans had been eliminated.

The expertise developed was subsequently diverted to Jewish extermination and a number of doctors, drivers and technicians of death were transferred to other extermination centers.

The concentration camp system

The nazi period created several disturbing associations in the popular imagination. The swastika, the SS, the Gestapo and the nazi salute are some of them. The concentration camps, which materialized the most barbaric system of terror that a government could organize under the cover of legality, were added to this dark list. Modern concentration camps are a reminder that the declaration of human rights proclaimed in many civilized countries was insufficient to protect people against barbarism. The mere fact that a modern and civilized nation was able to take this path shows that the German social disintegration and the political deadlock that existed in the country after 1930 generated an instability likely to awaken the barbarism inside of us. The concentration camp system was not limited to Germany. It also appeared in Russia around the same time, but it was much less publicized.

The first concentration camps

There is a strictly logical escalation based on the requirements of racial purity between the concentration camps and the Jewish genocide. No one was safe from Hitler, if he was a threat to the master race. The racial requirements warranted the sacrifice of German citizens with physical or mental disabilities that could be passed on to future generations. Therefore, sterilization was legalized first and euthanasia of the sick later.

We often forget that the concentration camps were first created for the Germans. The first camps received mostly political opponents, such as communists, social democrats and strong-minded individuals who challenged the government policies. In fact, the nazi regime targeted anyone whose beliefs or political ideas could generate a passive, active, real or imaginary resistance to the activities or objectives of the government.

Dachau: The first concentration camp

The village of Dachau is located a few miles from Munich, in Bavaria, and used to host the arts community. It is where the first concentration camp was established in 1933. The smooth running of the camp was ensured by SS volunteers, who were later known as the Death's Head unit.

The communists were the first to experience life in the concentration camps. After the Reichstag fire in 1933, four to five thousand activists were imprisoned in those camps, which were then aimed at discipline by labor and re-education through indoctrination. Their existence did not raise strong objections within the population.

The SS Death's Head units, which comprised about thirty thousand to forty-five thousand men, were assigned to guard the concentration camps. They swore to never reveal what was going on in the camps where they were posted. In theory, the SS guards were not allowed to abuse or kill a prisoner. The commander of the camp was the one who could decide if a detainee would live or die. But in practice, the guards had the possibility to delegate the acts of violence to other inmates, forcing them to beat or kill a prisoner.

The organization of the concentration camps focused on the psychological destruction of the individual for the political prisoners, and then the physical destruction, especially for the Jews, Slavs, Gypsies, and religious and political groups opposed to nazism. The need to destroy the two last groups was irrational. In the nazi doctrine, the destruction of the resistance forces took priority over the necessities of war. The concentration camps could have easily become huge camps of forced labor and a vital link in the war effort.

Himmler willingly let the rumor mill run about atrocities worse than those that already existed in the concentration camps. Since nearly half the population was opposed to nazism—in 1933, eight million Germans had voted for the Communist Party, he realized that it was impossible to detain one in two Germans, although he believed that fear was an effective repressive tool against political opposition. With the beginning of the war, the concentration camps that were modern hells started to multiply, especially in Poland.

Life in the concentration camps

The concentration camps were all surrounded by electrified barbed-wire fences and had watchtowers every two hundred feet, constantly manned by armed guards. The blocks were arranged in various ways, but overlooked the roll-call ground where the countless checks of prisoners and the torture took place publicly. Part of the blocks were reserved for the newcomers, who were quarantined before being identified and introduced to life in the camp, and to ensure that they did not have contagious diseases such as typhus spread by lice that the SS feared most of all.

The camp commander reported to Heydrich, and later to his successor Kaltenbrunner. He was directly responsible for the security of the camp and had the right of life and death over the prisoners. They were all SS and hardcore Nazis. Some of them, like Rudolf Höss, had a criminal record, but were appointed after being noticed for their zeal.

Each camp had a political section responsible for updating the prisoners' files, conducting interrogations and managing repression. The head of the section reported to the RSHA. Prisoners executed the secretarial work and sometimes discreetly advised some newcomers to change their statements, since a manual worker had a better chance to survive. The prisoner was then assigned a number that became his identity.

The detention section supported all prisoners' activities, especially the attendance check that lasted for hours, if not accurate. Clothing, food, work, offenses, sanctions, everything was recorded. Some prisoners known as kapos, often common law prisoners or criminals, were assigned responsibilities, such as keeping order in the barracks, and had power of life and death over the other prisoners. In the event of an infringement, they were punished. To avoid being caught, they hit other inmates.

A day in the camp began at 4:00 am with a piercing howl, a siren, or the screaming of the block leader, terrified that the prisoners under his responsibility be late, which could earn him a penalty. The daily diet consisted of a bowl of warm juice in the morning, a beet or turnip soup at lunch and, in the evening, a piece of bread with a dab of margarine or a synthetic sausage. Their caloric deficit being always about 30 percent, the prisoners who were undernourished and exhausted from work lost weight every day.

The forced labor camps and the extermination camps

Railway convoys from Germany, France, Belgium and the Netherlands transported their human cargo to the forced labor camps or the extermination camps. For the former, death was deferred; for the others, it was immediate. The concentration camps were located in Eastern Europe, especially in Poland. Transit camps housed prisoners awaiting the extermination camps. In April 1944, twenty concentration camps and one hundred sixty-five labor camps were officially recorded.

In the forced labor camps, the prisoners were used for construction projects or worked in German factories. They died from exhaustion, malnutrition, illness or as a result of medical experiments. They worked twelve hours a day and those who were unable to keep up were executed.

When the victims were brought to the extermination camps, officials welcomed them with shameless lies. They were led to believe that they would form a new state and learn new skills, but they first had to comply with the hygienic measures. They were asked to undress so that their clothing could be disinfected. They also had to divest themselves of their belongings, jewelry, watches and rings against an official receipt. The men were then separated from the women. The men had to undergo a quick physical examination. The strongest were assigned to work while the others waited to be informed of their fate. The women were sent to a hairdressing room where their hair was cut off. Then the human columns were led to the gas chambers that looked like shower rooms. Deadly gas crystals were deposited in a basin located above the ceiling where death followed the piping and escaped through the fake shower faucets. The victims, understanding the misconception, screamed, cried, and huddled together. Piles of bodies formed quickly, bathed in the urine and excrement of the dying. Fifteen minutes later, the heavy silence and fetid smell testified that the work of the executioners was completed. Six death camps were reserved for the massive and organized extermination of the Jewish population. They were Auschwitz, Sobibor, Treblinka, Belzec, Majdanek and Chelmno. The population of those camps rarely exceeded one hundred thousand prisoners since almost all newcomers were murdered upon arrival.

The Wannsee conference and the Final Solution

When the Nazis rose to power in 1933, there were a little more than five hundred thousand Jews under German control. The enactment of the Nuremberg laws excluded them from social life, and the persecutions that turned ever more vicious were intended to clean up the nation of the Jewish presence by forcing their emigration. In 1941, eleven million Jews were under German control in the occupied territories. Due to the war, emigration being no longer a viable option, it became necessary to find another solution to the problem.

Madagascar was a French colony conquered by the Germans, who had planned to establish Jewish ghettos on the island. But the state of war was an obstacle hindering maritime transportation. On July 31, 1941, faced with the failure of the Madagascar solution, Göring called Heydrich to tell him that the Jewish immigration policy was abolished and granted him full powers to create and execute a plan for a final solution to the Jewish problem.

On January 20, 1942, Reinhard Heydrich convened a meeting with Eichmann and fifteen senior officials at Wannsee, a suburb of Berlin. The conference was intended to develop the technical details of the final solution by coordinating the activities of the government agencies whose involvement was essential to the realization of the project. It was to be the last important meeting of Heydrich, who died two months later, following an attack by the Czech resistance on March 27, 1942.

Reinhard Heydrich presented the problem of the Jewish question in Europe. Since the beginning of the war had put an end to the Jewish emigration, he explained that Hitler had suggested the possibility of evacuating all the European Jews to the eastern territories. The deported Jews should be assigned to forced labor, such as the construction of roads, until the highest number of Jews was eliminated naturally. The survivors will be the strongest through natural selection and should receive proper treatment to prevent that they be components of a more resistant reconstruction of the Jewish people. Eichmann became responsible for the technical supervision of the final solution. He will later declare that the extermination of five million Jews was for him a source of great satisfaction. He was to become the specialist of special treatments.

We do not know what was the reaction of the participants since all the documents were carefully disposed of after the conference. It may be assumed that such a despicable project could have led to a strong reticence or opposition among some participants who did not necessarily share the fanaticism of Heydrich. But he was not a man to compromise. Hitler is often considered as the incarnation of evil. Sadistic, cruel, merciless and of an above average intelligence, Heydrich fits this image much better than Hitler. The mere fact that a SS leader with a rank as high as his conducted the conference suggests that reticence and opposition on the part of the participants were probably swept away by threats of physical retaliation. The SS were above the law and could at any time arrest, detain, torture or kill a person cleared in court. The threats of the SS were always taken seriously and knowing influential people did not ensure immunity.

The Final Solution: The case of the SS

The Wannsee Conference officially materialized a firm policy of extermination of the European Jews. Himmler's SS troops implemented the project. Rudolf Höss, commander of the Auschwitz concentration camp, and Adolf Eichmann, director of the RSHA section IV B 4 and expert on Jewish affairs, were in charge of developing an extermination program known as the Final Solution. The policy was not to be applied only in Germany, but also in all countries under German rule.

The implementation of the program was not that obvious. Several members of the SS commandos who executed the prisoners could not bear to see men, women, and children bleed to death. Several of them committed suicide. Many others became heavy drinkers as a means to support those horrors. Some SS asked not to participate in executions and their reticence was accepted. Carbon monoxide was experimented, but the facilities did not allow for the execution of enough prisoners. Ultimately, while experimenting on Russian prisoners, Captain Karl Fritzsch discovered accidentally the rapidly lethal properties of the prussic acid—Zyklon-B, manufactured by a subsidiary controlled by I.G. Farben. The chemical was used to exterminate vermin. After reviewing the effectiveness and speed of the product, Eichmann and Höss extended its use to other concentration camps. Six months later, in early 1942, the extermination of the Jewish populations of Europe began.

Several German industrialists were competing to get the crematoria order for the deadly Zyklon B gas previously used by the army as a pesticide, even though the call for tenders explicitly mentioned the goal of exterminating human life.

The concentration camps are frequently regarded as a tool specifically used for eliminating the Jews. In fact, approximately six million Jews were executed in the death camps. However, two caveats are in order. The concentration camps were the last and most effective means of extermination. On the other hand, the number of murdered Jews reached six million, about 60 percent of the Jews in Europe before the war, but the number of non-Jews who were executed was even higher. Ten million victims, mostly Poles and Slavs, were killed in the gas chambers by the Death's Head squads. The Nazis also killed a large number of Germans. They were opponents of the nazi regime, homosexuals, mentally ill, chronically ill, individuals who could transmit hereditary defects, communists, Jehovah's witnesses and Catholic priests. Finally, more than three million Slavs from the Russian army were captured by the Germans and died in captivity. Therefore, the total number of victims attributed to the nazi regime probably exceeds twenty million, and less than a third were Jews. The concentration camps were not meant to eliminate only the Jews, but also all those likely to oppose or slow down the march of Germany toward the Thousand-Year Reich, capable of imposing its order across Europe. The Jews and the Communists were for Hitler the greatest obstacles to the achievement of those objectives. The Jews had too much power. As for the Communists, their ideology was quite contrary to that of the Nazi Party. They needed to be eliminated.

From the beginning to the end, the Final Solution was executed with a detachment that stunned the world at the end of the war. When an organization transforms the absence of ethics and morality of its members into a selection criterion, there is no limit to the nature of the tasks it can perform. Josef Kramer was a SS. He had been trained in the techniques of execution in Auschwitz and Dachau. He quickly rose through the ranks and became commander of the Bergen-Belsen camp in 1944. He was one of the executioners who pushed eighty-six prisoners in the gas chambers after undressing them. When asked at his trial what he felt during the executions, he replied that he felt no emotion since he was merely following the orders, and that was the way he had been brought up.

We owe to Theodor Eicke the order based on terror that prevailed in the concentration camps. Appointed commander of the Dachau concentration camp in 1933, he soon implemented a surveillance, discipline and punishment system based on hatred and a total lack of pity for the prisoners.

Rudolf Höss said that Eicke urged the SS affected to the concentration camps to be merciless and warned his recruits that every SS was to be able to destroy even the members of their own family if they transgressed Hitler's beliefs or rebelled against the state.

Although it is true that some of the guards of the concentration camps were pathological sadists, most of them were ordinary people of average intelligence, chosen for their limited sensitivity and their ability to undergo the necessary training. They were prompted to consider the prisoners as vermin that needed to be exterminated to purify Germany and Europe. Their assignment was linked to racial hygiene.

In the final pages of his book, Höss repeats almost word for word the rhetoric of the Nuremberg defendants to excuse the atrocities committed under his responsibility at Auschwitz. He sees himself as a cog in the wheel of the transmission chain of authority that came from Adolf Hitler and ended when received by the soldiers.

Höss explained that the designation of prisoners responsible for the other prisoners was a key factor in the control of the masses crammed into the concentration camps. Called kapos, they tyrannized their companions insofar as their merciless attitude was likely to improve their own life when they demonstrated their value to the guards. Their brutality and ferocity for their fellow prisoners were worse than those of the guards.

The executioners were not recruited exclusively among those responsible for the concentration camps. Ilse Koch was the wife of Colonel Karl Koch, commander of the Buchenwald camp. She loved to ride her horse with naked prisoners aligned, looking for distinctive tattoos. When she discovered one, she hit the prisoner with her whip. The guards immediately took the victim to the infirmary. To prevent damage to the skin, the victim was killed by injection and the piece of skin showing the tattoo was carefully taken and sent to be tanned. The tattoos were subsequently assembled to make lampshades or book covers. Ilse Koch committed suicide during her trial in 1947.

The medical experimentation

Forty-five percent of the German physicians were members of the Nazi Party and twenty-two percent had joined the SS group.

The prisoners in the concentration camps were used as objects of medical experiments. During the Nuremberg trials, several witnesses argued that those people were to die anyway and were promised a death without suffering. This is why hundreds of prisoners were murdered, so that their skeleton could be used by the nazi *Ahnenerbe* Foundation or legacy of ancestors to study the morphology of the skull of those unfortunate people in an alleged scientific research.

The medical experiments falsely supported by research needs caused the death of tens of thousands of prisoners. The experiences had a military connotation since they were meant to determine the survival factors in conditions such as extreme cold or environments with reduced air pressure. To evaluate the consequences on the sailors or pilots who fell into the sea, they measured the time of death after exposing naked prisoners in snow or icy baths. To assess the risks associated with high altitude flights, the prisoners were placed in low pressure rooms until they suffocated after extreme suffering caused by intracranial decompression. They studied the reactions of the body when injected with typhus germs, gas gangrene bacteria and mustard gas.

Other experiments examined the most efficient mass sterilization processes. Some experiences such as vivisection, which consisted in dissecting living victims, had no apparent purpose other than satisfy the needs of sadism and voyeurism.

Dr. Josef Mengele

Dr. Josef Mengele, in charge of the medical services at Auschwitz, was the best known among the two hundred doctors assigned to the concentration camps. He will be remembered as the evil physician who dishonored the medical profession, altering humanitarian objectives for criminal purposes by exploiting and torturing prisoners who were under his responsibility. Born into a wealthy family of Bavarian industrialists, doctor of philosophy and medicine, this small man with a discreet strabismus was an educated person who liked the high society and to be with women. While studying in Munich, he was seduced by the theory of Rosenberg advocating the superiority of the Aryan race. He believed in classifying and experimenting with human beings, using a pedigree as if they were animals. After his medical studies, he joined Himmler's Ahnenerbe (Ancestral Heritage) research organization, specializing in the study of twins. He joined the Waffen-SS in 1939 and became chief medical officer of the Auschwitz camp in 1943. Without wasting time, he ordered that all prisoners with a deformity be executed and dissected upon their arrival. He was said to have sewn eleven sets of twins together to create Siamese twins. He escaped to South America in 1945 where he lived in Brazil and died of a stroke at the age of sixty-eight.

A prisoner's point of view

When Bruno Bettelheim was released from a German concentration camp, he proposed to a British publishing house a book relating his own experiences. They refused to publish it on the grounds that his story was not credible. Bettelheim had noted that the SS *Totenkopf* units responsible for administering the concentration camps were not only cruel bullies. Obviously, they applied very specific orders. Violence, torture and insults were not with some exceptions the expression of poorly controlled passions. They were coolly planned measures.

The period of his life spent in the concentration camp was the only time during which he did not experience depression and only later, after being secure again, did he start thinking about suicide. He said that he never before had the knowledge that he could cope with difficult conditions.

Bruno Bettelheim spent two years in concentration camps before the beginning of the war (1938-1939). To survive, he sought to understand the dynamics of the relationship between the executioners and the prisoners. He claims that the SS projected in a Jewish stereotype their negative tendencies and that some general remarks have to be made about the cruelty of the SS. Those who were really sadistic took pleasure in hurting or at least in demonstrating that they had the power to hurt, and any request for compassion increased their pleasure. Since they gained satisfaction from the reaction of the prisoners, there was no need for them to be harder. But to satisfy their sadistic impulses, they continued to abuse their victims. When a SS guard was doing what he considered his duty, any appeal to pity made him furious because the prisoner was creating distress and the guard was torn between the desire to do his duty and the idea that it was wrong to abuse others. The conflict irritated him and he sought to deny it and offload his anger by exercising greater cruelty. The more the prisoner was able to move the SS guard, the more the latter became frustrated and expressed his anger through violence.

Bettelheim said that some Jews had managed to escape and reach Warsaw to inform the others of the Jewish extermination. They were harshly reprimanded for spreading rumors that could only increase the anxiety of the Jews. Therefore, the voice of witnesses was silenced by a reassuring denial.

The denial was not limited to the Jews or the European countries. Between 1933 and 1939, the United States and other countries severely limited Jewish immigration on the grounds that the situation of the Jews and the cruelty of the Germans were exaggerated. It is easier to deny reality when facing it provokes unpleasant, difficult or costly reactions.

Those who saved Jews

At the time, antisemitism was strong throughout Europe and several countries, including Norway, applied zealously the anti-Jewish laws required by the nazi occupiers. However, several examples of humanitarian principles simultaneously appeared in Europe.

Even in Germany, German people hid Jews or helped them leave the country and risked their lives or lost them in the process. They were German soldiers or ordinary people. The best-known example is Oskar Schindler.

Born in 1908, Oskar Schindler was a German industrialist and a member of the Nazi Party. He made his fortune after setting up a kitchenware factory where employees were Jews. Shocked by the cruelty against the Jews, he purchased an enamel and ammunition factory in Czechoslovakia, where he allowed them to escape the extermination camps by buying them to work for him. In 1944, with the help of his Jewish accountant Itzhak Stern, he submitted a list of names of Jews waiting to be sent to an extermination camp and requisitioned them to work in his factory. An administrative error sent the convoy directly to the extermination camp. Using all his influence, he managed to convince the officers that the prisoners had to be released since they were considered essential to the functioning of his ammunition factory. More than a thousand Jews were saved and still today this is considered to be the only reported case where a large number of Jews having reached their destination escaped the gas chambers. Until the end of the war, he wasted his fortune in bribes that he distributed to German officers in order to win the support required for his projects. Oskar Schindler died in 1974. In 1993, he was recognized as a Righteous Among the Nations, the highest distinction awarded by Israel to celebrate the courage of those who risked their lives to save Jews. His story was popularized in *Schindler's List*, a historical novel published in 1982 by the Australian Thomas Keneally and adapted into a movie by Steven Spielberg in 1993.

Denmark, an occupied country, accomplished the amazing feat to save almost its entire population of Jews and protect the assets and properties of the Jews who left the country. The Danes offered a brave resistance against the Germans and created problems for the occupants with deliberate acts of sabotage. Several Danes were sent to concentration camps.

In Finland, the government refused to comply with the orders from the Nazis and helped the Jewish population to move to Switzerland for the duration of the war.

In France, the Vichy government actively cooperated with the Nazis. However, there were exceptions. A small village in southern France called Le Chambon-on-Lignon sheltered approximately five thousand Jews through the collaboration of citizens, the Church and the monasteries of the region.

Somewhat surprisingly, Spain, which maintained relations with Germany, accepted about forty thousand Jews for the duration of the war. Morocco, traditionally hostile to the Jews, protected its three hundred thousand Jews against the Vichy French government. The assistance from Japan was even more amazing. Japan, which occupied part of China, allowed thousands of Jewish refugees to escape from the German concentration camps.

As of January 1, 2018, twenty-six thousand nine hundred seventy-three individuals who risked their lives to save Jews during the Holocaust have been honored by the state of Israel with the title of Righteous Among The Nations.

The programming of the extermination of human lives on an industrial scale by a well-educated and culturally developed nation raises concerns about the destructive potential that dozes in the depths of each of us. But the heroic actions of those who risked their lives and that of their family to provide assistance to the victims of nazism remain a source of hope and demonstrate our capability to correct the deviations of human nature in order to build a better world.

Chapter 9

The resistance

In an election, the citizens' vote may reflect the choice of a program or a type of management proposed by a political party. This is usually what happens in times of peace and prosperity. However, when a nation goes through major upheavals, the popular vote can reflect a grumbling addressed to the ruling party and the emergence of marginal or extremist political groups. This is how the political, social and economic chaos provided the Nazi Party with an opportunity to make significant gains.

In the 1928 election, five years before they came to power, the Nazis formed a marginal party, garnering only a measly 2.6 percent of the votes. From 1931 onward, unemployment and poverty became chronic in Germany. The five largest banks collapsed, taking with them twenty thousand German companies. Misery had a grip on the middle class, opening the door to extremist political parties. Years of misery had proven favorable to the growth of intolerance, violence and hatred.

In a small German town such as Neindenburg, where the people had never seen Hitler and where there was no nazi organization, the Nazi Party garnered 2.3 percent of the votes in 1928 and 25.8 percent in 1930. The Nazis were not the only ones to take advantage of the economic crisis. The Communist Party also gained the support of the electorate. The rise of extremist parties clearly reflected that the electorate had lost confidence in a democratic form of government. The German culture had never assimilated the rules of the democratic system. The German emperor had fled at the end of World War I, leaving the democratic Weimar Republic with the heavy burden of managing the post-war with the mortgage of the

Treaty of Versailles. The experience had been quite catastrophic and the old popular reflex to support an authoritarian system simply because it is in power was ever present.

The German population never predominantly supported the nazi government, even when Hitler played his trump cards. In the election of March 5, 1933, after the crisis caused by the burning of the Reichstag and despite the imprisonment of many Communists and the reign of terror maintained by the Nazis, the NSDAP was unable to get a majority vote. The election gave the party 43.9 percent of the popular vote and two hundred eighty-eight of the six hundred forty-seven seats.

The popular dissent in Germany

There were many good reasons to oppose the policies of Hitler and there were many dissatisfied people in pre-war Germany. Citizens were concerned about the loss of rights and freedoms, the racist laws and the brutal and repressive measures carried out by the regime against those who created obstacles to the nazi government's plans. Many Germans, mostly Jews, left Germany and saved their lives. But the worst was yet to come.

Years	Number of convictions for political crimes
1933	40,000
1934	70,000
1935	85,000
1936	90,000

Table 1 – Number of convictions for political offenses at the beginning of the nazi regime

There were also good reasons to silence one's opposition to the nazi regime. Repression against the opponents was ruthless and merely expressing doubts about the outcome of the war regularly led to a death sentence. Active participation in political resistance was a rocky road. The clandestine networks were constantly threatened by a denunciation from a member, as a result of a dispute regarding the operations or to garner favor with the regime. The networks were also threatened by the recklessness of their members that could lead to arrests and confessions extracted through torture. Therefore, heroic courage was necessary to become an active opponent of the regime in nazi Germany. In 1935, the Gestapo arrested at least fifteen thousand people per month and eighty-five thousand Germans were imprisoned for political crimes. Goebbels' propaganda maintained confusion between the nationalist feeling anchored in the German collective consciousness and the support given to the Nazi Party. At first glance, the opposition to the latter and the love of the homeland appeared to be contradictory attitudes.

Hitler managed to become popular and develop an unexpected credibility in restoring basic elements like social, economic and political stability. The price to pay in terms of suppression of individual and collective freedoms did not appear disproportionate compared to the suffering that the nation had known for fifteen years. He also returned to the German nation a sense of pride lost with the Treaty of Versailles by recovering the territories sequestered after World War I. The Germans applauded the great dictator who had been able to recover their land using political rather than military strategies, without a single drop of blood being shed.

The Germans were fundamentally opposed to a new war. Popular indifference at the military parade in Berlin on September 27, 1938, in the midst of the Sudetenland crisis, spoke for itself. But the outbreak of war a year later forced the population to close ranks behind Hitler. And, in the middle of the war, the Allied raids posed a threat more serious than the political police.

In the German population, the dissent was disorganized and rather individual. By the very nature of its objectives and because of the cruelty of the repression it created, all opposition to nazism was to remain hidden. Those who criticized the regime endangered their own safety and that of their loved ones. The available evidence probably represents only a small fraction of the resistance operations and it is clear that many victims took their secret projects to the grave.

The only organized group that escaped the political police was the army, whose counterintelligence services headed by Admiral Canaris were conducting operations that were not accessible to Himmler. This is where the main resistance came from.

Hitler had carefully eliminated the sociodemocratic structures that could have channeled opposition. On coming to power, he dissolved the unions and disbanded the political parties.

The only successful spontaneous popular resistance was the one that followed the implementation of the euthanasia program of German patients considered incurable. The policy led to such a protest that Hitler ordered to terminate the program on August 24, 1941, after having exterminated a hundred thousand patients.

Hitler's providential chance

It must be noted that Hitler had an incredible chance. Between 1921 and 1945, he escaped about forty attacks. On November 8, 1939, barely two months after the declaration of World War II, Hitler was delivering a speech at the *Bürgerbräukeller* for the commemoration of veterans' day. He always had a busy schedule, speaking in more than one place on the same day. He constantly changed his schedule and this habit saved his life several times. The dissident Georg Elser had placed a powerful charge of explosives close to the speaker. But since Hitler wanted to be in Berlin the next morning, he shortened his speech in order to fly earlier so that the morning mist did not prevent his plane from landing in Berlin. When the bomb exploded and killed several members of the party, Hitler was long gone.

On March 13, 1943, Hitler flew to the Russian front. German soldiers had arranged for a package containing explosives to be placed in the luggage compartment. Due to the low temperature, the bomb did not explode. Hitler's life was saved once again.

On March 21, 1943, Hitler visited an exhibition of war materials. A German army officer was to guide him on a tour that would last at least ten minutes. The officer was carrying two explosive devices that he set off upon Hitler's arrival. However, the Führer was in a hurry and quickly moved through the room, leaving the officer behind him. His visit lasted about two minutes and the officer had to defuse the devices.

On March 11, 1944, a military officer armed with a gun was to attend a meeting with Hitler, during which he planned to shoot the dictator. At the last minute, he was denied entry into the room. Hitler was once again safe and sound.

On July 20, 1944, he escaped once more an attack planned by the military. Colonel Stauffenberg had placed a briefcase containing a powerful explosive near Hitler's feet. An attentive general decided that the briefcase was in his leader's way and moved it behind a leg of the table. Hitler suffered minor injuries, but he was spared. He was then convinced that the Providence had protected him so that he could carry out his plan.

The real resistance movements probably started when Hitler swept away the illusions of the Germans with the invasion of Poland, therefore launching World War II. Signs of resistance soon appeared. Opposition movements to the nazi policies arose in almost all environments—the church, the universities, the arts and communications, the army and even the population. The reactions of the nazi government were subjected to a power struggle. He gave up the programs that aroused the hostility of the population, tolerated public denunciations when the speaker was a well-known public figure, and engaged in ruthless repression when the opponents were defenseless.

Resistance in the academic community was severely repressed. Karl Saller, an anthropologist at the University of Munich, was prohibited from teaching at this university by the Chief of Gestapo Reinhard Heydrich, after the publication of a text in which he criticized the racial ideology as being a specified biological entity. The specialist had the temerity to insist that, in all races, there was a continual change in the gene pool or a perpetual state of flux, and that the German race had become entwined with many others and contained extensive Slavic influences. His fellow colleagues remained silent. As a result, he felt rejected and avoided by them.

In the last two years of the regime, the allied bombings combined with the SS repression confined the German population in a dazed and resigned silence. Denunciation, developed into a system and consecrated as a civic duty, efficiently reduced dissent, especially since special care was taken to make public the treatment of those who deviated from the nazi orthodoxy. Mrs. Elfrid Scholz, a seamstress in Dresden, had expressed doubts to her landlady about a possible victory of the German army on the eastern front. The latter, who worked for the Gestapo on her spare time, reported her right away. Mrs. Scholz was arrested, tried, found guilty of defeatist propaganda and sentenced to death in 1943. One word too many, shared thoughts, the mere fact of expressing doubts or a simple misunderstanding could send any German to the gallows, even if he was a member of the Nazi Party. Dr. Geiger, who was a member of the Nazi Party and a medical doctor engaged in private practice in Spiegelau, confided to one of his patients his doubts about a speedy victory of the German army. He was arrested, sentenced to death and hanged.

The resistance to the extermination policy of the useless eaters

The extermination policy was fully in keeping with Nietzsche's philosophy and the race-biological standpoint defended by Konrad Lorenz. Therefore, the nazi doctrine was aligned with the principle that the natural forces of evolution require that the weak be eliminated to give the nation the possibility to become stronger. Those principles of natural selection and racial purification by the extermination of morally inferior individuals were to be provided by human organizations.

The programs, gradually applied, began with the sterilization policy for people with disabilities of all kinds. There did not seem to be much opposition to sterilization. The Catholic Church disapproved of it, but avoided confronting the issue. However, it requested that Catholic judges and doctors be exempted from enforcing the law. The Nazi Party defended the moral of the policy, stating that the life of the nation took precedence over dogma and conflicts of conscience, and also that opposition to the government's program would be met with strong retaliation. Carried away by the nazi ideology, Dr. Rudolf Ramm, leading medical expert at the University of Berlin, proposed that each doctor was to be no longer merely a caretaker of the sick, but was to become a cultivator of the genes, a physician to the *Volk* and a biological soldier serving the nation. The essence of the nazi ideology, which favored the life of the nation over the individual life, triumphed again and relegated to the back burner the medical oath giving to human life an inalienable value.

Most of the German physicians joined the nazi ranks. A few ones, such as psychiatrists Hans Gerhard Creutzfeldt and Gottfried Ewald, opposed the nazi extermination policies and publicly criticized the regime. Due to their status and because they were protected by influential men, the Nazis tolerated them. Several other health professionals more discreetly participated in the modification of their patient records to conceal their health problems and enable them to escape death.

Nowadays, the concentration camps are still the symbol of the nazi extermination policies. An absolute necessity for a government that tolerated no opposition, they were built in the weeks following the seizure of power by Hitler. Dachau, the first concentration camp, opened on March 20, 1933, in order to keep in preventive detention the undesirable such as the vagrants, incorrigible alcoholics, prostitutes, homosexuals, Jehovah's witnesses and enemies. After the burning of parliament on February 27, a large number of Communists held accountable for the disaster had the dubious honor of being the first occupants. The camps were entirely under the responsibility of Heinrich Himmler and not accountable to legal or judicial authorities.

Die Weisse Rose

The episode of the White Rose remains the most emotional testimony of the strength of moral conscience and the breath of freedom that lived in the heart of the German youth in the face of tyranny. It is the story of Hans Scholl and the resistance movement that he created at the University of Munich. Like all the young people in those days, he joined the Hitler Youth, seduced by the government promise to give birth to a powerful and proud Germany, which was constantly repeated on the radio and in the newspapers. All Germans were now to have a job and bread on the table.

Inge Scholl, sister of Hans and Sophie, mentioned the initial enthusiasm that followed Hitler's election as chancellor. Hans was fifteen and Sophie twelve years old. Hitler's rise to power raised enthusiasm and gave the Germans hope that things would change in their country.

Inge described the astonishment of the Scholl kids before the reluctance of their father who objected to those activities and warned them not to believe what they were told. Hans loved the comradeship spirit that prevailed in his group. He played the guitar and sang German, Russian and Norwegian folk songs. One day his group leader formally forbade him to sing foreign songs. Hans burst out laughing, asking if it was because the composers were not Aryans. In response, he was threatened with disciplinary measures. Hans gradually ceased to be the driving force of the group and locked himself in a disturbing silence. As the months progressed, he gradually distanced himself from the Hitler Youth.

Hans had always believed that people are different in imagination, talent and personality. According to him, those differences enriched the group. He felt more and more uncomfortable in the Hitler Youth, which imposed on him an ideology closed on itself. One day, a group leader took a book away from him under the pretext that the author was not approved by the Nazi Party. A break with the system was only a matter of time.

On June 2, 1942, the BBC informed the world that Hitler's government had set up a plan for systematically exterminating the Jews. That year, Munich, which had a significant population of university students, had become a hub of opposition to the government policies.

The case of the White Rose came to light in the aftermath of the Stalingrad defeat in early 1943. Disillusioned with the excesses of the nazi regime, several students openly challenged the Nazis and wanted to take advantage of the Stalingrad defeat to awaken the Germans. At that time, Hans Scholl was a medical student. He took the head of the protest movement with his twenty-two-year-old sister Sophie, who was studying biology and philosophy. The students published *The White Rose* leaflets that criticized the policies of the nazi regime, and urged the German nation to rise up against the immorality of their leaders.

Things began to go wrong in February 1943 when the Gauleiter Paul Giesler to whom the Gestapo had given the White Rose file met the Munich intellectual youths to inform them of his disapproval and intentions. Known for his natural stupidity, he threatened to send the recalcitrant young males to the front and suggested that the women should bear a child each year to boost the population, with the collaboration of one of his men. Infuriated by such nonsense, the students threw Giesler out of the meeting room and he was forced to beat a hasty retreat under the protection of his SS bodyguards.

In the days that followed, anti-Hitler protests were organized in Munich, calling people to revolt. The students published six clandestine White Rose leaflets stating that Germany was headed toward an eventual disaster in the hands of a madman.

After a call for revolt by Hans and Sophie Scholl from a balcony of the University of Munich, the SS troops arrested several students. Then, on February 18, they arrested Hans Scholl, his sister Sophie, and a twenty-four-year-old medical student, Christoph Probst. Sophie was tortured by the SS and, when taken to court, she was forced to stand on a broken leg. On February 22, after a mock trial that lasted four hours, the three scholars were sentenced to death. Hans and Sophie had their head cut off. The night of the execution, the authorities of the University of Munich gathered the students and requested that they profess their nazi faith once again.

Two other medical students were arrested later, Alexander Schmorell and Willi Graf, respectively twenty-six and twenty-five years old. Kurt Huber, Sophie's professor of philosophy, was also arrested and sentenced to death.

The movement of Hans and Sophie Scholl did not change the course of the war. However, after the war, it helped prompt collective awareness among the Germans, and the White Rose became a symbol of courage and fidelity to one's own values. Today, nearly one hundred fifty schools and a large number of streets, public places and community centers have been named after the Scholls.

The resistance within the Church

In the 1930s, almost half of the Germans claimed to be Protestants. The Catholics ranked second with 25 percent of the population. A good many Catholics supported the Nazi Party and Hitler himself was Catholic.

Between 1933 and 1937, Hitler tried to limit the power of organized religion and get control of the Protestant church, less monolithic than the Catholic church. He gave Hermann Göring the mandate to take the necessary measures to subordinate the church to the state. The election of Friedrich von Bodelschwingh, a widely respected churchman and by no means a National Socialist—instead of Ludwig Müller of nazi allegiance as the Reich bishop, was an open insult to Hitler, because Bodelschwingh was the director of a famous home for the feeble-minded, caring for those people who, in Hitler's opinion, should have been exterminated for the good of the race. It broke the link between the church and the party. Due to a serious divergence of opinion, Göring ordered Bernhard Rust, Prussian minister of Education, to resolve the dispute. Members of the clergy were soon eliminated, Bodelschwingh was forced to resign and, in July 1933, the party had control over the German Evangelical churches. However, on June 29, 1933, President Hindenburg met with Hitler and shared with him his concerns about the decline of freedom of the Protestant church. He also put his concerns in writing and published them thereafter. He argued that if the attacks on the Protestant church remained, the nation, the country and the national unity would inevitably be affected. It was the first public rebuff for Hitler, who had done as much as he could without serious resistance. After the intervention of the president, he backed off and took away from Göring the responsibility for the church affairs that he gave to Frick, whose stance was more moderate.

Another friction appeared between the Nazi Party and the church when the German Christians demanded the exclusion of the non-Aryans from the church, especially for the clergy. The Catholic church, for its part, rejected the notion that the non-Aryans were no longer Germans. In a pastoral letter dated June 10, 1933—the last of its kind for many years to come, the Catholic bishops declared that national unity could be achieved, not only by like blood, but also like mentality, and that the exclusive consideration of race and blood in judging state membership led to injustice. It was to be the last edit of the church for a long period of time. The break with the Catholic church was complete when Pope Pius XI published on March 14, 1937 an encyclical denouncing the difficulties of the Catholic church in Germany.

After the outbreak of war, the different denominations locked up in cautious neutrality when they were not benevolent. Gradually, the church withdrew from political life in order to preserve its spiritual power in Germany. Hitler agreed to tolerate the church insofar as it self-excluded from political interventions.

The persecutions and intense surveillance by the Gestapo were meant to prevent religious organizations of any political activism. If there was resistance to the nazi policies, the initiatives remained local or individual. The Protestant pastor Martin Niemöller, who had served in the submarine fleet during World War I, was one of the few critics of the Nazi Party who survived the Gestapo. His sermons vigorously denounced the nazi attacks on the church and triggered Hitler's anger. Niemöller was arrested in 1937. Niemöller took advantage of his trial to roundly criticize the regime. His great popularity in Germany saved his life. He remained in prison and concentration camps until the end of the war.

During a homily, Clemens August von Galen, bishop of Münster, preached against the nazi extermination policy of the sick and mentally ill. He managed to mobilize the public around him in such a way that Hitler had to put an end to the euthanasia programs. The SS wanted to arrest him, but Hitler was hesitant. Goebbels eventually convinced the Führer that the execution of the bishop would have a negative political impact on the population of Westphalia. The bishop continued to criticize the nazi methods of work. He was finally arrested and kept under house arrest after the July 1944 conspiracy. While his life was spared because of his notoriety, several lesser known pastors were arrested and executed for subversive activities. According to the German historian Hans Rothfeld, eight hundred Catholic priests and three hundred fifty Protestant pastors were executed at Dachau between 1941 and 1945.

The resistance and the German army

Ludwig Beck was a central figure in the military resistance. He was born in 1881 and had pursued a brilliant military career. He was deeply respected by all those who approached him. He was an intellectual who thought carefully before undertaking a risky military operation and analyzed all the possibilities before supporting a specific strategy. He did not embrace the nazi delusions about the master race and the myth of the German blood. He saw the Wehrmacht as a politically independent organization governed by its own set of laws.

In November 1937, when Hitler announced his expansionist projects and asked his staff to begin the military preparations, Beck, who was chief of staff of the ground forces (OKH) had serious reservations and expressed them to his immediate superior, Fritsch, supreme commander of the army. The latter shared Beck's feeling, but he was removed from his post at the same time as the Minister of War von Blomberg. This is when Hitler appointed himself commander in chief of the army. He was assisted by Keitel, who was only a puppet, and Jodl, who did not dare oppose the views of the Führer. Beck proposed to Walter von Brauchitsch, the successor of Fritsch, a mass resignation of the generals in order to avoid war and eliminate the nazi dictatorship. The officers ignored the proposal. Beck resigned on September 1, 1938. He said that a soldier's duty to obey ends when his knowledge, his conscience and his sense of responsibility forbid him to carry out a certain order.

Several German generals, especially Blomberg, Fritsch and Beck, felt that Hitler was a dangerous madman who could drag Germany into a disastrous military adventure. Just before the invasion of Czechoslovakia, a group of German generals led by General Beck tried to stop Hitler and, in a proclamation, explained to the German people that their gesture was an attempt to save the nation. But when Chamberlain returned to Great Britain triumphantly holding a document expressing Hitler's desire for peace, he had not saved the peace. He had saved Hitler from his generals who could not decently arrest a man who was about to make conquests by peaceful means. In the months that followed, the prestige of Hitler increased considerably. The opportunity to overthrow Hitler will not present itself again before 1943.

The Abwehr, a thorn in the side of the Nazis

Beck remained in contact with military leaders who hardly concealed their animosity toward the regime. Admiral Canaris, head of the Abwehr—the Military Intelligence Service, was one of them.

Apart from the Abwehr, few areas in Germany escaped the vigilance of the Gestapo. Responsible for detecting spies in Germany and infiltrating European countries with its secret agents, the German counterintelligence service conducted top-secret activities that even Himmler could not access.

This very broad autonomy of the Abwehr allowed its leaders to choose the high command of the organization based on the distance that the officers maintained from Hitler's regime rather than their loyalty to the Nazi Party.

The head of the service, Admiral Wilhelm Canaris, of Italian origin, but German by birth, was a cultured, intelligent and pleasant man who had an outstanding service record in the German Navy and had been involved in right-wing and left-wing politics. In June 1934, in the Night of the Long Knives, Canaris seized the criminal potential of the nazi organization when Hitler solved his problems in a bloodbath. With great art, Canaris led to believe in his loyalty to Hitler and, in January 1935, he was appointed head of the Abwehr.

His deputy, Colonel Hans Oster, was as fiercely opposed to the Nazis as was his chief, Admiral Canaris, who trusted him completely. Naturally bold, he did not hesitate to do things that could have compromised him. During the war, he repeatedly passed strategic information to the Allies, but the latter did not take them into account, believing that he was one of the many deceits of the nazi government.

In that context, nearly three thousand officers of the Abwehr reporting to Admiral Canaris were engaged in secret activities. Many of them participated in the development of projects designed to thwart the plans of the nazi government and the senior officials of the party had no input regarding those activities.

On May 9, 1940, Oster informed Belgium that a German invasion was scheduled for the next day. However, the German intelligence services had managed to decode the message and informed Hitler that there was an important leak of information within his staff. Angered, Hitler assigned the investigation to Admiral Canaris, who was unable, we can guess why, to identify the source of the leak.

During that time, using his influence, Canaris was able to torpedo some German military projects to discourage activities that he considered unsustainable.

In the fall of 1942, clouds began to accumulate above the Abwehr when a Canaris agent was arrested at the border while attempting to go to Switzerland. Since he was carrying foreign currency whose source he could not explain, the customs officers handed the suspect to the Gestapo. The investigation dragged on, but the agent eventually admitted that the currency was to be handed to a group of Jewish refugees in Switzerland. The currency came from Josef Müller, an Abwehr agent. A wave of arrests followed, dangerously undermining the German resistance network. Canaris managed to convince Himmler that a court procedure against the Abwehr would show the army in a bad light and have far-reaching consequences on the political level. However, Hitler ordered its dissolution in 1944, after German secret agents had sought asylum in Great Britain.

Oster and Canaris were hanged on April 9, 1945, one month before the end of the war.

The assassination attempt by von Stauffenberg

As early as 1938, Beck had begun to gather around him a core of conspirators: Admiral Wilhelm Canaris, Colonel Hans Oster, Generals Erwin von Witzleben, Erich Hoeppner, Carl-Heinrich von Stülpnagel, Eduard Wagner, Franz Halder and Kurt von Hammerstein-Equord. The group was responsible for the attack of July 20, 1944.

The most serious attack was the work of Count Claus Schenk von Stauffenberg, from an old aristocratic Catholic family. He joined the army at the age of eighteen. He learned about the scandal of the Crystal Night and discovered the gangsterism of the National Socialist Party when he was twenty-nine years old.

He joined the resistance around the time when Sophie and Hans Scholl were executed in Munich for having appealed to the conscience of the Germans. On April 7, 1943, he was in North Africa when his car was attacked by an enemy aircraft. He was severely wounded. He lost his right arm, two fingers on the left hand and the use of his left eye. During his convalescence, his thinking led him to believe that, among the conspirators gathered around Beck, he was the man for the job since his position gave him the opportunity to be in direct contact with Hitler. The bombing plan provided that the army reserve would be mobilized to seize power and establish a transitional government.

The attack was planned to take place on July 20, 1944, at the Wolf's Lair. Stauffenberg and his adjutant, Lieutenant Werner von Haeften, brought a briefcase containing a powerful explosive device at a meeting scheduled to start at 1:00 pm. Since Mussolini was to arrive later in the afternoon, Hitler had rescheduled the meeting about thirty minutes earlier. At the beginning of the meeting, Stauffenberg left the room and armed the device with the three fingers in his left hand, ensuring that the bomb would explode ten minutes later. He returned to the room and positioned the briefcase under the table, close to Hitler's feet. After a few moments, he mumbled an excuse and left the room claiming a call from Berlin. At 12:42 pm, a powerful explosion shook the house where Hitler was holding the meeting with his staff. Stauffenberg and Haeften immediately got into their car and easily crossed the first two points of verification. At the third and final point, the maximum alert had been given and Stauffenberg, using his powers of persuasion, was able to leave without being troubled in any way. Nine miles away, a plane was waiting for them and they flew to Berlin, convinced that their mission was a success. It was discovered later that Hitler had been miraculously saved by one of the participants at the meeting who had moved Stauffenberg's briefcase since it was in the Führer's way.

The last hours of the day gave rise to a confusion from which Goebbels took advantage.

When they learned that the attack had failed, the conspirators' allies withdrew one after the other and Stauffenberg was arrested that very evening with his closest collaborators. The military were shot dead without any further ado. Shortly after, two hundred suspects were arrested and died slowly hanging from meat hooks, filmed by the SS at Hitler's request.

The conspiracy mainly involved military belonging to the Prussian aristocracy and not the bulk of the officers. It was criticized by the army as a whole who found nothing to say about the wild and ruthless repression that followed. Four hundred investigators were assigned to the case until the end of the war. About seven thousand people were arrested and many of them had nothing to do with the bombing. Five thousand suspects, including seventeen generals, were executed, some of them after months of torture. All the Stauffenbergs in Germany, women, men and children, were arrested. The children or babies were taken away from their mothers and given for adoption under a false name. This brutal repression was meant to burst the abscess of resistance by eliminating the actual or potential anti-nazi movement leaders. Hitler took that opportunity to deal a mortal blow to the groups of officers who belonged to the aristocracy.

The Jewish resistance

The Jewish resistance was never organized, except in rare cases. Most often, the Jews met death with resignation. Extreme antisemitism, expertly orchestrated by the nazi propaganda, made the Jewish population very vulnerable, dehumanized, disorganized and overwhelmed by the feeling that the situation was irreversible.

However, the heroic Jewish resistance of April 1943 cannot be ignored since it remains a symbol of courage and dignity in the face of tyranny in the Jewish history.

The Warsaw ghetto was home to the Jews of the capital and a large number of Jews deported from the regions of occupied Poland. All social and economic classes were represented, workers and artists living with merchants and professionals. The ghetto was overcrowded, each room accommodating about ten people. After the invasion of Russia in 1941, the population of the ghetto reached five hundred thousand people. Due to the severe food rationing imposed by the Nazis, the Jews suffered from starvation or typhus and death soon became an everyday occurrence. The streets and alleys were filled with bodies.

An eight-foot brick wall topped with barbed wire completely isolated the Jews from the Polish population. No Jew could enter or leave the ghetto without formal permission. The guards were ordered to shoot on sight anyone trying to escape. However, despite the fact that they were kept under close watch by the Nazis, the prisoners of the ghetto managed to maintain external contact using the underground sewers whose galleries were running under the city. A Hebrew Council called *Judenrat* was responsible for administering the ghetto.

Several Jews in the ghetto tried to deal with their bad fortune and denied the most pessimistic information that came from the outside warning them that suffering and death awaited them. A number of them had no illusions about their fate and began selling their lives dearly.

On the night of July 21-22, 1942, the SS began to raid the ghetto. Armed with bayonets, they took contingents of Jews to an unknown destination from which no one ever came back. In the summer of 1942, more than three hundred thousand Jews had gone missing. Several of them were hiding in underground sewers, hoping to escape their executioners.

In January 1943, winter was difficult for the Wehrmacht, which was headed toward a disaster at Stalingrad and required a maximum of material and military resources. The population of the Warsaw ghetto was down to sixty thousand and the Gestapo was irritated by the lack of cooperation of the Jews who were not always showing up in the forced labor shops where the production constantly decreased. This is when Himmler ordered the destruction of the Warsaw ghetto, to be leveled after the deportation of its last inhabitants.

Resistance was organized around a young and brave Jew with a strong leadership whose name was Mordechai Anielewicz. The ghetto prepared for a siege. Trenches were dug and light weapons were scrounged through contacts with the Polish resistance.

When the SS troops invaded the ghetto on April 19, 1943, they faced a resistance that was admirably organized despite the limited resources available. Every street, every lane, every house became a threat to the SS who showed up. They seemed infested with men and women who were disappearing into the underground bunkers of the sewer system. The resistance fighters, who were equipped with rifles, automatic pistols, a few grenades and improvised Molotov cocktails, drove back several times in twenty-eight days the Waffen-SS troops supported by tanks, automatic machine guns and flamethrowers.

The Germans systematically destroyed the city section by section, torching the blocks and killing the wounded who tried to escape. Running out of food, water and ammunition, the besieged sent a final message to the Polish resistance on May 15, 1943, asking for help. No one replied and the next day the Warsaw ghetto no longer existed.

The resistance of the Warsaw ghetto inspired the Jews in the Bialystock and Czenstochowa ghettos. In the extermination camps of Treblinka and Sobibor, the Jewish resistance spilled German blood. In August 1943 in Treblinka, Jews who managed to get weapons attacked the German SS and their Ukrainian auxiliaries. Several of them managed to neutralize the guards in the watchtowers and escaped by crossing the barbed wire. Most died in a battle or were captured, but about a hundred of them took refuge in the forests nearby and were found by the Russian troops in July 1944.

The resistance in occupied territories

Many occupied countries such as Denmark and Norway remained fiercely opposed to the German policies and avoided mass deportations. Few countries assumed their responsibilities like Denmark, which showed to the world that courage still existed and that it was possible to openly resist the German persecution of the Jews. The statement by the King of Denmark, Christian X, went down in history: "If they try to enforce the yellow star here, the King will be the first to wear it."

Other countries such as France, Czechoslovakia and Norway formed a government in exile. In all those countries, the resistance movements damaged the German war effort through the end. Hitler had to maintain a permanent force of three hundred thousand soldiers in Norway.

In Holland, longshoremen confronted Dutch collaborators who were persecuting Jews during a police raid in a Jewish neighborhood. A police officer was killed during the confrontation and Himmler arrested four hundred Jews between twenty and thirty-five years of age who were repeatedly hit with gun butts on February 22, 1941. Three days later, the Dutch workers went on a two-day solidarity strike. Leaflets denouncing the nazi brutality were distributed to the population. The nazi authorities immediately declared a state of emergency and arrested the labor leaders. They also executed eighteen members of the resistance and sent the Jewish hostages to concentration camps where they died under torture.

The French resistance

On June 17, 1940, Marshal Philippe Pétain broadcasted an hourly message announcing that the French government had surrendered to Germany and urging the French nation to stop fighting. The next evening, the BBC in London aired the message of an obscure French General, Charles de Gaulle, asking the French resistance to continue the struggle against the German invader. Churchill had officially recognized de Gaulle as the leader of free France. The appeal of de Gaulle was heard not only in France, but in all the occupied European countries. London became the capital of pockets of resistance in Europe.

Pierre Laval, head of the Vichy government in 1940, sacked by Pétain in December 1941 and recalled by him under German pressure in April 1942, set up a government that actively collaborated with the Nazis. Well informed about the woes of German troops and despite the fact that the United States had joined the Allies, Laval stubbornly believed in the German victory. Recognizing that the majority of the French population was opposed to a policy of collaboration, he said that if he was right, he would have a statue erected in his honor, and if he was wrong, he would be shot. He was not that far from the truth. He collaborated at all stages of the persecution of the French Jews, whose census was ordered on September 29, 1940. Three weeks later, the order of October 18 announced the expropriation of the Jewish businesses and their aryanization. Then, the regime forced all Jews over six years of age to wear a yellow star sewn on their outer clothing, on the left side of the chest. In early 1942, the Final Solution was ready to be applied. In June 1942, the Gestapo decided the deportation of one hundred thousand Jews. In a dishonorable haggling, Laval decided to exchange the Jewish refugees in France as a bargaining chip for the promise to save the French Jews. The French police arrested seventy thousand stateless Jews, thus handing them a death sentence.

In France, the resistance did not get organized immediately. The French were hesitant between their loyalty to the Vichy government that collaborated with the Nazis and an appeal for resistance from London by General Charles de Gaulle. The problems faced by the British, who were bombarded in their own territory and crushed by Rommel's troops in North Africa, inspired a painful resignation. However, as of August 1940, several French colonies stood with the free France government-in-exile, reinforcing the legitimacy of de Gaulle as head of state. The entry of the United States into World War II, after the bombing of Pearl Harbor on December 7, 1941, offered a glimmer of hope and the French resistance quickly started to organize around Captain Henri Frenay and Jean Moulin.

Defying the Gestapo and infiltrating all organizations and trades, the clandestine networks tried to sabotage the nazi propaganda and instill in the population the desire to resist the invader. Criminal attacks derailed freight trains on their way to Germany. It was a game of cat-and-mouse between the resistance and the Gestapo. Captured resistance members were regularly tortured to force them to denounce their comrades. Each German military assassination resulted in the execution of hostages in the population to serve as a warning. Three, five and then ten French hostages or more were killed for every German shot by members of the resistance. In October 1941, fifty French hostages were executed to avenge the death of one German officer.

On 21 June 1943, Jean Moulin, betrayed by a traitor, was arrested by the Gestapo and tortured to death by Klaus Barbie, a sadistic officer known as the butcher of Lyon. Moulin died without revealing his secrets.

The resistance in Europe was due to a large number of women and men whose initiatives forced the nazi government to mobilize a large force of military and police, depriving the fronts of a valuable workforce. Until the end of 1941, the French resistance focused its activities on espionage rather than sabotage.

The *Nacht und Nebel* or Night and Fog Decree promulgated by Hitler on December 12, 1941 and signed by Marshal Keitel shows the sinister side of the nazi terror regime. The Decree was targeting the resistance movements in the occupied territories. In France, five thousand resistance members vanished without a trace. Kidnapped without warning by the Gestapo mostly in the night, the victims were taken to Germany, where nobody ever heard about them.

Belgium, the Netherlands and Luxembourg had their own resistance networks, which helped many allied military or British agents flee from Europe.

The most spectacular episode of resistance in Europe was the assassination of Reinhard Heydrich by Czech partisans in 1942.

The assassination of Reinhard Heydrich in Czechoslovakia

The events surrounding the killing of Heydrich deserve to be known because they demonstrate vividly the back room games and cruelty of the nazi regime.

Heydrich was one of the few nazi officials who embodied the physical characteristics of the master race. Blond hair, blue eyes, aquiline nose, thin, excellent musician, Heydrich charmed his entourage. He was a man of much greater intelligence with quick reflexes, but totally devoid of any sense of morality, of human feelings, and capable of the most vicious measures to meet the goals he had set for himself. Appointed by Himmler head of the RSHA, the central security bureau of the SS secret police, he was part of all the political intrigues, from the Night of the Long Knives in June 1934 to the false flag operation against the Gleiwitz radio station in 1939. He was the architect of the Final Solution and the one who summoned the Wannsee meeting on January 20, 1942, where Eichmann and a few senior officials developed the technical details of the Final Solution. It was to be his last important meeting since he died as a result of an assassination attempt against him on March 27, 1942.

On September 1941, Martin Bormann suggested to Hitler that Heydrich be appointed Reich Protector of Bohemia-Moravia, the former Czechoslovakian state, in replacement of von Neurath, who was unable to put an end to the political unrest that was annoying Berlin. Bormann was well aware of Heydrich's intelligence, machiavellianism and inordinate ambitions. To him, Heydrich was a dangerous rival who was becoming more and more important in the closed circle of the Führer, and he had a powerful weapon—the secret police. The appointment of Heydrich sent his rival away from Berlin, at least temporarily, even though he kept his post in the RSHA.

Heydrich moved quickly. Upon his arrival in Czechoslovakia, he arrested General Alaïs Elias, former Prime Minister of the Czech government, suspected of being in contact with President Beneš, who had taken refuge in London. After submitting him to the usual torture ranging from punches, kicks, cigarette burns and suffocation by head immersion in icy water, he hanged him after a parody of a trial. To quell the unrest, he managed to get the power to make preventive arrests to ensure the security of the protectorate.

On December 28, 1941, seven Czech resistance members took off from London and were parachuted in the Pilsen region where they split into three groups whose mission was to deliver the Czech people from Heydrich. The latter used to travel to Prague in the surrounding countryside, in his convertible Mercedes with no protection other than the gun he carried on his belt.

In the following months, the members of the commando watched Heydrich's comings and goings. He regularly toured the countryside of Prague often taking a winding road with light traffic. On May 27, 1942, around 10:00 am, Jan Kubis and Joseph Gabcik pretended to fix a streetlight. When Heydrich's Mercedes slowed down to start the turn, Gabcik took a concealed machine gun, pulled the trigger and aimed at Heydrich. Unfortunately, the weapon jammed and the driver sensing the attack accelerated. Meanwhile, Kubis threw a grenade that exploded under the rear fender. The car stopped. The two occupants jumped out and exchanged gunshots with Kubis, who used his automatic weapon. The driver was wounded in the thigh and collapsed. And then, Heydrich collapsed in turn. Metal shards from the grenade had penetrated into the lumbar region up to his spleen and perforated the diaphragm. After the operation, Heydrich's condition seemed to improve, but deteriorated gradually thereafter. He died on June 4, 1942.

Exploding in anger, Hitler sent the heads of the security service to Prague. Arthur Nebe, Heinrich Müller and Water Schellenberg questioned the witnesses to the attack, but no one had seen anything. Sixty thousand police officers were sent to Prague to search the houses from top to bottom. The investigation languished and the terrorists were nowhere to be found despite the ten million crowns offered to anyone who would denounce the culprits. Exasperated, Hitler ordered collective reprisals and dozens of members of the Czech intelligentsia were summarily executed daily. Cleansing operations were undertaken and five thousand towns were systematically searched. Seven hundred people were executed.

Dissatisfied with the outcome of the investigation, Hitler ordered more brutal retaliation measures. On the night of June 9, SS troops invaded Lidice, a small medieval village surrounded by fields of wheat, with about a hundred houses. The inhabitants were woken and made to gather outside the village while their houses and barns were burned down one by one. The women and children were taken to death camps, and the men were gathered at a farm that had been spared to serve for their execution. The one hundred seventy-three men of the village were shot in groups of ten and the next victims had to stand two steps in front of the bodies lying on the ground. Lidice was not rebuilt and remains the silent witness of modern barbarism.

The Czech commando members were tracked throughout the country and finally found refuge in the crypt of a church close to Prague. Frustrated because they were unable to track down the culprits, the nazi officials offered amnesty and a large amount of money to anyone who would allow them to find Heydrich's killers. One of the Czech resistance fighters, Karel Curda, left the group to inform the Nazis of the place where the commando was hiding in exchange for the reward and a change of identity. The Czech commando members hidden in the Church resisted the attack of eight hundred SS for eight hours and none of them fell alive into their hands. As for the informer, he was arrested and tried by the Czech government in 1945. He was executed two years later.

In early 1944, the price paid by the Czechs for the assassination of Heydrich was estimated at three hundred sixty thousand victims. Those events were made into two Czech movies in 1964 and 1975: *The Assassination* and *Operation: Daybreak.*

Chapter 10

The Nuremberg trials

When the Allied troops entered Germany and Poland, disbelief, dismay and horror struck the first witnesses of the vision of hell in the concentration camps. Dead bodies of children, old people, women and men were lying on the ground, many of them with sunken cheeks and sunken eyes. The Nuremberg trials, the largest trial of war criminals ever held, took place in a climate of painful emotions.

The German surrender was officially signed by General Alfred Jodl, at Reims on May 7, 1945, before the representative of General Dwight Eisenhower, since the latter had refused to negotiate directly with a Nazi. According to the instructions of Grand Admiral Karl Dönitz, the new head of the German government, Alfred Jodl, delayed the signing of the document of surrender to allow the German military to escape the Russian troops and surrender to the Americans or the British.

The creation of an international criminal law

The Allies did not wait the end of the war to put in place the legal structure required to judge the nazi war criminals. In the fall of 1941, representatives of several occupied countries gathered in London, answering the call of the international community made by the Polish and Czechoslovakian governments. On January 13, 1942, a Joint Declaration was signed at St. James' Palace in London, in which the signatories stated their determination to prosecute, search, judge and condemn the criminals, regardless of their origin, and ensure the enforcement of the sentences by an International Court. The signatories were Belgium, Czechoslovakia, Greece, Luxembourg, Holland, Norway, Poland, the United States, Great Britain, Russia, and a committee representing the free France.

It was agreed that the court would be sitting in Nuremberg. It was one of the few German cities to have a courthouse, a jail and relatively intact accommodation facilities. Ironically, it was also the ceremonial birthplace of the Nazi Party where its large annual gatherings were held. France was getting back at Germany for being forced to sign the surrender in the boxcar where Germany had signed the infamous Treaty of Versailles.

The establishment of an international tribunal to judge war criminals

At the time, a number of prominent people spoke against the idea of laying war crime charges.

General Montgomery said that it was the trial of the vanquished by the victors, who were as guilty of war crimes as the accused. The American writer Taylor Caldwell estimated that it was a despicable conduct on the part of civilized countries that bore their share of blood and crime. The brother of President Eisenhower, lawyer Edgar N. Eisenhower, estimated for his part that the Nuremberg trials were a black page in the history of the world. In 1976, H.K. Thompson and H. Strutz published a book, *Dönitz at Nuremberg: A Re-appraisal*, arguing that a soldier on duty cannot be a war criminal.

The trial raised at the time the problem of legal technicalities that the accused themselves formulated to their judges. Even before the hearings, defense lawyers argued that, contrary to prevailing practice, their clients were charged under an *ad hoc* retroactive law.

It seemed strange to many that Russia was part of the court when political leaders still in office had signed with Germany less than a decade ago a Treaty of non-aggression that included a partition of the Polish territory in the event that Germany would go to war with Poland. We might add that a government that exterminated more than twenty million of its own citizens a few years earlier has little credibility when judging a crime such as systematic extermination.

It is worth mentioning that the United States were also in a position difficult to justify, after having dropped two atomic bombs on civilians in Hiroshima and Nagasaki in 1945.

As for Great Britain, we may ask ourselves if the exclusion of the London bombing from the charges was an attempt to avoid the mention of the British bombardment directed to civilian populations, when those with phosphorus bombs in Dresden would have been unprecedented. Even today, the historic debate remains open on the actual need of this aggression, which was a first and hopefully a last. We may wonder whether such a decision would have been taken, had it not been for Pearl Harbor.

The Russians were the most difficult to convince. It is said that on November 29, 1943, on the evening of the Tehran conference, Stalin invited Roosevelt and Churchill to dinner. Stalin simply suggested the execution of fifty thousand senior officers in order to behead the German military power. He knew what he was talking about. Roosevelt replied with a smile that forty-nine thousand executions would be quite sufficient.

Upon the death of Roosevelt, Truman became president of the United States. He appointed Attorney General Robert H. Jackson to conduct the trials of the German war criminals. A few days before, Jackson had said that a trial cannot be conducted if the defendant is found guilty before the disclosure of formal evidence, and that world opinion would denounce a mockery of justice if the Court ratified a decision taken in advance.

On August 8, 1945, the four allied powers agreed on the rules of procedure for the conduct of the Nuremberg trials. We owe to the insistence of the United States this large-scale trial, which was far from having unanimous support. The Russians, for whom the law was somehow at the service of the political power, already felt guilty about the German war criminals and were in favor of an expeditious procedure that would allow for specifying the responsibility and sentencing of each accused. And Great Britain would have preferred by far a brief and simple procedure, believing that the problem of the German crimes was a political rather than a legal issue.

However, the United States felt more at ease in a trial examining in depth the circumstances of war crimes, since they had disassociated themselves from the terms of the Treaty of Versailles imposed on Germany, because they considered them to be abusive and provocative.

Finally, we can also note the strangeness of the decision to entrust the victors with the responsibility to judge the vanquished. No serious court would allow a judge to sit on the trial of the murderer of his own son. There is no doubt that the revelation of the concentration camp horrors brought to the court the support of the public opinion and legitimized its existence. In fact, many documents from the Nuremberg trials attest that the guilt or innocence of several accused was the result of haggling between Russia and the three other allied countries.

However, one of the accused, Albert Speer, recognized the need for the trial and said that there is a common responsibility for such horrible crimes, even in an authoritarian system.

The hunt for war criminals

For the Allies, the end of the war marked the beginning of the hunt for the nazi war criminals. They had prepared a list of the major criminals who should be tried before the Nuremberg Tribunal. Twenty-three German leaders were hunted down and Martin Bormann was the only one who was never found. He was long believed to have fled to South America, but there is compelling evidence that he never left Berlin and was shot in the back by the Russians.

There were twenty-four names on the list of wanted criminals. On the opening day of the main trial on November 20, 1945, twenty defendants took their seats. Martin Bormann was tried in absentia. Dr. Robert Ley, Reich minister of Labor, had committed suicide a month before the beginning of the trial. Ernst Kaltenbrunner suffered a stroke and showed up on the sixteenth day of the trial. As for Gustav Krupp von Bohlen, he was exempted from the trial due to his age, health condition and mental deterioration.

1. Hermann Göring

Reichsmarschall Hermann Göring, the second-highest-ranking nazi official, was without a doubt the most colorful and maybe the most popular character of the nazi regime. This Bavarian was an air force hero who distinguished himself by his prowess during World War I. After the war, he was attacked on the street by revolutionary Communists who ripped off the decorations from his uniform, something he never forgave them. Later, he lived in exile in the Scandinavian countries. In Sweden, he married a Swedish countess, Carine von Fock, who died of tuberculosis. To perpetuate her memory, he built a lavish residence called Carinhall. He joined the National Socialist movement in 1922 and was injured during the Beer Hall Putsch. After a medical treatment, he became addicted to narcotics for the rest of his life. He was one of the first to be elected to the Reichstag, of which he became president on August 30, 1932. We owe him the creation of the Gestapo that he will pass on to Himmler on his appointment as head of the Luftwaffe in 1935. He authorized the bombing of civilian targets in Great Britain during the war. Vain and boastful to a grotesque degree, he prized exotic clothes and works of art, bringing together the largest collection of paintings in Europe through confiscation and theft. He occupied positions of responsibility that he assumed with little success. He fell out of favor with Hitler after the defeat at Stalingrad. Ten days before Hitler's suicide, he spoke to him for the last time and left the bunker under the pretext of organizing the defense of what remained of Germany. In the following days, he withdrew from his safe the decree issued by Hitler in 1941, naming Göring his successor in the event of his death. He immediately sent a telegram to Berlin advising them that he was taking over from Hitler as head of the German nation, unless otherwise advised by the latter. Hitler became furious and Martin Bormann quickly signed the death warrant for his opponent. When Göring heard on the radio that a warrant had been issued against him, he drove his Mercedes to the American lines and surrendered to the Allied forces the day before Jodl signed the surrender of Germany.

2. Martin Bormann

Martin Bormann was the manager of a large estate before joining the Nazi Party. He assisted Rudolf Höss after the seizure of power in 1933 and, at the beginning of the war, he became responsible for the liaison between the party headed by Höss and the Führer. A skilled manipulator, he became increasingly necessary to the Führer and gradually assumed the role of Rudolf Höss. He had a special talent for making Hitler look good and transformed his wildest projects into well-structured orders ready to be signed. In April 1943, Hitler appointed him his private secretary. He soon assumed other responsibilities and quickly became for the party and state leaders alike the mandatory entry door to meet the Führer. He was arrogant, loathed, but feared. In 1944, Hitler gradually retired in a relative solitude and Bormann consolidated his power, becoming the strong man of the regime. When the Russians attacked the Reich Chancellery, Bormann had already disappeared. It was believed that he had fled to South America. However, according to the testimony of Max Amann, who was part of his group when he escaped from the bunker, he was shot in the back on the streets of Berlin. Amann claimed to have identified his body with certainty. The Allies insisted on keeping his name on the list of the major war criminals and he was tried in absentia.

3. Rudolf Höss

For Rudolf Höss, who was Hitler's secretary and his representative within the National Socialist Party, the war ended early. In order to avoid that Germany be caught between two fronts, he took on himself to bring a peace proposal to Great Britain a few days before the German invasion of Russia. Unbeknownst to Hitler, he borrowed a Messerschmitt on May 10, 1941. To avoid being shot in flight, he parachuted at an altitude of 20,000 feet and landed in Scotland, where he asked to meet with the Duke of Hamilton to present him with his peace offer. No one took him seriously and he was officially disavowed by the Führer in the following days. Registered as a prisoner of war, he was sent to Nuremberg on October 9, 1945 to be tried as a war criminal.

4. Ernst Kaltenbrunner

Austrian by birth, Ernst Kaltenbrunner was a physically imposing man. Six foot six, broad-shouldered, he had a thick square chin and a deep scar on his left cheek caused by an accident when he was drunk. Shaking his large hands was almost painful. He was cold, ruthless, fanatic and brutal. He succeeded Heydrich as director of the Reich Main Security Office after his assassination in Czechoslovakia. Less polished and ambitious than his predecessor, he was however of the same species, capable of the most horrible tasks. Hoping to keep away Himmler in whom he saw a powerful rival and taking advantage of the tasks that kept Himmler far from Hitler, Bormann used his power to bring Kaltenbrunner closer to Hitler, who eventually transmitted his orders directly to him, bypassing Himmler's chain of command. Kaltenbrunner, who was in a cottage in the Austrian Alps, was arrested without resistance by a patrol of American soldiers on May 15.

5. Joachim von Ribbentrop

Son of a German officer, Ribbentrop served with distinction during World War I. He entered the upper class when he married the daughter of a wealthy champagne merchant and later added the nobiliary particle *von* to his name. Vain and arrogant, he became part of Hitler's cabinet in 1933 because of his international contacts. Appointed minister of Foreign Affairs in 1938, he negotiated the Non-Aggression Pact between Russia and Germany in 1939. In 1945, Joachim von Ribbentrop's photograph was distributed by the Allies in Europe when his name was added to the list of most wanted war criminals. His wife, acquaintances and collaborators were questioned extensively. He was living a peaceful life in the suburbs of Hamburg when he was denounced by the son of a wine merchant who was aware of his presence. On the evening of June 14, 1945, a British officer knocked on the door of the address he had been given. As soon as the door opened, the officer quickly toured the house and found Ribbentrop in his pajamas in bed. He was arrested on the spot. Upon his arrival at the security office, he was examined by a doctor who discovered a poison in a tiny container hidden on his lower limbs.

6. Karl Dönitz

The new German government established its headquarters in Flensburg a few days after the death of Hitler. That is where Grand Admiral Karl Dönitz formed the first provisional cabinet. Dönitz enlisted in the German Imperial Navy in 1913 and was assigned to the submarine units in 1916. A friend of Göring, who convinced him to join the National Socialist Party, he commanded the submarine fleet at the beginning of the war and was appointed Commander in Chief of the German Navy in January 1943. Hitler chose him as his successor before ending his life. On May 23, 1945, British soldiers came to the headquarters of the new government and asked the officials to meet in the lounge. This is when Lowell W. Rooks, on behalf of General Eisenhower, announced the dissolution of the new government and gave the list of the German personalities who were under arrest for trial as war criminals. Karl Dönitz, Alfred Jodl, Wilhelm Keitel, Alfred Rosenberg and Albert Speer were immediately arrested.

7. Alfred Jodl

Born in Bavaria and a career officer, Jodl impressed his superiors with his talent for military planning and administration. He quickly won the confidence of Hitler and served as Reich minister of the Interior in 1935. On August 22, 1939, he was appointed Chief of Operation Staff of the High Command of the Armed Forces. He had much influence as strategic advisor to Hitler and remained one of the men that Dönitz trusted after the death of Hitler. He signed the surrender of Germany on May 7, 1945. He was arrested with Dönitz at the transitional government headquarters.

8. Wilhelm Keitel

This farmer's son was part of the German general staff during World War I, before becoming Chief of Operation Staff of the High Command of the Armed Forces (OKW) in 1938, directly under the authority of Hitler. He represented Hitler for the surrender of France, which was signed in the boxcar where Germany had been forced to sign the humiliating Treaty of Versailles twenty-two years earlier. Renowned for his slavish submission to Hitler, of whom he approved the most ridiculous plans, he was known as *Lakeitel*, from the word lackey. Hitler exercised his authority through Keitel, who signed the orders for the execution of the prisoners of war, which were contrary to the international laws.

9. Alfred Rosenberg

Born in Estonia and one of the pioneers of the National Socialist Party, he studied in Russia and earned a degree in architecture from the University of Moscow. Driven by anticommunist and antisemitic convictions, he was one of Hitler's thought leaders. He developed racist theories and published in 1930 *The Myth of the Twentieth Century,* a nebulous book on the superiority of the Nordic race that Hitler himself considered unpalatable. Official ideologue of the party and publisher of the *Völkischer Beobachter,* he had a limited influence on the party, due to the lack of consideration from his colleagues. Minister for the Occupied Eastern Territories between 1941 and 1945, he indulged in murder and looting activities. He was arrested on May 23, 1945 at the new government offices.

10. Albert Speer

One of the younger members of Hitler's inner circle, Speer was a gifted architect and a technocrat, before his rise due exclusively to his talent and undeniable skills. Fallen under Hitler's spell in 1931, he owed to his simple and reserved personality to remain in the inner circle of the Führer to the end of the war. He was the inspiration behind the extravaganza at the annual meeting of the party in Nuremberg and the architect of the new Reich Chancellery in Berlin. In February 1942, he was appointed Reich minister of Armaments and Munitions and, in September 1943, minister of Armaments and War Production. He performed admirably in this position, allowing Germany to support an amazing war effort. He was arrested in May 1945 in the small town of Glucksbourg, where he had established the industrial production services. He was one of the few to recognize his mistakes and those of Germany.

11. Erich Raeder

Grand Admiral Erich Raeder, predecessor of Dönitz and inactive since 1943, and Hans Fritzsche, deputy to Goebbels in the ministry of Propaganda, were prisoners of the Russians when they were registered on the list of war criminals for the Nuremberg Tribunal. Born in Wandsbek, Schleswig-Holstein, he enlisted in the Navy in 1894 and stood out on the basis of his military exploits during World War I. Appointed Rear Admiral in 1922, he contributed to secretly rearm Germany and Hitler appointed him Admiral of the German Navy in 1939. He did not share

Hitler's opinion about the role of the Navy and was uncomfortable with the demands of the Nazis. Hitler relieved him of his position of commander of the German fleet in January 1943. On June 23, he was arrested in Babelsberg by a Russian detachment and imprisoned in Moscow.

12. Hans Fritzsche

Born in 1900, Fritzsche was an ordinary soldier during World War I. At the age of twenty-three, he became a journalist who wrote articles and editorials, and he was a radio commentator, well-known for his popular radio program, Hans Fritzsche Speaks. In 1933, he joined the press section of the ministry of National Education and Propaganda, and he became cabinet director in 1943. He was one of the architects of the nazi propaganda. Arrested by the Russians, he joined Raeder in Moscow before being transferred to Nuremberg, where he was tried in place of the deceased Paul Joseph Goebbels.

13. Julius Streicher

This elementary school teacher, small, stocky and bald, fiercely anticommunist and antisemitic, had a strange destiny. He attracted crowds and eventually had enough followers to create an antisemitic political party after World War I. Hypnotized by a speech of Hitler in 1921, he joined the National Socialist Party in 1922, taking the members of his party with him. He worked on promoting hatred of the Jew, in particular in the *Der Stürmer* pornographic and slanderous weekly that he founded in 1923, a favorite of Hitler. Corrupt, sadistic, brutal, obscene and despised by the other nazi leaders, he kept quite curiously the support of Hitler and was Gauleiter of Franconia between 1929 and 1940. He was one of the few Nazis to be on a first-name basis by Hitler. He retired in 1940, but kept his job as publisher of his newspaper. He was arrested by the Allied forces in the Bavarian Alps while he was painting a canvas on the side of a hill. At the Nuremberg tribunal, he had the lowest IQ score when assessed.

14. Arthur Seyss-Inquart

Seyss-Inquart was born in Moravia in 1892 and for several years he lived in Vienna, Austria, where he was a prominent lawyer. He was interested in politics and admired Hitler, with whom he shared the desire to link Austria to Germany. He did not belong to the Austrian Nazi Party and acted as an intermediary in the negotiations that led to the annexation of Austria to Germany. Under pressure from the German nazi government, he was appointed Austrian minister of the Interior in February 1938 and became responsible for the Austrian police service. After the Anschluss, he was appointed governor of Austria. In May 1940, he became commissioner of the Reich to the Netherlands. He sent one hundred seventeen thousand Jews to death and five million Dutch to forced labor. Between 1939 and 1945, he was also minister without portfolio in Hitler's cabinet. Foolishly back home at the end of the hostilities, he was relaxing near the fireplace when he was arrested by a Canadian detachment.

15. Hans Frank

A lawyer by training, Frank was an educated man and a gifted pianist. He joined the Nazi Party in 1927 when he was defending at no cost the SA prosecuted for homicides or physical attacks. He became two years later the most important jurist of the party. After his election, Hitler appointed him Reich minister and commissioner for justice. In October 1939, he became responsible for the general government of Poland, a position that he held until the end of the war. Called the Butcher of Krakow, he tried to go unnoticed by donning a corporal's uniform in a prison camp. During the call, he fainted and was carried to the infirmary where two capsules of cyanide were discovered in his pocket. As a clue that he was an important figure, he was questioned by the French forces and he quickly confessed. He joined a group of other war criminals at the American detention center of Montdorf-les-Bains in Luxembourg before being brought to Nuremberg.

16. Baldur von Schirach

At the trial, Schirach was thirty-nine years of age and the youngest among the accused. Son of the director of the Court Theater in Weimar, he was seduced by a speech of Rosenberg in 1924 and joined the Nazis. In 1926, he moved to Munich, where he campaigned with the National Socialist German Students' League, of which he became the leader in 1929.

Hitler appreciated his enthusiasm and appointed him Reich Youth Party leader in 1931 and head of the Hitler Youth in 1933. After seven years in that position, he became Gauleiter of Vienna until the end of the war, when he decided to find a job as interpreter for the United States Army. Unable to bear his hiding, suffering from insomnia, loss of appetite and dizziness, he denounced himself to the Americans.

17. Hjalmar Schacht

Born in 1877, Schacht studied finance in the United States, Germany and France. He worked for the Dresdner Bank before entering the public service in 1923 as currency commissioner. He became president of the Reichsbank, but he resigned in 1930 due to a disagreement with the budgetary policy of the Brüning cabinet. In December, he met Göring, who aroused Schacht's interest in the nazi political program without the latter immediately adhering to the ideas advocated. But Schacht was a convinced nationalist humiliated by the Treaty of Versailles and he helped Hitler to take power in raising funds for his election. Minister of Economics under the nazi regime, authoritarian and stubborn, he quickly came into conflict with Göring. When the latter was appointed plenipotentiary for the Four Year Plan in October 1936, it became clear that the two men could not reconcile their differences. He resigned as minister of Economics in 1937 and was dismissed as president of the Reichsbank in 1938, after having proposed a reduction of military spending to pay the debts of the state. Walther Funk inherited the two positions. Schacht remained minister without portfolio. However, he was hostile to Hitler. He was arrested by the Gestapo in July 1944 and sent to a concentration camp until the end of the war. He had been in Ravensbrück, Flossenbürg and Dachau before being arrested by the British troops.

18. Robert Ley

A chemist by training and an aviator during the war, he became a member of the National Socialist Party in 1925. After having dismantled the German trade unions, he founded the German Labor Front in 1933. He established difficult working conditions for the Germans. He was a heavy drinker. Despite the precautions taken by the Allies, he hanged himself with his briefcase in the Nuremberg prison on October 25, 1945.

19. Wilhelm Frick

Born in 1877, a lawyer by training, Frick was an official in the Munich police administration in 1920. After joining the ranks of the National Socialist Party, he was alongside Hitler at the failed Munich putsch. He was an accomplished bureaucrat, stiff, unimaginative, taciturn, but his experience as an administrator was appreciated by Hitler during his rise to power. In 1933, he was appointed Reich minister of the Interior where he drafted and signed laws and decrees enacted by his government. In 1943, he became *Reichsprotektor* of Bohemia and Moravia.

20. Walther Funk

Born in 1890 into a merchant family of Königsberg, he studied political science, literature and music at the University of Berlin. In 1922, he became editor of a major German financial magazine in Berlin, a position that earned him a certain prestige in financial circles. In 1931, he gave up this position and got a job as an economic and political analyst. The same year, he joined the Nazi Party. Thanks to a substantial business contact list, he remained an important intermediary between the German industrialists and Hitler. When the Nazis took power, Funk was appointed chief press officer of the Third Reich attached to the Chancellery. Six weeks later, Hitler created the ministry of Propaganda directed by Goebbels, where Funk performed administrative functions until 1939. Appointed minister of Economics and president of the Reichsbank between 1939 and 1945, he kept all the assets confiscated from the Jews in the concentration camps. He was arrested by the French forces. Known as a happy-go-lucky person during the years of nazism, he collapsed completely during the trial. He appeared as a wreck and inspired some degree of leniency to the judges.

21. Fritz Saukel

Born in 1887, Saukel was a small man who followed a strange path to find himself among the twenty-four accused of Nuremberg. He joined the merchant marine when he was fifteen and worked as a laborer in a factory after World War I. He joined the Nazi Party in 1925 and was appointed Gauleiter of Thuringia in 1927. In 1933, he became Reich Regent of Thuringia and, despite his limited education, made hundreds of speeches and signed articles and two books. In 1941, the Wehrmacht had operated significant punctures in the workforce and Saukel was appointed Reich defense commissioner for labor deployment due to his experience in that field.

22. Konstantin von Neurath

Born in 1873, von Neurath was from the German aristocracy whose ancestors had held important political positions or been officers of the Imperial Army. He occupied various diplomatic posts. After the Nazis came to power, he was appointed minister of Foreign Affairs and replaced by Ribbentrop in February 1938. Not wanting to spread the word that von Neurath had resigned due to differences of political opinion, Hitler named him president of the Secret Cabinet Council, a body that existed only on paper. In 1939, von Neurath was appointed Protector of the Reich of Bohemia and Moravia, probably more out of ambition than political conviction, and was used as a puppet applying the directives of Berlin. In 1943, he refused to cooperate with Heydrich and resigned. He was arrested by the French troops at the end of the war.

23. Gustav Krupp von Bohlen und Halbach

Born in The Hague in 1870, he became a career diplomat in 1889. He married the Krupp heiress and added the Krupp name to his own. He became chairman of the board of the company during World War I and his firm thrived during the war. During World War II, he was one of the main armament suppliers to the nazi regime, and he made extensive use of forced labor. Due to his old age and ill health, he was tried in absentia.

24. Franz von Papen

The elder of the defendants, von Papen was a German nobleman. When asked for a brief overview of his life, he began by declaring that he was born on land owned by his family for nine hundred years. A trained officer, he was appointed military attaché to the German ambassador in Washington in 1913. A clumsy diplomat, he was expelled from the United States two years later. After World War I, he left the army, acquired an estate in Westphalia, entered politics, and eventually joined the Center Party. He was elected to the parliament of Prussia. Educated and charming, he developed a large network of politic and military contacts, but lacked political clout and was not taken seriously. His appointment as chancellor of Germany in 1932 was short-lived. The anti-nazi speech that he gave at the University of Marburg definitively contributed to his political downfall. He was appointed ambassador to Austria in 1936 and ambassador to Turkey in 1939, a role that he performed remarkably well until the end of the war. In the last days of the Reich, he lived in a temporary residence in Gemünden, where the Gestapo had an oversight on his comings and goings. On March 15 at 3:00 am, he was awakened by a German army officer asking him to follow him. He was transferred to Stockhausen in Westphalia, where he lived in a wooded area with his daughter. On April 9, a United States detachment invested the village and he was immediately arrested, despite his protests about his old age and the fact that he did not belong to the army.

The stage of the trials

On November 20, 1945, at 10:00 am, the war crimes trial began. Two hundred journalists took place in red chairs arranged in tiers and attended the debates translated simultaneously in English, French, Russian and German. The room was monotonous, covered with dark woodwork and sober curtains blocking daylight.

At the back of the room, to the left, a dozen helmeted and gloved white policemen, baton in hand, stood behind two rows of ten defendants dressed in civilian clothes. Four of them were missing: Robert Ley had committed suicide, Bormann was never found, Kaltenbrunner had suffered a stroke and would attend only the sixteenth day, and Krupp von Bolne had been exempted due to his physical and mental health.

Across the floor, to the right, facing the accused, the four flags of the allied powers were a reminder that this was an international tribunal.

Sitting in front of the flags, the president of the tribunal, British judge Sir Geoffrey Lawrence, and the four judges representing the allied powers: Francis Biddle, attorney general of the United States; Sir Norman Birkett, judge of the High Court of Great Britain; Henri Donnedieu de Vabres, international criminal law specialist and professor at the Sorbonne of Paris, France; and Soviet judge Major General Ion Timofeevich Nikitchenko.

Separated from the court by the clerks and stenographers, the defendants' lawyers were sitting in the middle of the courtroom. The prosecutors occupied almost the full width of the room between the spectators and the tribunal.

Date of beginning	November 20, 1945
Date of closing	October 1, 1946
Number of defendants	24
Number of sessions	403
Number of witnesses (prosecution)	33
Number of witnesses (defense)	61
Number of volumes on the trials	24
Number of volumes of documents produced	17
Number of additional trials at Nuremberg	12

Table 1 – Statistical data from the Nuremberg trials

The indictment

On November 20, 1945, at 10: 00 am, the trial opened with the prosecutor reading out the four main charges:

1. Crimes against humanity
2. Crimes against peace
3. War crimes
4. Participation in a conspiracy to commit any of these crimes

Crimes against humanity included, namely, murder, extermination, enslavement, deportation and other inhuman acts committed against any civilian population, before or during the war; or persecutions on political, racial or religious grounds in the execution of or in connection with any crime within the jurisdiction of the Tribunal, whether or not in violation of the domestic law of the country where perpetrated. In short, this crime referred to any act of persecution resulting or not in death, against individuals or groups, on the basis of their race, nationality, religion or political opinions.

Crimes against peace were related to the participation in a war of aggression and were defined as being, namely, planning, preparation, initiation, or waging a war of aggression, or a war in violation of international treaties, agreements or assurances, or participation in a common plan or conspiracy for the accomplishment of any of the foregoing.

War crimes were violations of the laws or customs of war. There was a list of thirty-two offenses that included a variety of activities such as torture of civilians, internment in atrocious conditions, usurpation of the sovereignty of occupied countries, forced conscription of their populations in the German army, plunder of public and private property, wanton destruction of cities, towns or villages or devastation not justified by military necessity, ill-treatment of prisoners of war and so forth.

Conspiracy was an offense under the common law of Great Britain and Wales, which stated that the voluntary and conscious preparation to commit a crime was punishable.

Beyond individual responsibilities, the tribunal also recognized that belonging to an organization deemed to be criminal, namely, the Reich Cabinet, the high command of the German armed forces, the Stormtroopers (SA), the Secret State Police (Gestapo), the Security Service (SD), the Elite Guard (SS) and the leaders of the Nazi Party was punishable.

Finally, the indictment rejected outright traditional immunity conferred on the representatives of a state as well as the individual justification of those crimes under the pretext of the obligation of obedience to superior orders.

The conduct of Tribunal hearings

The trial extended through four hundred two sessions and lasted almost ten months. The tribunal heard thirty-three witnesses for the prosecution and sixty-one for the defense. Nineteen defendants were also heard. The transcripts of the proceedings were published in twenty-four volumes.

The Nuremberg trials left little room for spontaneity and lyricism. The texts were written in advance with determined slowness, set by the translators who slowed down the speakers with yellow lights and stopped them with red lights. In the first days, while the indictments were read, several defendants were sleeping or snoring on their bench. Between the end of November 1945 and the middle of March 1946, the prosecutors read the indictments with an inevitable monotony. However, this procedure trivialized the extent of the crimes committed by the nazi government in drowning them in a list of endless and repetitive criminal actions.

The defendants' replies

According to G. M. Gilbert, the accused had different reactions. Obedience to orders and ignorance of the extent of the brutality and sadism demonstrated by the nazi leaders summarize the justification presented by the men who were people of authority during the twelve years of the dictatorship.

The main defense argument: Obedience to orders

During the trials, SS judge Konrad Morgen, who had been charged by Himmler to investigate and prosecute corruption in the concentration camp system, was cited as a witness for the prosecution. He recounted in detail the circumstances in which the Jews were exterminated in the crematoria.

Unquestionably, the trial played an important role in the management of the emotions of horror and pain that the democratic countries felt when the reality of the concentration camps came in broad daylight. Deny, that could have been used before, was totally inoperative when objective evidence was produced. Without a doubt, the designation of culprits in the months that followed helped to locate and delineate the evil, whereas their execution helped purify the collective unconscious of those nations.

Hermann Göring	The victor will always be the judge and the vanquished the accused.
Wilhelm Keitel	I obeyed orders.
Ernst Kaltenbrunner	I obeyed orders.
Franz von Papen	I had no knowledge of those horrendous crimes.
Von Neurath	I was not aware of anything.
Fritz Saukel	I did not know.
J. von Ribbentrop	The defendants are not the real culprits.
Alfred Jodl	I regret the mixture of justified accusations and political propaganda
Rudolf Höss	I do not remember anything.
Baldur von Schirach	The main problem was the racial policy.
Hans Fritzsche	It is the most terrible indictment of all times.
Albert Speer	This trial is necessary. There is a common responsibility for such horrible crimes in an authoritarian system.
Hans Frank	This is God's judgment meant to end the suffering that people endured under Hitler.
Erich Raeder	I have no comment.
Julius Streicher	This trial is a triumph for world Jewry. I want to be defended by an antisemitic lawyer.

Table 2 – The defendants' replies

At the Nuremberg trials, the SS were considered a criminal organization. The representative of the United States Attorney, commander Warren F. Farr, described the SS as a unified organization in which some functions were performed by specific services, although no one was involved in all those activities. But all those services were necessary for the whole range of activities to function.

The Russians have a problem

The Russians led the debate on February 8, 1946. Rudolf Höss' lawyer, Dr. Seidl, tried to bring the tribunal on the minefield of the German-Soviet non-aggression pact that resulted from talks in Moscow between August 15 and 21, 1939 with a German delegation led by Ribbentrop. This protocol kept secret and seized in Berlin by the Russians determined the partition of Poland between Russia and Germany after the invasion of the troops of the Third Reich. Even without the original document, Dr. Gaus, head of the Foreign Affairs Legal Department, attempted to reconstruct the protocol from memory. Finally, a copy of the original certificate was given to Dr. Seidl by an anonymous source. The Russian prosecutors, caught off guard, made constant obstruction to the use of the document as a piece of evidence. The Court gave them satisfaction. The president of the tribunal rejected the document on the ground that it was not the original document and that it should have been filed in advance for the prosecutors.

Subsequently, another defense lawyer questioned Margarete Blank, personal secretary to Ribbentrop, about the agreement. Soviet prosecutor Rudenko objected again, arguing that the Court could not make reference to a so-called treaty, unless it was part of the documents accepted by the tribunal. The Court granted Mrs. Blank the right to testify and admitted at least that such an agreement existed. The Soviet prosecutor was no longer able to deny the existence of the protocol. However, he attempted to deny the relevance of the document for the procedure and refused its admissibility as evidence. A legal embarrassment resulted from this evidence that the defense insisted on filing.

After the German attack on Poland, Russia deported two million Poles to the gulags of Siberia and Kazakhstan, and the Gestapo imprisoned two million Jews in the ghettos pending the development of the extermination technology. The journalists covering the trial revealed to the world the sordid dealings between Germany and Russia.

The defense of the accused

Almost all of the accused pleaded not guilty to the charges laid and justified their actions by their obedience to orders. Two main arguments were sustained by the accused: the ignorance of the facts and the duty of obedience. The first argument was mostly the excuse of the leaders while the second was that of the military.

Questioned by prosecutor Sir David Maxwell-Fyfe, Hermann Göring denied any knowledge of the extermination of millions of Jews murdered in concentration camps. He said that he knew nothing about what took place and what methods were used in the concentration camps later. Göring argued that the Final Solution for him was the emigration of Jews outside Germany and the occupied territories. Conducting a direct examination, the prosecutor tried to get Göring to admit that Hitler knew what was happening in the concentration camps. The accused replied that the Führer was not informed of the details. Sir David Maxwell-Fyfe countered that he was not talking about the details, but the murder of four to five million people. Göring still maintained that Hitler did not know the numbers.

As for the military, they were four: Field Marshal Wilhelm Keitel, General Alfred Jodl, and Admirals Erich Raeder and Karl Dönitz. At the Nuremberg trials, almost all the defendants repeated *"Befehl ist Befehl!"* "An order is an order!" That was true for the army and the SS questioned by the prosecutor about the executions by the *Einsatzgruppen*. SS General Otto Ohlendorf, head of the D Group in Ukraine, admitted having had reservations about carrying out the orders. However, they were given by a higher authority and had a legal dimension due to the oath of loyalty and obedience to those who gave the orders.

The Nuremberg trials: The verdicts

In his speech delivered on December 11, 1945, Sir Hartley Shawcross summed up what was to become the conclusion of the tribunal. He first pointed out that the criminal law does not recognize as admissible the excuse that a crime was perpetrated on the order of an officer. The defendants were not in a different condition because the alleged acts were on a national level. No criminal act becomes legal when perpetrated out of political loyalty or military obedience. Even an ordinary soldier may refuse to execute an order perceived as an illegal activity. But the defendants were not ordinary soldiers. They were leaders who chose to violate all the conventions regulating the relations between nations and the international law, and brought death on a scale never achieved so far on the basis of racial superiority.

A conviction or sentence required three votes out of four. The Soviet judge, General Nikitchenko, wanted to condemn all the defendants to death. Negotiations and compromises between the judges became necessary.

On October 1, 1946, the accused paraded one by one before the Court. Among the twenty-two accused, twelve were sentenced to death and hanged, seven to prison terms and three were acquitted. After the sentencing, the judges left the tribunal for the last time.

Two convicts escaped the tribunal: Göring committed suicide a few hours before he was scheduled to be hanged and Bormann was never found. Ironically, the executioner John Woods died accidentally four years later, when attempting to repair an engineer lighting set.

Name	Birth	Category	Verdict	Sentence
1. Hermann Göring	1893	Minister	Guilty	Death (suicide)
2. Martin Bormann	1900	Leader	Guilty	Death
3. Rudolf Höss	1894	Minister	Guilty	Life in prison
4. Ernst Kaltenbrunner	1903	Police	Guilty	Death
5. Joachim von Ribbentrop	1893	Diplomat	Guilty	Death
6. Karl Dönitz	1891	Military	Guilty	Prison: 10 years
7. Alfred Jodl	1890	Military	Guilty	Death
8. Wilhelm Keitel	1882	Military	Guilty	Death
9. Albert Speer	1905	Leader	Guilty	Prison: 20 years
10. Alfred Rosenberg	1893	Publisher	Guilty	Death
11. Erich Raeder	1876	Military	Guilty	Life in prison
12. Hans Fritzsche	1900	Journalist	Not guilty	Acquitted
13. Julius Streicher	1885	Publisher	Guilty	Death
14. Arthur Seyss-Inquart	1892	Leader	Guilty	Death
15. Hans Frank	1900	Leader	Guilty	Death
16. Baldur von Schirach	1907	Leader	Guilty	Prison: 20 years
17. Hjalmar Schacht	1877	Minister	Not guilty	Acquitted
18. Robert Ley	1890	Minister	——	Suicide
19. Wilhelm Frick	1877	Minister	Guilty	Death
20. Walther Funk	1890	Minister	Guilty	Life in prison
21. Fritz von Saukel	1894	Minister	Guilty	Death
22. Konstantin von Neurath	1873	Minister	Guilty	Prison: 15 years
23. Franz von Papen	1872	Diplomat	Not guilty	Acquitted
24. Gustav Krupp von Bohlen	1870	Industrialist	——	——

Table 3 – The verdicts of the Nuremberg trials

265

The seven convicted criminals sentenced to terms of imprisonment were transferred to the Spandau prison in Berlin.

Name	Date of release	Date of death
Rudolf Höss	August 7, 1987	August 17, 1987
Karl Dönitz	September 30, 1956	December 24, 1980
Albert Speer	September 30, 1966	September 1, 1981
Erich Raeder	September 26, 1955	November 6, 1960
Baldur von Schirach	September 30, 1966	August 8, 1974
Walther Funk	May 16, 1957	May 31, 1960
Konstantin von Neurath	November 6, 1954	August 14, 1956

Table 4 – The terms of imprisonment

As for the three acquitted defendants, they were sued pursuant to a denazification order by the new German authorities and sentenced to eight years in a labor camp. They all obtained a mitigation of their sentences.

What have we learned from Nuremberg?

Despite the procedural difficulties of the trial and the awkward position of the Allies as judges and juries, especially Russia, this very long trial left to mankind a phenomenal amount of documentation constituting the most detailed story of all the horrors and atrocities that man is capable of. From Stalin to Pol Pot, no war crime has been more scrutinized. For that reason, the trial was justified.

Documents reviewed	100,000
Documents filed (exhibits)	2,000
Photographs reviewed	25,000
Photographs filed (exhibits)	1,800
Films:	100,000 feet
Official court records	17,000 pages
Text of the judgment	50,000 words

Table 5 – Documentation of the Nuremberg trials

Edmund A. Walsh noted that the documents produced during the Nuremberg trials are an irreplaceable testimony demonstrating an abuse of power. He wanted the memory of crimes against peace and humanity to become an integral part of the thinking, education and international moral. This story issues a stern warning about the real dangers of intolerance, hate propaganda, institutionalized racism and dictatorship. It reminds us that democracy remains the least imperfect of government modes.

It may also leave an insoluble ambivalence among many Germans for whom Hitler was at the same time a source of great pride regained and indescribable shame. They were torn between their admiration for the Führer, who crafted the socioeconomic progress that other European nations envied, and their repugnance for the monster who orchestrated without a shadow of remorse the murder of millions of innocent men, women and children. The fact that the liberation of Germany was the result of an external rather than inner intervention increased the feeling of guilt of the German people.

As for the Jews who were the selected target of an intense racism never seen before, the trial was a clear denunciation, however insufficient, to start a full grief process.

A repetition generates a sense of déjà vu and déjà vu triggers boredom. The horror stories patiently gathered by the prosecutors ended up creating tolerance, some sort of moral numbness that was called the evil of the Nuremberg laws.

This trial was one cog in a gigantic war and extermination machine that brought Germany to its knees over a period of twelve years and whose main components, Hitler, Himmler and Goebbels, had already been eliminated. It left the impression of an unfinished business that also resulted in strong criticism from the press in the aftermath of the acquittal of three defendants. While the Nuremberg Tribunal was not perfect, it enabled Germany and other countries involved in judicial rituals to begin the healing process in channeling their feelings of revenge through rational procedures that neutralize violence created by violence.

Chapter 11

A portrait of Hitler

Hitler is probably the most fascinating personage in modern history.

There is something unusual and unimaginable in a man's life, whose road map virtually guaranteed that he would be a failure until his entry into politics, when he became the dominant figure of the twentieth century. The probability that an itinerant artist would exercise a power with global reverberations was simply nonexistent.

Despite the tremendous number of biographies of Hitler published in all languages, it remains difficult to capture the essence of the man behind the head of state.

Part of the problem lies in his personality rich in contrasts hard to reconcile: he was a messy student, but a determined soldier; a shy person, but an aggressive speaker; a Bohemian artist, but a methodical organizer; a social parasite, but an influential politician; an undisciplined statesman, but a dictator who imposed a strict order. Unemployed until the age of twenty-five, fifteen years after his entry into politics, he gained supreme power in a country that was not even his, negotiated with world leaders, transformed a democracy into a dictatorship, drew eighty million Germans into a global conflict, replaced with his own the moral conscience of a nation that became an accomplice in his project and approved without hesitation the most horrific crimes perpetrated by humankind.

Hitler's personality remains mysterious. He made small talk, but rarely talked about himself. We get to know people when we listen to them, but we know them better through their emotional reactions. Hitler seldom showed emotions.

An additional difficulty in analyzing the character lies in the fact that he was essentially a cheater. He explicitly used lies as a power tool and it became difficult to distinguish between reality and deceit. He had intense bouts of anger when he was frustrated. However, historians are still debating two interpretations: was it really hysteria or a simple staging to mystify his interlocutors? For Hitler, the end justified the means.

Finally, this approach is complicated by his untimely death. Thousands of Nazis were held accountable for their actions before an international tribunal. In committing suicide, and due to the fact that his body was burnt, the main architect of the worst crime against humanity abruptly closed a chapter of history, depriving the world of a testimony that could have clarified a large number of unanswered questions.

Hitler's domination tools

Hitler carried in a latent state several attributes that were only waiting for favorable circumstances to surface. He did not miss his appointment with history. Table 1 lists the ingredients that largely explain the extreme power that he held and his supremacy over the people who surrounded him. It is worth noting that during the Nuremberg trials, none of the defendants blamed Hitler for the atrocities committed by the Nazis.

An irresistible magnetism
An undeniable speaker talent
A prodigious memory
A fanatical determination
A shameless opportunism
A golden chance in risky situations

Table 1 – The ingredients of Hitler's power

1. An irresistible magnetism

With the exception of Caesar and Hitler, few people generated so much enthusiasm that their name was associated with a greeting. From 1926 onward, the Hitler salute was mandatory in the Nazi Party. This decision reflected more a marketing operation than a popular consensus since the number of militants did not reach one hundred thousand at the time. But this mark of distinction gave Hitler a mythical prestige.

Obviously, the National Socialist Party needed Hitler more than Hitler needed the party. In 1922, the cult of Hitler's personality became apparent in the introductions before his speeches. He was presented as the hero of the German nation, the leader that the Germans were looking for, the long-awaited Messiah. After the failed putsch of November 1923, the theme of the hero who gives himself to the nation was exploited, his book *Mein Kampf* was advertised and he was surrounded by bodyguards like an important official figure.

The most striking element that emerged from Hitler's personality was his amazing magnetism that many called hypnotic. After the death of Hitler, his secretary Gertrud Traudl Junge was astonished by the radical change of atmosphere in the bunker. In the moments that followed, the people there began to smoke, drink alcohol and talk aloud. His death was for many the end of a collective hypnosis. Suddenly, they were discovering the light. They had a crazy desire to live, to be themselves, to find again a normal human condition. They were no longer interested in Hitler. In fact, they even felt a violent hostility toward him.

His magnetism did not come only from his ideological convictions. Prompted by his students, Albert Speer attended a speech by Hitler in 1930. He was instantly deeply moved almost physically by the delirious applause that regularly punctuated the end of each sentence. In Hitler's speech he found new ideals, a new understanding and new societal projects. A few days later, in January 1931, he became member 474,481 of the National Socialist Party. Rereading the speeches of Hitler in his prison after his conviction at the Nuremberg trials, Albert Speer noted with bitterness that the text that had raised his enthusiasm before was now lacking vision as well as common sense.

His magnetism even touched the non-Germans. In the summer of

1936, Charles Hamilton was listening to the radio with a Jewish friend fluent in German. Hitler gave an antisemitic speech with the intonations of anger and strength that characterized his style. At the end of the speech, she squeezed the arm of Hamilton and muttered horrified that he had almost made her hate the Jews.

Several senior nazi leaders, such as Hans Frank, Alfred Rosenberg, Paul Joseph Goebbels, Baldur von Schirach and Rudolf Höss, put the past behind them and joined their destiny to that of Hitler from their first encounter with him. Later, Goebbels wrote in his diary "Adolf Hitler, I love you", and he became one of his most unconditional supporters. Goebbels and his wife Magda poisoned their six children before killing themselves the day after the suicide of the Führer. Student at the University of Munich, Höss wrote in his thesis that Hitler embodied a personality of his own, able to resolve the major issues of the day in a bloodbath, even killing his best friends to achieve his objectives. Baldur von Schirach listened to a speech by Hitler in 1925 for the first time and immediately joined the party, convinced that Hitler was the savior of Germany.

During the trial following the failed Munich putsch, the judges seemed seduced by Hitler. They gave him a public speaking platform the he used brilliantly to position himself as the champion of German nationalism across the country. Even in the Landsberg prison, he rallied the support staff to the National Socialist Party, including the prison director and his wife.

In the spring of 1932, Hitler was invited to a dinner at the home of Joachim von Ribbentrop and made a lasting impression on his host. At the Nuremberg trials, Ribbentrop mentioned having been struck by his blue eyes, his way of expressing himself and the character of his ideas. He was convinced that if anyone could save Germany, it was him. Ribbentrop's wife, Annelies, who had a strong personality, embraced his cause from day one. When the psychiatrist Douglas Kelley and the psychologist Gustave Gilbert visited him in prison during the Nuremberg trials, Ribbentrop said that even with all he knew, if Hitler came to him in his cell and said "Do this", he would do it.

In a recent interview, actress and director Lina Riefenstahl, who produced films about the Nazi Party, made a clear distinction between the politician and the man she met privately, describing him as modest, discreet and even reserved. She was astonished that this man was the same who was screaming and gesticulating before a crowd in a trance. She claimed that he exuded a sense of power and determination related to the fact that he had the unwavering conviction of what was good, what was not and what was needed to carry out his mission.

Hermann Göring heard Hitler for the first time in October 1922. He later explained that he was seduced by the clear and specific objectives of the speaker. He felt that the words spoken by Hitler came from his own heart.

Whatever the ingredients of this mysterious magnetism were, they allowed Hitler to gather twenty staunch collaborators, entirely subject to his authority, who became his power conveyors on the members of the party at first and on Germany after 1933. Each nazi leader collaborated within his own sphere of competence to promote, with ruthless determination and total loyalty, the cult of personality of Hitler and the nationalist objectives proposed by the Führer. Without the support of his troops brilliantly led by Ernst Röhm, the National Socialist Party would have remained a marginal organization. Without the genius of Goebbels, who organized a massive propaganda until the end of the war, it would have been very difficult for Hitler to access a mythological status. Without the police structure invented by Göring, the political opposition would have been much stronger. Without the coldly operational and ruthless mind of Heinrich Himmler, the large-scale extermination program would have been less effective. Without the remarkable sense of organization of Albert Speer, the war effort would have collapsed long before 1945. All those men, united around their leader, embracing his doctrine, his objectives and sharing his determination, had a powerful effect on the German nation.

2. An undeniable speaker talent

His talent was not based on his rude tone of voice, but on the enthusiasm that he communicated to his audience with a scholarly dose of pauses and oratorical flights, punctuated with gestures whose effect was calculated. Kurt Lüdecke was emissary to Hitler before his seizure of power. He said that he was blown away by the conviction conveyed by Hitler to the extent that he completely lost his critical faculty and became a member of the National Socialist Party. He later distanced himself from the Nazis. He was arrested by the Gestapo on May 9, 1933 and sent to a concentration camp.

Hitler was not addressing the rational side of the crowd that listened to his speech. He challenged with conviction the emotional vulnerability of the audience, using words that put a face on their panic and frustration. He finished his speech by saying with certainty and in a triumphant tone that a happy ending was awaiting the German nation.

Political assemblies were addressed with extreme care to impress the participants and increase the emotions in a crowd. A journalist, was attending a political assembly in Cologne just before the election held on November 6, 1932. The assembly was scheduled to begin around 8:30 and the doors to the Messehallen were opened around 7:00. When the journalist arrived at 7:10, five or six thousand participants were around the podium, in an enormous room where the walls were plated with nazi flags, the black swastika standing out on a white circle. The walls were covered with slogans to capture popular imagination: Germans, join Hitler, death to marxism, long live Germany; Hitler for freedom, work and food. While the excited crowd awaited the arrival of the Führer, musicians played military bands awakening precious memories in the older participants. Young boys walked around in the crowd to sell photographs or souvenirs of Hitler. The security service, managed by the SA, was friendly. After a wait of two hours and a half, the Führer finally showed up preceded by flags and framed by a double row of SA, the crowd chanting Heil Hitler. Hitler calmly walked up to the podium, stared at the crowd, raised his right hand and began to speak. During forty-five minutes, the crowd listened religiously to the Führer in an absolute silence. He spoke in a voice sometimes quiet and easy to understand, sometimes screaming in a hoarse voice, frantically waving his arms and his hands to emphasize important points. He spoke little about the program, but brilliantly refuted the attacks of those who blamed him for not having accepted the vice-chancellorship a few months earlier.

At the end of the speech, thousands of hands waved frantically in the air while the participants sang vibrant songs to the glory of Germany and the memory of the party heroes who gave their lives for the nation. Impressed by the spectacular staging and bewitched by the magic words of Hitler, thousands of Germans returned home that evening with the conviction of having finally discovered the man who could restore Germany to power and greatness.

3. A prodigious memory

Hitler is a perfect example of the power conferred by knowledge. His innate ability to communicate was effectively supported by a prodigious memory, allowing him to sprinkle his speeches with quotes, dates, and numerical data that gave a lot of strength to his theses and often sowed confusion amongst his opponents. In political assemblies as well as in meetings around a table with his generals, his phenomenal memory gave Hitler a significant advantage over his interlocutors. Since he was correcting the statements of stakeholders in political assemblies, those who did not share his opinion looked bad, and he projected the image of a leader who proposed sound political options based on a thorough knowledge of the situation. His knowledge of military armament specifications, whether tanks, aircraft or naval vessels, gave him superiority over several generals.

He also had a natural knowledge of mass psychology, which made him a formidable manipulator. When he joined the NSDAP in 1921, he was about to discover his talent for organization, which jumpstarted the party, and his political flair, which enabled him to navigate successfully until his accession to power.

In an era of social and economic instability, it was comforting for the average German to find a leader who knew exactly what path to follow to get Germany out of that slump.

4. A fanatical determination

Hitler was convinced to be the holder of a divine mission. The promotion of a superior race to achieve the greater good of humanity appeared to be the only absolute criterion of good and evil. The achievement of this objective justified the use of all necessary means and tolerated no compromise. From this perspective, the objectives reciprocated the most basic humanitarian rights recognized in human rights charters. Compassion and pity should in no way determine decision-making choices, and suffering and human lives sacrificing were no match.

5. A shameless opportunism

Political opportunism refers to the attitude of one who, in politics, does not have much use of principles and takes advantage of the circumstances. Hitler was a calculating politician who routinely ignored the principles to which most of the other heads of state committed to. A treaty is an agreement in good faith between two countries seeking mutual benefits. For Hitler, good faith was the tool of the weak. A treaty signed by him was essentially a manipulation tool allowing him to take advantage of a situation. As soon as the treaty became cumbersome, he denied his signature. In establishing his own rules without the knowledge of his interlocutor, Hitler could not lose the game of international relations. In a very calculated way, he knew how to take advantage of the weaknesses of the countries with which he dealt.

The cynicism that Hitler demonstrated while he was in power considerably misled Europe, which aspired to peace and asked for nothing more than to believe the promises of the Führer.

Examples of blatant lies and half-truths abound in the statements of Hitler. It is a hundred times easier to quote his lies than to find a single honest, sincere and firm statement.

On September 1, 1939, in a speech to the Reichstag, Hitler denounced the oppression suffered by the Germans in the Danzig Corridor, with the obvious aim of justifying a German attack. Ignoring the Jewish and Communist repression in his own country, Hitler said quite seriously that the minorities living in Germany were not persecuted or deprived of their rights.

In the same speech, Hitler made a solemn declaration in which he formally denied having expansionist intentions. With consummate cynicism, he assured that the border between Germany and France was final. He even said that he had no ambitions for the future. And he guaranteed solemnly and with sincerity that Germany would respect the neutrality of its borders.

On May 10, 1940, nine months after this statement, Hitler aligned about one hundred divisions and three thousand tanks on the western border of Germany. He occupied Paris one month later.

On August 23, 1939, a short Non-aggression Treaty between Germany and Russia was signed in Moscow by Ribbentrop and Molotov. The first of seven articles stated that the parties to the treaty were to refrain from any aggressive action or act of violence on each other, either individually or jointly with other powers.

On June 22, 1941, twenty-two months after the signature of the treaty, three million German soldiers violated the Russian border and began the conquest of Russia. That treaty gave Hitler the respite he needed to invade Great Britain, but Russia was next in his plans of military conquest.

6. A golden chance in risky situations

Quite incredibly, luck played a significant role in his political career. He miraculously escaped many attacks as a result of delays or unexpected changes in his schedule. His luck not only saved his life several times, but it also fed his conviction that he was the carrier of a divine mission.

He was lucky again in the first military operations, when he decided to go forward despite the disagreement of his generals who felt that the army was ill-prepared to ensure a victory. The success of the blitzkriegs, combined with the fact that there was no loss of German lives, made the German general staff look bad and convinced a significant part of the population that the Führer was the man who could restore the order, the prosperity and the power that the country had known in the past.

The elements of the Hitlerian doctrine

As ill-founded as it can appear today, the nazi doctrine needs to be examined in depth since it is based on the internal logic of the behaviors that is difficult to explain. Built on sophisms, fraught with half-truths and articulated around a megalomaniac delusion, it leaves the feeling of an inspirational social project insofar as it proposes to build a new and better world.

The doctrine was simple and therefore more accessible. It involved four main elements that came back tirelessly in political speeches:

1. Supremacy of the Aryan race
2. Glorification of brute force as a survival tool
3. Precedence of the nation over the citizen
4. Concentration of the power in the hands of one leader

We will use two main sources to examine the nazi doctrine. The six hundred-page book entitled *Mein Kampf* recounts the childhood memories of Hitler, mixed with a repetitive and poorly organized discussion on various topics related to biology, sociology, philosophy, education, politics, the art of war, racial theories, et cetera. His conversations at night, recorded between 1941 ad 1944 at the request of Martin Bormann, are also an important and more reliable source of information, since the secretary to the Führer was known to have high expectations of his staff.

1.   Supremacy of the Aryan race

The cultural domination exerted by the German minority in Austria convinced Hitler of the German superiority. According to him, the foundation of civilization was based on the Aryan race.

The theory of a superior Aryan race is at the center of the nazi ideology and it is very difficult to understand Hitler without a precise knowledge of his racial beliefs. Many of his inexplicable behaviors, contradictory attitudes and seemingly irrational decisions were rooted in his mystical belief in the value of the Aryan race.

However, this master race needed and will continue to need the help of inferior races, due to a technical inadequacy that it had to replace with a human workforce, in the same way that the horse has been the faithful servant of man. Therefore, the presence of men of inferior race was an essential condition of civilization, compensating the shortage of material resources. That is why Hitler brutally wiped out the Polish intelligentsia after the outbreak of the war, sparing the other Poles, but ensuring that they would never have access to education and would remain slaves subject to the dominant race.

He believed that the supremacy of the Aryan race required the suppression of certain individual liberties, with or without the approval of the parents.

Freedom of thought was the second sacrifice requested. A massive propaganda presented at all levels ensured the uniqueness of the Aryan thought. The chosen race needed to be protected from anything that may impair its strength and he advocated that the purity of the race ensured the production of better quality individuals. Echoing principles gleaned from his readings, he founded his beliefs on nature observation. He observed that animals mate with their own species, such as a cat with a cat or a finch with a finch. Therefore, a cross between two human beings of different value would give a medium term value.

Speaking about miscegenation, Hitler concluded that the destiny of humanity was facing a serious danger and that his final project was to safeguard civilization.

According to him, the offspring produced by the mating of a superior being with an inferior being will be inevitably doomed to failure in his struggle against the superior race and such mating contradicts the will of nature toward the selective improvements of life in general. The stronger must dominate and not mate with the weaker. The general tendency of nature is to seek and maintain the purity of the breed. The resulting superior race ensures its survival for daily bread, thanks to its struggle against inferior human beings.

The planet is inhabited by superior races and inferior races. It is the rule of the *Völkischer*, the racial community. The Aryan race is a superior race whose origin is lost in the mists of time and whose mission is to ensure the development of civilization by dominating Europe first and then the world. Trustees of Nordic blood must ensure the perpetuation of their genetic heritage while preserving the blood purity. Any mixture with other breeds, especially Slavic and Jewish races, can only impoverish the Northern blood and weaken the German nation. Once those objectives are adopted, a simple internal logic will determine the legitimacy of the actions taken to achieve them.

When the optimal development conditions and racial purification are reached, the primacy of the Völkischer requires a selection to eliminate the weak links. Adolf Hitler immediately mentions the elimination of the sick individuals or those suffering from flaws, but he states that it is important to prevent their reproduction.

Elevated to the rank of religion, the racial rule was neither compromise nor opposition and did not spare the Germans. The deviants, the handicapped, the sick and even the military would be the victims of the Aryan doctrine.

In 1933, sterilization became a compulsory measure for individuals with a genetic disorder. By extension, that measure applied to the deviants of society, like homosexuals and gypsies. In 1939, Hitler established a euthanasia program to eliminate the physically or mentally handicapped. In 1941, the Nazis organized the extermination of the Jews, the last and most cruel measure taken to ensure the purity of the Aryan blood.

The Jews, who were often the designated victims of nazism, posed a particular problem. In addition to threatening the Aryan purity, German Jews were educated and powerful. Hitler was to eliminate them the same way he wiped out the Polish intelligentsia. Antisemitism remained present in Europe and it was easy for Hitler to stir up hatred of the Jew since the German population liked nothing better than having a scapegoat to blame for its woes. It did not suspect that its chosen path led to genocide. Antisemitism and antimarxism may be regarded as tools for the construction of an all-powerful Germany. The Jews of Europe represented an economic obstacle, wereas communism was a political obstacle. And since many Jews belonged to the Communist Party, the obstacles blended in many cases.

For Hitler, it was a striking reality that the responsibility of the Aryan race to protect civilization justified the use of all means to fulfill its role. The Führer knew what to do and had the determination to do so. He brazenly lied to the Germans to bring them into war without their consent. He signed peace treaties to gain time and tore them without remorse once they became cumbersome. Although he made himself the standard bearer of physical and moral values, he assassinated millions of people. He let entire divisions die in combat when they were facing defeat, denying the generals to retreat to save German lives.

2. Glorification of brute force as a survival tool

If the Aryan race was to dominate the world, it was necessary to ensure that all Germans could live in a great Germany with enough space to grow.

Germany was limited by a territory without any possibility of expansion. However, the German nation needed living space to grow, the lebensraum, inseparable from the Völkischer, the racial community. That space could not be gained without confrontation with the less developed peoples. For Hitler, war was inevitable since nature knows no political border. Adequate space for people does not belong to those who advocate peaceful blindness, but to those who use force to secure a territory that meets their needs.

Justifying the German expansionism by the need to give the world the mark of the Aryan civilization, Hitler claimed that he was an idealist who realized during World War I that life is a cruel fight and the real issue is the survival of the species. He added that he preferred to avoid causing pain, but when faced with a threat of extinction, he did not hesitate to impose sacrifices on individuals in order to save their community.

He was convinced that war was a necessary part of the regeneration of the active forces of the nation. Then, during the night of September 25 to 26, 1941, he justified his lack of compassion by his strong belief that the German race was endangered and the sacrifices of tomorrow would be more painful than those of today.

3. Precedence of the nation over the citizen

In his racial doctrine, Hitler radically changed the social stratification. In 1918, the Weimar Republic economic groups replaced the social classes of the second Reich monarchy. In 1933, Hitler introduced a theoretical equality based on the Aryan race. It implied that German citizenship was no longer determined by territorial limits, but by the race. As a result, individuals of Aryan origin from neighboring countries were considered full German citizens living in Germany, whereas those of non-Aryan origin lost the attributes of the German citizenship. His ultimate goal was to bring all the Germans together in a greater Germany. In his opinion, the nation was a fabric and the individuals were its fibers. In itself, the individual had value and importance insofar as he was an element of the race, and his physical and psychological characteristics were determined by his blood. Any fiber in the fabric that deviated from the orthodoxy of the nation was a potential threat that needed to be re-educated or removed at any price. In the middle of 1944, one hundred seven thousand soldiers were brought before the courts for absence without cause and forty-nine thousand others for disobedience. More than seven thousand German soldiers were executed for desertion and subversion compared to forty-eight during World War I. The individual had no purpose in himself, but took his meaning and value in contributing to the development of the nation. Unlike the democracies where the government is at the service of the citizen, in Hitler's system, the individual was at the service of the government.

For Hitler, the foundations of the action laid in the sense of the *Volk*, the people as an organic unity at the center of life. The German citizens were important due to their affiliation to the nation, and the individual was never to take precedence over the public good. The values of good and evil derived from that eternal value. The collective needs of citizens justified the laws abiding individuals.

The government, so important in the nazi machine, was only an intermediary ruling the life of the citizens for their greater good. And the Führer represented the legitimate guardian of the values of the people to whom he answered with his life. There was no room in that system for the rules of democracy that weaken the power. For Hitler, the progress of humanity could not be explained by the game of democracy, but by the intervention of energetic leaders ready to fight and die for their cause. The political leaders should not be elected, but appointed by the holder of the supreme power, and their value could not be linked to their social status. It had to be determined by the strength of their convictions. It was one of the reasons why Hitler maintained Julius Streicher's leader status even though the Nazis viewed him with open contempt. It was the only way to ensure that the good of the people would not be subject to the existing laws for the sole purpose of promoting the existence of the Volk. It appeared quite natural to use physical force when necessary, to compel individuals to contribute to the survival of the nation. To Hitler, human life was a technical component.

In the Third Reich, religion was confused with the *Volksgemeinschaft* or racial community. The individual was at the service of the community and not the opposite as in democracy. He was therefore subject to a systematic indoctrination from school age and imposed a program of activities and mandatory work focused on the racial community service.

Hitler explained that the secret of the Aryans is not only their intelligence, but also their ability to sacrifice their individuality for the greater good of the community.

"The greatness of the Aryan is not based on his intellectual powers, but rather on his willingness to devote all his faculties to the service of the community. Here the instinct for self-preservation has reached its noblest form; for the Aryan willingly subordinates his own ego to the common weal and when necessity calls he will even sacrifice his own life for the community."[3]

The fact that many cruel and barbaric behaviors involve an explicit racial theory, no matter how naive, becomes very important when attributing a certain color of patriotism to gestures that are ultimately atrocious war crimes.

The lives of six million Jews had no more value than the hundreds of thousands of German lives lost unnecessarily during the battle of Stalingrad, when Hitler denied his generals a defensive retreat. Worse yet, when he had to admit that the war was lost, Hitler ordered Speer to destroy all the infrastructure of civilization in Germany. The destruction of the Aryan dream no longer justified the existence of individuals who belonged to the fallen race.

4. Führerprinzip: Concentration of the power in the hands of one leader

When Hitler arrived in Vienna, he was fascinated by the mayor of the city, Dr. Karl Lueger, whom he described in *Mein Kampf* as the most eminent type of German Burgermeister. He ran the Christian Socialist Movement and enjoyed an undisputed popularity with the Viennese petty bourgeoisie. If Hitler was critical of Lueger's moderate antisemitism and rather timid nationalist thinking, he had an unspoken admiration for his genial capacity to mobilize masses, to win them over with his speech, to use an effective propaganda and to navigate with skill to win the support of the institutions.

Hitler's conception of the role and function of the government finds its inspiration in the writings of two German philosophers. Emmanuel Kant lived at the end of the eighteenth century and was interested in metaphysics. His book *Critique of pure reason* is perhaps the best known and looks

---

[3] Hitler, Adolf; *Mein Kampf* (James Murphy Translation), p. 232.

at the limitations of human knowledge. When discussing the political system, he strongly argued for dictatorship as a mode of government and was highly critical of the democratic system. Hegel was interested in human knowledge. He proposed the domination of the government over individuals and believed that citizens had to submit to it. He wrote that Germany would have its heyday when a hero emerged and brought the nation at the top of glory. Marx had to use his theories to promote the dictatorship of the proletariat, and Hitler, his own dictatorship. For Hitler, nothing else but the firm and unwavering commitment of a leader who had all the powers could spare the nation the unnecessary dithering that goes on in all the parliaments.

Opinions are varied on the true role of Hitler in the nazi government. Some argue that Hitler consciously had a divide and rule attitude while others suggest that Hitler distanced himself from risky political choices so as to keep his charismatic image clean.

One thing is clear. When faced with a dilemma, he made every effort to have it both ways. When the minister of the Interior, Wilhelm Frick proposed a reform plan to keep a centralized government control, he was opposed by the Gauleiters, the regional governors under the direct authority of Hitler, whose discretionary power was broad enough to implement the policies of the Nazi Party. The Gauleiters who did not like the addition of a decision-making body between them and the Führer made strong representations to Hitler. The latter solved the problem by allowing the Gauleiters to appeal directly to him on political issues and the authority of Frick remained a reality on paper. Therefore, Hitler avoided a constitutional restriction of his absolute power, which depended more on the absolute loyalty of the Gauleiters—who were getting huge benefits, than on a more or less effective bureaucracy.

Hitler and the war

Hitler concealed a morbid fascination for war. He deeply regretted being born at a time when the world had manifestly decided that halls of fame were for shopkeepers and public servants. He would have liked to be born a hundred years earlier, at the time of the liberation wars. When World War I broke out, he fell on his knees and thanked God for the grace granted to him. But he always denied making war for war's sake. To those who opposed pacifism, a concept that he attributed to the Jews, he replied: "The pacifist-humanitarian idea may indeed become an excellent one when the most superior type of manhood will have succeeded in subjugating the world to such an extent that this type is then sole master of the earth."[4]

He read carefully the works of Prussian General Karl von Clausewitz published in 1833. They described the military strategy that led to the victory of Germany over France in 1870.

Another German philosopher of the nineteenth century, Heinrich von Treitschke, advocated that war is a necessity logically stemming from the very essence of the state, power. He also said that it was absurd and immoral to banish war, because it represents the sublime force of the human soul.

Hitler admired Otto von Bismarck, the chancellor of the Second Reich. His authoritarian government had managed to bring together Germany under Prussian domination, excluding Austria from the German Reich. However, Hitler did not recognize behind the apparent inflexibility of Bismarck his capacity to adapt to difficult situations by negotiating a compromise.

He had a military knowledge that stunned the generals themselves. His phenomenal memory enabled him to discuss the features of a jet fighter or a tank with an amazing accuracy.

His relationship with the generals was tense. Upon his accession to power, he eliminated the military leaders likely to disagree with him. Self-appointed Supreme Commander of the Armed Forces, he surrounded himself with Wilhelm Keitel, who never dared contradict him, and Alfred Jodl, whose military skills were recognized.

However, he was a bad strategist. Many of his decisions bordered adventurism and, if he came out winning repeatedly, it was due to the fact that the other European countries could not imagine going to war with Germany, whose military potential very was limited in 1939.

Despite the disagreement of his generals and trusting his lucky star, he launched operation Barbarossa in the late summer of 1942. Like all other military operations, the attack and the victory had to be quick. The events seemed to prove him right. A week after crossing the Russian

---

4 Hitler, Adolf; Mein Kampf (James Murphy Translation), p. 225.

border, when the German troops were almost halfway to Moscow, he took the incomprehensible decision to attack Stalingrad instead, and the troops changed their trajectory. Since Russia is a vast country, it became more and more difficult to get supplies, and the Russian winter proved to be more dangerous than the Russian army. The difficulties of the German troops gave the Russians the break they needed to regroup. That is where his military strategic expertise proved to be insufficient.

Aggravating the situation with his foreign policy, he contributed to the creation of an unholy East-West alliance that contributed to the inevitable defeat of Germany faced with two superpowers.

The affective life of Hitler

The quality of his affective life provides a wealth of information about his personality. In-depth relationships involve an ability to expose one's vulnerability and negotiate workable tradeoffs. However, Hitler had no real interest in women. We know that in his youth he longed for a young woman to whom he never spoke. He had developed a certain friendship with the aviatrix Hanna Reitsch, who visited him at the Reich Chancellery at the end of April 1945.

It is said that he became infatuated with Geli Raubal, the daughter of his half-sister Angela, but the relationship he had with her remains obscure. She often accompanied him in his travels and Hitler had an apartment set up for her in Munich. Was Hitler attached to her because he was seeking in her his mother Klara, or was there an incestuous attraction? We will never know. Hitler had several arguments with her and, on September 18, 1931, she was found dead in her apartment, shot through the heart. It could have been a suicide or a murder ordered by Himmler, who had scabrous information that threatened the rise of Hitler. We will never know. But Hitler seems to have truly suffered the loss of his niece. After her death, he kept the apartment where she lived.

Two years earlier, he had met Eva Braun, a seventeen-year-old blonde beauty who was to become his mistress. One evening in October 1929, Hitler stopped at the studio of Heinrich Hoffman, his personal photographer whose assistant was Eva. She was a woman with a sporty look, unobtrusive, with whom he enjoyed a peaceful and quiet life that contrasted with the turmoil of politics. She remained relatively invisible until the final two years of the regime, when Hitler allowed her to come to Berlin. She never tried to interfere in politics or to exert some influence over him. Hitler claimed that his relationship with her was friendship. To ensure her financial independence, he granted her and Hoffman the exclusive sale of his photographs. For about twelve years, she had an ambiguous status, being neither Hitler's wife or his mistress and, in Hitler's intimate circle, she was referred to as EB. On April 15, 1945, sensing the impending end of the regime, she came to the Reich Chancellery without being invited and refused to leave at the request of Hitler. She had decided to be part of the final act of the nazi drama. This is how she became Eva Braun-Hitler, twenty-four hours before sharing her husband's suicidal destiny.

It seems that love was never important in his life, since he married her moments before ending his life. Eva Braun had to convince the Führer to marry her, at a time when Hitler had become depressed and abulic.

In summary, Hitler's emotional balance sheet shows significant difficulties in his personality structure. He focused his energies on the mission that he firmly believed to be invested with, leaving out any other significant emotional investment. We should not be surprised by his lack of enthusiasm toward his marriage with Eva Braun and even less by his suicide the next day. In fact, the only significant connection that he developed seems to be with his dog Blondi that he took with him in death.

The Parkinson's disease

Hitler suffered from Parkinson's disease, a slowly progressive, degenerative disorder of the central nervous system. The observation of video films shows the first signs of the disease as early as 1934. There is a decrease in the mobility of the left arm. Toward the end of the war, he had the classic symptoms of Parkinson's disease, such as slow movement, facial stiffness, monotone speech and a tremor in the right upper limb that he tried to conceal by keeping his hand in his pocket. J. Thomas Hutton, a neurologist, believes that this disease may have contributed to the defeat due to the loss of mental flexibility, the difficulty to reconcile conflicting reports and the daytime fatigue weakening his decision-making capabilities. It is obvious that during the second part of the war he avoided public appearances and lost a large part of the link he had created between him and the German population.

The complexity of a psychiatric diagnosis

A psychiatric diagnosis is sometimes a laborious exercise for several reasons. First, the diagnosis is based on a subjective collection of clinical data. The information usually comes from a contact with the affected individual, and some people are better historians than others. For Hitler, we have only indirect information made up of historical documentation. On the other hand, to be meaningful, the symptoms must interfere with the person's ability to function. The line between the normal and the pathology is not always well defined and several observers can have different views in the presence or absence of a dysfunctional state of the person. Also, several psychiatric conditions share the same symptoms. Anxiety, irritability, aggressiveness, fatigue and insomnia are examples of symptoms that may be present in a variety of psychiatric conditions, and they create some confusion in the research of a diagnosis. In addition, psychiatric issues tend to attract each other and psychiatric comorbidity is the rule rather than the exception. When the person has two or three psychiatric conditions interacting, symptomatology becomes complex and may induce the clinician in error when validating the diagnosis. Finally, the psychiatric diagnosis is based on criteria identified by a consensus of mental health experts proposing a cluster of specific symptoms and a determined period of time for each mental condition. The validity of this tool is often challenged and it is suggested to use the classification of psychiatric illnesses as a guide and not in a dogmatic way.

A detailed and thorough psychiatric history remains the best tool to get a valid diagnosis. A proper psychiatric evaluation usually allows 80 percent for the collection of historical data, the remainder of the document presenting an explanation of the diagnosis and the treatments offered. Therefore, the fact that this book focuses on historical data should not come as a surprise.

A very important error factor should be mentioned. Several doctors have been appointed as Hitler's personal physicians: a surgeon, Dr. Karl Brandt; an internist, Dr. von Hasselbach; and Professor Theodor Morell, specialized in venereal diseases. His colleagues considered Morell as a quack who financially benefited from his proximity to Hitler. It is hard to understand the interest of Hitler for this doctor who had menial attitudes, communicated badly and never gave evidence of complete cleanliness. Disregarding scientific medicine, he preferred to try mixtures of drugs, recommending to Hitler, among other things, a battery of calming, hypnotic, stimulating and cardiotonic potions.

Between 1936 and 1945, Morell remained in the inner circle of Hitler. In the last years, he treated everything by injection without a therapeutic plan. He injected Hitler up to five or six times a day to prevent a cold, or even on the eve of a speech. Dr. Brandt reported that his colleague never disclosed the nature of the injections and that, in the last years of the regime, Hitler seemed increasingly dependent on the drugs he injected him. Around 1943, Hitler showed a worsening of the Parkinson's disease symptoms and Morell became Hitler's primary physician, after he successfully eliminated Dr. Brandt, who fell into disgrace in October 1944.

Dr. Morell was giving Hitler oral medication and regular injections. The ignorance of the nature of that medication calls for reservations in the discussion of psychiatric diagnoses, since the physician could have used drugs that may have interfered with the psychological functioning of Hitler or induce withdrawal reactions, complicating the search for a diagnosis. Even today, it would be unthinkable to produce a psychiatric assessment that would not include the list of drugs.

Mental illness

Contemporary psychiatry recognizes different categories of psychological disorders and makes a difference between mental illness and personality disorders. Mental illness can be considered as an accident occurring in a lifetime. It can be acute and of limited duration, or chronic and long-term, and cause suffering that will affect the ability of the person to function normally. The illness is usually caused by difficulties in everyday life or a genetic vulnerability. It often responds to psychological therapy and appropriate medication.

The psychiatric history of Hitler does not show a sudden rupture of its level of psychological functioning that would indicate the presence of a mental illness. His frequent outbursts of anger were triggered by annoyances, highlighting a low frustration tolerance threshold. His grandiose ideas did not show a break in his way of thinking and his megalomania was shared with several of his close collaborators. Hitler's way of thinking, emotional life and behaviors remained stable throughout his life and suggest the absence of a mental disorder.

In his book published in 1998, *Hitler: Diagnosis of a Destructive Prophet*, Dr. Fritz Redlich, professor emeritus of psychiatry at both Yale University and the University of California at Los Angeles, reported the results of a ten-year research on the physical and mental health of Hitler. He concluded that Hitler had a multitude of psychosomatic symptoms, but there was no evidence of mental illness that may explain his behavior.

The personality disorders

In psychiatry, a personality disorder is a clinical entity different from mental illness. Unlike the disorders that create a break in the psychological functioning of the individual, the personality disorders are a functional impairment that begins early in life and remains stable. They are characterized by an enduring pattern of inner experience and behaviors that deviate from what is expected in the culture and must appear in two or more of the following areas: anomalies in the perception of oneself, others and events, in the emotional control, in the interpersonal functioning and in the impulse control. Those patterns are long-lasting and lead to distress or a functional impairment in the social or personal life, or other important areas.

Obviously, Hitler significantly stood out from the people around him with regard to his self-perception. He was convinced to be a man with a divine mission who was allowed behaviors opposed to the cultural standards of the time. This conviction led him to make regular use of deceit and lies in dealing with others. In his opinion, it also justified his decisions that resulted in unnecessary casualties, like when he denied a defensive withdrawal of his troops in critical situations. He felt no remorse when he used murder as a political management tool.

Patterns and personality disorders

Personality disorders are common. They affect nearly 10 percent of the population. What causes personality disorders? We all use patterns, which are core beliefs reflecting our perception of ourselves, others and the world in general. Those patterns are the result of the interaction between genetic and environmental factors.

We inherit from our parents the personality traits that will determine how we react to the stimuli in the environment. Those stimuli determine, among other things, our level of activity, attention, vulnerability to anxiety and emotional sensitivity. Thus, we say that an individual is calm, aggressive, angry, apathetic, timid or happy according to the dominant way this person thinks, reacts or behaves in various situations. As for the environment, it participates in the development of our thought patterns in the course of happy or unhappy, pleasant or painful life events, giving a color to our experiences in the familial, social, cultural and religious contexts, especially in the first years of our life. The interaction of temperament and life experiences etches a prism through which we approach our reality that will determine our attitudes and behavior. It is the same reality that many try to impose on others as an objective reality, ignoring that it is not recorded but transformed by our perception.

A healthy individual has nuanced and relative basic beliefs. He sees himself as reasonably interesting and competent. He lives in a world where people around him can be benevolent, indifferent or malicious. He acknowledges his strengths and weaknesses, and correctly identifies the situations that will be favorable and those where more difficulties may arise. He will then use a repertoire of responses adapted to each situation, and this ability to modulate his response allows him to adapt reasonably well to changing circumstances. A person with a personality disorder has internalized extreme negative and global beliefs. Therefore, one who suffers from low self-esteem may adopt self-defeating attitudes and behaviors, even when the difficulty is trivial and requires little adaptive resources. Devoid of confidence in his abilities, he keeps asking for help, becomes a burden to his family and perpetuates with his accumulated failures the low self-esteem he feels about himself. His repertoire of responses to the demands of the environment is rigid and limited.

These patterns may not result in major functional difficulty. We then talk about personality traits and they represent a preferred way of reacting to the events of our being. Depending on the way he usually reacts, an individual is defined as being aggressive, perfectionist, introvert, extrovert, choleric, dependent or narcissistic, but he keeps an adequate level of adaptation. When those beliefs generate a dysfunctional state in many areas of his life or if they result in significant suffering among relatives or the people close to him, we talk about a personality disorder.

For example, it may be normal to feel threatened when entering a criminalized neighborhood. But this threat should fade when leaving the area. Back home, the individual with a paranoid personality disorder will continue to be very suspicious of the people around him, even if the objective facts and his own experience indicate that they are probably trustworthy. His attitude may lead to disputes with his neighbors, tired to be around a person who gets angry easily and multiplies legal letters for trivia. Interestingly, we need to realize that, in some cases, a personality disorder can become an advantage. The same individual with a paranoid personality disorder can be considered a good manager if he works for a company where the leaders encourage the use of bullying as a management technique. His distrust and aggressiveness can even be an advantage if he joined the criminal world where might makes right. Personality disorders are a handicap, but they can have a positive impact in some environments, as was the case with Adolf Hitler.

The criteria for mental disorders

There are criteria for a diagnosis of mental disorder. In America, the DSM-5 (*Diagnostic and Statistical Manual of Mental Disorders, 5th revision*), published by *The American Psychiatric Association*, is the preferred tool. The suggested diagnosis criteria have no absolute value, but they are based on a consensus reached by groups of psychiatrists drawing from their experience of the aggregations of symptoms that seem compatible with a specific diagnosis. These criteria can be changed from one edition to another and should be considered as guides or benchmarks. Criteria can be shared with several diagnoses, but the appropriate DSM table should be used to diagnose a specific condition.

Hitler was a carrier of a narcissistic personality disorder

Traudl Junge, Hitler's secretary, often had lunch with him. One day, she asked him why he was not married. She was stunned by his answer. He explained that he would not be a good father and would be unable to devote enough time to his wife. He added that he did not want children of his own because the offspring of a genius have a hard time following in the footsteps of their genitor. People would not forgive them for being average and most of them become morons.

On April 26, 1942, in an enthusiastic speech at the *Sportpalast* in Berlin, Hitler announced to the Germans the victory in Russia. Proclaiming his superiority over Napoleon, he claimed having defeated Russia, where the French emperor had failed more than a century earlier. He and he alone had been able to take carefully calculated risks through his military genius that nobody else could equal. He asked that a seventh or eighth title be attributed to him. He wanted to be an *Obserster Gerichsheer* or Supreme Law Lord. In fact, he was asking to be given the power of life and death over every German, whether Nazi or not.

Convinced to have an exceptional talent, he dreamed of grandiose achievements. He endlessly discussed his plans until the morning with his exhausted guests. Hitler had grandiose plans to beautify Berlin. He wanted the visitors to see breathtaking monuments that would give them the impression that they were in the city of the master of the world. As for the Reich Chancellery, he fantasized about a building that would make St. Peter's Square in Rome look like a toy next to it.

The prevalence of the narcissistic personality disorder is less than one percent in the general population.

Hitler meets almost all the criteria for this disorder. Carriers of the narcissistic personality disorder have an exaggerated opinion of themselves. They have a grandiose sense of their importance, expect unlimited success, and believe that they are unique and understood only by special people. They gladly exploit others, convinced that everything is due to them. They frequently lack empathy.

Narcissism refers to the attitudes related to self-appreciation. It is desirable to have a good appreciation of ourselves. But when those attitudes become an investment that distorts the perception of reality and individuals remain focused on themselves to the point where they constantly need attention and admiration, when they are transported by fantasies of success, impressive projects and unlimited power, when they become haughty, arrogant and believe that they are superior to others to the point of exploiting them, they meet the criteria of this disorder. However, as soon as we analyze their immediate surroundings, we discover their difficulties in interacting with others. They are unable to listen, to negotiate compromises and to treat others as equals. Affected individuals have behaviors reflecting a grandiose perception of their own importance. They constantly exaggerate their abilities as well as their achievements. They are inhabited by fantasies of uninterrupted success or unlimited power and frequently engage in extraordinary missions, which are manifestations of megalomania. They identify with the cause they defend and criticism of their organization is perceived as a personal insult. They tend to minimize or even devalue the contribution of others from whom, however, they require a constant admiration. They show an extreme egocentrism with a profound lack of sensitivity to the needs or opinions of others. As a result, carriers of this personality disorder show a flagrant lack of judgment. They resent contradictions and quickly feel threatened by individuals whom they perceive as superior to themselves. Therefore, they usually surround themselves with people they can control or whose profile is so low that it will not cast a shadow over them.

Building on his initial successes with the blitzkriegs and his in-depth knowledge of military technology, Hitler treated his staff with authority and contempt, ignoring the advice or opinions of his generals. He lashed out in rage when his orders were not followed or when the German troops were unable to get the expected results on the battlefield. Driven by an unlimited self-confidence, he made the disastrous decision to open a Russian front, counting on a quick victory and ignoring the defeat of Napoleon one hundred years earlier. His rigidity and his stubbornness in refusing to allow German troops to retreat resulted in hundreds of thousands of casualties.

Hitler's narcissism bordered on the ridiculous. But he had another problem with more significant consequences.

Hitler was also a carrier of an antisocial personality disorder

The prevalence rates of the antisocial personality disorder are estimated at 3 percent for men and 1 percent for women. It is characterized by a flagrant lack of moral conscience and a marked difficulty to comply with social norms accepted in the living environment. The individuals seem unable to integrate the social standards in their behaviors. To keep up appearances, they could say that those standards are important, but that admission is purely verbal. They are regularly in conflict with others. They show contempt for the laws, which may cause prison stays. In 1921, Hitler was imprisoned for three months for having assaulted a speaker in a political assembly that he intended to sabotage at the head of his SA troops. Often very intelligent, optimistic and gifted with a great sense of humor, the initial contact with them can be nice. But the relations deteriorate quickly due to their manipulative behavior, since they exploit others to achieve their ends. Without a second thought, they use lies, deceit and fraud on a daily basis, regardless of the rights of individuals. They also display impulsive behaviors and do not pay attention to the risks and consequences for themselves or others.

From an early age, Hitler refused to conform to social norms. He showed oppositional behaviors with his father, sabotaged the subjects that did not interest him in school, took a sabbatical at the age of sixteen under dubious circumstances and he scrounged on his mother without finding stable employment in Vienna.

Antisocial personality disorder and psychopathy

Antisocial personality disorder is not a homogeneous condition. Before the 1980s, this disorder and psychopathy were considered equivalent terms. Subsequently, the latter was considered a category of antisocial personality disorder. All psychopaths have an antisocial personality disorder, but carriers of this personality disorder are not all psychopaths.

It would seem that the antisocial personality disorder represents a continuum of symptoms of a similar category, indicated in a clinical table from light to severe, psychopathy representing the most severe form of this disorder that may be associated with violent and cruel behaviors, such as torture or the murder of a victim with no other benefit than adrenaline stimulation.

The definition of the term psychopath is ambiguous, which makes it difficult to ensure a reliable diagnosis. Although the prevalence of affected individuals can be as high as 1 percent of the population, they are over-represented in prison environments where they amount to 25 percent of the prisoners. The popular imagination presents them as serial killers, taking sadistic pleasure in torturing their victims before ending their lives. The drama of those behaviors promotes the setting of the psychopath as a violent individual, and their recruitment in prison circles where they are more easily identified by those doing research in this area is likely to reinforce this image. In fact, we regularly come across psychopaths who can remain invisible in their environment. They can be a friend, a neighbor, a parent. Some may even occupy an important place in their environment.

Two Canadian psychologists, Paul Babiak and Robert Hare, wrote a book describing how business leaders can occupy senior management positions and engage in psychopathic behaviors by using their power for their own benefit, regardless of the difficulties and suffering that they cause to those who are in daily contact with them.

Violence is not the trademark of psychopaths. In fact, most violent individuals are not psychopaths. Personality traits and undesirable social behavior must also be part of the clinical picture.

Psychopathy refers to a mental disorder manifested by devoid of moral and antisocial behaviors. The individuals seem impervious to guilt and the suffering of others. Devoid of compassion, they are focused on themselves and abuse people, using lies and manipulation well hidden behind their magnetism and a charming attitude. In a study published in 2009, psychologist Stephen Porter examined the records of three hundred nine individuals who spent more than two years in prison between 1995 and 1997. Ninety of them met the criteria for psychopathy. He discovered that the carriers of this diagnosis were two and a half times more likely than other prisoners to be released on parole. He explained this fact by their manipulation power and their ability to impress their interlocutors. Many of those individuals have a wealth of information about the diagnosis, are skilled in the art of deceiving the scientists and present a reassuring face.

We all need stimulation, otherwise life would be boring. In our daily life, we get it in various ways: sport competition, fast driving and suspense movies are common examples. Psychopaths have a boring life due to their inability to react to those stimuli. Their brain requires sources of anxiety much more intense to feel the surge of adrenaline and, to get it, they are willing to significantly endanger their lives or their safety as well as that of others. This might explain the pathological fascination that war had on Hitler and also his interest in volunteering for the most dangerous missions with complete disregard for his life during World War I.

Psychopaths often take a bold stand and are always right, unable to recognize the harm they do to others. They do not learn from experience and return to their illicit activities more often than other criminals. They do not suffer from perceptual disorder. They know what they are doing and they act impulsively by manipulating those around them without worrying about their suffering and the consequences of their actions. Suffering from affective poverty, they are incapable of empathy, compassion and love. They do not emotionally bond with others and live as predators. The absence of fear and anxiety makes them unable to integrate the social norms of their environment. But it also allows them to be comfortable before the cameras and they perform better than healthy individuals in situations that generate stress, like a presentation before an audience.

The difference between the antisocial personality disorder and psychopathy is not obvious at first glance. Since the antisocial personality disorder is mostly characterized by unlawful and antisocial behaviors, many criminals meet the criteria of this disorder. In a pleasant individual, the difficulty to create stable emotional ties and the total lack of fear, regret and compassion add up and transform the psychopathy in an extreme form of antisocial personality disorder. Exposed to a threat of violence, the carrier of an antisocial personality disorder feels a surge of adrenaline associated with an increased heart rate, shallow breathing and agitation. The psychopath does not feel any of those changes. This is what generates a deep malaise in murders committed by carriers of this disorder: the psychopaths exhibit profound indifference to the suffering and agony of their victims, whom they can kill with a relaxed smile. The emotional emptiness that is a characteristic of the typical psychopath prevents him from developing deep emotional bonds and makes his learning experiences inoperative.

Fear and anxiety play an important role in the development process of the moral conscience and the learning of desirable social behaviors. Very early in life, society uses those emotions to bring an individual to comply with social norms: fear of rejection and criticism enable people to internalize social norms of behavior to avoid the threat of social pressure. It is important to remember that studies have highlighted that the emotional reactivity of psychopaths is impaired: they have no fear or anxiety. However, those emotions are controlled by of a group of brain cells in the limbic system—the emotional brain or amygdala. An animal in which this structure is removed becomes indifferent to the stimuli associated with fear. The amygdala, the alarm system that reacts to a threat, seems to be off in psychopaths. Studies have been done on the brains of people exposed to anxiety-generating situations. Radiological examination of the exposed individuals showed in a group of psychopaths very little reactivity of the amygdala compared to a control group. In addition, research indicates that the prefrontal cortex of the brain has an inhibitory effect on aggressive behavior. However, several groups of researchers have highlighted a reduced volume of gray matter in the brain of psychopaths. The combined effect of a reduced fear and the curbing of aggressive behaviors could provide the neurobiological basis of this condition.

It seems clear that psychopaths show structural brain abnormalities that are probably genetic. The identical twin of a psychopath and a child born to a psychopathic parent, but adopted by normal parents, both have a high chance of developing this problem.

This deficiency is accompanied with a physiological peculiarity: the heartbeat of psychopaths is slower than that of the average population. In a threatening situation, the psychopath does not have the normal physiological reaction of fear or an emotional response like the normal population. Studies have shown that a slow heart rate in children is associated with an increased risk, independent of all other psychological variables, of antisocial personality disorder during his adult life.

If genetic factors are involved, the influence of the environment probably plays a very important role in the expression of the psychopathy in the affected individuals. Therefore, being exposed to violence in the family could condition people to use in turn violent behaviors in their environment. Furthermore, a higher level of education could reduce in the individuals the risk of crime and imprisonment by providing access to more favorable social life conditions.

Was Hitler a psychopath?

Hitler was clearly a carrier of an antisocial personality disorder. Was he a psychopath? It is possible. His complete lack of empathy and his difficulty to establish meaningful relationships showed a marked emotional poverty. His contempt for suffering and death takes a variety of forms. His refusal to use the defensive withdrawal in his war strategies claimed a large number of German lives. The ease with which he ordered the murder of those suspected of violating the nazi orthodoxy, the assassination of Ernst Röhm to whom he owed his political rise, but who had become a nuisance, and the execution of Hermann Fegelein, Eva Braun's brother-in-law, who had left the bunker without his permission, clearly show the low value he attached to human life. The failed Stauffenberg attack, where several defendants died slowly in extreme pain, pierced by meat hooks to which they remained suspended while the SS were filming their agony, demonstrate the brutality of his repressive measures.

However, all those behaviors could be explained by a blind adherence to the nazi doctrine advocating a ruthless approach totally subjecting the respect and safety of individuals to the requirements of a huge project. On the other hand, Hitler showed behaviors that do not align with a philosophical explanation, which could be associated with the neurologic abnormalities of psychopaths. His morbid interest in war, his complete lack of concern for his safety when he volunteered for the most dangerous missions and his refusal to use his days of leave because he wanted to stay on the battlefield suggest abnormalities in the perception of fear and anxiety.

Hitler's total lack of empathy, his marked lack of affective life, his inability to create stable emotional ties and the absence of anxiety showing in his morbid attraction to war as well as his propensity to self-exposure to death when volunteering for dangerous missions during World War I all favor a diagnosis of psychopathy. On the other hand, the stability of the ideology that mobilized him, the consistency he showed in the pursuit of his objectives and the importance he gave to his personal safety raise doubts as to the soundness of this diagnosis. Moreover, his secretaries who were in daily contact with him claimed that he acted more like a protective father than a tyrant.

Additional consequences of narcissistic and antisocial personality disorders

In fact, these two personality disorders complement each other. In the narcissistic personality disorder, the individual develops the wildest dreams, whereas in the antisocial personality disorder, he uses fraudulent means to achieve them with total disregard for the rights of others and human life.

Hitler had something very important to sell: the product of his narcissism, which was the megalomaniac dream of a Thousand-Year Reich. He attracted clients who were not asking so much, but had a huge need to avenge the defeat of World War I and restore the socioeconomic stability, the power and the national pride of yesteryear. Focusing on the patriotic side of the crowds who bought that kind of line, he gave free rein to his most utopian pandering in front of an audience unable to distinguish between dreams and reality. His conviction that he was the carrier of a divine mission proved to be contagious and the excessive enthusiasm of the crowd fed his narcissism. Convincing, Hitler claimed to be able to deliver the goods. What Hitler never said was what the price would be.

In the logic of his antisocial personality, Hitler authorized his executioners to use in a cruel and relentless way the necessary means to achieve his objectives, totally ignoring the human rights and human life. Arbitrary arrests, torture, summary executions and mass exterminations became the daily reality in Germany. But Hitler was not the only one involved. The SS, the Gestapo and all the parallel organizations contributed to the brutal repression that followed.

We should wonder about the reasons for which many Germans from all walks of life idolized the Führer, even though they hated the Nazi Party. We should question the fact that none of the accused in the Nuremberg trials blamed Hitler for the atrocities committed by the Nazis. We should also try to understand why many of our contemporaries, who live in a society where human rights are respected, but who are frustrated by the challenges of democracy, support with great conviction that we would need another Hitler to restore social order. Finally, we should question the reasons why extremists create neo-nazi groups all over the world.

There seems to be a gap between the nazi brutality and the character of the Führer, as if those two elements were not linked. This dichotomy is typical of the relationship between a crook and his victim.

Adolf Hitler: A top-notch crook

Fraud is using a false name or a false quality, abusing a true quality or using fraudulent activities to mislead a person or entity and induce this person, to his detriment or to the detriment of a third party, to transfer funds, valuables or any property, to provide a service or to consent to an act incurring or discharging an obligation.

The difference between a thief and a crook is subtle. The thief illegally appropriates property belonging to another. There is no relationship between the thief and his victim. The crook appropriates property that does not belong to him, but he uses lies and deceit to get the cooperation of the victim. The crook is often a brilliant, charming and charismatic person. Heinrich Hoffman, the personal photographer of Hitler, had to produce photographs showing a favorable and reassuring image of the Führer.

There is always something realistic in what the crook says. The sophisms and half-truths are integral elements of his thinking. He skillfully gets the confidence of his victim. He knows what words to use so that the latter recognizes his thoughts. The victim knows that nothing is free, and everything has to be paid for. The crook knows that if he explains to his victim that nothing is free, and everything has to be paid for, it will be easier for him to defraud that person. This is likely what Hitler thought after the Munich putsch failure. He quickly realized that to achieve his ends, it was better to go with rather than against the system. An alliance with the army seemed like a trump card to rise to power and he had to go into politics to achieve his objectives.

To gain his victim trust, the crook will ensure that this person makes a minimal profit, but out of proportion to the expected gains for himself. Whatever one thinks of Hitler, the result of his twelve years as head of Germany was not uniformly negative. He was the voice of the country and he expressed accurately the German resentment following the defeat of World War I and the humiliation of the Treaty of Versailles. He demonstrated a contagious enthusiasm in his struggle to achieve the objective of a Germany that was to reign over Europe. He amazed the Europeans when he got the economy moving during the Great Depression. He introduced an impressive decorum for the officials and the military, granting them an unquestionable prestige. Fascinated by the reconstruction of Germany after Hitler's election, taking pride in the expeditious military victories won without bloodshed from 1938 onward, many Germans welcomed the election of a magician at the head of the nation.

He showed his best performance between 1933, when he came to power, and 1939, at the outbreak of World War II. Even though it was a period of major political blunders, several historians consider that Hitler gave the impression of being a good state leader, in view of his speed and efficiency to take Germany out of the socioeconomic slump in which it was stuck since the end of World War I. The return to traditional values such as discipline, obedience and patriotism, the reconstruction of Germany, the development of the military force and the recovery of the territories lost after World War I were sufficient to erase the humiliation of the Treaty of Versailles and allow the Germans to hold their heads high again.

This scenario takes the form of a monumental scam at the expense of the German nation. For the Germans, restoring the power of the nation was an end in itself. For Hitler, it was an essential step to achieve his plan of a superior race that would extend its dominance across Europe. The militarization of Germany was aiming at a war across the continent. Going to war required roads, armament plants, and especially a hardened population prepared to follow orders unquestioningly. He therefore put Germany back to work in a very effective way. He ordered that all the trade unions be dissolved and replaced with a single union reporting to the Nazi Party. He also imposed less favorable working conditions. German workers became feudal serfs under the authority of the manufacturing industry leaders, who no longer worried about higher wages or strikes. The party even determined the retail price in stores and all price increases had to be approved by the appropriate authorities. The Germans decided that the cost of socioeconomic stability and eradicated unemployment was not too high. But that was before the war began.

Hitler even managed to cause a mutation of the traditional social rules for several Germans. The respect of authority and obedience are universal values and they were firmly established in the German culture. A programmed perversion of social standards was now favoring violence and cruelty under a pseudo-patriotism dedicated to the promotion of the Aryan race. Paradoxically, respect of authority and obedience became incentives for a criminal behavior. In the nazi philosophy, the humanistic principle that promoted respect for the human dignity was against all laws of nature, which favored the domination of the strong over the weak. Defenders of those values were weakening the race and exhibiting an unpatriotic behavior that warranted a brutal crackdown. It took unusual courage and strong moral values to oppose this distortion of traditional standards.

Following a financial scam, the victims realize the extent of their loss and hold a grudge against the crook who manipulated them, but they also regret their naivety when they collaborated with him. This ambivalent attitude of the victims may also reflect a form of denial due to their participation in the scam process. They are surprised that such a good person initiated the scam, but they remember that, in spite of everything, they received some benefits.

Hitler's suicide may have had an impact on his image. His premature death did not provide an opportunity to carefully analyze in a war crimes tribunal the operating mechanisms of the nazi system and the specific role of Hitler. It is clear that the nostalgia of a nazi government shows the perverse effect of the crook scheme with his victim. The meager benefits for the victims and the charming attitude of the crook lead to overlook the extremely heavy cost of the nazi project.

What did Adolf Hitler teach us?

It is often said that we must remember those events to ensure that they will not be repeated. Unfortunately, similar disasters will continue to haunt the human consciousness. But we can draw from five observations related to Adolf Hitler's passage in history.

1. Honest citizens can be programmed to become serial killers.

Hitler demonstrated that a perverted reward and punishment system cleverly programmed and used consistently can change human behavior in an amazing way and wake up an unsuspected potential of aggressiveness. Apparently normal citizens may be led to react like murderers in well-structured interventions like those used by the SS troops where not just anyone could become a SS. The admission criteria were very severe and required a clean psychological and criminal record. Therefore, it is likely that this elite group did not have a significant number of individuals with antisocial personality disorder. Their intensive training remodeled their moral values by making obedience to orders an absolute rule. This is how a large number of Germans were programmed to ruthlessly murder innocent victims, convinced that it was their duty to follow orders. Despite the fact that they were assigned to criminal activity, the SS proudly sported their membership in a brotherhood that provided for its members a certain prestige in the German society.

2. The adoption of the Charter of Rights did not end barbarism.

Man is by nature a gregarious human being. Life in communities allows for a distribution of tasks intended to ensure the safety and well-being of the members. But community life also includes many frustrations and exposes individuals to the aggressive impulses that lie dormant within us until the proper conditions awaken them. Man has always been the most dangerous predator for his species. The potential for aggression, violence and cruelty remains firmly locked in many individuals. But there are people in whom the repression of those impulses seems to be less effective, for temperamental or psychiatric reasons, and who may be capable of cruelty and sadism under adequate circumstances.

We probably believe that the proclamation of the Universal Declaration of Human Rights brought a new era in history and that this humanist current would definitely put an end to barbaric behaviors in human beings. Over the past century, three episodes of racial extermination have been recognized as such by the United Nations. In 1915 and 1916, the Armenian genocide claimed over one million victims. Between 1942 and 1945, six million Jews were murdered in nazi concentration camps. And in 1994, one million Tutsi men, women and children were slaughtered over a period of one hundred days, because they were not the pure Rwandan race.

This rather heavy toll greeted the arrival of civilization. In fact, far from eliminating violence, the modern era seems to have refined the methods of torture and improved the efficiency of mass extermination.

Hitler definitely demonstrated the fragility of the gains made with the proclamation of human rights. The nazi doctrine looked back and exchanged the humanist philosophy for that of Nietzsche: brute force gives way to the strongest and collective rights take precedence over individual rights. For the advocates of humanism, the respect of the individual rights and freedoms is more than a negotiable convention. It represents a societal choice incompatible with a totalitarian police state.

The proclamation of human rights and freedoms confirms a choice of values adopted by a society in which emphasis is given to citizens to ensure their well-being and protection. It reflects an awareness of the aggressive potential of human nature, but does not represent a progress on the individual level. Today's barbarian is no longer the individual with an unkempt beard, armed with a club or a sword. He is a face in the crowd who probably is not even aware of his own aggressive potential.

3. Power is a dangerous weapon.

We all have a perception of reality that allows us to distinguish between good and bad and decide what is desirable or undesirable for our well-being. We also believe that the reality that we perceive is the objective reality and, therefore, the reality perceived by others should necessarily be similar to ours. One man's vision of the reality cannot summarize that of the community members. However, those in power can guide the decisions in directions that favor them.

The nazism episode highlights how difficult it can be for the human being to live with others who may be their guardians, but also their executioners when they abuse their power. Yesterday's victims may become tomorrow's executioners. And it is the power that determines who the executioner and the victim are. Since a dictatorship badly fits in a pluralist society advocating freedom of opinion, repression gradually increases in order to stop by force any discordant note in the imposed orthodoxy.

Dictatorship helps achieve seemingly unreachable goals in a more efficient manner than a democratic government. It represents an apparently desirable alternative in the event of a large and persistent social unrest. Such situations favor the emergence of a radical intervention, and then, many people are convinced that the power needs to be entrusted to one man. But the political directions of the dictatorship are invariably those of repression and corruption.

However powerful it may be, a weapon without ammunition is harmless. With no power, Hitler would probably have remained an obscure socially-inept Austrian, an annoyance for his peers, unable to adapt in a productive manner. His extraordinary charisma and his sharp political instinct would have found no room to express themselves. Through power, he became the most dangerous man of the twentieth century, responsible for the ruin of Germany, for the profound and brutal change in the geopolitical balance in the world and for the biggest man-made tragedy. Hitler clearly demonstrated that it is better to be ruled by a majority of people who can evade their responsibilities than by one man who takes full responsibility for his decisions.

Could history repeat itself? No doubt it could. Personality traits similar to Hitler's should raise concerns about a possible abuse of power in individuals fulfilling these characteristics:

- Their political views are polarized and reject the principles of democracy.
- They are convinced that they know better than you what is best for you.
- They do not tolerate those who disagree with them.
- They are condescending toward media communication and have a low tolerance to criticism.
- Their public statements focus on emotions rather than content.
- Falsehood is their working tool.
- They show little humanitarian concern.
- They are unreliable political partners.

Although we should not pull the alarm each time we are faced with those situations, we must keep in mind the explosive potential of a disproportionate power in the hands of such individuals.

Aware of the dangers of political power, many democracies

constitutionally limit the duration of the head of state's mandate. Democracy is far from being a perfect political system. It tries to identify opinion convergences, but it is often paralyzed by conflicting public pressures. Democracy is a political system that requires compromises. Very few projects are completed without any change to the original plan, because those who are responsible must ensure that the interests of the majority are respected. Furthermore, political leaders have a short-term vision that rarely exceeds the period of time until the next election. However, based on respect and equality of rights for all, democracy is the system that guarantees more effectively the security of the citizens. Given the unpredictability of human nature in a situation of power, the health of a democracy is not measured by the degree of integrity of the leaders, but by the ability of the political regime to identify and correct their deviant behaviors. The access to information and the freedom of the press play a counterbalance role that protects against the excesses of power. They are two reliable markers of a democratic society.

Unfortunately, the democratic model is not exportable without distinction, and is much more difficult to implement in countries marked by persistent ethnic, tribal and ancestral divisions like Africa. To perform, the model requires a minimum of consensus in terms of values and traditions. Nevertheless, democracy appears as the least imperfect political model in reasonably homogeneous societies.

4.   Hatred is often disguised under a veneer of patriotism.

Hatred is an intense anger coated in malevolent intentions, usually resulting in a strong frustration caused by unsatisfied needs. It has a virtual destructive potential that can become reality when it is associated with power.

Hatred is a contagious emotion. Hatred awakens the aggressive impulses that lie dormant in each of us and may encourage individuals and communities to undertake actions beyond the control exercised by social norms or individual morality. Hatred is a declaration of war against someone and rejects the social rules allowing us to live in groups. Individuals with a higher aggressive potential may show a behavior of unexpected violence. Every day, newspapers report tragedies involving ordinary people: a friendly neighbor murdered his wife and another shot his employer at work.

In politicians' speeches, hatred often hides beneath a veneer of patriotism. In any country, patriotism reflects the commitment of citizens to their country and constitutes a very noble value. We must remain vigilant when using this term. Demagogic politicians widely use this value to rally behind them their intended audience. Patriotism is the willingness that brings members of a country together under one flag. When expressing intolerance toward the differences, it becomes nationalism. When it is based on racial characteristics and it leads to contempt, it becomes ethnocentrism. When associated with hatred, it is racism.

5. The scam is a subtle exercise from which Hitler still derives benefits.

The crook draws more sympathy than the thief due to the seductive image that he conveys and the co-benefits for his victims. The turning around of the economy after Hitler's rise to power in 1933 was the incidental benefit of his Thousand-Year Reich project and it still impresses many observers. Some even say that had he died before the war began, he would have been considered one of the greatest politicians of the twentieth century. But we should not forget that his enviable achievements have been made possible through the abolition of trade unions, the elimination of political parties, the suppression of freedom of the press and a ruthless repression of opponents. A stunned admiration at Hitler's achievements between 1933 and 1939 validates the principle upheld by Hitler that the end justifies the means.

Baldur von Schirach, sentenced to imprisonment at the Nuremberg trials, wrote that the disaster did not come only from what Hitler did to the German people, but also from what the German people did to him. He was the man that they had expected for a long time and he told them what they wanted to hear.

This opinion reflects the subtleties of the scam mechanism. It always begins with a seduction operation to win the trust of the victim through lies and trickery, which corresponds to a break-in of the victim's environment. Once there, the crook recommends that the victim put in place a system that will bring him clear benefits, which will however end up being at his expense. The game will continue until the victim's tolerance level is reached and he realizes that the crook's profits outrageously exceed his own. The declaration of Schirach amounts to ignoring the break-in and saying to the victim: "What are you complaining about? Did you not open the door to him? Did you not consent?"

The economic prosperity of Germany and the disappearance of unemployment that followed Hitler's rise to power often hide the reprehensible means that have been used to achieve those results. By analogy, we should not forget that the financial support provided to a small village by narco-traffickers who live there comes from the drug market, which benefits from the dependence of millions of addicts.

Chapter 12

How was it possible?

The explanation could very well be hidden behind anyone of these possibilities: a consequence of Adolf Hitler's insane mind; a release of the intense collective aggressiveness generated by the defeat in World War I and the socio-economic turmoil that followed; the passive tolerance of the European countries toward the German expansionism and the Jewish genocide; the abnormal psychosocial environment created by the state of war; the systematic indoctrination that began at an early age; the intoxication by a simplistic ideology hammered in by a systematic propaganda; the unbridled nationalism requiring the sacrifice of individuals to promote the master race; the military culture that numbed the individual consciousness; the tradition of respect for authority; the loss of a global perspective created by a segmentation of duties in the Jewish genocide project; the negative reinforcement of human values assimilated to a form of cowardice; the positive reinforcement of hard, sadistic and cruel behaviors; the excessive indulgence of human consciousness; the aberration of social standards; the conspiracy of silence on the part of the German institutions; the refusal to transfer to others the weight of a painful collective task; the fear of ostracism; the exaltation of honor in blind loyalty to the regime; the perverted social idealism; the release of individual sadistic impulses under the guise of group responsibility; the outburst of pure racism equating Jews with sub-humans and legitimizing their extermination; a collective psychosis; a mass phenomenon; the threatening surveillance by the political police; the brutal sanctions against the opponents of the regime; or the hermetic isolation of international bodies of opinion created by a pseudo-totalitarian state.

All those factors helped create an unlikely historical momentum, opening the door to an explosion of violence on a scale never reached before.

There are probably several additional hypotheses that may provide avenues for further reflection. We have to be realistic. The reality is likely to remain elusive in its entirety since the human mind can only apprehend it bit by bit and does not resist the temptation of linear explanation. Therefore, integrating as many variables in a set accepted by all is an impossible task because of the complexity of human behavior.

The reader looks at history with eyes tinged by his own subjectivity. The historical truth is factual, but the determinism that we perceive behind the events and the interpretation that we give to them belong to our personal apprehension. Our vision of things is distorted by the prism of our subjectivity. Carved by our education, culture, personality, life experiences and the values that we hold, it exaggerates or minimizes what it sees. We give varying degrees of value to the factors involved in order to get a clear meaning of the events analyzed. The important thing is not to agree on a common perspective, but to find answers to our questions. The horrors caused by nazism challenge us to do the trial of human nature. As human beings, we are caught between the role of the accused and that of the judge looking for the truth. In fact, we are looking for a history that conveys a reassuring meaning to the events. We want to believe that in a similar situation, we would have acted differently.

Times have changed and history will not repeat itself on such a scale. Computers have transformed the world in a large village where it is no longer possible to partition the populations in sealed enclosures. However, ethnocentrism is always present in human nature and outbreaks of violence and cruelty based on racism will continue to torment humanity. Few countries have experienced more than a hundred years of peace throughout history. War has always been the preferred tool to resolve conflicts when dialogue fails to find acceptable compromises.

There is a large number of factors whose layout and interactions have allowed nazism to emerge. The absence of one single factor could have changed the course of history. How were those factors juxtaposed to put the planet to the edge of the abyss?

The linear perspectives are advantageously replaced by formulations using a grid that distributes the contributing elements in subsets whose interaction provides benchmarks on the why and how of crises. The distribution of the factors into predisposing, precipitating and perpetuating elements helps to further qualify the formulation of the problem. Predisposing factors are usually multiple and create instability in a system. The Treaty of Versailles, the German nationalism and the cult of the authority are a few examples. Triggers critically increase the instability of the system, upset its functioning and force the system to reposition itself. The simulated attack on a German radio station by SS dressed in Polish uniforms unleashed World War II and the Japanese attack on Pearl Harbor brought the United States into the war. Finally, the perpetuating factors are elements that impede the resolution of the problem. Systematic denunciation, nazi observers in the citizens' immediate surroundings and the brutal repression of dissidents played a crucial role to prevent an effective resistance to the nazi project.

However, the images capture the movements of a system much better than the abstract concepts. The resentment toward the humiliating Treaty of Versailles, the German nationalism, the culture of submission to the authority and the socioeconomic and political instability of Germany contributed to transform the German nation into a potentially devastating source of energy. With his magnetism and communication skills, Adolf Hitler channeled those explosive forces in the Nazi Party that had become a powder keg. Carrier of a narcissistic and antisocial personality disorder and therefore capable of falsehood, deceit and cruelty—and devoid of compassion, Hitler became the wick in the keg. By giving him absolute power, the Germans lighted the wick without realizing the consequences. From then on, everything was set for the explosion. And it is exactly what happened.

A third perspective that could help visualize with greater precision Hitler's behavior and the loss of control of the nazi regime would be to consider this page of history as a disastrous scam on a massive scale. A campaign of seduction, lies, deceit, brutality and cruelty of that magnitude cannot be found elsewhere. The characteristics and mechanisms of the crook's behavior fit remarkably well with those of the nazi era. By rejecting the behavioral rules with the German citizens and the representatives of the European countries, Hitler benefited from a power that enabled him to bring suffering and death on the continent for several years while pursuing his delirious and unrealistic objectives of racial purity and Aryan hegemony. He mobilized the most degrading impulses of human nature in hundreds of thousands of people, making them believe that they could build a better world on millions of dead bodies. His modus operandi was so effective that the extremists of the next generations were seduced by his model and attempted to create movements using similar scenarios. This trend is so obvious that several democratic countries enact a legal ban on neo-nazi movements within their borders.

The vulnerabilities of the German society

Many observers believe that the German temperament with his nationalist fervor, his sense of duty and his military tradition contained all the ingredients for a technologically organized racial slippage. We cannot deny that the nazi seeds fell on fertile ground and that Hitler took advantage of this German specificity.

The German nationalism

For centuries, Germany felt cramped on the European continent. Caught between powerful neighbors, the country could rely on a burning patriotism to ensure a strong cohesion between the Germans. At the end of the nineteenth century, Germany ranked among the top industrial powers in the world and its culture shone through several European countries. After the Treaty of Versailles, the German nationalism slid into intolerance toward Jews and became fanaticism and racism when World War II began. Taken to the extreme, German nationalism soon became an exclusion rather than a rallying tool. All the forces hindering the expression of nationalism were to be eliminated. Fanatical nationalism is a religion that conveys its own ethics and morally justifies all that will likely bring it closer to its objectives. That type of nationalism distorts its original purpose, which is the benefit of a community, and becomes an ideology that is accountable only to itself and no longer to the citizens it was meant to serve. Nationalism contains the seeds of racism.

We need to remember that the unbridled nationalist wave that swept Germany was not unique, and did not represent a specific German trait. Around the same time, an identical nationalism emerged in Japan between the two wars. The similarities between those two nationalisms are so striking that we sometimes have the impression that only the names have been changed. From school age, the young Japanese learned to venerate the family, the nation and the emperor. They learned that they were a chosen race and that the emperor was invincible. To be in the Imperial Army and to fight and die were seen as the ultimate glory. The Samurais with their code of honor were somewhat reminiscent of Heinrich Himmler's SS formations. As in Germany, the Japanese propaganda brazenly lied to the people. When in 1942 the four Japanese aircraft carriers were destroyed in the Battle of Midway, the military government hid the disaster and praised the victory against the Americans. To complete the picture, after having lost a large number of soldiers in the battle, Japan mobilized young citizens to replace the soldiers killed in combat.

Adolf Hitler knew how to simplify a message so that it was understood by the least gifted in his listening audience. He knew how to choose the appropriate words to reach hearts. He knew that the masses were mobilized by emotions, not intelligence. He knew how to lie when it benefited him and stated that a big lie is more difficult to challenge. He knew the importance of an impressive staging in his speeches or military parades, to impress the crowds and show his power. His solitary personality added an aura of mystery around him. Few people really knew him, except for Ernst Röhm. Almost nobody who spoke to him used the familiar form *du* in German, which indicated a more personal relationship.

The hypertrophy of the sense of duty

The German culture deeply valued authority, in the family and in society. Psychologist Gustave Gilbert, who treated the Nuremberg defendants, realized that the Germans formed a nation conditioned to obey all levels of authority: parents, teachers, religious leaders, employers, superiors and government officials. Since early childhood, the Germans were raised in an environment where authority was a stable value. To produce a Dachau, an Auschwitz or a Buchenwald, a few sadists were not enough: they needed the assistance of thousands of Germans blindly submitted to the authority.

At the Nuremberg trials, SS Major-General Otto Ohlendorf was questioned about the murder of ninety thousand Jews in Russia while he was leading an Einsatzgruppen commando. He admitted having felt scruples during that operation, but argued that he was only following orders.

That excuse, repeated ad nauseam at the Nuremberg trials, shows how the nazi propaganda had managed to stifle the personal consciousness of the Germans and substitute the voice of authority. How did the Nazis manage to silence any form of criticism?

Culturally, Germans valued discipline, authority, organizational skills, efficiency and performance. Adolf Hitler embodied those values with the Führerprinzip, based on the principle that authority flows from top to bottom. He personified efficiency when he subordinated the means to the objectives. He delighted the Germans with successive victories in the first military expeditions, despite the warnings of his staff who felt, quite rightly, that they were not ready to support a war effort if the European countries had responded.

After the death of President Hindenburg on August 2, 1934, Hitler merged the positions of chancellor and president of the Reich and required an oath of allegiance of the army to him and not to the constitution. When candidates were admitted to the prestigious ranks of the SS, they had to swear loyalty to the Führer until death. One day Himmler was addressing the SS and, to mitigate the moral gestures that would be required from them when killing an enemy of the regime, he said that he was the one holding their rifle and no SS would be reprimanded or prosecuted.

The vast majority of soldiers under the age of twenty-five who fought during World War II had undergone massive indoctrination in the Hitler Youth. In 1936, the Hitler Youth membership was mandatory for all young Germans. At the end of the year, more than five million young Germans had joined the groups. They were taught unconditional love of the homeland, wholehearted dedication to the Volk and blind obedience to their leaders, whose authority had been vested in them by the Führer and who knew what they had to do. Baldur von Schirach described the objectives of the organization. From the age of ten, those who joined the Hitler Youth learned to set aside their own needs and follow the state guidelines to prevent chaos and destruction. Blind obedience strengthened the group and allowed to achieve important objectives for the nation.

The strong Prussian military tradition spread across the country a choice of values based on discipline and respect of authority. Most training programs had mechanisms to encourage the candidates to obey without discussion. During the training period, haircuts and identical clothing were imposed to remove individual differences and create a homogeneous group. Then, the recruits were asked to achieve the highest level of physical fitness, and they were frequently the object of denigration and verbal abuse on the part of their superiors. The punishments were degrading and focused on the uselessness of the work they were forced to do. Recruits saw their self-esteem take a quick drop. However, due to their intensive training, good hours of sleep and food intake, they became capable of an unusual physical performance that stimulated a better perception of themselves. Finally, the sergeant recognized that the group was not so bad and praised the group rather than the individuals. The recruits had more leave time and a prestigious uniform to strengthen their new identity that made them reliable and effective armed forces members. Then they were ready to obey orders and serve their country.

The socioeconomic and political instability

A prosperous and stable population is no fertile ground for chaos. But we all know that poverty and unemployment weaken the social fabric and are associated with rising crime levels.

Hitler offered to the distraught German nation what it was looking for. To a nation wracked by political turmoil, he offered stability. To a nation faced with unprecedented unemployment, he offered employment. To a financially ruined nation, he offered economic recovery. To a nation in total disarray and faced with huge social problems, he offered a social project focused on reconstruction with work and discipline. To a nation deeply humiliated and embittered by the Treaty of Versailles, he embodied the refusal to abdicate Germanic pride and proposed to develop a master race.

Faced with those problems, he pointed at the Communists, and especially the Jews who, in any case, were linked to the Communist Party. But, above all, despite the dreams that Hitler was dangling, the German nation had few alternatives and faced a hopeless political vacuum. The usual duration of the political regimes was calculated in months, sometimes in weeks.

The daily life in nazi Germany

Out of context, the impact of those circumstances may be difficult to grasp. Let us take a moment to draw a quick picture of the reality in Germany after Hitler came to power.

After 1933, nazism had infiltrated all spheres of daily life, whether or not one was a member of the National Socialist Party, man or woman, young or adult, worker or employer. From sunrise to sunset, the Germans lined up their activities and ways of being on the nazi creed. Everyone had to possess their own copy of *Mein Kampf,* which had become the orthodox reference like the *Little Red Book* of Mao in China, the Koran for the Muslims or the bible for the Christians. The Nazi Party was the gateway for employment, leisure, culture, education and access to social benefits. It used the machinery of the state to give an apparent legality to bodies accountable only to the party and responsible for ensuring that the activities of each citizen contributed to the achievement of its racist objectives.

Work

The disappearance of all employers' associations and trade unions regulating labor was followed by a complete reorganization of the structures, controlled by the party. The German Labor Front, led by Dr. Robert Ley and legally created on October 24, 1934, replaced all pre-existing structures and controlled the lives of the workers, from hiring to termination, including unemployment insurance and workplace accident programs. The worker became theoretically equal to his employer, but, in reality, he had the status of a feudal serf submitted to the will of his boss, himself under the control of the state. The workers and the employers formed a community whose services were for the greater good of the nation. The already low wages were subject to mandatory contributions to nazi charitable organizations or the workers risked losing their jobs for hostile behavior toward people. Lower labor rates allowed employers to do successful business, free from threats of strikes as they were banned.

A branch of the German Labor Front, called *Kraft durch Freude* or Strength through Joy, governed the personal time of the employees, providing them with opportunities for meetings, sports and cultural activities, in a framework maintaining a propagandist pressure even in their leisure time. Through subsidies from the organization, the Germans could enjoy to go on a cruise or to the beach at competitive prices during their vacation time. In 1934, nine million workers took part in those activities and that number increased to fifty-five million in 1939.

Education

The nazi leaders realized that their ideology would survive if it was reinforced by education. They changed the school curriculum in Prussia first and then throughout Germany. The guidelines issued on January 29, 1935 by the Minister of Education Bernhard Rust stated that racial education should begin at six years of age to allow the students to have a broader notion of the need and signification of racial purity.

After March 1, 1938, all the school books had to be approved by the party. The education was becoming national socialist. Courses in racial biology were made mandatory and the students learned about the evolution of the Aryan race up to their days. Practical work allowed them to become familiar with the physical traits that determine the race of an individual. They had to research the special achievements of Aryans. *Mein Kampf* became the most important history book. It was to be studied chapter by chapter and summarized after the last pages. Mocked by many, Rosenberg book, *The Myths of the Twentieth Century*, became the second most important book, and physical education, a leading subject, took up to five hours a day in order to build character, develop discipline and, of course, prepare for military objectives.

The girls had a different education that prepared them for their function of motherhood. In a speech to the National Socialist Women's Congress on September 13, 1936, Hitler reminded them of the role of the

German women. He claimed that a mother with six or seven children, healthy and well-brought-up, accomplished more for Germany than a female jurist with amazing achievements.

An article published in the *Völkischer Beobachter* on May 27, 1936 was a reminder that Hitler did not want women in school but in the kitchen and raising children for Germany.

The Hitler salute: A trivial gesture with serious consequences

From the seizure of power in 1933, the Hitler salute with the arm stretched out accompanied by the greeting Heil Hitler became the trademark of the National Socialist Party and a gesture of courtesy to greet someone. A trivial gesture that could be repeated twenty or thirty times during the day, the Hitler salute had a much more pernicious role than what could be seen at first glance. It helped to quickly identify the dissidents and those who lacked political fervor. Reluctance to make the Hitler salute immediately drew the attention of the political police. The citizen who dared show his opposition to nazism brought the Gestapo at his home and threatened the security of his parents and friends. To have a friend who was an enemy of the regime was reprehensible and sufficient to justify an interrogation session by the Gestapo. It opened a door to a transfer to a concentration camp and no legal or judicial body could protect the individuals against the excesses of the state. As a result, even if the friends of one who opposed the regime shared his anti-nazi feelings, they exerted pressure to make him comply with the requirements of the state or they took their distance from him and stopped talking to him or seeing him. In all cases, the recalcitrant individual was under extreme social pressure to conform and, the peak of refinement, even from those who disagreed with the national socialist ideology. Finally, the dissident surmounted his reluctance and most of the time conformed to the requirements of the party.

However, a gesture that goes against one's beliefs creates a stalemate. The only way to resolve the impasse was to silence one's own political beliefs. After having made the Hitler salute about ten thousand times over a period of one year, some confusion appeared in the value system of the dissident due to the fact that he displayed externally and repetitively his belonging to the National Socialist Party in which he did not really believe.

Bettelheim established a correlation between the totalitarian state and mass society, where consumption is driven by advertising (read propaganda) that leaves little room for individual freedom and atrophies the sense of identity. In the mass society, neighbors read the same books, watch the same TV shows and enjoy the conformity, until they suddenly realize the emptiness of a life that offers no individual experiences.

The poisonous atmosphere of systematic denunciation

In nazi Germany, the poison of denunciation had infiltrated the most vital social institutions. The children were encouraged to denounce their parents and teachers, and employees their bosses. The family unit, a source of individual stability and security, could no longer fulfill its role. Denunciations within the family sphere were rare, but the publicity that they were given was sufficient to amplify the phenomenon and undermine the peaceful trust of several families. In many cases, children had a hard time resisting the urge to use this power and threatened their parents of denunciation without really intending to do so. However, these threats undermined the confidence that could have strengthened the family unit. Also, a representative of the Nazi Party was assigned to every fifty residential unit. Since each German constantly felt scrutinized, it is plausible that a mental block contributed to create in many people a form of censorship that allowed them to avoid dangerous indiscretions.

The genius of Hitler: The water drop strategy

Albert Speer admitted in his memoirs that he could perceive less acceptable elements in Hitler's speech, but regarded them as excesses of language as there were in all revolutions and he did not think that they would materialize. His options were communist or socialist, since more moderate alternatives no longer existed. He believed that Hitler was a moderate, not realizing the opportunism that he showed. As for the Jewish question, he strongly believed that Hitler was mostly denouncing the undue Jewish influence over the cultural and economic spheres of life in Germany, and it seemed reasonable to ask that those influences be reduced proportionally to the percentage of the population represented by Jews.

> Hitler's strategy to achieve his ends was pretty much like the drop of water, which, from brooks to rivers, becomes imperceptibly a destructive torrent.

Hitler knew how to convince people to accept unacceptable facts by proposing a series of actions starting with the more tolerable, but leading inexorably toward the unacceptable decisions. That strategy remained his trademark. We should not forget that the German nation and the *Reichswher* were certainly in agreement with Hitler's expansionist policy. The decision to recover the territories owned by Germany before World War I was unanimous. However, the conquests in Europe that represented the end of the war for the German nation were only the beginning for Hitler. To achieve the conquest of the pre-war German territories, Hitler established an absolute power that allowed him to exceed the goals of the German people and the army.

He first applied it during the seizure of power. He was appointed chancellor in the most democratic way. Then, he merged the two offices of chancellor and president with the strong support of 89.9 percent of the vote in a referendum held on August 19, 1934. That merger represented a concentration of power extremely dangerous in the hands of one man. The decision was not clearly illegal. Hitler could use at will and without obstruction the principle of governmental decrees, as was the practice in previous governments. But the oath of allegiance that the Führer asked the Armed Forces to swear clearly represented a breach in the democratic rules and broke the tradition of allegiance to the Constitution. It seemed acceptable to the population, given the enthusiasm and hope that Hitler inspired. When shortly after Hitler made the military his accomplices in the assassination of the SA leaders in the Night of the Long Knives, the Germans were faced with a fait accompli that was clearly illegal and unacceptable. But they were the logical consequence of previous decisions, all accepted by the people, after the institutions that could have exercised a corrective influence had been muzzled. Hitler had introduced the Führerprinzip clearly described in *Mein Kampf.*

He applied the same principle with the concentration camps. Initially, the camps were meant for preventative detention of the state enemies, which in itself was a common and accepted practice in the European countries.

Then, they were used for the antisocial, alcoholics, prostitutes and Gypsies. That immediately became less acceptable, but in a country promoting order and discipline, there was little criticism. When the country went to war, all the structures needed for the imprisonment and the elimination of the undesirables were in place and those responsible for the camps were prepared to use the machine for purposes that were clearly unacceptable in a democracy, which in fact no longer existed in Germany. He therefore proposed in a plan of war to eliminate the unproductive eaters by murdering in a disguised way people with physical and mental disabilities. Everything was ready for the last step, the systematic elimination of the European Jews.

He used a similar principle when he implemented his expansionist policies. He first installed his troops in the Rhineland, the German territory occupied by the French army since the end of World War I. That move was looked upon favorably by the German population and had some legitimacy in the eyes of the European countries, aware of the frustrations caused by the Treaty of Versailles. Then, there was the annexation of Austria, which although less acceptable in Europe, had some logic for the German population.

In fact, Hitler was using routinely a cleverly balanced proportion of propaganda, deceit and opportunism. The annexation of Austria was carefully prepared by a propaganda presenting the German Austrians as eager to return to the homeland. When Hitler wanted to invade Czechoslovakia, he encouraged the Germans living in Czechoslovakia to make excessive requests to the government, which was forced to refuse them, and he used the abusive treatment of the Sudeten Germans to justify the invasion of Czechoslovakia. As for the invasion of Poland, Goebbels had prepared the popular opinion by presenting in the cinemas images of German refugees chased by the Poles. And to fully justify the intervention in Poland, Hitler put Himmler and his SS in charge of a fake attack on a German radio station on the German-Polish border. On the morning of the German invasion, the citizens of Germany were wondering why Poland was at war with their country.

This strategy, referred to as the straw that breaks the camel's back, succeeded brilliantly even outside Germany. After the invasion of Holland in 1940, Arthur Seyss-Inquart was appointed governor. The latter managed to reassure the population that life would continue as before, the Dutch laws would be maintained, all the government officials would retain their positions, and the nazi ideology would not be imposed on people. The first year of occupation was devoted to establishing a civil registration system. At first glance, the information requested seemed trivial: name, address and whether or not there were Jewish grandparents in the family. The identification of the Jews appeared to be a relatively harmless measure, but it was a prerequisite for further racial eradication.

It is only one year later, when the Dutch Jews were forced to wear the star of David and the persecution began, that the Dutch realized that by agreeing to complete the civilian identification forms, they had, without their knowledge, put part of their fellow citizens in the hands of the Nazis. In the following months, the Jews were gradually expelled from the arts, literature and business community. A clever propaganda created a climate of fear and repulsion for everything Jewish. In the movie theaters, Pavlovian conditioning techniques were used when showing sequential images of hordes of rats and groups of strange-looking, badly dressed and unkempt Jews who inspired aversion. Finally, the ruling regime proceeded to spread the purity of the breed ideology and one hundred five thousand of the one hundred forty thousand Dutch Jews died in the gas chambers. That concluded the genocide of the Dutch Jews, initiated by a trivial question in an identification form. This is how Holland was nazified despite Seyss-Inquart's formal promise to the contrary.

Nazism had all the attributes of a religion

The German National Socialism had all the attributes of a religion. It had a God: Hitler. It had its bible: *Mein Kampf.* It had its cross: the swastika. It had its sign of faith: the nazi salute. It had its priests: Goebbels, Göring, Himmler, Ribbentrop, Höss, Rosenberg, Darré and many others. It had its liturgy: large-scale parades culminating with the spectacular annual rallies in Nuremberg. It had its dioceses, the Gau, and a church hierarchy, the Gauleiters, the Reichleiters and the Blockleiters, who were responsible for ensuring the faithful orthodoxy. It had its infidels whom it needed to fight: the Jews and the Communists. It had its martyr: Horst Wessel, murdered in January 1930 by Communist opponents and who was presented by the propaganda as a man of honor, but who was in reality a pimp living on the avails of a prostitute, his mistress. The Nazi Party had its official rally song to celebrate his memory: the Horst Wessel song. Above all, nazism had its racial doctrine based on the greatness and purity of the Nordic blood that it needed to protect from the infiltration of Jewish blood and the threats of bolshevik communism. Those beliefs were supported by a pseudo-scientific literature embellished by scientific institutes and historical research groups. Finally, it had its moral code that determined the criteria of good and evil by the impact of behaviors on the racial doctrine.

All fundamentalists share the honest and sincere conviction that their fight is for the greater good of their members. This conviction perniciously gives false nobility to their gestures and allows for the more condemnable excesses. The priests have the knowledge of good and evil and take responsibility for protecting the faithful against themselves. In the fundamentalist doctrine, opposition is a crime and disagreement a heresy. Accordingly, it is legitimate to use all available means to bring back the lost sheep for their greater good. Most modern fundamentalist movements are religious and their judicial and political powers to correct the deviations from orthodoxy are limited. They must exercise their domination by imposing penalties of relative severity, the worst being the exclusion from the group. Political fundamentalism automatically inherits control of the judicial and legal authorities, which provides unlimited means of pressure in their nature and consequences. Then the concentration camps appear as a natural and almost inevitable consequence.

The nazi liturgy

Nazism also had its liturgy built in a staging that was likely to capture the popular imagination. All political meetings were held in banner, flag and slogan dominated gathering places. The nazi leaders favored particularly the torchlight walks where participants sang war songs.

The impact of the huge protests organized by the Nazi Party to capture popular imagination cannot be overemphasized. At all times, from Caesar with his Roman legions to Khrushchev with his nuclear warheads, men liked to use parades to show and spread their power. But in human history, the magnificence and the excesses of the annual political rallies in Nuremberg probably ranked first. Many of those who attended the rallies claimed that they never saw anything more majestic: Hitler standing on a huge platform, a gigantic eagle behind him, reminding of ancient Rome, surrounded by the nazi leaders in their uniforms with their decorations in front of hundreds of thousands of soldiers lined up in perfect order. This photo of the 1934 Nuremberg rally shows the Führer making the nazi salute, Himmler on his right, Lutze on his left, in front of nearly one million Nazis arranged in fourteen long rows. In the background, there are three huge banners at nearly one hundred feet above the ground. This single image provides a breathtaking view. The spectacular show culminated with over one hundred anti-aircraft searchlights installed around a large gathering space, drawing on the night the columns of a huge cathedral whose clouds represented the vault. A documentary of Leni Riefenstahl, *Triumph of Willens* or The triumph of the will, shows images of the September 1934 Nuremberg rally. It still has a dramatic impact on those who view it today. We see Baldur von Schirach in front of the massive ranks of Hitler Youth, swearing eternal loyalty to the Führer on behalf of his troops. He takes one step forward and tells them that they have to learn to obey and respect peace while being hard and resistant.

Photograph 1 – Nuremberg annual rally of the Nazi Party, 1934

Those who saw Hitler, alone and magnificent on the podium in the distance, dominating the nazi legions, immobile and perfectly aligned in solemn silence, got a clear and simple message: that man knew what he was doing and he was capable of great things.

Spectacular events produce an intense emotional mass mobilization that a skilled manipulator can easily use for his personal benefit. Large-scale events being quite rare nowadays, it may be difficult to imagine the emotional vulnerability that they would likely create. The grandiose staging of the annual rallies of the Nazi Party also surpassed what the world had seen and created a sense of national unity that we find today in the opening and closing of the Olympic Games ceremonies. They feed a sense of national pride in the host country and obscure the inevitable rivalries within the communities. The impact of that spectacular event on the Germans was more powerful since they were in the aftermath of a long period of humiliation and misery. They were thirsty for those things that nourish the collective memory and arouse national pride. Those large-scale shows provided a clear indication of the movement of the nation toward an exciting societal project that would give back to Germany the supremacy and power of the past.

Strength, power, discipline, strong leadership and a sense of organization surround those images. Those values are all prized by people who have experienced anarchy and social unrest for several years. They indicate a return to stability and peace. But those values are also sought by far-right citizens who favor a racist ideology that does not tolerate differences of opinion.

The delusional aspect of Hitler's project was not a source of concern because many large projects stem from crazy dreams. The brutal shock of reality would certainly bring the Führer back down to earth. As for the racist nazi theories, they pleased many Germans who felt that the Jews had enjoyed a privileged socioeconomic status during the crisis compared with the average Germans. Therefore, they were only getting their fair share of suffering.

Hitler was a communication genius. He knew instinctively that critical thinking is an intellectual process, whereas emotions are amoral. He delivered a simple intellectual message, summarized in a few repetitive slogans, but he attached the utmost importance to formulas that hit German imagination and created a feeling of elation that brought the people along with him, convinced that they were involved in an unparalleled historic event.

Dictatorship becomes fundamentalism when it imposes a doctrine seemingly aimed at supporting human or social growth, which is in reality a self-justified end. It is a sham projecting an illusion of good for human beings and it has extremely serious consequences. If the doctrine found its rationale in the greater good of those on whom it is imposed, then it could be challenged in whole or in part when not delivering the expected favorable changes. If the doctrine exists for mankind, it determines the inherently good or bad in an act by its propensity to reach growth or development goals. But when the doctrine is an end in itself, it becomes the criteria of good and evil. Then, the doctrine allows to brutalize, torture and even kill if ultimately those acts allow the doctrine to expand for the greater good of those who benefit from it.

Hitler had long recognized the need to feed the masses a spiritual ideal that would mobilize them. A Reich millennium of a pure Aryan race, gathered in a large Germany dominating the rest of the world that it fed through an advanced civilization, summed up the megalomaniacal dream that it was forbidden to criticize.

If the doctrine had been a series of words in a bible, the average German would probably have shrugged in front of this painting of the future Germany. But Hitler had already provided a preview. During the twelve years the Nazi Party was in power, Hitler put up a grandiose staging that strongly struck the imagination of the participants at political rallies or parades. After coming to power, he achieved what was called a military and economic miracle. He literally took Germany out of recession while the rest of Europe was in serious trouble and rebuilt the German military power despite the prohibitions of the Treaty of Versailles. In addition, he successfully invaded several neighboring countries without effort and recovered German populations excluded from the homeland. But for Hitler, that spiritual ideal was an end in itself. When he realized that the war was lost and the Russian divisions were at the gates of Berlin, he ordered Speer to destroy the infrastructure in Germany—the roads, the bridges, the power plants, the industries. The German people did not deserve to survive the shattered dream. For Hitler, his dream took precedence over the Germans for whom he lived.

"The instinct for the preservation of one's own species is the primary cause that leads to the formation of human communities. Hence the state is a racial organism, and not an economic organization. The difference between the two is so great as to be incomprehensible to our contemporary so-called statesmen. That is why they like to believe that the state may be constituted as an economic structure, whereas the truth is that it has always resulted from the exercise of those qualities that are part of the will to preserve the species and the race. But these qualities always exist and operate through the heroic virtues and have nothing to do with commercial egoism; for the conservation of the species always presupposes that the individual is ready to sacrifice himself.

(...) The sacrifice of the individual existence is necessary in order to assure the conservation of the race. Hence it is that the most essential condition for the establishment and maintenance of a state is a certain feeling of solidarity, wounded in an identity of character and race and in a resolute readiness to defend these at all costs."[5]

For Hitler, there could be no compromise with the opponents of the nazi doctrine, to avoid creating a protest movement that could weaken the momentum. In 1942, after the execution of two hundred thirty Jehovah witnesses who refused to join the army for religious reasons, he justified the mass execution decision by the need to destroy anyone who chose not to get actively or passively involved in state activities for religious reasons or lack of courage when the nation was threatened.

---

[5] Hitler, Adolf; Mein Kampf (James Murphy Translation), pp. 127-128.

Fanatical leaders

In order to ensure a real coercion, it is necessary to recruit fanatical groups that will be able to ensure the application of the doctrine and will execute the punishment deserved by the deviants. Fundamentalist religious groups have their army of zealous advocates and the nazi Germany had fanatical leaders and troops, which were probably the best trained and conditioned in global history. Those groups were responsible for the implementation of the sanction measures in an arbitrary environment where the individual right to freedom of opinion was denied with no legal recourse. We must simply bear in mind that the Gestapo had a power superior to that of the tribunal and a citizen acquitted in court could still be imprisoned or even executed with no legal recourse. The nazi leaders totally shared the megalomaniac delusion of their leader. Goebbels, Göring and Himmler defended the nazi doctrine with as much enthusiasm and as little scruple as Hitler himself.

Obviously, Hitler would have never been able to achieve many of his objectives without the unconditional support of the SS troops. Those troops committed their first official criminal act in the Night of the Long Knives. They also were the instigators of the attack scam of a German radio station on the Polish border that triggered World War II. They were responsible for the concentration camps and executed nearly ten million Jews, Slavs and opponents of the regime. Toward the end of the war, they were the most feared divisions on the battlefield. In Germany and the occupied territories, they ensured a climate of permanent fear that annihilated all possibilities of organized resistance. In fact, it is in the army, independent of the SS, that the best organized core resistance against the nazi regime developed.

Those men had for a large part been trained and conditioned by the Hitler Youth that all young Germans were forced to join from 1933. That organization was not only a fantastic indoctrination school for the Nazis, but also a valuable recruitment field to detect the most promising elements who could be incorporated into the SS troops.

The background: The state of war

A state of war is one of the most severe strains that could affect a community. It changes radically not only the relations between the individuals, but also the rules that build the social fabric of a society.

The psychology of a state of war oversimplifies human relations by assigning two categories mutually exclusive: friend or enemy. In Russia, by the end of the czars' era, there were the Whites and the Reds. Those who were not white were necessarily red and vice versa. In time of war, the shades of opinion and the gray areas immediately raise mistrust, since non-supporters are automatically suspected of collusion with the enemy. This polarization of human relations calls for violence between the enemies and sows the seeds of repression inside each of them. However, in many cases, the nations at war see a drop in tensions generated by societal problems, insofar as social aggressiveness is moved to an external target. And the presence of a common enemy helps citizens to stick together. In fact, the Germans never stood together along the Führer as much as when they were bombed day and night by the Allies in 1943.

The actors in a drama where civilians are relegated to the role of extras, the military are conditioned to perform duties on a collective rather than individual basis. The collective mission is usually to exterminate the enemy or, at the very least, put him out of action. In time of war, most of the rules structuring human relations between belligerents lose their meaning. Even the few internationally accepted rules intended to preserve some semblance of civilization in the battles are regularly ignored. To win the war, means are less important than the end. That situation is understandable. In many cases, international rules governing the behaviors of the combatants can become dangerous constraints. In the Pacific, the Japanese, who had developed an ultranationalism reminiscent of Germany, were programmed to die in battle. Some United States units were deceived by Japanese soldiers carrying the white flag as a sign of surrender while other armed and hidden Japanese soldiers were waiting for Americans soldiers to show up. We suppose that, subsequently, even the white flag carriers were shot point-blank. Similar experiences clearly establish the primacy of the jungle law and open the door to an extreme degradation of human behaviors.

A potential or definite hazard in the environment of the soldiers whose life is threatened stimulates the coping mechanisms that numb the moral conscience when re-aligning the choice of behaviors that become subordinated to the danger of death. Protecting the civilian population remains one of the rules more widely accepted by the international community. Several war criminals were tried for having violated that ban. But the majority of those acts escape collective condemnation. The death of hundreds of thousands of civilians in Hiroshima and Nagasaki speaks for itself.

War and atrocities go hand in hand. When armed men are sent to kill their fellow human beings, it is clearly foreseeable that brutality will occur despite the humanitarian rules proposed to humanize the battlefields. War crimes are far from being a nazi specialty. John Dower reported that American units in the Pacific boasted that they never took prisoners and collected Japanese body parts as war souvenirs.

In fact, a state of war has unavoidable consequences. Carrier of violence exacerbated by survival instincts, a war unleashes behaviors completely beyond the standards that usually govern human relations, and they have practically no rule or limit. In addition, it lulls individual consciousness under the shroud of the collective consciousness of the battalion, which depends on that of its hierarchical superiors. It creates a context that defeats corrective social mechanisms and promotes destructive behaviors that would be utterly inconceivable in times of peace. Alone, a state of war does not explain anything. However, it creates an extreme instability in the individual relations and leaves the door wide open to an uncontrolled outbreak of the more demeaning behaviors. It is the decor in which the Jewish genocide took place and it adds a striking depth to the actors' performances in this monstrous drama.

The racial war

As mentioned earlier, the rationale for a state is the conservation and promotion of a group of individuals who are physically, psychologically and culturally similar. However, in Europe, due to the immigration and the instability of the borders that were moving with each clash, many states housed a variety of ethnicities competing for power.

For the national socialists, the notion of race remained unclear, despite the development of institutes for the study of race and the pseudo-scientific classifications put forward. There were attempts to use morphological measurements to distribute men in an arbitrary classification system. Himmler was particularly interested in those studies. His training as an agronomist and his work as a chicken farmer were very helpful. He designed the racial cleansing as if it were for livestock. The mating had to be between purebred individuals, their offspring would be handed to institutions to help them grow healthy and sick offspring should be exterminated.

A racial war deserves special considerations because it increases in an extreme way the disintegration of relationships inside a community and is conducive to worse atrocities than conventional wars. A war usually breaks out in agitated times leading to intense social strains. The resulting aggressiveness finds in the enemy camp a target that allows the transfer of the collective aggressiveness outside the community. In a way, a conventional war stabilizes the social tensions by increasing cohesion among the individuals. Unlike a civil war, where groups are fighting for the recognition of certain rights or privileges, a racial war supports the ideology of inequality among human beings and, therefore, of inequality of rights in society. In a conventional war, the enemy is identified as one who threatens the geographic boundaries or the political power, but peace can be restored if the enemy abandons his territorial claims. In a race war, the enemy is defined by his ethnic identity rather than a hostile behavior, and he must disappear regardless of his involvement in the well-being of his community. In fact, German Jews played an important role in the German society despite their limited number. Many were professionals, university teachers, or held administrative positions. Once identified, the Jew could not escape his fate since he was a nuisance, not because of what he was doing, but for what he was. This notion of inequality based on race has no scientific value and is in total contradiction with one of the most important values of modern societies. A community under significant social strains blames a specific category of citizens for its social problems. This instability in the social fabric increases when someone tries to solve the problem, when the univocal solution remains the disappearance of the identified sources of evil. In a racial war, the enemy is not on the other side of the borders and he becomes a target that is part of the social fabric of the nation. The enemy is seen as an insidious germ that creates damages from the inside like a worm in an apple. To eradicate the evil, the germ needs to be removed along with the healthy tissue around it. Therefore, citizens who lived in relative harmony with each other must be made to feel mistrust, fear and hatred of each other. The majority must be convinced that a well-identified minority is directly the source of important socioeconomic problems, and that this minority prevents the majority from flourishing. The right of the majority justified the mistreatment imposed on a minority.

In this process, the excision of a healthy tissue was inevitable. Citizens who did not share the racist ideology, or who supported or protected directly or indirectly the enemy, or those who were believed to do so, faced a merciless repression. Denunciations, personal vendettas and abuses of all kinds increased and became an outlet for the less noble feelings of human nature.

To achieve this objective, it was necessary to exacerbate in brothers, neighbors and citizens their hatred for each other—and this is one of the ugliest aspects of a racial war. There needs to be an ideology that denies the principle of human equality.

The Nazis did not have at the time the monopoly of racist theories. In a book published in 1940, five years before the end of the conflict, Sir Nevile Henderson denounced the inhumane practices of the Gestapo. With a certain naivety, he argued that the Anglo-Saxon is a lovely person who, when at war, does not use persecution and torture. The average German is also very kind in normal circumstances. But when placed in an unusual position of authority, most of the time the German will abuse it. It could be because a considerable proportion of Slav blood flows in his veins.

Likely involuntarily, the author mentions the racial theories that the nazi doctrine invoked in a very different way to explain the superiority of the German blood. We must keep in mind that it is reassuring to say that the germ of cruelty lies more in someone else's genes rather than in the human nature that we all share.

The conflict between the individual and collective moral

Gerhard Boldt, cavalry captain in the German army, revealed the difficulties encountered by those who dared deviate from the nazi ideology.

He had joined the Hitler Youth after Hitler's rise to power in 1933, attracted to the movement by some idealism, a sense of camaraderie and the emphasis placed on training and sport. He quickly became a leader within his group. However, due to ideological conflicts with local officers, he was forced to resign from his post. He subsequently had problems in school, with the police, and he was finally rejected by the infantry despite the fact that he had successfully passed the officer examinations. He had just experienced a conflict between the individual standard and the social standard.

The individual standard is based on the choice of personal values. Those choices result from the integration of childhood conditioning derived from the models of parenting roles, the style of education, pleasant or traumatic experiences, and the values exemplified by the sociocultural environments. However, people integrate that conditioning differently. Behavior determinants, like temperament and the type of personality, modulate the influence of each conditioning experience of human beings. Individual moral conscience and the ability to stay faithful to those values are the result of a unique combination of genetic and social influences.

When social and individual standards collide, people face two options: stay true to their values and expose themselves to community sanctions or deny their own beliefs and endure feelings of guilt. There are very few Hans and Sophie Scholl. Our societies are made up of a handful of heroes and a mass of ordinary people who much prefer struggling with their conscience than being blamed by society.

During the twelve years of the nazi regime, under a veneer of legitimate patriotism, the German social standards were transformed into intolerance for dissenting opinions, bloody repression and racial discrimination for the honor of the nation and the survival of the Aryan race. Social sanctions are much more powerful than those of individual consciousness to determine the behaviors of individuals. It is a known fact that we are always more lenient with ourselves than we would be with others. In nazi Germany, very effective pressures were stifling the moral conscience of individuals. With the omnipresent propaganda, the Germans were forced to follow a code of behavior contrary to the humanist philosophy.

In human populations, there is a latent respect for authority that seems independent of its coercive potential and defines power as an instrument of social control that the citizens find necessary. In general, the official standards of behavior and the sanctions associated with a deviance are reasonably defined in the legal codes of most societies.

The nazi code was based on decrees never subjected to public debates. It included important gray areas that kept many Germans in limbo and required a defensive stance. Helping a Jewish neighbor to escape or even doubting the ultimate victory of Germany were crimes that called for punishment whose severity could include execution. The arbitrary aspect of the charges, the absence of legal remedies and the potential severity of the sanctions against the deviants instilled in most Germans the fear of getting seriously in trouble. Yet in many cases, the refusal to participate in a mass execution or obey an order involving free brutality did not necessarily lead to the imposition of an official sanction. For example, a policeman participated in the visit of a ghetto hospital. When his colleagues opened fire on bedridden patients, he felt a deep sense of shame and disgust. He aimed all his shots wide, intentionally avoiding any human target. His sergeant had noticed his marksmanship. When the killing was over, he took him apart, called him a traitor and a coward, but never reported the incident to the captain.

Major Wilhelm Trapp, head of the Reserve Police Battalion 101, met with his men and informed them of the assignment the battalion had received. There were one thousand eight hundred Jews in the village of Józefów. The male Jews of working age were to be taken to a work camp. The remaining Jews—women, children and the elderly were to be shot on the spot by the battalion. Major Trapp explained that they were to perform a very unpleasant task. However, he invited the older men who felt unable to execute the order to step out. After some hesitation, a policeman stepped out while his captain was hurling insults at him. Trapp interrupted the captain and took the man under his protection. A dozen police officers followed and stepped out as well.

Under Hitler, the definition of legality was modified to blind obedience to the Führer and to all those who held his authority by proxy. Even the most sordid decrees followed the usual route of administration with the signatures and seals of the appropriate administrative authorities confirming their legality. In the mind of the executor, those documents conferred legitimacy to acts, which, under normal circumstances, would have seemed unacceptable on a moral or humanitarian standpoint. As for those feelings, they became signs of weakness and pusillanimity threatening the revival process of the new Germany.

It is worth noting that war criminals such as Höss and Eichmann perceived themselves as honest public servants performing their job with as much dedication as possible, transferring the morality of their acts on their immediate superiors as if their own morals were confused with blind obedience to orders. Rudolf Höss was the first to use Zyklon-B for mass exterminations in the gas chambers and he slew over two million Jews. He argued that he assumed his responsibilities in executing the orders of his superiors with diligence and dedication. Adolf Eichmann participated in the Wannsee meeting to develop the organization of the Final Solution. He was in charge of the extermination of over five million Jews in the concentration camps. When the inhuman character of his work was questioned, he replied that no one was to be sentimental when it came to the Führer's order. In this way, the morality of the actions could be transferred to the top of the pyramid, from the immediate superior to the next, and no one was guilty. In the pyramid, only one person was guilty, Hitler, and the hundreds of thousands of executors were all innocent of the crimes ordered by Hitler.

The pressure from authority

The results of a psychological research on the influence of external situations, such as a position of authority and institutional support to help understand aberrant individual behaviors, are thought-provoking. How do ordinary people respond to unhealthy situations?

For ethical reasons, there are relatively few experimental studies on aggressive behaviors. Most people think that they are immune to the aggressive impulses that lie dormant in their brain. But the results of those studies show that we substantially underestimate the impact of aggressive impulses on our behaviors.

The Milgram studies

In 1961, Stanley Milgram examined the elements influencing individuals when acts requested by officials in a position of authority may raise moral problems. In experiments conducted at Yale University in the early 1960s, Milgram observed the behavior of subjects giving electric shocks to another person at the request of an experimenter. The subjects (called teachers) were told that they were participating in a study on learning through punishment. Behind a glass, there was an alleged learner who needed to recall a pair of words or face electric shocks of increasing intensity. The teacher had an electroshock generator that he could use starting with 15 volts and increase by 15 volts for each wrong answer, up to a maximum of 450 volts. The learner behind the glass did not receive an electric shock, but he mimicked a growing pain as the shock intensity increased in order to create for the teacher a conflict between his conscience and the request from the experimenter. Up to 150 volts, the learner showed signs of pain. At 150 volts, he pleaded to be allowed to stop the session, but the experimenter encouraged the teacher to continue. At 285 volts, the learner screamed in agony. The teacher was then caught between the learner, who showed intense suffering and the experimenter, who encouraged him to continue administering electric shocks to the learner. If he wanted to end the session, the teacher had to clearly refuse to comply with the request from the authority figure (the experimenter).

The results of the first experiment indicate that 62.5 percent of the participants carried through the experiment and inflicted a shock of 450 volts three times. All participants reached 135 volts and the maximum shock average was 370 volts. It is interesting to note that when the experience was the responsibility of two people who were in conflict, one favoring the continuation of the session and the other showing his disagreement, no participant exceeded 150 volts. In a variant of the experimental protocol where the participants were not pressured and could choose the intensity of the shocks, barely 2.5 percent of them used 450 volts and the average was 82 volts.

Obedience to authority is an essential element of life in society. It helps ensure that individuals' needs are met. These results highlight the significant weight of authority that determines human behavior. They suggest that when authority is perceived as legitimate, the majority of people are tempted to abdicate their personal choice and comply with the request, silencing their conscience and turning off their critical sense. The ability to disobey seems to be true for a small minority of subjects.

Protocol	Percentage of participants who used 450 volts	Average voltage used by participants
The study was under the supervision of an experimenter who encouraged the participants to apply electric shocks up to 450 volts.	62.5%	370 volts
The study was not supervised and the participants controlled the conduct of the experiment.	2.5%	82 volts

Table 1 – The results of Milgram's experiment

Milgram was criticized for the ethical issues created by those experiments. Concerns were raised about the long term psychological impact on the subjects who were convinced that the electric shocks were real.

Milgram asked 40 psychiatrists to predict the outcome of his study before undertaking his experiences. There was a consensus of opinions on the prediction that virtually no subject would dare use the maximum force of the generator. Milgram concluded that we grossly underestimate the power of situational factors as determinants of human behaviors.

The Burger's study

Wanting to know if attitudes had changed forty years later, Jerry Burger of Santa Clara University in California published the results of his studies replicating the Milgram's experiment. The results were comparable. In the Milgram study, 17.5 percent of the subjects continued to administer electric shocks at the 150-volt level or less while 82.5 percent continued to administer shocks at a level greater than 150 volts. In the Burger's study, the percentages were respectively 30 and 70 percent.

The docility of the subjects in the Burger experiment was even more noteworthy, since the pressure to obey was not as strong as in the Milgram experiment. Participants had been informed three times that they could withdraw from the experience at any time without risking to lose their compensation, and they had to stop the experiment at 150 volts at the learner's first cries of pain, although the subjects could go to the 450-volt level in the Milgram study. Burger explained that taking responsibility for the experimenter facing the victim made him the sole reference point for the participants. He also noted that the only participants who were likely to refuse to obey unacceptable orders were those with a dominant personality marked by a desire to control their environment.

Those studies highlight three important data. Firstly, the subject inflicting pain sees himself as an instrument in the execution of a task whose responsibility belongs to the person who made the request.

Secondly, obedience reaches high levels when the demand increases gradually. The subjects began the experiment with an intensity of 15 volts and gradually increased by 15 volts each time. It may have seemed difficult to refuse to inflict a 165-volt shock after the previous 150-volt. The gradual increase in the demands is an effective tactic to change the attitudes and behaviors. By using the strategy of the straw that breaks the camel's back, Hitler demonstrated that he had an intuitive knowledge of human nature.

Finally, when a plan involves many steps, those who execute the various phases of the project focus on the step assigned to them and do not clearly see the global result. It is a phenomenon that can be illustrated in many other areas. Hence, to each citizen, voting is an important civic duty that allows each and everyone to participate in democracy. In many cases, a significant percentage of the population does not fulfill their duty because one vote rarely changes the outcome of an election and will not affect the proper functioning of democracy. However, if each citizen abstains from voting, democracy, which is based on the choice exercised by each citizen, will no longer exist.

Those studies suggest that the ease with which a human being can become a torturer is due to environmental factors and personality traits. Most people would likely participate in an activity that could hurt people.

The arrival of civilization has not modified the reactions of human nature and compassion does not seem powerful enough to stop those behaviors. However, the strength of personality and the desire to control one's environment appear as major determinants to resist orders considered unacceptable.

The Stanford prison experiment

In 1971, Philip Zimbardo, professor at Stanford University, conducted a research funded by the United States Office of Naval Research to verify the impact of personality traits among prisoners and guards, in order to shed light on the abuse situations in prisons. He recruited twenty-four participants who were divided into two groups; twelve subjects played the role of prisoners and twelve the role of prison guards. The experiment was to last two weeks. The participants belonged to the middle class and the selection criteria were a lack of criminal history and psychological or medical problems. The guards received a nightstick, not to hit the prisoners, but to establish their identity as guards. They also wore sunglasses to avoid eye contact. As for the prisoners, they wore ankle chains to remind them of their status and they had to be called by their identification number rather than their name. In a preparatory briefing, guards were informed that they were not to inflict physical violence on the prisoners. As for the latter, the protocol specified that they were arrested at their homes for armed robbery and brought to the prison by local police forces.

The first day of the experiment occurred without any incident. On the second day, a revolt broke out when the three prisoners in a cell refused to step out. The guards requested the assistance of other colleagues who had completed their shift and attacked the prisoners with fire extinguishers without being supervised by authority figures. The guards came to the conclusion that they needed to use psychological tactics to control the situation and improve the conditions of the prisoners not involved in the revolt. The latter refused in solidarity with the rebels. Thirty-six hours later, one of the prisoners flew into a fit of rage. At first, the guards tried to control the prisoners with physical punishments. Then they made their living conditions more difficult. They removed some mattresses and the prisoners had to sleep on the cement floor. The guards stopped emptying the stool and urine containers and some prisoners had to stay naked in their cells. The situation deteriorated thereafter, one-third of the guards showing cruel and sadistic behaviors to the point that the experiment had to be ended prematurely on the sixth day.

The researchers drew the conclusion that situational factors, such as the tendency to obey when there is a legitimate ideology supported by social and institutional bodies, are likely to lead to abusive behaviors, regardless of the personality of the subjects. Those conclusions are in line with the work of Milgram. This experiment also points out that the potential for abuse is high when the subjects are placed in a position of power, even if they are ordinary people.

The group pressure

There is a fundamental conflict in the human mind between the need for conformity and the need to be unique, different from the others. In fact, social groups consist of dominant and dominated individuals who have complex relationships in an environment where the first determine the rules and the latter comply with those rules to avoid marginalization. The need for conformity is linked to the need to be accepted by our peers while the need to be unique is mainly a positive self-perception and confidence in one's values and ability to make a judgment on the environment. This is referred to as constructive aggressive impulses, which lead to narcissism when pushed to the extreme, as opposed to destructive aggressiveness, which can be powered by sadistic impulses or a desire for dominance over an individual or a group.

Participating in a collective gesture greatly dilutes the individual responsibility and confers some immunity to the members of the group. It is much more difficult to impose sanctions on a group than on an individual. All great revolutions had their lot of summary executions without the guilty being brought to justice.

Social conformism, or peer enforcement, has always been an extremely powerful control mechanism, similar to political power, because it has a legitimacy considered to be the voice of the majority. Most people are not aware of their need to conform. When they find out that their ideas are shared by the majority, the consensus is a proof that they are right. Very often, the opinion of others has a major impact on their self-image and endorsing the group ideas or values gives them the collective approval of its members. Marginalization or exclusion represents a severe penalty that hurts the individual vital need, which is herd instinct. However, mass behavior escapes this control since the individuals within the group have no peer accountability.

Unlike the control exercised by the authority, groups rarely use physical punishment to ensure the conformity of their members. By way of socialization, individuals internalize the standards that seem to be important for the group to which they belong. Fearing above all individualism that would have generated critical attitudes toward them, the nazi leaders gave great importance to the organizations governing the activities of the Germans, both at work and in their spare time. The sense of belonging to a group was a very powerful force that brought individuals to break their own code of moral behavior. For many police and military, the strength of conformity was sufficient to overcome the inhibitions imposed by their moral conscience, even in situations where transgression of moral rules was evident.

The orders to kill Jews were given to the battalion, not to the individuals. Despite their reluctance and feelings of horror, 80 to 90 percent of the policemen executed the orders. It was easier to shoot the Jews than adopt a non-conformist attitude. If they left the others to do the dirty work, they risked ostracism. Isolated abroad and facing a hostile population, the support and human contact became an essential need for those men.

The voice of conscience and the mental block

The nazi plan for the extermination of the Jews was adopted two years and four months after the beginning of the war. On July 31, 1941, Hermann Göring gave Reinhard Heydrich the mandate to find a solution to the Jewish problem. The Final Solution was officially presented at Wannsee on January 20, 1942, during a meeting of officials to be involved in the project. The date coincides with a turning point in World War II. Six weeks earlier, the Japanese had destroyed the American fleet in the Pacific at Pearl Harbor. The next day, the Congress voted in less than twenty minutes the entry of the United States into war. The United States mobilized their powerful industry for military purposes and the first Allied bombers were seen in the European sky on July 4, 1942, about three months after the beginning of the Jews extermination in the concentration camps.

To Hitler, individual moral conscience was an important potential obstacle to the unquestioned obedience he required from the Germans. However, when faced with the dangers of resisting the political power, many Germans shelved their personal code of ethics, not only for themselves, but also for their family.

Caught between the external threat of the Allies who were attacking the Germans on their home ground and the repressive political system that punished by death any citizen suspected of questioning the nazi ideology or even doubt the outcome of the conflict, the German population was in a rather uncomfortable situation. It was expected that most Germans were more concerned about their security and that of their family rather than the fate of thousands of Jews deported to concentration camps, particularly since those camps were located in Poland rather than in Germany.

The human soul has the ability to evacuate from the conscience anything leading to deadlock in times of conflict with personal values.

The Germans knew about the concentration camps. The nazi regime had informed the public of the existence of re-education camps, but the details about their activities were kept secret. The fact that no one knew what was happening in the camps made them even more terrifying. Those who feared them most were those who felt more strongly the need to believe that the camps did not exist.

Physicians regularly see patients who wonder about the cause of their problems. When it comes to a serious disease, those patients frequently react by listening carefully, but they may be unable to manage the information received. They do not seek clarification, but go back to the description of their symptoms and keep asking questions about the nature of their problem.

In 1945, when General Patton freed the prisoners of the Ohrdruf concentration camp, he was so horrified at what he saw that he vomited. Disgusted, he questioned the people of Gotha, a nearby village. The villagers said that they did not know what had been going on in the camp. He forced the villagers to come and witness the horror of the situation. That evening, the mayor of the village and his wife hanged themselves.

A psychologist who lived in the United States for about twenty years told me about her 1988 trip to Hungary, where she stayed a few weeks. Member of a Jewish family stigmatized by World War II, she had been reprimanded repeatedly for her light hearted comments or discussions with close friends about the political system. While she was in Hungary, she sent a dozen postcards to American friends with comments that she considered harmless about the Hungarian government. The people with whom she was staying had anxiously urged her to tear up the postcards. Determined not to inconvenience her guests during her stay, she concentrated during the following days on repressing all thoughts or reflections that could lead to a tense atmosphere in the house. After a week of self-censorship, this psychologist noticed a spontaneous thought blocking process, as if it were too painful in the long run to filter her thoughts constantly in order to eliminate any idea that would be detrimental to her entourage if it was expressed. Questions about the political system did not exist anymore, or at least they were not crossing the boundaries of consciousness without apparent effort, which she interpreted as a coping mechanism. The thought-blocking appeared automatically, even though she did not feel the need to react that way. Two weeks after leaving Hungary, during a stay in Nice, the thought blocking disappeared spontaneously.

It is possible that a similar thought blocking may have contributed to render inoperative in some people their ability to make a value judgment on the nazi political regime, given the climate of terror initially established by the SA and subsequently maintained by the SS. Or, viewed in a different light, the brain coping mechanisms simply suppressed their curiosity about the value of the political regime. There is no doubt that the repressive pressures exerted by the Hungarian family on her American visitor have nothing in common with the magnitude of the nazi terror and the length of time it was exerted on the German population. The possibility that the Germans were able to encapsulate the unacceptable policies of the nazi regime becomes highly plausible.

There is a similarity between this mental block process and the dissociation frequently found in children who have experienced severe psychic trauma, such as sexual violence. It is as if the painful events experienced were somehow lived by someone else, dissociated from the personality of the child. On reaching adulthood, childhood memories are almost non-existent. A survival mechanism of the psyche, the mental block isolates intolerable events in the subconscious, which transforms the reality by removing from the conscious events that it would be unbearable to evoke. The victims may continue to live normally with parents or other relatives that they should hate, without making value judgments about them.

How does one become an executioner?

This question is not simple, given the complexity of the human psyche. We can however provide some thoughts likely to shed a little light on those extreme behaviors.

One amazing fact is the absence of an apparent pathological trait in most of them. The torturers are recruited among ordinary people, sometimes highly educated, who torture and murder in a nine to five routine. They justify their actions by obedience to orders and feel little guilt toward extremely sadistic behaviors. It is difficult to determine if this submission to the hierarchical authority is only an alibi allowing them to release aggressive impulses that lie dormant in them, or if it meets a linear view of things under which a given order must be executed blindly. However, it is important to remember that, after the Nuremberg trials, the International Court recognized for the first time the right to dissent for the executioners. It clearly established the individual responsibility in the execution of a task related to torture and murder, which can no longer be justified by the obedience to orders.

Another constant found among torturers is their dehumanized perception of their victims. They are no longer men or women, fathers, mothers or members of a family. They become objects to destroy, bugs to crush under the foot, anonymous enemies to kill. This distorted perception of the human being is a feature of the war, but not exclusive to war. It is also found in totalitarian regimes, in religious dictatorships, in racist societies and in ethnic clashes when the people in power systematically repress the opposition. This distorted perception of the human being, rightly or wrongly considered as the enemy in time of war, allows for mass behaviors that would call for very stringent sanctions in times of peace in a democratic society. In the history of humanity, from the beginning, the killing of women, children, elderly, the gang rape, the looting, and the destruction of villages are called collateral damage of armed conflicts and raise very few concerns. In this respect, we could recall the lack of importance given by history to the systematic rapes of German women by Russian soldiers when the Soviet army entered Germany at the end of World War II. In a television interview, a torturer from the Argentinean dictatorship said that he felt guilty to perform his tasks, but he knew that he had the right to refuse to follow orders when he realized that his victims were human beings.

Although the executioners are recruited among ordinary people, we cannot conclude that all ordinary people would be good torturers. It is likely that a large number of people have enough moral sense to refuse to perform such duties. A large number of Germans lost their lives because they did not share the nazi goals that were not aligned with their personal moral values. However, the dissent was not exclusive to the Germans who were not engaged with the nazi system. Many high-level officials, such as Admiral Canaris and General Rommel, paid the ultimate price for their refusal to compromise the moral values they were fighting for. Somehow, their behavior was diametrically opposed to that of the torturers in the system. Far from being the servile executer of orders, Admiral Canaris used his power to sabotage the nazi system. Due to the secret status of military counterintelligence, he remained for some time beyond the reach of the SS services, which suspected him of treason. He made repeated attempts to win the cooperation of the Allies, but remained unable to convince them that, as a high-ranking officer in the military hierarchy, he actually wanted to collaborate in the destruction of his own system. Toward the end of the war, he was arrested and executed by the SS. As for General Rommel, he was forced to commit suicide. Due to his military hero status, the Nazis did not dare execute him as a criminal for his participation in a plot aimed to assassinate Hitler in 1944.

By analogy, we could examine the characteristics of the spouses in couples affected by domestic violence. Those people are neither sadists nor psychopaths. Those characteristics are usually found in individuals for whom the exercise of power seems important, and more often among police officers and doctors. The victim tends to be a vulnerable person with little outside support. Even though it is risky to associate the characteristics of domestic violence with torture, it is difficult to avoid highlighting the similarities of the dominant-submissive relationship in those two situations. We can believe that the victims of torture are being murdered more commonly perhaps than the victims of domestic violence simply because the perpetrators can count on impunity in times of war, whereas a sanction is the punishment for a violent spouse in times of peace.

One might be tempted to conclude that a more or less pronounced potential for barbarity is latent in all of us. In many people, a strong moral sense is sufficient to repress those urges. For others, their aggressive impulses are expressed more strongly and their control requires powerful social pressures to keep them in check. Despite those two levels of control, it still happens in our society that people lose their lives, killed by a violent spouse. Torture and murder are common when the social pressure disappears and they take place with the blessing of the state or under the guise of defending one cause.

The contemporary Germans still carry a burden of guilt for the actions of their parents nearly eighty years ago. A large number of people are convinced that something in the German temperament or in the German culture was already preparing the ground, allowing the nation to release its destructive impulses and engage in an extermination program, in which unimaginable atrocities were committed against human beings. The swastika has become the best-known icon of cruelty and sadism that can live inside of us.

Was the German nation victim or guilty?

What was the role played by the Germans during the nazi period? Five types of responses can be identified, but it is impossible to assess the percentages since the brutal and systematic repression of dissent forced the population to stifle any criticism about the regime.

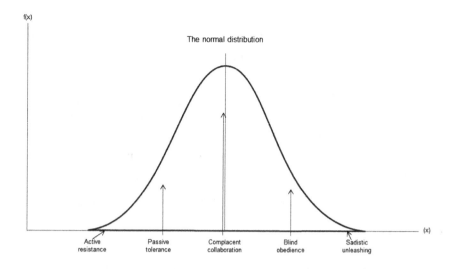

Table 2 – Types of responses to the nazi dictatorship
(These categories are not distinct and individuals could
have moved in and out of the categories over time.)

However, in the event of a breakdown following the normal curve, the range of behaviors should be distributed according to a continuum of responses, such as illustrated in Table 2, where the two extremes occur in a minority of individuals at each end of the curve.

1. Active resistance

The heroes are in this category: Germans with a strong personality and strong personal values, able to resist the nazi propaganda. Those men and women actively opposed the nazi regime and many were executed. For example, Hans and Sophie Scholl, Admiral Wilhelm Canaris, Colonel Claus von Stauffenberg, General Ludwig Beck, Pastor Martin Niemöller, and all those who anonymously risked their lives to defend freedom and the values of democracy.

It is difficult to determine how many Germans remained faithful to their moral conscience. In Germany, six hundred sixteen people risked their lives to save Jews and received the Righteous Among The Nations award. Moreover, it is estimated that three thousand army officers took

347

advantage of the protection of the Abwehr—which was beyond Himmler's control—for operations against the nazi regime. Also, there were nearly three hundred thousand convictions for political crimes between 1933 and 1936.

We find heroes in all societies, but they remain invisible even in their own eyes. We discover them in crisis situations, when they have the courage to help people in danger despite major personal risks. We would like to believe that the number of Germans who remained loyal to their convictions and acted accordingly was much higher than it may seem at first glance.

2. Passive tolerance

A large number of Germans did not approve the incitement to racial hatred and the brutal repression of the nazi government, but openly disagreeing involved significant risks for the individual, his family and the loved ones. The Germans were not talkative and many of them lived in fear that their half-heartedness toward the regime became apparent and threatened their security. Hundreds of Germans were executed for attitudes or behaviors that would be viewed as ordinary in a democratic regime, among other things, helping a Jewish neighbor, listening to the BBC, showing contempt for the Nazis and doubting the final victory. The story of a pharmacist told by Anna Ornstein illustrates the dilemma between his loyalty to his moral values and his duty to protect his family.

Dr. Anna Ornstein, in a speech delivered on Remembrance Day in memory of the six million Jews who perished in the Holocaust, said that it was difficult for the citizens living in our democratic societies to imagine what would have been their behavior under the extreme circumstances that prevailed in Germany and in the occupied territories under the nazi regime. She asked specifically where each of us would be in the behavioral repertoires if we were facing the same moral dilemma. After the war, she had a meeting in Heidelberg with Herr Pabst, with whom she lived with her husband for two years.

Herr Pabst had five children in their teens. He had a National Socialist Party membership card, essential to exercise his profession. His children were in the Hitler Youth, in order to enjoy benefits such as social status, sports facilities and travel that the Nazi Party was offering to those who joined the organization. He told Anna Ornstein that at the beginning, he promoted Hitler's policy, but that his sense of belonging became a moral dilemma after seeing the nazi slippage. His priority being to ensure the safety of his family, he was in no position to withdraw his support from the party. Confronted to an authoritarian and totalitarian political system, he felt trapped in a dead-end.

3. Complacent collaboration

Most Germans should theoretically belong to this category combined with the previous. We know that a project like the Final Solution required the participation of a large number of citizens. They could have ignored the real fate of the Jews who were sent to concentration camps, but could not turn a blind eye to their persecution. The voice of authority, the brutality of the repression and the fragmentation of tasks were enough to silence the voice of their conscience. Some of them showed antisemitic attitudes. They considered that the Jews had benefited from better living conditions in earlier years and that the pendulum was finally swinging the other way.

For the average German citizen, the outbreak of World War II came as a surprise and was bad news. Until 1939, he dealt with the domestic threat of the political police. From 1939 onward, he sustained a painful wartime effort as well as continued Allied air raids. In that context, he was concerned with his survival and that of his family, which left little space for other people's survival.

4. Blind obedience

A large number of executors subject to the authority contributed in many ways to the proper functioning of the nazi machine by blindly following orders. The SS embodied the perfect prototype of the fanatics transformed into killing machines. Without them, Hitler would have been unable to achieve his destruction plans. Conditioned to unquestioned obedience, they had to be able to murder their own family in cold blood, should they be ordered to do so. The SS troops executed the most sordid tasks with a brutality and cruelty that would have paralyzed a normal individual. Obedience to orders was a must and they executed the most disgusting tasks, convinced that they had fulfilled their duty.

But the SS training was not mandatory to kill. The Reserve Police Battalion 101, a unit of five hundred, mostly family men too old to be sent to the front, participated in the killing of eighty-three thousand Jews between July 1942 and November 1943. Resisting the pressure of social conformism, about 15 percent of them refused to execute the victims while 85 percent chose to obey the orders.

Submission to the authority is not the only element involved. Environmental factors may be sufficient to explain the outbreaks of extreme violence and cruelty. The results of the Zimbardo prison experiment are very similar to those of the Browning study on Battalion 101.

In this category, the violence and cruelty are based on conditioning factors, environment factors, and probably also on genetic factors—about 3 percent of the male population are carriers of an antisocial personality disorder likely to result in a propensity for violence.

5. Sadistic unleashing

Several nazi leaders such as Himmler, Kaltenbrunner, Rudolf Höss, Adolf Eichmann and many SS executioners followed in Hitler's footsteps by planning without pity or remorse the execution of men, women and children, as if they were bulky items that they had to get rid of. Some like Dr. Josef Mengele engaged in unnecessary medical experiments under the guise of science to conceal their sadistic impulses. Sadism was not exclusively masculine. Ilse Koch, known as the witch of Buchenwald and the wife of the camp commander Karl Koch, ordered selected prisoners to be murdered and collected their tattoos to make lampshades.

We also find in this category most of the executors of the torture procedures related to politics or medical experiments. Despite the difficulties of diagnosing, it is more than likely that the psychopaths of the nazi regime would be in this category. In fact, the specific traits of this psychopathology, such as a lack of empathy, senseless cruelty and ruthless fanaticism, were valued by the authorities.

If nazism became a symbol of cruelty, it is simply because it relates to acts that are the most extensively documented. Many other nations were guilty of abuses as bad as those of the Germans. Cruelty and sadism are inherent to human nature.

A historical and significant fact rarely recorded in history books deserves to be recalled. Jedwabne is a small Polish village with a little more than three thousand inhabitants. The population, comprising Catholics and Jews in equal proportions, was living in a climate of cordiality until the summer of 1941, when strong antisemitic feelings suddenly emerged. With chilling details, Jan T. Gross recounts in his book *Neighbors* how the Catholic half of the village spontaneously slew the other half—men, women and children. A Polish couple hid seven Jews who escaped the massacre and praised the courage and greatness of soul of their rescuers. Although many historians do not share the belief that this pogrom was prepared by the villagers themselves, it is recognized that a number of Catholics participated in the massacre.

Cruelty and sadism were not exclusive to the Germans. The Japanese committed similar atrocities. And Americans were not immune to those behaviors. On March 16, 1968, a platoon of one hundred five American soldiers entered the village of My Lai and brutally killed five hundred unarmed civilians, in many cases with a bayonet. Women were sodomized and raped and some had their vagina slashed with a knife. Bodies were scalped. Only William L. Calley, head of the platoon, was tried and sentenced.

The choice of a system of values and being true to them appear to be two different processes. The choice of values would be based more on environmental factors from the family and the community in which people develop. Skinner's operant conditioning likely has a decisive influence on the transmission or even the modification of the chosen values, as well demonstrated by the nazi system.

On the other hand, our loyalty to our system of values might be more dependent on the genetic makeup of individuals or on the temperament we inherit at birth. Some people are more combative or stubborn or altruistic than others and those personality traits are obviously reflected in the way we convey our values. We may be convinced that in a given situation we will react in a specific and predictable way. But in fact, most of our choices are determined by our emotions rather than our reason. The real test is the exposure to an extreme situation that will reveal our true human nature. Jean Moulin died under torture without ever revealing information incriminating the French resistance members. How could we predict such a deep loyalty to a system of values?

The question is not "Were the Germans guilty or victims in this disaster?" but rather "Had we been in their position, would we have acted differently?" Current knowledge supports the view that the physical and social environment plays a key role in determining human behavior. The American psychologist B. F. Skinner wrote that we underestimate the environmental factor when explaining the behaviors. This statement is strongly supported by the erroneous belief of the forty psychiatrists in the Milgram's study, that virtually nobody would use the maximal range of the generator to produce electric shocks inflicted to a comedian faking intense pain. In Skinner's opinion, people are extraordinarily different in different locations, and if we interchange the location of two people at birth, they would follow a behavior in line with the place where they have been relocated.

The fascination exerted by Hitler on the German nation is still alive today among our contemporaries in a somewhat surprising way. I came across a ten-minute speech delivered by Hitler and, at the time, three hundred seventy-two thousand three individuals, mainly from the United States, the United Kingdom and Sweden had viewed the video. In this group, 39 percent of the visitors had checked one of the two boxes indicating I like or I don't like. The percentage of people who had enjoyed the video was 73 percent against 27 percent. In addition, one thousand three hundred people had left a comment. In the first twenty-eight comments that I read, twenty-five were positive (89 percent), calling Hitler a genius, expressing their admiration, saying that we still needed him, highlighting his intelligence and his performance as a speaker. Two comments were neutral (7 percent) and one was negative (4 percent).

Almost all favorable comments applied to the form rather than the content of the speech. The strong and passionate voice was hammering words interspersed with pauses filled with the roar from the crowd, and the apparent sincerity of the speaker seemed to create pure magic in the audience who was totally silent as soon as Hitler spoke again. It illustrates perfectly the governing principle of Marshall McLuhan for whom the medium and not the message is the real determinant factor of communication. If our contemporaries are lured by the speech of a character who killed millions of people, we can try to imagine the impact that Hitler produced in a population worn by social, economic and political chaos, and unaware that the path it was following led directly into a hell inhabited by destruction, suffering and death. Speaking to emotions rather than reason, this power of seduction defeats the critical sense of the targeted victims and is one of the most valuable tools in a crook's toolbox.

Conclusion

The fragility of civilization

To give a meaning to the nazi derailing, it is not enough to examine the mental health and the personality of Hitler. It is also necessary to explore the booby trapped relationship model maintained by Hitler with the German nation and the European leaders, which allowed the dictator to use an almost unlimited power to set the continent on fire with the intention to impose a wacky racial purity and the Aryan hegemony project that was not supported by a majority of Germans. Attention must be given to the weaknesses and vulnerabilities of human nature as well as the determinants of behavior that helped transform respectable citizens in ruthless murderers. Finally, we must clearly realize the dangers of power, which gives to those in positions of authority a variety of tools enabling them to exert a physical, psychological, social or material dominance on their fellow human beings.

The tragic advent of nazism challenges human nature about the dangers of power with its potential for abuse and the vulnerability of people within the communities. Man's best friend can become his worst enemy. Although human contacts are essential to the well-being and safety of everyone, they can be a source of suffering and death. Winston Churchill said: "The power of man has grown in every sphere, except over himself." World War II and all the steps that led to it highlight the multiple facets of human nature in all its noblest and most perverse manifestations.

Contrary to popular belief, in the battle between heart and mind, the heart generally wins. If the reason was dominant, it is likely that a large number of human conflicts would easily find a solution. Many people claim to be rational, but the reasons given to justify their behavior appear to be post hoc justifications. When we are faced with a situation, our brain verifies in a fraction of a second if we had a similar experience in the past and analyzes the impact on our well-being. It gives an emotional tone that colors the perception of reality and guides the decision-making process. In general, everyone seeks the maximum benefits to meet his needs. The problem is aggravated by the fact that what is perceived as a benefit for one is not necessarily a benefit for all. Many artists say that they are totally at ease on the stage in front of hundreds of spectators, but very uncomfortable in interpersonal relationships. For others, it is the opposite. Those who are in power are able to impose on members of the community objectives that find little resonance among some but are clearly unacceptable for others. A relationship of strength is established between the leader and the members, the first trying to impose his project and the latter being reticent to endorse it. Hitler was deeply convinced of the German superiority over the rest of the world. His divine mission was to purify the German nation of its contaminants in order to produce a pure breed of masters of the world. Hitler's beliefs reached the point of religious fervor and had a dogmatic character that could not be questioned. Blinded by his narcissism, he determined that the well-being of the nation had precedence over the individual rights and security of the Germans.

The German support to the Nazi Party

The population support for the Nazi Party was more apparent than real. Hitler never won an election by a majority vote. His best performance was 43.9 percent of the votes in the March 1933 election, despite the crisis caused by the Reichstag fire a few days earlier—which he blamed on the Communists. The election of November 1932, four months earlier, had given him only 3.2 percent of the votes, since two out of three Germans had dissociated themselves from the nazi politics. We know perfectly well that the social order of a nation can be significantly disrupted by a minority of individuals who are actively engaged in public demonstrations. The strength of the nazi movement was primarily due to the activist nature of the members of the party, particularly the SA. In 1932, the SA had four hundred thousand members. As for the Nazi Party, it had eight million members in 1933, barely 11.4 percent of the population. Throughout that period, the Germans understood that something unusual and potentially terrifying was going on. The police forces had abandoned the citizens at the hands of the SA who could choose their victims and murder them in cold blood. The Germans tried to reassure themselves pointing out that, despite the appointment of Hitler as chancellor on January 30, 1933, the Nazis were in a minority situation with only three departments out of ten. What they never expected was that Hitler intended to quickly get rid of the parliamentary system and impose a dictatorship. No more than 18 days after the election of March 5, 1933, Hitler managed to have the Reichstag vote a law giving him full powers for four years. With absolute power, he was to use all means at its disposal to carry out his project, from the abolition of individual rights to the genocide.

Who knew what?

If the Germans knew about the abuses suffered by the Jews, they were probably unaware of their extent. The high-ranking officers in the army were certainly informed of the mass murders, and the soulless civil servants and technocrats who prepared the documents and printed the lists of victims could not ignore everything.

It was widely agreed that the more credible among the Nuremberg defendants was Albert Speer, Hitler's architect. Speer candidly accepted responsibility for the nazi crimes and found that the trial was necessary, admitting a shared accountability for the leaders despite the authoritarian system in which they were working. Questioned by Gustave Gilbert, the psychologist assigned to the war criminals during the Nuremberg trials, he claimed that he had no knowledge of the crimes listed in the indictment and that as minister of Armaments and War in 1942, he knew about the concentration camps no more than his other colleagues knew about the secret weapons such as the V-2, whose characteristics were clothed in secrecy.

The commander of the German Navy, Grand Admiral Karl Dönitz, was sentenced to ten years in prison for crimes against peace and war, but he was acquitted of the charge of crimes against humanity. A few days after the surrender, Dönitz learned in the newspapers the atrocities of the concentration camps. On May 15, he enacted a decree intended to arrest those responsible for the crimes and bring them before German courts. He was short of time since he was put under arrest by the Allies and tried as a war criminal.

Dr. Traut Lafrenz-Page, who was a medical student with Hans and Sophie Scholl and currently lives in the United States, was against the nazi policies. In March 1943, she was arrested and imprisoned by the SS for her distribution of leaflets in Hamburg. Released a year later, she was imprisoned again until April 1945. In an interview published on January 28, 1998, she said that she knew nothing about Auschwitz at the time.

Gustave Gilbert also interviewed half of the thirty-eight war criminals imprisoned in the fortress of Landsberg until their execution for their crimes committed at Dachau. Physicians, administrators, guards, all functions were represented. They could not deny that they knew everything. Dr. Klaus Schilling admitted killing hundreds of prisoners, but justified them by the need to find a serum against malaria. He admitted that his experiments were unnecessary, but considered them more relevant than those implemented by other colleagues. Josef Seuss, an administrator, Walter Langleist, a regimental commander, and Anton Endres, a supervisor described as a sadistic psychopath, justified their actions by obedience to orders. Endres said that those who acted otherwise risked death.

Was the population's indifference part of the range of normal human reactions?

The beginning of the war coincided with a sharp increase in violence against the enemies of the Nazis, especially the Jews and the Slavs. The violence took the form of a deportation of the Poles to the concentration camps and of the Jews to the ghettos. The executions by the Einsatzgruppen commandos and the exterminations in gas chambers began toward the end of 1939. The SS executed victims by the hundreds. It is reported that those behaviors were condemned by the army, but the denunciations were more a smear technique used in a power struggle than a real humanitarian gesture.

It may seem surprising and even scandalous to see that those executions did not raise a wave of indignation in the population. However, we must place ourselves in the context of that time and remember that serial executions were almost part of daily life in Germany. Examples include hundreds of executions after the burning down of the Reichstag in 1933 and the beheading of the SA in 1934. The bloody repression of thousands of Germans after the failed attack of Stauffenberg in 1944 did not raise waves either. The German indifference seems selective since the extermination of their mentally ill provoked the opposition of the population and forced the nazi government to backtrack.

The extermination techniques appeared to be improvised when the number of victims to be executed amounted to millions and the ghettos became overcrowded. The problem was entrusted to Adolf Eichmann and the technical details of the Final Solution were developed at the Wannsee conference on January 20, 1942. However, barely twelve months later, the Stalingrad defeat in January 1943 predicted the collapse of the Third Reich. Shortly after, Allied bombings combined with political terrorism forced the population to adopt an attitude of resigned apathy. In 1943, it is likely that the German citizen was more concerned about the daily Allied bombings than the fate of the victims in the concentration camps. The world of people experiencing problems narrows down and the misfortune of some overshadows that of others.

We can finally believe that the average German who would have heard about the concentration camps and their medical experiments, and the cruel torture and the systematic extermination of the Jews in the crematoria and gas chambers would have been completely incredulous. At that time, human history had never documented comparable facts and the charters of human rights promulgated in America and Europe less than a century earlier appeared to be the guarantors of a new civilization where such barbarism would be inconceivable. After being released, when Bruno Bettelheim proposed a book recounting his stay in the concentration camps in Poland, the British editor refused to publish it on the grounds that the story was implausible.

Despite overwhelming evidence that the horrors in the concentration camps were real, there is in historical literature an ideological current called denial, which minimizes or questions the existence of such cruelties. Anne Grynberg reported that a document from Pierre Vidalnaquet quoted the German lawyer Manfred Roeder as establishing the loss of Jewish lives during World War II to two hundred thousand, mostly attributed to natural causes. Despite the fact that history is behind us and compelling evidence of the reality of the horrors in the concentration camps, many contemporaries continue to express doubts about the truthfulness of the facts. Was such cruelty possible at the time when history was being made?

Were the Germans the only ones accused?

If the Holocaust is a specifically German drama, it would be unfair to say that it is an exclusively German phenomenon. The astounding number of publications on the topic produced in recent years suggests that the Nuremberg trials have not eased the collective conscience in limiting and eliminating evil after the conviction of the guilty. No one yet has convincingly shown that we are collectively totally blame-free. Should we expand the scope of responsibilities to those who indirectly contributed to the implementation of the mechanisms that created this disaster? For the war to engulf the entire world, elements external to Germany necessarily sinned by act or omission.

What about the passive resignation of the Allies toward Hitler's pranks? Driven by the desire to avoid a new war, they allowed the execution of the projects detailed in *Mein Kampf*, published ten years earlier.

What about the participation of the populations of more than a dozen European countries who joined the SS ranks to the point that at the end of the war the Germans were a minority in several divisions of the Waffen-SS?

The need for a scapegoat

Psychologists observe that the frustration of the individual or collective needs in achieving highly desirable objectives generates aggressive behaviors. In accordance with our internal logic, it is against nature to blame ourselves for our own difficulties. No one will knowingly make his own misfortune. When for multiple reasons aggressiveness cannot be directed to the real cause of frustration, individuals or masses seek to move their anger to other individuals or other groups who usually belong to their immediate environment and will unlikely react forcefully to their aggressiveness.

The identification of a scapegoat goes with a fanciful rhetoric—since it misses the real target, it seeks to blame the person presumed guilty. A vicious verbal one-upmanship compensates the simplistic aspect of the charges. Hitler used extremely offensive and vulgar terms toward the Jewish people. Newspapers—in particular those of Julius Streicher, as well as the movies, with Paul Joseph Goebbels' blessing, amplified the hate propaganda, thus channeling the collective resentment of the Germans toward the Jews.

There was a catastrophic misunderstanding of the real issues of the German militarization. As the nation sought to erase the humiliation of the Treaty of Versailles and recover the lost territories, Hitler was preparing his weapons with the view to achieve a comprehensive ideological plan of racial domination. The expansion of the German vital space or lebensraum at the expense of Russia was already a priority set out in *Mein Kampf* a decade earlier. But the false German-Soviet pact signed with much fanfare in 1938 misled both Stalin and the Germans. The Jewish populations represented a convenient outlet for the frustration of the Germans. Hitler used that outlet as a catalyst for rallying the population to support his cause and eliminate at the same time a significant obstacle on his path.

This staging describes the subtlety of the scam mechanism. The operation always begins with a seduction phase to gain the trust of the victim with lies and deceit, similar to a break-in in his or her environment. Then, the crook makes recommendations to the victim so that this person can establish a system that will have positive results for the crook at the expense of the victim. The scam goes on until the threshold of tolerance of the victim is reached and he or she realizes that the crook's benefits largely exceed his or hers.

The fragility of civilization

The history of World War II reminds us that the achievements of civilization are much more fragile than we imagined. The nazi ideology took root in the same soil where the world's greatest thinkers, composers and scientists flourished. It demonstrates clearly that the development of a society is not enough to maintain humanist values enshrined in the charters bearing on human rights. The principles of the value of man and respect for the dignity of the human being were simply dismissed by the German nationalism. It took only a period of political instability to mobilize the primitive attributes of the mass social conscience and lead to the madness of World War II.

The totalitarian dictatorship was not an exclusively German phenomenon. After World War I, the collapse of parliamentary democracies and the ensuing social chaos encouraged the emergence of dictatorships with a strong executive power. Before 1914, Europe had seventeen monarchies and three republics. After 1918, there were thirteen monarchies and as many republics. In 1939, there were seven monarchies and five republics left. The other forms of government were dictatorships.

In Germany, totalitarianism was particularly aggressive, even though it relied on a racist nationalism. Using the legal basis of the decrees, Hitler deprived the citizens of all their rights and democratic privileges, expanding at the same time his hold on the nation. However, societies are made up of a few heroes, a small number of mobsters and a mass of ordinary people with a great force of inertia, whose movements can determine the course of history.

Hitler's firm resolve and shrewd political style were sufficiently powerful to make the German society deviate from the humanist principles adopted a century earlier. The social buffers that civilization needed to preserve its gains collapsed one after the other. With the denial of the fundamental principle of the equal value of all human beings, regardless of their race, language, religion or sex, the door to barbarism was wide open. The stakes of the conflict were not simply limited to territorial borders. The real issue became the humanist ideal of freedom of man and the peoples.

Can we imagine the consequences of a nazi victory, enslaving the European populations to its ideology and using all the industrial resources of the continent to ensure the military supremacy of the Aryan race in the world? It would have sufficed for Hitler to get a foothold in Great Britain for the inconceivable to become possible. The German-Soviet Pact would have ensured peace in the East and the United States would have been deprived of their disembarkation platform in Normandy. It is difficult to avoid feeling a deep anguish in the face of scenarios that could have woven the history of the twentieth century in the event of a German victory, when we are inspired by the pages already written with the blood of millions of innocent people whose death did not influence in any way the outcome of the war. Those deaths still tarnish our collective conscience.

The nazi barbarism remains today a reference point for crimes against humanity, since it was the most technically refined, collective crime in its organization and the best documented in history. However, the massacres of civilian populations at the hands of soldiers belonging to very civilized countries did not end after 1945. Those responsible for killing civilians are usually not bloodthirsty psychopaths, but more often ordinary people in the line of duty. In fact, the nazi crimes have allowed us to uncover the most troubling aspect of human nature. Hitler is not dead: he simply has a different face.

The Nuremberg trials were meant to put an end to one of the saddest chapters in human history. Evidence was filed, the accused were heard, the oral arguments were recorded, the defendants were sentenced and the faults were atoned. However, there is something strange in the fact that the Americans, who dropped two atomic bombs on civilian populations in Japan, accused of mass murdering the Germans who had dropped the Zyklon-B crystals over the heads of Jewish civilians. There was also something absurd in the Russian indictments denouncing the Nazis. Those who blamed the Germans for the extermination of ten million people had themselves exterminated twenty million citizens in the Stalinist purges. Clearly, the men demonstrated to the end of this tragedy the limits of civilization and of its humanitude.

The human nature that we share conceals destructive forces in the depths of our unconscious, allowing outbursts of aggressiveness, hatred and cruelty that coexist with noble impulses, allowing the expression of loyalty, generosity, tolerance and altruism. Our behaviors are the result of a complex interaction between the genetic influence of our temperament and the influence of our living environment. In our daily life, we project an image that we try to improve to give a good impression to the people around us. But in extreme situations threatening our psychological or physical integrity, those concerns become secondary and fade to give free rein to our natural impulses.

The link between human nature and democracies

Human nature and democracies have several characteristics in common. They are both imperfect. Democracies react to surveys and human nature is vulnerable to social pressures. Pushed to the right and left, they mainly go where the wind blows. They are both capable of extraordinary achievements, but they persist in projects that are clearly hopeless. They both tend to blame others to justify their failures rather than assume their responsibilities. They both make mistakes that they try to hide and come up with excuses for their wrongdoings. Democracies seek peace, and human nature happiness. They often use the wrong tools to achieve them.

Human nature and democracies are also complementary. They are both at risk of getting out of control and they are each other's watchdog. Communities use access to information and freedom of press to monitor and prevent democratic abuse. Despite inevitable exceptions to the rule, those who assume this responsibility are usually credible representatives of the community, able to fulfill their mission properly. Democracies play a similar role for the citizens through the legislative and judicial systems. Justice within the democracies often has gaps, but it protects the rights and fundamental freedoms of every citizen. There is a close relationship at this level: the abolition of the access to information and freedom of the press in dictatorships inevitably goes along with a suppression of the rights and freedoms of individuals, allowing at the same time the exploitation of man by man.

Civilization and barbarism belong to communities just like love and hatred belong to individuals. A similar distance separates them. And it is narrow.

Appendix 1

Closing address of Adolf Hitler to the Nazi Party Congress in Nuremberg, Germany, on September 14, 1934

Full transcript of this closing address at http://www.speeches-usa.com/ Transcripts/adolf_hitler-congress.html.

Bibliography

- Babiak, Paul & Hare, Robert D.; Snakes in Suits; Harper Collins Publishers, 2006.
- Bettelheim, Bruno. The Informed Heart, Penguin Books, 1991.
- Boldt, Gerhard. Hitler's Last Days: An Eye-Witness Account, First Sphere Books Edition, 1973.
- Browning, Christopher R. Ordinary Men, Penguin Books, 1992.
- Bullock, Alan. Hitler and Stalin: Parallel Lives, Vintage Books, 1991.
- Burger, J.M. Replicating Milgram: Would People Still Obey Today?, American Psychologist, 2009.
- Crankshaw, Edward. Gestapo, Instrument of Tyranny, Da Capo Press, 1994.
- Desroches, Alain. La Gestapo, Éditions de Vecchi, 1976.
- Erikson E.H. Enfance et société, Delachaux et Niestle, 6ᵉ édition, 1976.
- FitzGibbon, Constantine. 20 July, W.W. Norton, New York, 1956.
- Frei, Norbert. The Fuhrer State 1933-1945, Oxford, 1983.
- Frischauer, Willi. Himmler: The Evil Genius of the Third Reich, Odhams Press Limited, 1953.
- Gilbert, Gustave M. Nuremberg Diary, Da Capo Press, New York, 1995.
- Grynberg, Anne. Shoah: The Impossible Oblivion.
- Haffner, Sebastian. Defying Hitler: A Memoir, New York: Farrar, Straus & Giroux, 2000.
- Haffner, Sebastian. The meaning of Hitler, MacMillan Publishing, 1978.
- Hamilton, Charles. Leaders & Personalities of the third Reich, Vol. 1 & 2, R. James Bender, 1996.

- Heiden, Konrad. Der Fuehrer, Houghton Mifflin Company, 1944.
- Hilberg, Raul. The Destruction of the European Jews, Vol. 1, Holmes & Meier, 1985.
- Hitler, Adolf. Mein Kampf (James Murphy Translation), Hurst and Blackett Ltd., 1939.
- Hitler's Table Talk, Weidenfeld and Nicolson, 1953.
- Höss, Rudolf. Commandant of Auschwitz, World Publishing Company, 1959.
- Infield, Glenn B. Secrets of the S.S., Jove Books, 1982.
- Junge, Traudl. Until the Final Hour: Hitler's Last Secretary, Arcade Publishing, 2003.
- Keegan, John. Waffen SS: The Asphalt Soldiers, Ballantine Books Inc., 1970.
- Kershaw, Ian. Hitler 1936-1945: Nemesis; Penguin Books, 2001.
- Kershaw, Ian. The Nazi Dictatorship; Bloomsbury, 2015.
- Lewis, David. La vie secrète d'Adolf Hitler, Pygmalion, 1979.
- Lieberman A. Hitler's Parkinson disease began in 1933, Movement Disorder, 12; 239-240, 1997.
- Lifton Robert Jay. The Nazi Doctors, Basic Books, Inc., 1986.
- Maturana, H.R., Varela, F. The tree of knowledge: The Biological roots of Human understanding. 2nd edition. Boston New Science Library, 1992.
- Milgram, Stanley. Obedience to Authority, Harper & Row, 1974.
- Ornstein, Anna. Am I my brother's keeper: Reflections on the relationship between morality and politic. Speech delivered on Remembrance Day (Yom HaShoah).
- Overy, Richard. The Penguin Historical Atlas of the Third Reich, Penguin Books Ltd., 1996.
- Persico, Joseph E. Nuremberg: Infamy on Trial, Penguin Books, 1994.
- Redlich, Fritz. Hitler: Diagnosis of a Destructive Prophet, Oxford University Press, 1998.
- Schmidt, Paul. Hitler's Interpreter, William Heinemann Ltd., 1951.
- Scholl, Inge. The White Rose: Munich 1942-1943, Kobo ebooks, 2011.
- Shirer, William L. The Rise and Fall of the Third Reich, Simon & Schuster, 1960.

- Speer, Albert; Inside the Third Reich; Macmillan Publishing Company, 1970.
- Steinert, Marlis G. L'Allemagne nationale-socialiste 1933-1945, Éditions Richelieu, 1972.
- Steinert, Marlis G. Hitler et l'Allemagne nazie, Éditions Richelieu, 1972.
- Sutton, Nina. Bruno Bettelheim, A Life and a Legacy, Basic Books, 1996.
- Tamblyn, S. The Impending Influenza Pandemic, Can. J CME, Feb. 1999.
- Trevor-Roper, H.R. The Last Days of Hitler, Pan Books Ltd., 1952.
- Varaut, Jean-Marc. Le procès de Nuremberg, Librairie académique Perrin, 1992.
- Various. The War Years 1939-1945: Eyewitness Accounts, Marchall Cavendish, 1994.
- Von Papen, Franz. Memoirs, Andre Deutsch, 1952
- Wormser-Migot, Olga. L'ère des camps, Collection 10-18, Union générale d'éditions, 1973.
- Zimbardo, Philip. The Lucifer Effect: Understanding How Good People Turn Evil, Random House, 2007.

Printed in the United States
By Bookmasters